Allah Almighty is the Close Companion of His Loving Servants

Beautiful Names and Sublime Attributes of Allah Almighty from the Qur'an and Sunnah

Abdullah al-Qahtāni

Copyrighted by the author

Second Edition

1441 AH - 2020 AD

In the name of Allah, the Most Compassionate, the Most Merciful

Dedicated

to my parents..

This is only some of what you used to supplicate Allah Almighty for me. I would not be able to return even a small portion of your abundant giving and kindness to me.

It is then dedicated to every person who loves the Almighty Lord and seeks to draw close to Him.

To you, I dedicate the fruit of my effort, which I implore Allah Almighty to accept.

Introduction of the Second Edition

All praise is due to Allah Almighty, and may Allah's peace and blessings be upon His Prophet Muhammad.

I here present this second edition to my dear readers after the first edition, with its 6000 copies has been sold out over a short period of time, praise be to Allah. After the content of the book has been revised and subjected to some additions and omissions, hopefully the book will be more adequate for its readers, tackles the topic at hand, and achieves its desired objective.

I intend to spread useful knowledge in pursuit of reward from my Lord, hence, I permit printing of the book with conditions:

There should be no omission or addition; and it should be printed in a fine manner that befits its content. Moreover, correspondence should take place via the mobile number 00966564570117 or the e-mail ga.1440.ga@gmail.com

so as to make sure the book has not experienced any modification or addition. Indeed, no book whatsoever is perfect save the Book of the Almighty Lord.

I would also like to give thanks to Dar Ibn Al-Jawzi and Al-Mutanabbi Bookshop for their past efforts. I ask Allah Almighty for guidance, success, and acceptance,

and all praise is due to Allah, Lord of the worlds.

Author

Introduction

All praise is due to Allah, and may Allah's peace and blessings be upon Prophet Muhammad, his family, and Companions.

One of the best means of increasing faith is to know Allah Almighty through His names, attributes, and actions. Each name of Allah is like a door through which we can approach Him. {And to Allah belong the best names, so invoke Him by them...} [Surat al-A'rāf: 180]. If that is the case, then how about those who memorize them all!The Prophet (may Allah's peace and blessings be upon him) is authentically reported to have said:"Verily, Allah has ninety-nine names, one-hundred minus one. Whoever memorizes them all will enter Paradise."[Narrated by Al-Bukhāri and Muslim]

I used to implore Allah Almighty to grant me the honor of memorizing them. In 1430 AH, I began to recite them in a brief form. Thereupon, I perceived the eagerness of the listeners to know the names and attributes of Allah Almighty.

How could any believer not be eager to know them while his love for Allah and longing to meet Him grows upon knowing each name?!

How could a believer not long to know the names and attributes of his Lord when he knows that they are the lifeline for those who are distressed, wronged, sick, imprisoned, confused, or in debt?!

How could a believer not long to know the names and attributes of his Lord when he knows that they are the keys to relief, happiness, and opulence?! Indeed, those who know them well will always be in happiness.

Hence, I implored Allah Almighty to enable me to write down a book that will be a legacy for me and a spring from which good things are taken. So, I embarked upon my endeavor, adopting the approach of compiling and phrasing only, as I know that I am not a good author and my skills in this area are modest.

I compiled all what I laid my eyes on and recorded everything I felt comfortable about, hoping that I made the right choices, in which I was keen to stick to the beliefs of the righteous predecessors with regard to the names and attributes of Allah.

Then, I put it in beautiful and eloquent phrases, taking into consideration the different levels and types of learners and learned people and keeping away from the purely academic style.

I only cited Saḥīḥ (authentic) and Ḥasan (sound) Ḥadīths and did not explore traditions and biographies.

My intent is to make the reading easy and interesting and let the reader get the message through the easiest and shortest way.

I hope my book will bring happiness, relieve distress, comfort hearts, boost faith, increase knowledge, fill hearts with faith, and feed minds with knowledge.

All grace and praise are due to Allah Almighty alone, then the credit goes to the virtuous scholars from whom I collected these good fruits. Whatever I did right belongs to Allah and to Him I give thanks for it; and whatever I did wrong is from myself and from the devil. I intended nothing but good, and I ask for Allah's forgiveness and repent to Him.

Finally, I am humbled to offer you the product of my modest efforts and skills, praising Allah Almighty for helping me accomplish it and imploring Him to accept it. I hereby declare to Allah Almighty that I love and trust Him.

I implore Allah Almighty to give abundant rewards to me, to those from whom I collected the material, and to those who took part in revising, correcting, arranging, copying, and printing this book or shared with their advice or opinion.

I also ask Allah Almighty to render the content of this book right and to accept it as purely done for His sake; and I implore Him to make it a means for winning His love and drawing closer to Him and to forgive me, my parents, my teachers, my family, and all Muslims; indeed, He is All-Hearing, Responsive.

Yours,

'Abdullah ibn Mushabbib al-Qahtānī

My Lord...

How grave, serious, and weighty the situation will be!

Words cannot describe it, the heart shivers, the tongue stutters, and the mind gets perplexed. Your servant stands before You, weak and humble, wanting to praise You and reveal to You what lies hidden within himself, and You are the Knower of all things.

No matter how much we praise You, Your greatness is far bigger!

O Lord!

We know that our praise and glorification of You, our extolling of Your majesty, and our remembrance of You are but a blessing and a favor from You upon all of us. You are the One Who has guided us to this.

And We know that You, O Lord, are beyond the laudation and praise of anyone.

O Allah, accept from us the favors You have bestowed upon me and upon those who read these words, and pardon our shortcomings.

To Allah I extend my praise and good words that are pleasing to Him.

Allāh Al-ilāh (Allah; the God)

We begin with the greatest and best name humanity has ever known. It is the best name and the most beautiful letters to be uttered by the tongue. It is close to our hearts and souls and gives us a feeling of comfort and tranquility.

This is the name "Allah",{...Do you know of any that is given His namesake?}[Surat Maryam: 65]

The name "Allah" exclusively belongs to Him, apart from all else. No one else is called as such or claims to have this name. Allah Almighty prevented people's minds and tongues from using this name for anyone else.

Indeed, Allah Almighty is the Owner of majesty, beauty, grandeur, awe, and might.

No matter what we say to describe Your greatness, You are still far greater.

All Your attributes are holy, and we chant them in glorification of Your majesty.

When the name "Allah" is mentioned, what is little increases, fear goes away, distress and anguish are relieved, need turns into opulence, the weak become strong, the humiliated become honorable, the poor get rich, and the defeated become victorious.

It is the name by which distress is removed, blessings are brought, supplications are answered, good things occur, evil things are averted, and errors are forgiven. Nothing is greater than the Almighty Lord!

The name "Allah" comes from the word "ilāh", which means deity. Allah Almighty says:{O People of the Book, do not exceed the limits in your religion, and attribute to Allah nothing except the truth. The Messiah, Jesus, son of Mary, was only a Messenger of Allah, and His command that He conveyed unto Mary, and a spirit from Him. So, believe in Allah and in His Messengers, and do not say: "(Allah is a) trinity." Give up this assertion; it would be better for you. Allah is indeed just one God. Far exalted is He from having a son. To Him belongs all that is in the heavens and on the earth. Allah is sufficient as a guardian.}[Surat an-Nisā': 171]Ibn 'Abbās (may Allah be pleased with him and his father) said:"Allah is the God and Lord of all His servants."Allah, Blessed and Exalted, is the Loved and Extolled One for Whom people's souls yearn and they find tranquility and intimacy by remembering Him and drawing closer to Him.{And among the people are those who take other than Allah as equals [to Him]. They love them as they [should] love Allah. But those who believe are stronger in love for Allah...}[Surat al-Baqarah: 165]He is the One Whose help is sought at the time of disasters and afflictions.{And whatever you have of favor - it is from Allah. Then when adversity touches you, to Him you cry for help.}[Surat an-Nahl: 53]Minds and intellects get perplexed about Him and cannot grasp His essence, and His servants cannot encompass Him in knowledge.{...But they do not encompass Him in knowledge.}[Surat Tāha: 110]

Allah Almighty is the One Who is deified by people in love for Him and humiliation, fear, hope, glorification, and obedience.

He is the true God, and all beings worshiped apart from Him are nothing but false and helpless deities.

Allah Almighty is the Possessor of all divine attributes - the attributes of perfection, majesty, beauty, and greatness - and is far exalted above their opposites.

Hearts deify Him and souls yearn for Him.

So, when a person knows the meaning of the name "Allah", his heart gets attached to his Lord such as feeling such love, longing, and pleasure that are more beautiful and pleasant than all else. That is the greatest thing with which the worshipers worship Him and His pious servants get close to Him. {...He loves them, and they love Him...} [Surat al-Mā'idah: 54]. One's real happiness depends on the degree of his knowledge of Allah's names and attributes.

Shaykh al-Islam Ibn Taymiyyah (may Allah have mercy upon him) said: "There is a Paradise in the worldly life; whoever does not enter it will not enter Paradise in the Hereafter."

One of the knowledgeable servants of Allah said: "Sometimes my heart experiences certain status in which I say: 'If the dwellers of Paradise will be in a status like this, they will surely have a good life.'"

Ibn 'Uyaynah said:"Allah has not bestowed upon His servants a better favor than letting them know 'La ilāha illallāh' (there is no god except Allah). To them, 'La ilāha illallāh' (there is no god except Allah) in the Hereafter will be like water to them in the worldly life."

The believer knows that this condition can only exist through the power and will of Allah Almighty. If Allah loves a servant, He puts love in his heart; and when the servant loves Him, through guidance from Allah, He still rewards him with additional love, and that is utter benevolence from the Almighty Lord, as it all comes from Him.

The greatest name:

Al-Qurtubi mentioned that some scholars said: "The name 'Allah' is the greatest name, which if He is invoked with, He answers the invocation, and if He is asked with, He gives."

The Messenger of Allah (may Allah's peace and blessings be upon him) heard a man saying: "Allāhumma inni as'aluka bi'anni ash-hadu annaka anta Allāh la ilāha illa ant, Al-Ahad As-Samad al-ladhi lam yalid wa lam yūlad wa lam yakun lahu kufuwan ahad (O Allah, I ask you by the fact that I testify that You are Allah, and there is no god but You, You are the Eternal Refuge, Who neither begets nor is He begotten, nor is there any equivalent to Him)." Thereupon, the Prophet (may Allah's peace and blessings be upon him) said:"By the One in Whose hand my soul is, he asked Allah by His greatest name, which if He is supplicated with, He answers the supplication, and if He is asked with, He gives."[Narrated by the Compilers of Sunan as well as Ahmad in his Musnad; Sahīh (authentic)]

It is the only name that occurs in all the Hadīths in which the Prophet (may Allah's peace and blessings be upon him) informed about the greatest name of Allah.

It also occurs in and is closely associated with most reported Dhikrs like Tahlīl (saying: La ilāha illallāh (there is no god except Allah), Takbīr (saying: Allāhu akbar (Allah is the Most Great), Tahmīd (saying: Alhamdulillāh (praise be to Allah), Tasbīh (saying: Subhānallāh (glory be to Allah), Hawqalah (saying: La hawla wa la quwwata illa billāh (there is no power nor strength except through Allah), and Basmalah (saying: Bismillāh (in the name of Allah).

This name is the root of all the beautiful names of Allah. It is not attributed to any of them; rather, they are all attributed to this great name. No one says, for example: "Allah" is one of the names of the Most Compassionate or the Most Merciful; rather, we say: "The Most Compassionate" or "the Most Merciful" is one of the names of Allah.{And to Allah belong the most beautiful names...}[Surat al-A'rāf:180]

The form by which Allah Almighty is most frequently supplicated is: "Allāhumma" (O Allah). The Messenger of Allah (may Allah's peace and blessings be upon him) would often supplicate Allah Almighty saying: "Allāhumma" (O Allah).

Al-Hasan al-Basri (may Allah have mercy upon him) said:"'Allāhumma' (O Allah) is the comprehensive form of supplication. If a supplicant says: 'O Allah, I implore You,' it is as if he said: 'I supplicate Allah, to Whom belong the beautiful names and sublime attributes, by His names and attributes.'"

With this name, every affair is commenced in pursuit of blessing.

Moreover, it is the first name in the first verse of the Qur'an: {In the name of Allah, the Most Compassionate, the Most Merciful} or {Praise be to Allah, Lord of the worlds} [Surat al-Fātihah: 1]. It is also the last name mentioned in Surat al-Nās: {The God (ilāh) of mankind.} [Surat an-Nās: 3]

It is also the only name in the testimony of faith, which turns a person from disbelief into Islam: "Ash-hadu alla ilāha illallāh" (I testify that there is no god but Allah). This testimony is invalid without this name.

Due to the great honor attached to this great name, Allah will lift it off the earth at the end of time, after taking the souls of the believers. The Prophet (may Allah's peace and blessings be upon him) said:"The Hour will not come while there is anyone who says: Allah, Allah."[Narrated by Muslim]This is the name that occurs most in the Noble Qur'an.It occurs more than 2200 times.Commenting on the verse that says:{Say: "Call upon Allah or call upon the Most Compassionate"...}[Surat al-Isrā': 110],some scholars said: "He singles out these two names for mention in the above verse given their special merit, and He puts the name 'Allah' first because of its additional honor."The Prophet (may Allah's peace and blessings be upon him) is authentically reported to have said:"Indeed, the dearest of your names to Allah Almighty is 'Abdullah and 'Abd ar-Rahmān."[Narrated by Muslim]

So, be with Allah and He will be with you.

If a person does not go to his Lord willingly, he will do so under the compulsion of need and necessity.

We should stand humble before Allah Almighty and call Him when we are in distress.

Indeed, the All-Generous Lord responds to those who call upon Him.

When people suffer hardships, distress, and severe crises and they become totally helpless, they call out saying: O Allah!

When a person becomes seriously ill and doctors cannot treat him, he calls out: O Allah! When the sea becomes rough and dark, those on a boat call out: O Allah! When the land becomes arid and people suffer famine and drought, they call out: O Allah!

He is Allah, the refuge at times of distress, the companion at times of loneliness, and the supporter at times of weakness.

People are too powerless to cause any harm or bring about any benefit not predestined by Allah Almighty. So, let your heart be deeply attached to Allah Almighty.

All ropes get cut off except for His rope, and all doors get closed except for His door.{Is He [not best] Who responds to the desperate one when he calls upon Him and removes evil...}[Al-Naml: 62]

Al-Nasafi (may Allah have mercy upon him) said: "Al-Wāsiti said: 'Whoever asks from Allah alone will not be in need, and whoever seeks honor from Allah will not be humiliated.'" Al-Husayn said: "A person becomes self-sufficient as much as he stands in need before Allah."

O you who are in distress, rejoice, for indeed your distress will be relieved. Despair may sometimes take its toll upon you; but Allah brings ease after hardship. So, if you are afflicted, put your trust in Allah and be content with whatever He wills, for you have none but Him.

Rejoice, for relief will come to you from Allah. Do not lose hope, for your needs will be fulfilled by Allah. Do not show impatience, for Allah is the One Who predestined all things and He is the One Who removes afflictions. So, Allah is sufficient for You in everything.

There is no god except Allah. O Allah, we have not worshiped You as properly as You deserve.

O Allah, I ask You Paradise and the words and deeds that bring one closer to it, and I seek refuge in You from Hellfire and from the words and deeds that bring one closer to it.

Ar-Rabb (The Lord)

Knocking on the door..

O Lord, we ask You by Your honor and our humiliation, by Your power and our weakness, and by Your lack of need for us and our need for You. We stand before You as wrongful servants. You have lots of servants apart from us, but we have no Lord except You. There is no refuge or escape from You but to You.

We supplicate and implore You as Your needy, humble, and fearful servants.

We stand before You in total submission and with tearful eyes and humble hearts. We implore You to forgive us and all Muslims and to admit us into Your mercy, O the Most Merciful of those who show mercy!

A servant has none but his Lord to seek help from.

He is the only One Who helps us at times of distress and hardship.

He is the Owner of the whole world and all that inhabits it.

Who can remove afflictions, near or distant?

Who can prevent disasters just before they strike?

It is only You, our Lord, Who does this.

In the lines to come, we are honored to speak about one of the beautiful names of Allah, namely "Ar-Rabb" (the Lord), Blessed and Exalted.

Allah Almighty says:{(He is) the Lord of the two easts and the Lord of the two wests.}[Al-Rahmān: 17]He also says:{"Peace", a word from a Most Merciful Lord.}[Yasīn: 58]

Our Lord is the Creator, the Owner, the Manager, and the Disposer of affairs. He is the Lord of lords and the deity of worshipers. He possesses the kingdoms, the kings, and all creation. He manages the affairs and interests of His servants, human and jinn, and He is the Sustainer in the worldly life and in the Hereafter.

His Lordship to His servants falls under two categories:

General Lordship: This comprises all beings, pious and wicked, believers and disbelievers, and even inanimate objects.

It means that He creates them, provides for them, manages their affairs, and bestows favors upon them.

Special Lordship: It means that He raises and educates His close and chosen servants through faith and guidance, and He reforms their hearts, souls, and morals and brings them out of darkness into light.

He guides them to every good and protects them from every evil.

All praise is due to You.

Allah Almighty praises Himself as the Lord of the worlds:{All praise is due to Allah, Lord of the worlds.}[Al-Fātihah: 2]He also praises Himself as the Lord of the Throne, saying:{Glory be to the Lord of the heavens and the earth, the Lord of the Throne! Exalted be He above all that they ascribe (to Him).}[Al-Zukhruf: 82]{Allah - there is no god but Him; He is the Lord of the Mighty Throne.}[Al-Naml: 26]And He praises Himself as the Lord of the heavens and the earth; He says:{Glory be to the Lord of the heavens and earth, the Lord of the Throne! Exalted be He above all that they ascribe (to Him).}[Al-Zukhruf: 82]Hence, all creatures extend praise to their Almighty Lord:{...And it will be said: "Praise be to Allah, Lord of the worlds."}[Al-Zumar: 75]So, He is praised in this life and in the Hereafter.{Their call therein will be: "Glory be to You, O Allah," and their greeting therein will be: "Peace." And the last of their call will be: "Praise be to Allah, Lord of the worlds!"}[Yūnus: 10]

Keys to the treasures..

As the prophets and righteous people knew that this name is the key to answering supplications, they supplicated Allah therewith.

Nūh (Noah) (peace be upon him) used it in his supplication:{My Lord, forgive me and my parents and whoever enters my house a believer and the believing men and believing women...}[Nūh: 28]Ibrāhīm (Abraham) (peace be upon him) used it as he supplicated:{Our Lord, accept from us. Indeed, You are the All-Hearing, the All-Knowing!}[Al-Baqarah: 127]And Prophet Muhammad (may Allah's peace and blessings be upon him) used it in his supplication:{And say: "My Lord, I seek refuge in You from the incitements of the devils,And I seek refuge with You, My Lord, lest they should come near me."}[Al-Mu'minūn: 97-98]

O Lord!

Whenever anything distressed the Prophet (may Allah's peace and blessings be upon him), he would say:"La ilāha illallāh al-'azhīm al-halīm, la ilāha illallāh rabbu al-'arsh al-'azhīm, la ilāha illallāh rabbu as-samāwāt wa rabbu al-ard wa rabbu al-'arsh al-karīm (There is no god but Allah, the Most Great, the Forbearing. There is no god but Allah, the Lord of the Mighty Throne. There is no god but Allah, the Lord of the heavens and the earth, and the Lord of the Honorable Throne)."[Narrated by Al-Bukhāri and Muslim]

If anyone does not supplicate using the Lord's names willingly, he will certainly use it by way of necessity. A person lying very ill in his bed would call out: "O Lord, O Lord!" And behold! Cure and recovery come to him from the Almighty Lord.

A person in abject poverty and misery would call out: "O Lord, O Lord!" And behold! He fulfills his needs and removes his poverty.

A starving person, in real suffering, would call out: "O Lord, O Lord!" And behold! Sustenance comes to him in abundance.

A wronged person, wiping off his tears and hiding his pain, would call out: "O Lord, O Lord!" And behold! He gets support and a good outcome for his suffering.

Al-Hāfizh ibn Rajab (may Allah have mercy upon him) said:"Persistently supplicating Allah by mentioning His Lordship is one of the best means for getting the supplication answered."

O Lord, relieve the distress of Your servant and put an end to his suffering.

Nonetheless, we do forget our Lord!

He is the Most Great, His dominion is so grand, His status is so high, and He is very close to His servants and so gentle with them.

His Lordship is that of greatness and majesty.{Exalt the name of your Lord, the Most High.}[Al-A'la: 1]His Lordship is about blessing, increase, and giving.{...Blessed is Allah, Lord of the worlds.}[Al-A'rāf: 54]His Lordship involves concealment and forgiveness.{... A good land, and a forgiving Lord.}[Saba': 15]His Lordship brings honor, strength, dominance, and invincibility.{The Lord of the heavens and earth and what is between them, the All-Mighty, the Oft-Forgiving.}[Sād: 66]His Lordship is mercy.{The Lord of the heavens and earth and what is between them, the Most Compassionate...}[Al-Naba': 37]His Lordship is generosity.{O man, what has deceived you concerning your Lord, the Generous One?}[Al-Infitār: 6]

There is no god except Allah, the One and Only God. We have not worshiped You properly as You deserve.

He who knows that Allah is the Lord of lords would not be pleased with other than Him as a Lord, and when he gets this pleasure, he tastes the sweetness of faith. The Prophet (may Allah's peace and blessings be upon him) is authentically reported to have said:"Whoever is pleased with Allah as a Lord, with Islam as a religion, and with Muhammad as a Messenger, has indeed tasted the sweetness of faith."[Narrated by Muslim]{And say: "My Lord, forgive and have mercy, and You are the best of those who are merciful."}[Al-Mu'minūn: 118]Ibn Rajab (may Allah have mercy upon him) said:"Persistently supplicating Allah by mentioning His Lordship is one of the best means for getting the supplication answered."

Our Lord, we hope for Your mercy. Do not leave us to our own devices, even for the blink of an eye, and admit us into Your mercy.

Our Lord, forgive and have mercy, for You are the best of those who show mercy.

Al-Ahad Al-Wāhid (The One and Only God)

The Prophet (may Allah's peace and blessings be upon him) said:"On the Day of Judgment, Abraham will meet his father Āzar whose face will be dark and covered with dust. Abraham will say to him: 'Did I not tell you not to disobey me?' His father will reply: 'Today I will not disobey you.' Abraham will say: 'O Lord, You promised me not to disgrace me on the Day of Resurrection; and what will be more disgraceful to me than cursing and dishonoring my father?' Then, Allah Almighty will say: 'I have forbidden Paradise for the disbelievers.' Then, he will be addressed: 'O Abraham, what is underneath your feet?' He will look and there he will see a blood-stained hyena, which will be caught by the legs and thrown in Hellfire." [Narrated by Al-Bukhārī]

--

Our merciful Lord will not accept the intercession of Abraham (peace be upon him) for his father, who died as a polytheist. This is because Allah Almighty forbade Paradise for all polytheists and disbelievers. However, since Allah promised Abraham that He would not disgrace him on the Day of Judgment, He will transform his father into a hyena, which will then be thrown into Hellfire. Thus, none will know this is Abraham's father. In this way he will be safe from disgrace.

If the intercession of Abraham, the intimate friend of Allah, for his polytheistic father will not be accepted, then what about any such intercession of another person less in rank than Abraham (peace be upon him)?!

Allah Almighty says:{Surely Allah does not forgive that a partner be ascribed to Him, although He forgives any other sin for whomever He wills. He who associates anyone with Allah has indeed forged a mighty lie and committed a heinous sin.}[Surat an-Nisā': 48]

Hence, the servant's most important duty is to worship Allah Almighty alone, with no partner.

Allah Almighty praises Himself as the One and Only God.{Say: "He is Allah, the Only One."}[Surat al-Ikhlās: 1]{...And they were not commanded except to worship one God; there is no god but Him...}[Surat at-Tawbah: 31]

Let's pause and reflect upon these two noble names, perhaps Allah will enable us to have sincere faith and proper belief in His Oneness.

Our Lord is the Sole Possessor of the attributes of glory, majesty, greatness, pride, and beauty.

He is One in His essence, and there is none like Him.

He is One in His attributes, and there is none equal to Him.

He is One in His actions, and He has no partner or helper.

He is One in His divinity, and there is none equal to Him in terms of love, glorification, humility, and submission.

He is the One God Who has excellent and great attributes and uniquely possesses all traits of perfection. None in His creation can ever grasp something of His attributes, let alone equally possess one of them.

Sound natural disposition..

Monotheism is the core of the messengers' call and the mainstay of their message:{Say: "It is revealed to me that your god is only one God. Will you then submit to His will?"}[Surat al-Anbiyā': 108]

Monotheism is the sound innate disposition upon which Allah Almighty created people; the covenant He took from people; the call of His messengers with which they were sent; and the message contained in the books He revealed.

For the sake of monotheism, Paradise and Hellfire are established, the Bridge will be erected, the Scrolls will fly around, the Scale will be put in place, the sword of religion is unsheathed, the flag of Jihad is raised, martyrs sacrifice their lives, and death becomes sweet.{Say: "I am only a man like you to whom it has been revealed that your god is but one God; so take a straight course to Him and seek His forgiveness." And woe to those who associate others with Allah.}[Surat Fussilat: 6]Establishing monotheism and affirming the obligation of devoting the religion sincerely to Allah, Allah Almighty says:{And they were not commanded except to worship Allah, [being] sincere to Him in religion, inclining to truth, and to establish prayer and give Zakah. And that is the correct religion.}[Surat al-Bayyinah: 5]Moreover, Allah Almighty ordained submission and humility to Him as the One and Great God:{...For your god is one God, so to Him submit. And give good tidings to the humble [before their Lord].}[Surat al-Hajj: 34]

Clear evidence:

Refuting the polytheists' beliefs, Allah Almighty says:{And Allah has said: "Do not take for yourselves two deities. He is but one God, so fear only Me."} [Surat an-Nahl: 51] {...Are separate lords better or Allah, the One, the Prevailing?}[Surat Yūsuf: 39]He responds to those who say that Allah is the third of three saying:{...And do not say: "Three"; desist - it is better for you. Indeed, Allah is but one God...}[Surat an-Nisā': 171]He negates the existence of anyone similar or equal to Him from any aspect. Indeed, He is the One God Who has no equal or peer.{...Do you know of any that is given His namesake?}[Surat Maryam: 65]

He has forbidden us from likening Him to any of His creation. He has informed us about Himself, and He knows Himself best.

Whatever occurs to people's minds about Allah Almighty, He is surely different from that. None is similar, like, or equal to Him.{...There is nothing like unto Him, and He is the All-Hearing, the All-Seeing.}[Surat ash-Shūra: 11]None of His creation resembles Him. To Him belong the beautiful names, sublime attributes, perfection, majesty, magnificence, glory, and pride.The polytheists said to the

Messenger of Allah (may Allah's peace and blessings be upon him):"Describe your Lord to us. Is He of gold? Is He of copper or brass?" Some of them would say: "Name for us the lineage of your Lord, O Muhammad."

The Jews used to say: "We worship 'Uzayr, the son of God." The Christians used to say: "We worship Messiah, the son of God." The Magians used to say: "We worship the sun and the moon." The polytheists used to say: "We worship idols."

So, Allah Almighty responded to them saying:{Say: "He is Allah, the Only One."}[Surat al-Ikhlās: 1]

Allah is far exalted above what they say!

They were bold enough to speak badly about Allah Almighty and commit such a heinous crime because of which the massive heavens would almost crack and the mountains collapse, as they ascribed a son to the Almighty Creator - far exalted is Allah above what they say!

They are all subject to His authority and power and will come to Him as individuals on the Day of Judgment.{Indeed you have brought forth a terrible evil thing.The heavens almost rupture therefrom and the earth splits open and the mountains collapse in devastation,that they attribute a son to the Most Compassionate.But it is not suitable for the Most Compassionate that He should take a son.There is none in the heavens and the earth but comes unto the Most Compassionate as a slave.Verily, He knows each one of them, and has counted them a full counting.And everyone of them will come to Him alone on the Day of Judgment.}[Surat Maryam: 89-95]The Prophet (may Allah's peace and blessings be upon him) said:"Allah Almighty said: 'The son of Adam belied Me and he had no right to do so. And the son of Adam reviled Me and he had no right to do so.

As for his belying Me, it is his saying that I will not resurrect him as I created him in the beginning. Resurrecting him is not more difficult for Me than creating him in the first place.

And as for his reviling Me, it is his saying that Allah has taken a son, but I am Allah, the One, the Eternal Refuge, I do not beget nor was I begotten, and there is none like unto Me.'" [Narrated by Al-Bukhāri]

Allah Almighty is one God, Who has no partner or anyone equal to Him in His essence, attributes, or actions.

The universe attests to His Oneness:

All the creativity, order, consistency, and harmony existing in the universe indicate that their Creator and Director is One. If there were more than one creator and director, the universe would fall into disorder and its laws in turbulence.{Had there been other gods therein besides Allah, they both would have been ruined. Exalted is Allah, Lord of the Throne, above what they describe.}[Surat al-Anbiyā': 22]

Consider the plants on earth, with all its different kinds, and have a close look at all the wonderful creatures in the world,

which clearly point to the One Creator, Who has no partner.

Allah is the farthest from need to have partners..

Allah Almighty alone is worthy of being worshiped. One should not turn to or devote any of his worship to other than Allah Almighty, be it prayer, supplication, sacrificial slaughter, vow, reliance, hope, fear, humility, or submission.{Say: "Indeed, my prayer, my rites of sacrifice, my living, and my dying are for Allah, Lord of the worlds.No partner has He. And this I have been commanded, and I am the first of the Muslims."}[Surat al-An'ām: 162-163]Our major concern should be devoting worship to Allah Almighty alone.{And I did not create the jinn and mankind except to worship Me.}[Surat adh-Dhāriyāt: 56]{...And they were not commanded except to worship one God; there is no god but Him...}[Surat at-Tawbah: 31]

Monotheism is the best, fairest, and purest thing ever. It can be scratched, tainted, and affected by the least thing.

The Prophet (may Allah's peace and blessings be upon him) is authentically reported to have said:"Allah Almighty said: 'Whoever does an act and associates others with Me in it, I leave him and his polytheism.'"[Narrated by Muslim]The Prophet (may Allah's peace and blessings be upon him) is also reported to have said:"When Allah assembles the first and the last on the Day of Resurrection, a day concerning which there is no doubt, a caller will cry out: 'Whoever associated anyone else in an action that he did for Allah, let him seek his reward from someone other than Allah, for Allah is so self-sufficient that He has no need for any associate.'"[Narrated by Ahmad in Al-Musnad; Hasan (sound)]

A Reminder..

There are numerous authentic Hadīths that urge us to adhere to monotheism and point out its merit. Examples include the following:

Abu Hurayrah (may Allah be pleased with him) reported that the Prophet (may Allah's peace and blessings be upon him) said:"Whoever says a hundred times in a day: 'La ilāha illallāh wahdahu la sharīka lahu, lahu al-mulk wa lahu al-hamd wa huwa 'ala kulli sahy'in qadīr (There is no god but Allah. He is One and He has no partner with Him; to Him belongs sovereignty and to Him belongs praise, and He is Omnipotent over all things),' he will have a reward equivalent to that of emancipating ten slaves, a hundred good deeds will be added to his record, a hundred of his sins will be erased, and he will be shielded against the devil on that day till the evening; and no one will exceed him in doing good deeds except someone who said more than that."[Narrated by Al-Bukhāri and Muslim]

Buraydah (may Allah be pleased with him) reported that the Messenger of Allah (may Allah's peace and blessings be upon him) heard a man say: "Allāhumma inni as'aluka bi'annaka anta Allāh la ilāha illa ant, Al-Ahad As-Samad al-ladhi lam yalid wa lam yūlad wa lam yakun lahu kufuwan ahad (O Allah, I implore You by the fact that You are Allah, there is no god but You, the One, the Eternal Refuge, Who has not begotten nor was He begotten, and there is none like unto Him)!"

Thereupon, he said:"You have implored Allah by His greatest name, which when asked therewith He gives, and when supplicated therewith He answers."[Narrated by Al-Tirmidhi and Abu Dāwūd; Sahīh (authentic)]

The Prophet (may Allah's peace and blessings be upon him) entered the mosque and heard a man supplicate Allah saying: "Allāhumma inni as'aluka ya Allāh Al-Ahad As-Samad al-ladhi lam yalid wa lam yūlad wa lam yakun lahu kufuwan ahad an taghfir li dhunūbi innaka anta Al-Ghafūr Ar-Rahīm (O Allah, I ask You, O Allah, the One, the Eternal Refuge, Who has not begotten nor was He begotten, and there is none like unto Him, to forgive my sins. Indeed You are the Oft-Forgiving, the Most Merciful)."

Thereupon, he said:"He has been forgiven, he has been forgiven, he has been forgiven."[Narrated by Ahmad in Al-Musnad; Sahīh (authentic)]Al-Hāfizh ibn Rajab (may Allah have mercy upon him) said:"Fulfillment of monotheism entails emancipation of slaves, which in turn entails emancipation from Hellfire."He (may Allah have mercy upon him) said:"Causes of forgiveness include monotheism, which is the greatest cause. Whoever lacks it misses out on forgiveness, and whoever fulfills it does possess the greatest cause for forgiving his sins."Imam Ibn al-Qayyim (may Allah have mercy upon him) said:"Monotheism is the first thing by which a person enters Islam and the last thing with which he leaves this life. The Prophet (may Allah's peace and blessings be upon him) said:'One whose last speech is: La ilāha illallāh (there is no god but Allah) will enter Paradise.'This is the first and last duty. Indeed, monotheism is the beginning and the end."He (may Allah have mercy upon him) also said:"Nothing is like monotheism for warding off hardships."He (may Allah have mercy upon him) said:"No polytheist will enter Paradise, only the monotheists will. Indeed, monotheism is the key to its gate."Ibn al-Jawzi (may Allah have mercy upon him) said:"Sufyān al-Thawri would go to Ibrahīm ibn Adham and say: 'O Ibrahīm, supplicate Allah to make us die as monotheists.'"The Prophet (may Allah's peace and blessings be upon him) saw a man supplicating with two fingers of his, and he said to him:"One, One."[Narrated by Abu Dāwūdj; Sahīh (authentic)]So, whenever wants to point during supplication, he should do so with only one finger.

O Allah, we implore You, O the One and Only God, the Eternal Refuge, to make us among those who supplicate You and You answer their supplication, and among those upon whom You bestow Your mercy and refuge as they invoke You and seek Your refuge from Hellfire; O Allah, make our last speech in this world "there is no god but Allah", for You are the Most Merciful of those who show mercy.

As-Samad (The Eternal Refuge)

If you are in need, turn to the Eternal Refuge. If you are in a humble and humiliating position, knock on the door of the Eternal Refuge. If weakness creeps into your body, seek strength from the Eternal Refuge.

Indeed, He is the One God and the Refuge upon Whom all creatures depend.

He is the owner of the beautiful names and sublime attributes, and He is the companion of those who feel lonely.

Allah's name "As-Samad" seldom occurs and is rarely mentioned, yet it enjoys special magnificence.

Allah Almighty says:{Say: "He is Allah, the Only One.Allah, the Eternal Refuge.He has not begotten and has not been begotten.And there is none like unto Him."}[Surat al-Ikhlās: 1-4]

It is our Lord upon whom all creatures, humans and jinn, depend. Indeed, the entire world and all that it contains turn to Him for the fulfillment of desires and take refuge in Him from disasters.

Our Lord is the Master with perfect glory, honor, majesty, forbearance, and self-sufficiency. These attributes belong to the Almighty Lord alone.

Our Lord has no hollow and He does not eat or drink, and He provides others with food. He stands in no need for others, yet all else do need Him. There is none like Him, and He is the All-Hearing, the All-Seeing.

The adequate answer..

In a Hadīth that was mentioned by Al-Bayhaqi and graded as Hasan (sound) by Al-Hāfizh, Ibn 'Abbās (may Allah be pleased with him and his father) reported: "The Jews came to the Messenger of Allah (may Allah's peace and blessings be upon him) and said: 'O Muhammad, name for us the lineage of your Lord Who has sent you.'So, Allah Almighty revealed:{Say: "He is Allah, the Only One.Allah, the Eternal Refuge.He has not begotten and has not been begotten.And there is none like unto Him."}[Surat al-Ikhlās: 1-4]

It is a short Surah that comprises Allah's attributes of perfection and majesty.

Given the greatness of this Surah, its recitation is like reciting one third of the Qur'an. The Prophet (may Allah's peace and blessings be upon him) said to his Companions:"'Is anyone of you unable to recite one third of the Qur'an in one night?' They said: 'How could anyone recite one third of the Qur'an?' He said: 'Surat al-Ikhlās equals one third of the Qur'an.'"[Narrated by Al-Bukhāri and Muslim; this is the wording of Muslim]Some scholars said:"The Qur'an was revealed in three parts: one third is about the rulings, another is about the promise and threat, and the last third is about the names and attributes of Allah. Surat al-Ikhlās comprises one of those thirds, i.e. the names and attributes of Allah. Hence, the reward of its recitation is made equivalent to the reward of reciting one third of the Qur'an."

A Companion used to recite Surat al-Ikhlās in all the prayers in which he led his companions. So, they mentioned that to the Prophet (may Allah's peace and blessings be upon him) who said: "Ask him why he does that." They asked him and he said: "Because it comprises the attributes of the Most Compassionate, and I like to recite it." Thereupon, the Messenger of Allah (may Allah's peace and blessings be upon him) said: "Tell him that Allah Almighty loves him." [Narrated by Al-Bukhāri]

Submission of the heart..

Love within the hearts of the righteous drives them to look for the love of their Lord.

This love within their hearts is only satisfied by bowing to Allah Almighty, circumambulating His House, standing before Him in prayer, getting up from sleep for His sake, and sacrificing one's soul in His cause.

Lovers' hearts feel tranquil only upon remembering Him and their souls will be calm only when they see Him.

If we fall ill, we get cured by remembering You; and when we fail to remember You at times, we suffer a setback.

Those people turn to Him at times of prosperity, and He helps them at times of hardship. The more they turn to and rely upon Him, the more He helps and elevates them.

For example, Prophet Abraham (peace be upon him) went through several afflictions, and as a result Allah Almighty raised his rank and he, thus, deserved to be the intimate friend of the Almighty Lord. Allah Almighty said:{...And Allah took Abraham as an intimate friend.}[Surat an-Nisā': 125]Another example is Ayyūb (Job) (peace be upon him) who suffered the severest afflictions and illness. He turned to his Lord, saying:{My Lord, adversity has touched me, and you are the Most Merciful of the merciful.}[Surat al-Anbiyā': 83]Response came from the Eternal Refuge, Blessed and Exalted, Who said:{So We responded to him and removed the adversity that afflicted him...}[Surat al-Anbiyā': 84]And Yūnus (Jonah) (peace be upon him), as he was in the whale's belly in three layers of darkness, he turned to his Lord saying:{...There is no god but You; Exalted are You. Indeed, I have been of the wrongdoers.So We responded to him and saved him from the distress. And thus do We save the believers.}[Surat al-Anbiyā': 87-88]

This was the case with all prophets and pious people. They knew Allah at times of ease, so He knew them at times of hardship.

They responded to the call of their Lord.

Moreover, our Lord, the Eternal Refuge, has opened His door not only to His pious servants but to all creation.

This stems from His kindness, mercy, and bounty. When the polytheists went into trouble and faced sure death, they resorted to Allah Almighty and called out: O Allah, O Allah! And behold! He saved them.{And when they board a ship, they supplicate Allah, sincere to Him in religion. But when He delivers them to the land, at once they associate partners with Him.}[Surat al-'Ankabūt: 65]

They acknowledge this fact. If the whole creation do not resort to Allah Almighty willingly, they will do so under the compulsion of necessity.

Rest assured!

Allah Almighty responded to the call of the desperate disbelievers. So, what about those who believed in Him as the One true God and in Muhammad as His Prophet?!

If you have any need or are in distress, turn to Him and call out: O Lord, O the Eternal Refuge, remove my distress!

So, do not be disturbed much by distress, illness, or debt. Your Lord is the Eternal Refuge. If you turn to Him, He will not let you down. Remember that the best form of worship is to wait for relief from the Almighty Lord. Indeed, nothing remains as it is; things must change. We do not know what lies ahead; and indeed ease comes with hardship.

The Prophet (may Allah's peace and blessings be upon him) entered the mosque and heard a man supplicate Allah and say: "Allāhumma inni as'aluka ya Allāh Al-Ahad As-Samad al-ladhi lam yalid wa lam yūlad wa lam yakun lahu kufuwan ahad an taghfir li dhunūbi innaka anta Al-Ghafūr Ar-Rahīm (O

Allah, I ask You, O Allah, the One, the Eternal Refuge, Who has not begotten nor was He begotten, and there is none like unto Him, to forgive my sins. Indeed You are the Oft-Forgiving, the Most Merciful)."

Thereupon, he said:"He has been forgiven, he has been forgiven, he has been forgiven."[Narrated by Abu Dāwūd; Sahīh (authentic)]Another narration reads:"You have implored Allah by the name which when asked therewith, He gives, and when supplicated therewith, He answers."[Narrated by Abu Dāwūd; Sahīh (authentic)]

My Lord, I seek Your mercy and refuge.

I pursue nothing but Your pleasure; so answer my supplication.

I call Your name, my Lord, and implore You.

If You do not answer my supplication, who will respond to my crying?

You are the All-Generous; so do not leave me stray.

I got tired of being so distant from You,

and I now implore You and turn to You,

in humiliation and humbleness; so do not turn down my invocation.

O Allah, the One and Only God, the Eternal Refuge, I ask You Paradise and the words and deeds that bring one closer to it, and I seek refuge in You from Hellfire and from the words and deeds that bring one closer to it.

Ar-Rahmān Ar-Rahīm (The Most Compassionate, the Most Merciful)

Allah Almighty says:{Say: "Invoke Allah, or invoke the Most Compassionate. Whichever you call upon, to Him belong the most beautiful names."}[Surat al-Isrā': 110]Whenever our Prophet (may Allah's peace and blessings be upon him) was distressed, he would say:"Ya Hayy ya Qayyūm birahmatika astagīth (O Allah, the Ever-Living and the All-Sustainer, I seek relief in Your mercy)."[Narrated by Ahmad in Al-Musnad; Hasan (sound)]How would a person not turn to the Most Compassionate while He is the refuge at times of hardships, the companion at times of loneliness, and the supporter at times of weakness?

He consoles the obedient servants and provides refuge to those who are fearful and fleeing to Him. Indeed, He is the Most Merciful of those who show mercy.

To Him only we should turn, and on Him alone we should pin our hopes.

{And your God is One God, there is no god but Him, the Most Compassionate, the Most Merciful.}[Surat al-Baqarah: 163]

Mercy is a divine attribute and characteristic. That is why Allah Almighty described Himself as Ar-Rahmān (the Most Compassionate) and Ar-Rahīm (the Most Merciful).

When we recite the Qur'an, we begin with these two noble and beloved names. We say: Bismillāh Ar-Rahmān Ar-Rahīm (in the name of Allah, the Most Compassionate, the Most Merciful).

These two noble names are derivatives and superlative forms of "Rahmah" (mercy).

Linguistically, "Rahmah" is a word that denotes tenderness, compassion, pity, and kindness.

So, our Lord is the Possessor of mercy that encompasses all creation.{...And My mercy encompasses all things...}[Surat al-A'rāf: 156]{...Surely Allah is indeed Ever-Compassionate, Most Merciful to mankind.}[Surat al-Hajj: 65]Allah devotes the greatest share of His mercy to the believers.{...And He has been Most Merciful to the believers.}[Surat al-Ahzāb: 43]

So, our Lord is Ar-Rahmān, which means that mercy is His attribute, and He is Ar-Rahīm, which refers to His mercy towards His servants.

Indeed, He is more Merciful to us than any merciful one, than our fathers, mothers, children, and even our own selves.

"A man came to the Prophet (may Allah's peace and blessings be upon him) with a child whom he embraced. The Prophet (may Allah's peace and blessings be upon him) asked him: 'Do you show mercy yo him?' The man said: 'Yes.' Then, the Prophet (may Allah's peace and blessings be upon him) said:'Allah is more merciful to you than you are to him, and He is the Most Merciful of those who show mercy.'"[Narrated by Al-Bukhāri in Al-Adab Al-Mufrad; Sahīh (authentic)]The name "Ar-Rahmān" belongs exclusively to Allah Almighty. No one else can be given or described with this name.{Say: "Invoke Allah, or invoke Ar-Rahmān. Whichever you call upon, to Him belong the most beautiful names"...}[Surat al-Isrā': 110]So, He equates it with the name "Allah", which exclusively belongs to Him; it cannot be used for other than Him. Some even said that it is the greatest name.As for the name "Ar-Rahīm", it can be used to describe created beings. For example, Allah Almighty says:{There has certainly come to you a Messenger from among yourselves. Grievous to him is what you suffer; [he is] concerned about you and is kind and rahīm (compassionate) towards the believers.}[Surat at-Tawbah: 128]We can say this is a "rahīm" man, but we cannot say a "rahmān" man.

The mercy of Allah falls under two categories:

General Mercy: It comprises all creatures. All created beings are shown mercy from Allah, as He has created them and raises and provides for them, in addition to other countless blessings that He bestows upon them.

{...Surely, Allah is Ever-Compassionate, Most Merciful to mankind.}[Surat al-Baqarah: 143]{Surely, He has been Most Merciful· towards you.}[Surat al-Isrā': 66]Special Mercy: It leads to happiness in this world and in the Hereafter. This kind of mercy is only shown to the believers.{...And He has been Most Merciful to the believers.}[Surat al-Ahzāb: 43]{Their Lord gives them glad tidings of mercy from Him, and blessed satisfaction, and gardens...}[Surat at-Tawbah: 21]

He is the Most Compassionate..

He is the most worthy of being remembered, worshiped, and thanked for His benevolence and mercy.

Wherever you look, you will see signs of Allah's mercy in this universe, the greatest of which is the divine revelation.{...And We have sent down to you the Book as clarification for all things and as guidance and mercy and good tidings for the Muslims.}[Surat an-Nahl: 89]If the land becomes arid, famine and drought hit, and afflictions get tough, the mercy of Allah descends.{And it is He Who sends down the rain after they had despaired and spreads His mercy. And He is the Protector, the Praiseworthy.}[Surat ash-Shūra: 28]When torment befell people, men wept, women screamed, children panicked, and horror prevailed, the mercy of Allah descended upon His sincere servants.{And when Our command came, We saved Hūd [Heber] and those who believed with him, by mercy from Us...}[Surat Hūd: 58]{And when Our command came, We saved Shu'ayb [Jethro] and those who believed with him, by mercy from Us...}[Surat Hūd: 94]

We cannot achieve our desires or get our needs fulfilled except through the Most Compassionate Lord. Everything happens according to His will. There is no power nor strength in the entire universe except through Him.

Out of His mercy, He sent His messengers to us.

Out of His mercy, He revealed His books to us.

Out of His mercy, He brought us out of misguidance into guidance.

Out of His mercy, He guided us out of blindness.

Out of His mercy, He taught us what we did not know.

Out of His mercy, He subjected the sun and moon for our benefit, created the night and day, and leveled the land.

Out of His mercy, He created Paradise and will admit its dwellers therein where they will lead a blissful life.

Out of His mercy, Allah Almighty created mercy as a hundred parts, each of it is as great as the distance between the heaven and earth. Out of these, He sent just one part of mercy to the earth, which He spread among His creation so that they can show mercy to one another. With this mercy, a mother shows compassion to her child. Indeed, the whole world and its system relies upon this mercy.

Glad tidings!

Let us talk about the vastness of Allah's mercy:{Say: "O My servants who have transgressed against themselves, do not despair of the mercy of Allah. Indeed, Allah forgives all sins. Indeed, it is He Who is the All-Forgiving, Most Merciful."}[Surat az-Zumar: 53]The Prophet (may Allah's peace and blessings be upon him) is authentically reported to have said:"If the believer were to know what is with Allah of punishment, no one would hope to enter His Paradise, and if the disbeliever were to know what is with Allah of mercy, no one would despair of entering His Paradise."[Narrated by Muslim]

This vast mercy stems from might, power, and dominance, not from weakness.

{And indeed, your Lord – He is the All-Mighty, Most Merciful.}

[Surat ash-Shu'arā': 9]

I bear witness that there is no god other than Allah. He is the Most Generous, the Most Merciful, upon Whom people pin their hopes.

Keys to mercy:

Allah is no need for us or our worship. We will not enter Paradise except with His mercy. This even applies to our Prophet (may Allah's peace and blessings be upon him).Abu Hurayrah (may Allah be pleased with him) reported that the Prophet (may Allah's peace and blessings be upon him) said: "'No one will enter Paradise by his deeds.' They said: 'Not even you, O Messenger of Allah?' He said: 'Yes, not even me, unless Allah encompasses me with grace and mercy from Him.'" [Narrated by Al-Bukhāri and Muslim]

Whoever knows this should engage in the worship of hope, and getting attached to Allah's mercy and seeking to attain it. This can be achieved through piety, faith, and acts of obedience.

By this we can attain mercy from our Lord.

{...And My mercy encompasses all things. So I will decree it [especially] for those who fear Me and give zakah and those who believe in Our verses }

[Surat al-A'rāf: 156]

Allah's mercy can be attained by obeying Him and obeying His Prophet. Allah Almighty says:{And obey Allah and the Messenger so that you may obtain mercy.}[Surat Āl-'Imrān: 132]Mercy can also be attained by doing good. Allah Almighty says:{...Indeed, the mercy of Allah is near to the doers of good.}[Surat al-A'rāf: 56]It is also obtained through seeking forgiveness. Allah Almighty says:{...Why do you not seek forgiveness of Allah so that you may receive mercy?}[Surat an-Naml: 46]

Allah's mercy can also be obtained through remembering and supplicating Him a lot.

The Prophet (may Allah's peace and blessings be upon him) said:"The supplication of a distressed one is: Allāhumma rahmataka arjū fala takilni ila nafsi tarfata 'ayn wa aslih li sha'ni kullah la ilāha illa ant (O Allah, Your mercy is what I hope for, so do not leave me to myself for a while, and put all my affairs in good order for me. There is no god but You)."[Narrated by Abu Dāwūd; Hasan (sound)]Allah's mercy can only be attained by the merciful among His servants. The Prophet (may Allah's peace and blessings be upon him) said:"Indeed, Allah shows mercy to the merciful among His servants."[Narrated by Al-

Bukhāri and Muslim]For example, a prostitute will enter Paradise by virtue of her mercy towards a thirsty dog as she gave it water in her shoes.

Do not let the devil daunt you!

Some people, when afflicted with disasters, crises, or saddening incidents, they give up their faith and fail to remember that Allah Almighty is more merciful to them than their own selves. So, they do not knock on the door of the Most Compassionate or hope for His mercy. That is why, they fall into the devil's misleading plots, which may ultimately lead them to ruin. Allah Almighty says:{...And do not kill yourselves. Surely Allah has been Most Merciful to you.}[Surat an-Nisā': 29]Do not ever think that your sin, no matter how great it may be, can be greater than Allah's mercy!The devil wants nothing but this from you; namely to make the sin look so big in your eyes that you belittle Allah's mercy in comparison.

Indeed, the mercy of Allah is greater than your sin and any sin. The man who killed 99 people and then completed them a hundred repented to Allah sincerely, so Allah forgave him.

I put all my trust in You, my Lord.

And I will not go through any door but Yours.

Allah Almighty says:{On the Day We will gather the righteous to the Most Compassionate as a delegation.}[Surat Maryam: 85]What a great promise, what a noble delegation, and what an excellent feeling! May Allah make us among this delegation.

O Allah, if we are not worthy of attaining Your mercy, indeed Your mercy is worthy of reaching us. So, encompass us in Your mercy in this world and in the Hereafter, O the Most Merciful of those who show mercy!

Al-Hayy (The Ever-Living)

When the clouds of grief attack and the shackles of distress unite together against you and you do not find a way out and things become too hard for you, as if your soul is departing through your throat and you are suffocating; at that moment when you feel life has become too harsh and restricted, people withdraw from your life leaving you alone, and you expect nothing but death,

at this moment Allah sends you relief and a window of hope, instills tranquility within you, extends a helping hand to you, and gives you life after you have almost seen death. Thereupon, you fall in prostration to Him, weeping and repeating: O the Ever-Living, the All-Sustainer, all thanks are due to You.

This can only happen when you rely upon Al-Hayy Who does not die.{And rely upon the Ever-Living who does not die, and exalt [Allah] with His praise. And sufficient is He as All-Aware concerning the sins of His servants.}[Surat al-Furqān: 58]Our Lord, Glorified and Exalted, established the attribute of life for Himself. His is a perfect and eternal life, neither preceded by nothingness nor will come to an end. It suffers no deficiency or defect and experiences no heedlessness, inability, or death. Indeed,{...No slumber or sleep can overtake Him...}[Surat al-Baqarah: 255]Far Exalted is Allah above this!His life is far exalted above being similar to the life of the created beings.{...There is nothing like unto Him: He is the All-Hearing, the All-Seeing.}[Surat ash-Shūra: 11]His is a life that entails possessing perfect attributes of knowledge, hearing, seeing, ability, will, mercy, and other attributes of perfection.Our Lord is the Ever-Living through Whom life came into existence and every living being became a living being. The life of everything apart from Him depends on His will to make it living. Allah Almighty says:{...When you were lifeless and He brought you to life; then He will cause you to die, then He will bring you [back] to life, and then to Him you will be returned.}[Surat al-Baqarah: 28]

Our Lord is the One Who gives life to our souls through the light of knowledge, guidance, and faith.

It is our Lord Who will grant the dwellers of Paradise the eternal and enduring life. He says:{...And indeed, the home of the Hereafter - that is the [eternal] life, if only they knew.}[Surat al-'Ankabūt: 64]

Clear evidence:

Allah is the Ever-Living Lord. There is no god but Him. He is sufficient for anyone who relies upon Him. None can overpower His will or escape His power. He removes harm, responds to the distressed, and brings the dead back to life as He created them in the first place, and that is easier for Him. He is the All-Wise Lord, Who does not create anything in vain or does anything without a purpose.

Ibn 'Abbās (may Allah be pleased with him and his father) reported: "Al-'Ās ibn Wā'il came to the Messenger of Allah (may Allah's peace and blessings be upon him). He got up, held a decomposed bone, broke it into small pieces with his hand, and said: 'Who will give life to decomposed bones?' - He meant to express denial of resurrection. Thereupon, the Prophet (may Allah's peace and blessings be upon him) said:'Yes, Allah will resurrect this and then He will cause you to die, bring you back to life, and then admit you into Hellfire.'Then, Allah Almighty revealed:{Does man not consider that We created him from a [mere] sperm-drop - then at once he is a clear adversary?}[Surat Yasīn: 77]To the end of the Surah."[Narrated by Ibn Jarīr, Al-Bayhaqi, and Al-Hākim, who graded the Hadīth as Sahīh and Al-Dhahabi agreed with him; Sahīh (authentic)]How ungrateful man is! He forgets his own creation and denies his Creator. Indeed, the One Who created him in the first place will repeat his creation and resurrect him. The second time is logically easier than the first one - and everything is easy for Allah Almighty.{And it is He Who begins creation; then He repeats it, and that is easier for Him...}[Surat ar-Rūm: 27]

To Allah belong might, power, majesty, pride, authority, the dominion, and judgment, and glorification and extolment. He is the Most Great, His dominion is magnificent, and His status is the highest.

Call of the universe..

Glory be to Allah Who has made for every created being a special life. The life of angels, for example, differs from the life of human beings, and the life of the latter is different from the life of jinn, and the life of animals varies from the life of humans, jinn, and angels.

Even some inanimate objects were influenced by Allah's name Al-Hayy and became living themselves. An example is the staff of Mūsa (Moses) (peace be upon him).{Then Moses threw his stick, and behold, it swallowed up all that they falsely showed.}[Surat ash-Shu'arā': 45]Even the trees have their special life. An example is the trunk that yearned for the Prophet (may Allah's peace and blessings be upon him)."The Prophet (may Allah's peace and blessings be upon him) used to deliver sermons while leaning on a trunk. Then, when he started to use the pulpit, the trunk made a sorrowful sound. So, he came to it and passed his hand over it." [Narrated by Al-Bukhāri]Another narration in Al-Sunan reads: "He came to it and embraced it, and it calmed down. Thereupon, he said:'If I had not embraced it, it would have continued to grieve until the Day of Judgment.'"[Narrated by Ibn Mājah; Sahīh (authentic)]

The emergence of life in this lifeless object is certainly one of the signs of Allah Almighty, which indicates that He is the Ever-Living Lord, besides Whom there is no god.

In everything there is a sign proving that He is the One God.

Hearts of lovers..

The Prophet (may Allah's peace and blessings be upon him) used to supplicate:"Allāhumma inni a'ūdhu bi'izatika la ilāha illa ant an tudillani anta Al-Hayy al-ladhi la yamūt wa al-jinn wa al-ins yamūtūn (O Allah, I seek refuge in Your honor - there is no god but You - that You should lead me astray; You are the Ever-Living Who does not die, whereas the jinn and humans die)."[Narrated by Muslim]Undoubtedly, guidance is the life of hearts, and it comes from the Ever-Living God, other than Whom there is no god. So, whoever wants guidance should seek it from the Ever-Living Lord, Who says:{He is the Ever-Living; there is no god but Him, so call upon Him, [being] sincere to Him in religion. Praise be to Allah, Lord of the worlds.}[Surat Ghāfir: 65]

When a person's heart abounds with belief in Allah and glorification of Him, life becomes beautiful in his eyes, he develops a clearer insight, and distress and grief go away.

The names of Allah Almighty fill the believers' hearts with love for Him and they lead, thus, a blissful life in this world and in the Hereafter.{Whoever does righteous deeds, whether male or female, while he is a believer - We will surely cause him to live a good life, and We will surely give them their reward [in the Hereafter] according to the best of what they used to do.}[Surat an-Nahl: 97]

On the other hand, the disbeliever leads a hard and an uneasy life in this world and in the Hereafter. Allah Almighty says:

{And whoever turns away from My remembrance - indeed, he will have a depressed life, and We will raise him on the Day of Resurrection blind.}

[Surat Taha: 124]

Although he is walking among the living, he is counted among the dead.

{They are, [in fact], dead, not alive, and they do not perceive when they will be resurrected.}

[Surat an-Nahl: 21]

He who dies and finds relief is not truly dead. But the true dead is the one who dies while still living.

Stand humble before Him!

Anas ibn Mālik (may Allah be pleased with him) reported: "When anything distressed the Prophet (may Allah's peace and blessings be upon him), he would say:

'Ya Hayy ya Qyyūm birahmatika astagīth (O the Ever-Living, the All-Sustainer, I seek relief in Your mercy)."

[Narrated by Ahmad; Hasan (sound)]

The Prophet (may Allah's peace and blessings be upon him) said to his daughter Fātimah (may Allah be pleased with her):

"What prevents you from listening to my advice! Say in the morning and evening: 'Ya Hayy ya Qayyūm birahmatika astagīth aslih li sha'ni kullah wa la takilni ila nafsi tarfata 'ayn (O the Ever-Living, the All-Sustainer, I seek relief in Your mercy! Reform for me all of my affairs and do not leave me to myself, even for the blink of an eye).'"

[Narrated by Al-Nasā'i; Sahīh (authentic)]

Ibn Mas'ūd (may Allah be pleased with him) reported that the Prophet (may Allah's peace and blessings be upon him) said: "Whoever says: 'Astaghfirullāh al-ladhi la ilāha illa huwa Al-Hayy Al-Qayyūm wa atūbu ilayh (I ask Allah for forgiveness, there is no god but Him, the Ever-Living, the All-Sustainer, and I repent to Him)', his sins will be forgiven, even if he fled the battlefield." [Narrated by Al-Tirmidhi and Al-Hākim; Sahīh (authentic)]

Anas (may Allah be pleased with him) reported: "A man supplicated saying: 'Allāhumma inni as'aluka bi'anna laka al-hamd la ilāha illa ant Al-Mannān Badī'u as-samāwāti wa al-ard ya Dhal-Jalāl wa Al-Ikrām ya Hayy ya Qayyūm (O Allah, I implore You by virtue of the fact that all praise is due to You, there is no god except You, the Bestower of Favors, the Originator of the heavens and earth, the Owner of Majesty and Honor, O the Ever-Living, the All-Sustainer).'

Thereupon, the Prophet (may Allah's peace and blessings be upon him) said:'He has implored Allah by His greatest name, which when supplicated therewith He answers, and when asked therewith He gives.'"[Narrated by the Compilers of Al-Sunan; Sahīh (authentic)]Ibn al-Qayyim (may Allah have mercy upon him) said:"The attribute of 'hayāh' (life) comprises and entails all attributes of perfection, and the attribute of 'qayyūmiyyah' (sustaining) comprises all the attributes of actions. That is why, the greatest name of Allah by which when asked He gives, and by which when supplicated He answers is 'Al-Hayy Al-Qayyūm'."

O Allah, I seek refuge in Your honor - there is no god except You - that You should lead me astray; You are the Ever-Living Who does not die, whereas the jinn and humans die.

O Allah, the Ever-Living, the All-Sustainer, I seek relief in Your mercy; reform for me all my affairs.

Al-Qayyūm (The All-Sustainer)

O Originator of the worlds, You are the One God, the Ever-Living, the All-Sustainer, You are the One upon Whom hopes are pinned.

All existence points to Your existence, and to Your majesty we fall in prostration.

The Prophet (may Allah's peace and blessings be upon him) heard a man supplicate, saying: "Allāhumma inni as'aluka bi'anna laka al-hamd la ilāha illa ant Al-Mannān Badī'u as-samāwāti wa al-ard ya Dhal-Jalāl wa Al-Ikrām ya Hayy ya Qayyūm (O Allah, I implore You by virtue of the fact that all praise is due to You, there is no god but You, the Bestower of Favors, the Originator of the heavens and earth, the Owner of Majesty and Honor, O the Ever-Living, the All-Sustainer)."

Thereupon, the Prophet (may Allah's peace and blessings be upon him) said:"By the One in Whose Hand my soul is, he asked Allah by His greatest name, which if He is supplicated therewith, He answers the supplication, and if He is asked therewith, He gives."[Narrated by Al-Tirmidhi; Sahīh (authentic)]

This is a message from our Prophet (may Allah's peace and blessings be upon him) to everyone leading a rough life; come to your Lord, empty your heart of anything apart from Him, and supplicate Him by His names Al-Hayy and Al-Qayyūm. He will surely respond to you and give you beyond what you hope for.

To Him alone we should turn.

And only upon Him we should pin our hopes.

We pause here with one of the beautiful names of Allah, namely "Al-Qayyūm" (the All-Sustainer).

Allah Almighty says:{And [all] faces will be humbled before the Ever-Living, the All-Sustainer...}[Surat Taha: 111]Our Lord, Exalted be He, He is self-subsisting and does not rely upon anyone for His existence or for His eternity. He is self-sufficient and is in no need for anyone.{O people, it is you who stand in need of Allah; as for Allah, He is the Self-Sufficient, the Praiseworthy.}[Surat Fātir: 15]

Our Lord, Exalted be He, sustains all creatures, whether in the heavens or the earth. None of them can remain alive without Him. They stand in need of Him from all aspects, and He does not need them in any way. Even the Throne and those angels who carry it, Allah Almighty sustains them.

Our Lord, Exalted be He, sustains the entire universe and all the creatures existing therein, in all their conditions. He preserves them, provides for them, and manages all their affairs at all times.

He also sustains His servants and records their deeds and words, the good and bad thereof, and He will recompense them accordingly on the Day of Judgment.{Is He who is a Sustainer of every soul, [knowing] what it has done, [like any other]? But to Allah they have attributed partners. Say: "Name them. Or do you inform Him of that which He knows not upon the earth or of what is apparent of speech?" Rather, their [own] plan has been made attractive to those who disbelieve, and they have been averted from the way. And whomever Allah causes to stray - there will be no guide for him.}[Surat ar-Ra'd: 33]As part of His perfect divinity, the heavens and the earth got established and settled by His command and power, without any pillars.{Indeed, Allah holds the heavens and the earth, lest they cease. And if they should cease, no one could hold them [in place] after Him. Indeed, He is All-Forbearing, All-Forgiving.}[Surat Fātir: 41]

The only Deity worthy of worship..

Allah is the Ever-Living, the All-Sustainer, the Lord of the worlds, the Most Merciful of those who show mercy, the Most Powerful of the powerful, the Most Wise of the wise, the One to Whom the creation and command belong and in Whose hand lie benefit and harm.

The sound natural disposition leads to Him, minds recognize Him, and all that exists points to His existence. Everything in the universe, still or moving, indicates His existence and the fact that He is the Sustainer of all existence. He is the One Who responds to those in distress, removes harm, relieves people of their anguish, and forgives errors.

He is the One Whose help is sought in dealing with any calamity and Whose favors and blessings keep descending.

He is the One to Whom all faces and voices will be humbled.{And [all] faces will be humbled before the Ever-Living, the All-Sustainer...}[Surat Taha: 111]

He is the One most worthy of being remembered, worshiped, and praised. He is the Best Supporter, the Most Compassionate King, the Most Generous Giver, the Most Forgiving and All-Powerful, and the Most Just in retribution.

His forbearance follows His knowledge, His pardon and forgiveness follow His ability and power, and His withholding is for a wise purpose.

He is Allah, the Ever-Living, the All-Sustainer, Who has no partner, and the One Who has no equal:{Allah - there is no god except Him, the Ever-Living, the All-Sustainer...}[Surat al-Baqarah: 255]

He has made some of His signs clear to those who contemplate, and some are clear to all. He has rebutted the excuses of the obstinate and the arguments of the deniers, thus brightly revealing the signs of His lordship and divinity.

Allah Almighty is the Sustainer of all creation. He does not need any of them, and they all stand in need of Him - the close angels, the carriers of the Throne, and the inhabitants of the heavens and the earth.{O people, it is you who stand in need of Allah; as for Allah, He is the Self-Sufficient, the Praiseworthy.}[Surat Fātir: 15]To Allah belong honor, power, majesty, pride, authority, the dominion, and judgment. Glorification and extolment are due to Him. He is perfect in His attributes and actions.{Allah - there is no god except Him, the Ever-Living, the All-Sustainer. No drowsiness or sleep overtakes Him. To Him belongs whatever is in the heavens and whatever is on the earth...}[Surat al-Baqarah: 255]Allah Almighty does not sleep, and it does not befit Him to sleep. The Prophet (may Allah's peace and blessings be upon him) is authentically reported to have said:"Allah does not sleep, and it is not befitting of Him to sleep. He lowers the Scales and raises them. The deeds done during the night are taken up to Him before the deeds done during the day, and the deeds done during the day before the deeds done during the night. His veil is light - fire - and if He were to remove it, the glory of his face would burn everything of His creation as far as His sight reaches."[Narrated by Muslim]

Glory be to the One Whose light brightened the heavens and the earth and Whose Face illuminated darkness. Glory be to the Ever-Living, the All-Sustainer!

Rest assured!

Whoever knows that Allah is the All-Sustainer, his heart will no longer be attached to created beings, rather his heart will feel at ease with His Creator, his Provider, and the Manager of his affairs. Within our souls, there is a need that cannot be fulfilled by wealth, prestige, pleasures, or fame.

It can only be fulfilled by having faith in Allah Almighty, feeling secure with Him, and relying upon Him. Glory be to Allah Who says:{Those who believe and whose hearts are assured by the remembrance of Allah. Unquestionably, by the remembrance of Allah hearts are assured.}[Surat ar-Ra'd: 28]

We implore You, our Lord, the Ever-Living, the All-Sustainer, to forgive our sins, conceal our faults, help us obey You, admit us into Paradise, and save us from Hellfire.

Al-Malik Al-Malīk (The King)

Ibn Mas'ūd (may Allah be pleased with him) reported: "A Jewish rabbi came to the Messenger of Allah (may Allah's peace and blessings be upon him) and said: 'O Muhammad, Allah will put the Heavens on one finger and the earth on one finger, the trees on one finger, water and dust on one finger, and the rest of the creation on one finger, and then He will say: "I am the King."'

Thereupon, the Prophet (may Allah's peace and blessings be upon him) laughed until his molar teeth became visible, in confirmation of the rabbi's words. Then, he recited:{They did not recognize the true worth of Allah. On the Day of Judgment the whole earth will be in His grasp, and the heavens shall be folded up in His right hand. Glory be to Him! Exalted be He above what they associate with Him.}[Surat az-Zumar: 67]" [Narrated by Al-Bukhāri]

No one knows what He deserves but He.

No one comprehends His knowledge but He.

No one knows His true worth but He.

No one can render the due praise to Him but He.

Words and eloquence fall short here and declare their incompetence.

Modesty fills our hearts at this moment as we seek to enumerate the excellent traits of the King of all kings. We would be honored to rub our noses in dust in exaltation of Him, and we are honored to move our tongues and pens in praise of Him. Whenever we glorify and extol Him, this is but a favor from Him upon us.

O Lord, none can praise You duly.

No matter what we say, You are still far greater.

Let us pause here with the name "Al-Malik" (the King):

{He is Allah, there is no god except Him, the King...}[Surat al-Hashr: 23]

Our Lord, Exalted be He, executes His commands in His dominion, and He is the Owner of all dominion. He is the King and Sovereign on the Day of Judgment and of all creation. There is no other king higher or equal to Him. All else are below Him. He is the Disposer of all things. None can resist His will or compete with Him - Exalted be He.

He is the All-Mighty King, Who owns every part and corner of the whole universe. All kings perish, but He is the Eternal King.

He is the One Whose forgiveness is sought and Whose dominion endures eternally.

The true dominion belongs to Allah Almighty alone, no one shares it with Him. Anyone who owns something is only given by the real Owner of all things. The Prophet (may Allah's peace and blessings be upon him) said:"There is no owner but Allah Almighty."Another narration reads:"There is no king but Allah."[Narrated by Muslim]{Say: "O Allah, Owner of Sovereignty, You give sovereignty to whom You will and You take sovereignty away from whom You will. You honor whom You will and You humble whom You will. In Your hand is [all] good. Indeed, You are Capable of all things.}[Surat Āl-'Imrān: 26]

Our Almighty Lord is the Owner of the treasures of the heavens and earth. All goodness lies in His hand, and He gives sustenance to whomever He wills.

He is the Sovereign over death, life, resurrection, benefit, harm, and all things.

He disposes of His dominion as He wishes. Every day He is upon some affair. The Prophet (may Allah's peace and blessings be upon him) is authentically reported to have said:"His affairs include forgiving sins, relieving distress, raising some people, and bringing others down."[Narrated by Ibn Mājah; Hasan (sound)]This is the dominion of Allah Almighty, and He gives it to whomever He wills.{...And Allah gives

His sovereignty to whom He wills...}[Surat al-Baqarah: 247]The Messenger of Allah (may Allah's peace and blessings be upon him) said:"Do not curse time, for Allah Almighty said: 'I am time. The days and nights belong to Me. I make them come and go and bring kings after kings.'"[Narrated by Ahmad, the first part is narrated by Muslim; Sahīh (authentic)]

Where are the kings who once wore magnificent crowns, yet they were later destroyed?

They could do nothing against the command of Allah and so they perished as if they had never existed.

The devil enticed them..

When Allah Almighty gave dominion to Pharaoh, he thought he was its real owner, so he acted arrogantly and tyrannically and oppressed people. He even attributed to himself the dominion and divinity.{And Pharaoh said: "O eminent ones, I have not known you to have a god other than me...}[Surat al-Qasas: 38]Thus, Allah Almighty destroyed him and made him an example and a lesson for all kings on earth till the Day of Resurrection so their authority would not make them forget their reality and weakness and the Day of Judgment.

Although kings have a semblance of dominion in worldly life, as they possess estates, palaces, gardens, gold and silver, they inevitably have one of two choices: either their possessions will go away and leave them, or they themselves will pass away. Indeed, their kingdom is a transient one, a loan to be paid back.

So, Allah Almighty reminds them that they will ultimately return to Him:{...And to Allah belongs the dominion of the heavens and the earth, and to Allah is the destination.}[Surat al-Mā'idah: 18]Also, the Prophet (may Allah's peace and blessings be upon him) forbade using the title "king of kings" for any human being. He said:"The meanest name in the sight of Allah is a man calling himself the king of kings." [Narrated by Al-Bukhāri and Muslim]

Sovereign of the Day of Recompense..

On the Day of Judgment, Allah Almighty will put the heavens in His right Hand and the earth in the other Hand. In the Qur'an, He says:{They did not recognize the true worth of Allah. On the Day of Judgment the whole earth will be in His grasp, and the heavens shall be folded up in His right hand. Glory be to Him! Exalted be He above what they associate with Him.}[Surat az-Zumar: 67]" [Narrated by Al-Bukhāri]Abu Hurayrah (may Allah be pleased with him) reported that the Prophet (may Allah's peace and blessings be upon him) said:"Allah Almighty will take in His grip the earth on the Day of Judgment and He will fold up the sky in His right hand. Then, He will say: 'I am the King; where are the kings of the earth?'" [Narrated by Al-Bukhāri and Muslim]'Abdullah ibn 'Umar (may Allah be pleased with him and his father) reported that the Prophet (may Allah's peace and blessings be upon him) said:"Allah Almighty will fold up the heavens on the Day of Judgment and then hold them with His right hand. Then, He will say: 'I am the King! Where are the tyrants? Where are the arrogant?'

Then, He will fold up the earths with His left Hand and say: 'I am the King! Where are the tyrants? Where are the arrogant?'" [Narrated by Muslim]

On the Day of Judgment, the Almighty Lord will call out: "To whom belongs the dominion today?" No one will answer Him!Then, He will respond to Himself: {...To Allah, the One, the Superb Vanquisher.} [Surat Ghāfir: 16]

His dominion is absolute:

Although Allah Almighty is the King and is in no need for our worship, He, out of His kindness and bounty, couples His name "Al-Malik" (the King) with other names that inspire assurance within our hearts and make us long to meet Him. He says:{The Most Compassionate, the Most Merciful.The Sovereign of the Day of Recompense.}[Surat al-Fātihah: 3-4]He also says:{...He is the Most Compassionate, the Most Merciful.He is Allah; there is no god except Him, the King...}[Surat al-Hashr: 22-23]Allah Almighty informs us that a kingdom does not become good and perfect without benevolence and mercy. He, Glorified and Exalted, is the Merciful King.The kingdom of our Lord is free from any deficiency.{Whatever is in the heavens and whatever is on the earth glorifies Allah, the King, the Most

Holy, the All-Mighty, the All-Wise.}[Surat al-Jumu'ah: 1]Since the kings of this world do have deficiencies and defects such as arrogance, indulgence in vain desires, and injustice, Allah Almighty informed us that His dominion is perfect and comprises all attributes of perfection and excellence. Hence, the Prophet (may Allah's peace and blessings be upon him) would always say after finishing Witr prayer:"Subhān Al-Malik Al-Quddūs (Glory be to Allah, the King, the Most Holy)." He would say it three times, raising his voice in the third one.[Narrated by Al-Nasā'i; Sahīh (authentic)]One is required to praise Allah Almighty for His kingship and mercy and to constantly glorify Him. Our Lord says:{...To Him belongs the dominion, and to Him belongs all praise...}[Surat at-Taghābun: 1]He is praised in His dominion. A dominion without praise entails deficiency, and praise without a dominion entails powerlessness. Indeed, praise along with dominion represent the utmost perfection and majesty.As an aspect of the magnificence of His dominion, He helps those who resort to Him, and none can help or protect anyone whom Allah wills to destroy.{Say: "In whose hand is the realm of all things - and He protects while none can protect against Him - if you should know?"}[Surat al-Mu'minūn: 88]

O the King, Who holds the forelocks of His creation, I seek refuge in You, O the Most Generous Lord.

Your predestination is sure to occur. I am Your servant, seeking Your refuge and protection.

O the One Whose dominion never goes away!

Biographers said: "When Hārūn al-Rashīd built his palace, whose magnificence was unmatched at the time,people came to congratulate him. Among them was Abu al-'Atāhiyah, who stood up and sang:

'Live as long as you wish, safe and sound. Whatever you covet comes to you and whatever you want happens. But when the soul is struggling to leave the body and you are in the throes of death, you will then know for sure

that your living in lofty palaces and great luxury was nothing but conceit and delusion!'

Thereupon, Hārūn wept so powerfully that he fell to the ground. Only a month later, he was dead."

That was Hārūn! The one who would address the cloud saying: "Drop your rain wherever you want. The yield will reach me." The one who used to perform Hajj in a year and conduct Jihad the following year.

'Abd al-Malik ibn Marawān, the ruler of the Muslim world in the past, when he was in the throes of death, he heard a washing man next to his palace singing in great joy. Thereupon, 'Abd al-Malik said: "I wish I were a washing man! Would that I did not know the rule or caliphate!" Then, he died.

Another man said: "O You Whose dominion never goes away, show mercy to the one whose dominion went away." Hearing these words, Sa'īd ibn al-Musayyib replied: "Praise be to Allah Who made them flee to us in the throes of death, and we do not flee to them."

Knock on the door of the King!

Dear reader, illness goes away, afflictions come to an end, sins are forgiven, debts are repaid, prisoners get released, absent people come back, sinners repent, and the poor get rich. All these lie in the hand of the King of all kings, Glorified and Exalted. So, let Allah be your refuge and source of hope at all times, especially in the last part of the night when He descends every night to the lowest heaven and calls out:"I am the King, I am the King! Who will supplicate Me, so that I will answer his supplication? Who will ask from Me, so that I will grant him his request? Who will ask Me for forgiveness, so that I will forgive him?" He continues to say so till dawn comes bright."[Narrated by Muslim]

Our Prophet (may Allah's peace and blessings be upon him), who is the most knowledgeable among people of the Almighty Creator and the most devoted in worshiping Him, urged us to constantly acknowledge the dominion of Allah Almighty right after the prayers and if we abruptly wake up in the night. We should make this part of our regular Dhikr in the morning and evening and upon return from journeys. Moreover, if we repeat this a hundred times during a day, we will be among the winners.

The Prophet (may Allah's peace and blessings be upon him) is authentically reported to have said:"Whoever says a hundred times in a day: 'La ilāha illallāh wahdahu la sharīka lah, lahu al-mulku wa lahu al-hamdu wa huwa 'ala kulli shay'in qadīr (there is no god except Allah. He is One and He has no partner with Him; to Him belong the sovereignty and praise, and He is over all things competent),' he will have a reward equivalent to that of emancipating ten slaves, a hundred good deeds will be added to his record, a hundred of his sins will be erased, and he will be shielded against the devil on that day till the evening; and no one will exceed him in doing good deeds except someone who says more than that."[Narrated by Al-Bukhāri and Muslim]

O Allah, the Sovereign of the Day of Recompense, render our last deeds to be the best ones, and make the reckoning easy for us, O Lord of the worlds.

As-Subūh (The All-Glorious)

Scholars said that Tawhīd of the names and attributes of Allah rests upon two foundations, which are the core of monotheism:

1. Establishing perfection in the names, attributes, and actions of Allah Almighty.

2. Exalting Allah far above any deficiency or defect that contradicts His perfect essence, attributes, and actions.

Out of Allah's mercy towards us, He taught us how to extol and glorify Him. He says:{And glorify Him in the morning and in the afternoon.}[Surat al-Ahzāb: 42]

Glory be to the One Who is constantly glorified!

Glory be to the One Whose remembrance brings contentment!

Glory be to Him alone, and never to anyone else!

The Prophet (may Allah's peace and blessings be upon him) used to say during his bowing and prostration in prayer:"Subbūhun Quddūs, Rabbu al-malā'ikati wa ar-rūh (the All-Glorious, the Most Holy, Lord of the angels and of the Spirit)."[Narrated by Muslim]

When we glorify Allah Almighty, this means we declare Him free from any deficiency or defect.

Indeed, our Lord is exalted above any defect or evil. To Him belongs the ultimate perfection.

You are more worthy..

The entire universe is a place for worshiping Allah. Everything therein glorifies the Almighty Lord, and this is the greatest form of worship.

The angels, inhabitants of the heavens:{They said: "Will You place upon it one who causes corruption therein and sheds blood, while we exalt You with praise and declare Your perfection?" He said: "Indeed, I know what you do not know."}[Surat al-Baqarah: 30]

There is nothing in the universe that does not glorify Allah Almighty, except the disbelievers among the jinn and humans.

Allah Almighty says:{The seven heavens and the earth and whatever is in them glorify Him. And there is not a thing except that it glorifies [Allah] by His praise, but you do not understand their [way of] glorifying. Indeed, He is All-Forbearing, All-Forgiving.}[Surat al-Isrā': 44]

Allah Almighty is the One worthy of being glorified, given His perfect essence and attributes.

Abu Hurayrah (may Allah be pleased with him) reported: "I heard the Messenger of Allah (may Allah's peace and blessings be upon him) say:'An ant had bitten a prophet; thereupon, he ordered that the colony of ants be burnt. Then Allah revealed to him: "You have burnt a community from amongst the communities that glorify Me because of an ant's bite!"'[Narrated by Al-Bukhāri - this is his wording - and Muslim]Mountains and birds also glorify Allah Almighty:{...And We subjected the mountains to glorify [Us], along with David and [also] the birds. And We were doing [that].}[Surat al-Anbiyā': 79]So, it is even more appropriate for us to glorify the Almighty Lord. One of the righteous predecessors said: "Would anyone of you not be ashamed that the animal he rides and the garment he wears mentions Allah more often than he does!"

Obedient hearts..

As pious people learned about the reward of good deeds and that glorification of Allah is the dearest speech to Him, they vied with one another in glorifying their Lord in all their situations. Indeed, that is the easy booty. The Prophet (may Allah's peace and blessings be upon him) said: "Two words are light for the tongue to utter, heavy in the scales, and are dear to the Most Compassionate: 'Subhānallāh wa bihamdih, subhānallāh Al-'Azhīm (Glory be to Allah and praise be to Him, Glory be to Allah, the Magnificent)."[Narrated by Al-Bukhāri and Muslim] The Prophet (may Allah's peace and blessings be upon him) is also authentically reported to have said: "Whoever says: 'Subhānallāh wa bihamdih (Glory be to Allah, and praise be to Him)' one hundred times a day, his sins will be erased even if they were as much as the foam of the sea."[Narrated by Al-Bukhāri and Muslim] He (may Allah's peace and blessings be upon him) said: "Is anyone of you unable to earn a thousand good deeds during a day?" One of those present asked: "How can one of us earn a thousand good deeds?" He said: "He glorifies Allah a hundred times, and thus a thousand good deeds will be recorded for him, or a thousand sins will be erased from him."[Narrated by Muslim]

Keys to happiness:

Glorification of Allah Almighty is one of the lasting good things.

Glorification of Allah comforts His obedient servants and provides refuge for the fearful among them, as they know that the One Whom they glorify and exalt above any imperfection or defect is their refuge at times of hardship, their companion in their loneliness, and their supporter when they are few and weak.

How could the supplications of those who glorify Allah a lot not be answered while they are the ones who know their Lord at times of ease?! How come He does not know them at times of hardship?!

Take Yūnus (Jonah) (peace be upon him) as an example. Allah Almighty says about him:{And had he not been of those who glorify Allah, He would have surely remained in its belly till the Day of Resurrection.}[Surat as-Sāffāt: 143-144] Ibn 'Abbās (may Allah be pleased with him and his father) said: "Fish in the sea would at times stay still, but he would not take rest from glorification of Allah. Frogs would keep silent, but he would continue to mention Allah Almighty." Al-Hasan said: "Yūnus (Jonah) did not offer prayer in the belly of the whale, yet the good deeds he had performed at the time of ease were the reason Allah took care of him at the time of affliction." Al-Karaji said: "This indicates that glorification of Allah and proclaiming His Oneness remove anguish and save one from distress and afflictions." A reported citation reads: "A righteous person gets recognized in heaven." This is because glorification of Allah is a righteous act and Allah Almighty says:{...To Him ascends good speech...}[Surat Fātir: 10] With glorification, a person is given sustenance. In Al-Adab Al-Mufrad, the Prophet (may Allah's peace and blessings be upon him) said: "...And 'subhānallāh wa bihamdih (glory be to Allah and praise be to Him)'; that is the prayer of everything, and with it everything is given sustenance."[Sahīh (authentic)]

Glory be to You!

Glory be to Allah as many as what He created in the heavens.

Glory be to Allah as many as what He created in the earth.

Glory be to Allah as many as the creation between them.

Glory be to Allah as many as what He creates.

Allah Almighty commands His servants to glorify Him a lot at the times of sunrise and sunset. He says:{So glorified is Allah when you reach the evening and when you reach the morning.}[Surat ar-Rūm: 17] He also says:{And glorify Him in the morning and in the evening.}[Surat al-Ahzāb: 42] Given the significance of glorification, Allah Almighty will inspire the dwellers of Paradise to glorify Him as naturally as breathing.{Their call therein will be, "Glory be to You, O Allah," and their greeting therein will be: "Peace." And the last of their call will be: "Praise be to Allah, Lord of the worlds!"}[Surat Yūnus: 10]Ibn Rajab (may Allah have mercy upon him) said:"Every deed comes to an end, except for the remembrance of Allah, which does not come to a halt. All deeds cease when the world ceases to exist, and nothing of it will remain in the Hereafter, except for the remembrance of Allah. The believer lives, dies, and gets resurrected upon the remembrance of Allah."

Glory be to the One Who is glorified by all creatures and all tongues.

Glory be to Him for the favors He bestows upon us.

Glory be to the One Who is glorified by those who knew that

glorification of Him is one of the best means of protection.

Glory be to the One Who disgraces the sinners or

forgives grave sins and minor ones if He so wills.

Glory be to the One from Whom we ask the forgiveness of a Mighty Lord

and seek refuge from severe retribution.

May Allah make us among those who glorify Him and extend praise to Him, and among the believers in His names and attributes who believe in His Oneness and extol Him; indeed, He is All-Hearing, Near.

{So glorified is Allah when you reach the evening and when you reach the morning.And to Him is all praise throughout the heavens and the earth. And [glorified is He] at night and when you are at noon.}[Surat ar-Rūm: 17-18]

Al-Quddūs (The Most Holy)

Go and buy today while the market is still there, while you can pay the price, and while the commodities cost little. There will come a day when this market and these commodities will not be available at any cost.{...That is the Day of Deprivation...}[Surat at-Taghābun: 9]{And the Day the wrongdoer will bite on his hands [in regret]...}[Surat al-Furqān: 27]

If you depart without a provision of piety, you will be in deep regret.

And on the Day of Resurrection you will see those with adequate provisions and know that you did not work for this day.

Let us spend some time with one of the beautiful names of Allah that brings us closer to Him, comprises the essence of monotheism, and constitutes one of the two pillars of the Tawhīd of names and attributes; namely "Al-Quddūs" (the Most Holy).

Allah Almighty says:{He is Allah, there is no god but Him, the King, the Most Holy...}[Surat al-Hashr: 23]The Prophet (may Allah's peace and blessings be upon him) used to say in his bowing and prostration:"Subbūhun Quddūs rabbu al-malā'ikati wa ar-rūh (The All-Glorious, the Most Holy, Lord of the angels and of the Spirit)." [Narrated by Muslim]It is also reported that when the Prophet (may Allah's peace and blessings be upon him) finished the Witr prayer, he would say:"Subhān Al-Malik Al-Quddūs, subhān Al-Malik Al-Quddūs, subhān Al-Malik Al-Quddūs (Glory be to the King, the Most Holy; glory be to the King, the Most Holy; glory be to the King, the Most Holy)." He would raise his voice in the third time.[Narrated by Ahmad; Sahīh (authentic)]

Linguistically, "Quddūs" means purity and integrity. It also means the blessed one.

Our Lord is the Most Holy, the One free from deficiencies and defects and exalted above having a wife, children, or equals. He is praised with the mention of His virtues and merits and His perfect attributes.

Our Lord is the source of all blessing, Whose favors and gifts exist on earth and in the heavens in abundance and at all times. Blessed is His name and blessed are His actions, essence, and sublime attributes. He is the One Who purifies whomever He wills from among His servants according to His wisdom.{...Allah intends only to remove from you the impurity [of sin], O people of the [Prophet's] household, and to purify you with [extensive] purification.}[Surat al-Ahzāb: 33]

Glorified is He!

Our Lord is the One worthy of being sanctified, glorified, and exalted by all creation far above any imperfection.

The angels, inhabitants of the heavens, worship Allah Almighty by sanctifying Him:{...While we declare Your praise and sanctify You?...}[Surat al-Baqarah: 30]The entire universe sanctifies and glorifies the Almighty Creator:{Whatever is in the heavens and whatever is on the earth is exalting Allah. To Him belongs dominion, and to Him belongs [all] praise, and He is Capable over all things.}[Surat at-Taghābun: 1]{The seven heavens and earth and whatever is between them glorify Him. And there is not a thing except that it glorifies [Allah] by His praise...}[Surat al-Isrā': 44]

You are more worthy..

The worthiest among the created beings of sanctifying the Almighty Lord are humans.

Sanctifying Allah Almighty is by

loving Him and exalting Him far above any deficiency or defect;

by affirming what He affirms for Himself or what the Prophet affirmed for Him;

and by holding Him far exalted above being similar to any of His creation:{...There is nothing like unto Him: He is the All-Hearing, the All-Seeing.}[Surat ash-Shūra: 11]

Sanctifying Allah Almighty is also by exalting Him above having partners, by referring to and being pleased with His Shariah as a source of rule and judgment, and by having good expectations about Him.

Whoever ascribes to Him other than what is established by Him or His messengers or denies any of the attributes by which He is described by Himself or by His messengers has thus mistrusted his Lord and thought ill of Him.

One of the attributes of the Most Compassionate Lord is that He is the Most Holy.

Your share in this name..

The believer can sanctify, or purify, himself by performing acts of obedience, avoiding sins, refining his heart, and keeping away from unlawfully gained money. Allah Almighty praises such attitude saying:{He who who purifies it has succeeded,And he who corrupts it has failed.}[Surat ash-Shams: 9-10]Allah Almighty clarified to Mūsa (Moses) (peace be upon him) the purpose behind sending him to Pharaoh, namely to purify himself by sanctifying Allah Almighty:{Go to Pharaoh. Indeed, he has transgressed.And say to him: "Would you purify yourself,and let me guide you to your Lord so you would fear [Him]?"}[Surat an-Nāzi'āt: 17-19]Hence, none can attain success without this spiritual purification.{He who purifies it has succeeded,And mentions the name of his Lord and prays.}[Surat al-A'la: 14-15]Moreover, Allah Almighty removes purity from the wrongful nations.The Prophet (may Allah's peace and blessings be upon him) is authentically reported to have said:"Indeed, Allah does not purify a nation where the weak do not take their rights from the strong."[Narrated by Al-Bayhaqi in Al-Sunan Al-Kubra; Sahīh (authentic)]The Prophet (may Allah's peace and blessings be upon him) is also authentically reported to have said:"How could Allah purify a nation where the rights of the weak are not taken from the strong?!"

When Abu al-Dardā' sent a letter to Salmān al-Fārisi (may Allah be pleased with both of them) inviting him to leave Iraq for the sacred land, Salmān sent him a reply eloquently clarifying the concept of sacredness saying: "Indeed, the land does not purify anyone. Rather, it is one's deeds that purify him."

Glory be to the One Who ceaselessly gives sustenance and grants the wishes of His creation.

The worlds depend on Him and feel assured about His provision.

O Allah, the All-Glorious, the Most Holy, we implore You to purify us, forgive our sins, and show mercy to us, O the Most Merciful of those who show mercy!

As-Salām (The Source of Peace)

Anas (may Allah be pleased with him) reported that the Messenger of Allah (may Allah's peace and blessings be upon him) said:"Indeed, 'As-Salām' is one of the names of Allah Almighty which Allah has put on earth. So, spread the greeting of peace among yourselves."[Narrated by Al-Bukhāri in Al-Adab Al-Mufrad; Sahīh (authentic)]

The believer should continue to ask Allah Almighty for safety in this world and in the Hereafter. Safety in worldly life is of two types: outward and inward.

Outward safety is good health and being free from ills and all unpleasant conditions.

Inward safety is religious soundness and freedom from disbelief, religious innovations, and disobedience to Allah.

That thing which the believer seeks is the firmest bond of faith. If he attains it, he will win himself a sound heart and will enter the abode of peace, i.e. Paradise.

Everyone seeks peace, and Allah is the Source of Peace, Blessed and Exalted.

Ibn Al-Qayyim (may Allah have mercy upon him) said: "Many have memorized this name but are unaware of such secrets and meanings contained therein."

Allah Almighty says:{He is Allah, there is no god except Him, the King, the Most Holy, the Source of Peace, the Giver of Belief (Security), the All-Controller...}[Surat al-Hashr: 23]

Our Lord, the Source of Peace, is the One free from any deficiency or defect, for He is perfect in His essence, attributes, and actions.

In Arabic, "salāmah" means innocence or well-being.

Allah Almighty is the Source of Peace and the One free from

any defect and He is exalted above any similarity to His creation.

In fact, our Lord is worthier of this name than anyone else.

Let us pause here with the name "As-Salām":

This name is reflected in the attributes of Allah Almighty, for His life is free from death, slumber, and sleep. He is the All-Sustainer and the All-Powerful Lord Who undergoes no fatigue or exhaustion.

"As-Salām" is reflected in His knowledge as well, for He is free from missing or forgetting anything and free from the need to remember or give thought.{...And not absent from your Lord is any [part] of an atom's weight within the earth or within the heaven or [anything] smaller than that or greater but that it is in a clear register.}[Surat Yūnus: 61]{...And never is your Lord forgetful.}[Surat Maryam: 64]His words are free from lying and injustice. Indeed, they are all truthful and just.{And the word of your Lord has been fulfilled in truth and in justice...}[Surat al-An'ām: 115]

His self-sufficiency is free from any need in any way. Rather, everyone and everything are in need of Him. Yet, He needs nothing.

His dominion is free from any disputant, partner, assistant, or supporter.

His forbearance, pardon, and forgiveness are free from being rooted in some sort of need, humiliation, or pretense on His part - as some created beings do.

Even His punishment and revenge are free from injustice, gloating, and undue severity or cruelty. Rather, they entirely stem from His wisdom and justice.{...And your Lord is not ever unjust to [His] servants.}[Surat Fussilat: 46]

His decree and predestination are free from frivolity and injustice.

His Shariah and religion are free from inconsistencies, contradictions, and flaws.{Then do they not reflect upon the Qur'an? If it had been from [any] other than Allah, they would have found within it much contradiction.}[Surat an-Nisā': 82]

His establishment above the Throne is free from need for any to carry it. Rather, it is the Throne that needs Him, and so do those who carry it. Indeed, He is in no need for the Throne or its carriers, or anyone else.

His hearing and sight are free from anything imagined by those who liken Him to His creation or claimed by those who deny any of His attributes.

Even His love for His pious servants is free from the casual things that arise in love between created beings, given that it stems from need, flattery, or benefiting.

Rewarding the lovers:

Allah Almighty gave the greeting of peace to His prophets and messengers for their faith and piety and to encourage people to take them as examples. Thus, none should speak badly of them.{And peace upon the messengers.}[Surat as-Sāffāt: 181]Then, Allah Almighty honored Yahya (John) (peace be upon him) by singling him out with peace in a number of situations, which are said to be the loneliest for people: the day he was born, when he saw himself leaving where he had been; the day he dies, when he would see those whom he has never seen before; and the day he will be resurrected, when he will see the tremendous gathering.{And peace be on him the day he was born, and the day he dies, and the day he will be raised alive.}[Surat Maryam: 15]Those who follow the guidance of Allah Almighty will be safe from His wrath and punishment. This is the meaning of the verse that says:{...And peace be upon he who follows the guidance.}[Surat Taha: 47]Paradise is the abode of peace:{They will have the abode of peace with their Lord...}[Surat al-An'ām: 127]Allah Almighty will greet His servants in Paradise:{"Peace," a word from a Most Merciful Lord.}[Surat Yasīn: 58]Moreover, the angels greet and reassure His righteous servants upon taking their souls:{Those whose lives the angels take while they are good and pure, saying: "Peace be upon you! Enter Paradise for what you used to do."}[Surat an-Nahl: 32]

Your share in this name..

We can worship Allah Almighty through His name "As-Salām" by purifying our hearts and tongues from any spite or offense against Muslims. The Prophet (may Allah's peace and blessings be upon him) said:"The Muslim is the one from whose tongue and hand the Muslims are safe, and the immigrant is the one who abandons what Allah has forbidden."[Narrated by Al-Bukhāri and Muslim]We should not merely stop at this level in terms of refraining from harming others. Rather, we should also fulfill the duty related to this great name. The Prophet (may Allah's peace and blessings be upon him) said:"Indeed, 'As-Salām' is one of the names of Allah Almighty which Allah has put on earth. So, spread the greeting of peace among yourselves."[Narrated by Al-Bukhāri in Al-Adab Al-Mufrad; Sahīh (authentic)]One of the merits of this greeting - "As-salāmu 'alaykum" (peace be upon you) - is that it leads to the abode of peace, i.e. Paradise. The Prophet (may Allah's peace and blessings be upon him) is authentically reported to have said:"You will not enter Paradise until you believe and you will not believe until you love one another. Shall I tell you of something which, if you do, will make you love one another? Spread the greeting of peace among yourselves."[Narrated by Muslim]

Note..

We should not say: Peace be upon Allah!

Indeed, peace comes from Allah and belongs to Him. When the Prophet (may Allah's peace and blessings be upon him) heard the Companions say: "Peace be upon Allah", he said:"Indeed, Allah is the Source of Peace. You should rather say: 'At-tahiyyātu lillāhi wa as-salawātu wa at-tayyibātu, as-salāmu 'alayka ayyuha an-nabiyyu wa rahmatullāhi wa barakātuh, as-salāmu 'alayna wa 'ala 'ibādillāhi as-sālihīn,ash-hadu alla ilāha illallāh wa ash-hadu anna Muhammadan 'abduhu wa rasūluh (All greetings, prayers, and good things are due to Allah. Peace, mercy, and blessings of Allah be upon you, O Prophet; and peace be upon us and upon the righteous servants of Allah.I testify that there is no god except Allah, and I testify that Muhammad is His servant and messenger).'"[Narrated by Al-Bukhāri and Muslim]Another narration adds: "If you say this, it will benefit every righteous servant of Allah in the heaven and on earth."[Narrated by Al-Bukhāri and Muslim]

O Allah, You are the Source of Peace and from You comes all peace. Blessed are You, O Owner of Majesty and Honor.

O Allah, grant us safety in our religion, which is the firm bond of protection; grant us safety in our worldly life in which we subsist; and grant us safety in our life in the Hereafter, which we are promised; and admit us into the abode of peace; indeed, You are competent over all things.

Al-Mu'min (The Giver of Belief/Security)

On top of the mountains, there is a rising sun of hope and relief that dispels darkness and grief.

Open your eyes and raise your hands in supplication to your Lord. Do not let grief or despair get the better of you. There is a Lord Who gives you safety and security. He is Allah, the Giver of Belief.

Fish, birds, and wild beasts all hope for safety and security from Allah Almighty, Al-Mu'min.

So, turn to the Giver of Belief and complain to Him, and relief will soon come to you from Him. His acts of kindness and relief do occur at every moment.

"Al-Mu'min" is one of the names of Allah Almighty, Who says:{He is Allah, there is no god except Him, the King, the Most Holy, the Source of Peace, the Giver of Belief (Security)...}[Surat al-Hashr: 23]

The name "Al-Mu'min" occurs once in the Qur'an, in the sense of security and safety to those in fear and distress.

Let us pause here with this great name:

Scholars said that "Al-Mu'min" has two meanings:

The first meaning is belief. Indeed, the greatest belief since the beginning of the creation till the Day of Judgment is Allah's belief in Himself and His confirmation of Himself as the One and Only God, in addition to the other perfect names and sublime attributes that He ascribed to Himself. In the Qur'an, Allah Almighty says about Himself:{Allah bears witness that there is no god except Him...}[Surat Āl-'Imrān: 18]This is the most sublime testimony that came out from the Almighty King, the Lord of the worlds, in relation to the greatest thing to testify about, namely belief in the Oneness of Allah and devoting religion sincerely to Him.

I bear witness that there is no god other than Allah. He is the Most Generous, the Most Merciful, upon Whom people pin their hopes.

He is the One Whose words and promises are true.{...And who is more truthful than Allah in statement.}[Surat an-Nisā': 122]

Allah Almighty confirmed the truthfulness of His prophets through clear signs and miracles that happened at their hands:

{...Indeed, I have come to you with a sign from your Lord...}

[Surat Āl-'Imrān: 49]

{And we have brought you the truth, and certainly we tell the truth.}

[Surat al-Hijr: 64]

Also, Allah Almighty fulfills His promise to His servants about victory and empowerment on earth and the reward in the Hereafter. He says:{Then, We fulfilled to them the promise. So, We saved them and those whom We willed, but We destroyed the transgressors.}[Surat al-Anbiyā': 9]He also fulfills His promise to the disbelievers about the punishment and humiliation in this world and in the Hereafter. He says:{And the people of Paradise will call out to the people of the Fire: "We have surely found what our Lord promised us to be true. Have you found what your Lord promised to be true?" They will say: "Yes." Then, an announcer will announce between them: "The curse of Allah shall be upon the wrongdoers."}[Surat al-A'rāf: 44]

All the speech, promises, and information given by Allah Almighty are true.

I place all my trust in the Almighty Lord and do not knock on a door but His door.

Allah Almighty loves those who keep their promises and speak the truth.{O you who believe, fear Allah and be with the truthful.}[Surat at-Tawbah: 119]The second meaning of "Al-Mu'min" is the Giver of Security.{And He gives them security against fear.}[Surat Quraysh: 4]

People experience fear from many things. They fear illness, lack of medicine, dominance of the enemy, poverty, and death. They always look for security in securing enough food, establishing castles and fortresses, and building hospitals and dams. Moreover, the weak, individuals or countries, resort to the strong for protection and security.

Yet, these powers may collapse in seconds and the protection goes away. In such a state, they can only resort to the Almighty Lord, the Giver of Security. They turn away from Him and then come back to Him. He is their Creator and the Creator of the whole universe, Who dominates everything and controls the entire creation.

So, if the punishment of Allah Almighty befalls some people, none can secure them or defend them against the Creator.{Do you feel secure that He who [holds authority] in the heaven would not cause the earth to swallow you and suddenly it would sway?Or do you feel secure that He who [holds authority] in the heaven would not send against you a storm of stones? Then you would know how [severe] was My warning.}[Surat al-Mulk: 16-17]

Three aspects:

People look for three aspects of security, all of which lie in the Hand of the Giver of Security, Exalted be He, Who has power over all things and Who grants it only to His pious servants.

First: Worldly security of all types,

{And if only the people of the cities had believed and feared Allah, We would have opened upon them blessings from the heaven and the earth...}

[Surat al-A'rāf: 96]

Second: Security needed at the time of death, as the angel of death descends, and in the grave upon seeing the two angels.

Here comes security and glad tidings for the believers:{Indeed, those who have said, "Our Lord is Allah" and then remained on a right course - the angels will descend upon them, [saying]: "Do not fear and do not grieve but receive good tidings of Paradise, which you were promised."}[Surat Fussilat: 30]Third: Security needed in the Hereafter at the time of the greatest panic. The greatest security will be afforded to the pious as Allah Almighty says:{They will not be grieved by the greatest terror, and the angels will meet them [saying]: "This is your Day which you have been promised"}[Surat al-Anbiyā': 103]Security is only given to the monotheists:{Whoever brings a good deed will have better than its worth; and they will be safe from the terror on that Day.}[Surat al-Naml: 89]The greater your faith is, the greater your security will be as Allah Almighty says:{They who believe and do not mix their belief with injustice – those will have security, and they are [rightly] guided.}[Surat al-An'ām: 82]

Your share in this name..

One of the benefits of this great name for the believers is learning that it is Allah Almighty Who secures them at the times of crises, hardships, and disasters; and learning that a person reaps what he sows, hence, they keep people secure from their own evil and harm in pursuit of security from their Lord and for fear of being deprived of this security on the Day of Judgment.

The Prophet (may Allah's peace and blessings be upon him) is authentically reported to have said:"Shall I inform you of the believer? He is the one from whom people are secure concerning their properties and lives; and the Muslim is the one from whose tongue and hand people are safe."[Narrated by Ahmad in Al-Musnad; Sahīh (authentic)]

O Allah, make us secure in our homes. O Allah, remove our fears, give us our books in the right hand, and make the reckoning easy for us.

Al-Muhaymin (The All-Controller)

Here is a message to everyone who feels bored of his life and finds difficulty therein. We give you the glad tidings that support, victory, relief, and ease are soon to come.

A bright hope, a good future, and a true promise lie ahead.{[It is] the promise of Allah. Allah does not fail in His promise...}[Surat ar-Rūm: 6]Indeed, your Lord and Creator says:{And to Allah belong the most beautiful names, so invoke Him by them...}[Surat al-A'rāf:180]If you invoke Him by them, what will the result be?{And your Lord said: "Call on Me and I will answer your prayer"...}[Surat Ghāfir: 60]

Let us draw close to our Lord by learning about one of His beautiful names; namely "Al-Muhaymin" (the All-Controller).

Knowing Allah Almighty through His beautiful names and attributes is the core of the religion and guidance and the best thing to be grasped by the hearts, souls, and minds.

Allah's name "Al-Muhaymin" occurs at the end of Surat al-Hashr:{He is Allah, there is no god except Him, the King, the Most Holy, the Source of Peace, the Giver of Belief (Security), the All-Controller.}[Surat al-Hashr: 23]Our Lord, the All-Controller, is the One Who manages all matters and affairs of His creation and knows everything, including secrets and innermost thoughts. He encompasses all things in His knowledge and watches over the words and deeds of His servants. Nothing of their actions escapes His knowledge, even an atom's weight, in the heaven or on earth, is not hidden from Him.{...And not absent from your Lord is any [part] of an atom's weight within the earth or within the heaven or [anything] smaller than that or greater but that it is in a clear register.}[Surat Yūnus: 61]All one's conditions, fluctuations, and activities during the day and night, be they public or secret, are known to the Knower of the Unseen and registered by Him.{...Indeed, He knows the secret and what is [even] more hidden.}[Surat Taha: 7]

For Him, private talk is a public one, secrets are open matters, and what is hidden is in fact apparent and revealed.

He is the All-Controller..

A group of hypocrites were planning evil and cunning plots against the Muslims, so the Knower of the unseen exposed them saying:{They conceal [their evil intentions and deeds] from the people, but they cannot conceal [them] from Allah, and He is with them [with His knowledge] when they spend the night in such as He does not accept of speech. And ever is Allah, of what they do, encompassing.}[Surat an-Nisā': 108]

'Umayr ibn Wahb and Safwān ibn Umayyah sat together by night at the Ka'bah, after the battle of Badr, plotting to assassinate the Prophet (may Allah's peace and blessings be upon him), but Allah Almighty informed him of their evil plot.

He is powerfully dominant over the Throne, and to His glory all faces are humbled and fall in prostration.

Yes, He is the All-Controller, the Preserver, and the Overseer of His servants and their actions.

Rest assured!

O you whose eyes flow with tears, wipe them and enjoy comfort and calm, for indeed you will get protection, care, and kindness from the Creator of the universe.

Rest assured, O servant of Allah, for fate has already been determined, everything has been decided, and relief is actually occurring.

How often do we fear death, and yet we do not die?!

How often do we face severe hardships and crises and darkness prevails our life, and then all of a sudden we find relief, victory, support, and hope?!{Say: "It is Allah Who saves you from it and from every distress; then you [still] associate others with Him."}[Surat al-An'ām: 64]How often do we feel that life has become so dark and narrow and then ease and abundance quickly emerge!?{And if Allah should touch you with adversity, there is no remover of it except Him; and if He intends for you good, then there is no repeller of His bounty. He causes it to reach whom He wills of His servants. And He is the Forgiving, the Most Merciful.}[Surat Yūnus: 107]

Our Lord is the All-Controller. All glory and power belong to Him, and from Him relief comes.

Ibn Kathīr reported a tradition from Wahb ibn Munabbih: "Allah Almighty said in one of His scriptures:'By My honor and majesty, if a servant of Mine resorts to Me and all those in the heavens and earth plot against him, I will certainly grant him relief and a way out. By My honor and majesty, if a servant of Mine resorts to anyone other than Me, I will certainly spoil the ground under his feet.'"

Our Lord, the All-Controller, Your majesty never goes away and Your judgment will sure come to pass regarding every matter.

Your dominion is enduring eternally, and nothing happens in this universe except according to Your will.

The lifeline..

Our Lord, Exalted be He, describes the Qur'an as a controller over the previous scriptures:{And We have revealed to you the Book in truth, confirming that which preceded it of the Scripture and as a controller over it...}[Surat al-Mā'idah: 48]

The Noble Qur'an is, thus, a controller and criterion over the preceding books. It has come with the best in these books and abrogated parts thereof, and it relates to the Children of Israel most of the things over which they differ, thus exposing their distortions and revealing the truth contained in those previous books.

Any Muslim who believes in this, his exaltation of the Book of Allah must yield within his heart feelings of love, joy, and gratitude to Allah for guiding him. Such guidance is the hope of every person and the pursuit of every believer in every Rak'ah of prayer as he says:{Guide us to the straight path.}[Surat al-Fātihah: 6]

O Allah, the All-Controller, guide us among those You have guided, take us as allies among those You took as allies, and forgive us, our parents, and all Muslims.

Al-'Azīz (The All-Mighty)

Al-Hākim mentioned in Al-Mustadrak that when 'Umar ibn al-Khattāb (may Allah be pleased with him) reached the Levant, he came across a ford. Thereupon, he dismounted, took off his shoes, held the halter of his riding animal, and crossed the ford.

Seeing him, Abu 'Ubaydah ibn al-Jarrāh said to him: "O Commander of the Believers, you have done something serious in the sight of the dwellers of the land! You have taken off your shoes, walked before your riding animal, and crossed the ford."

In response, 'Umar hit Abu 'Ubaydah's chest with his hand and said: "If only someone other than you had said it, O Abu 'Ubaydah!

You were the lowest of people, and Allah honored you with Islam. So, if you seek honor anywhere else, Allah Almighty will humiliate you."

Allah Almighty says:{Whoever desires honor - then to Allah belongs all honor...}[Surat Fātir: 10]Praising Himself, Allah Almighty says:{And indeed, your Lord - He is the All-Mighty, the Most-Merciful.}[Surat ash-Shu'arā': 9]{...There is no god except Him, the All-Mighty, the All-Wise.}[Surat Āl-'Imrān: 6]Allah Almighty commands us from above the seven heavens to know that and take it for sure:{...And know that Allah is All-Mighty, All-Wise.}[Surat al-Baqarah: 260]Our All-Mighty Lord, Who combines all meanings of honor in its most sublime and perfect form, says:{Whoever desires honor - then to Allah belongs all honor...}[Surat Fātir: 10]

To Him belongs honor by way of dominance, as He is the Vanquisher of His enemies.

To Him belongs honor by way of invincibility, as none can reach Him for He is Self-Sufficient.

And to Him belongs honor by way of power, as all difficulties and hardships are humble and easy before Him for His strength.

He is the All-Mighty Lord Who grants might and honor to whomever He wills of His servants.

He is the All-Mighty Lord Whose close servants and allies cannot be defeated or humiliated.

He is the All-Mighty Lord, the Vanquisher, the Dominant, the Owner of absolute and perfect power. None can target Him with any harm or overcome Him.

How could anything target the All-Powerful Lord with any harm or overcome Him?! He is the All-Mighty, and His might and honor are perfect in every way and free from any deficiency.

Sanctuary of the All-Mighty Lord:

As the believers know and believe that honor and might come from Allah alone, they stand humble before their All-Mighty Lord and turn to Him for refuge, protection, and honor because they are well aware of the verse that says:{Whoever desires honor - then to Allah belongs all honor...}[Surat Fātir: 10]Al-Madā'ini said in his book:"One of the people of Yemen went to Al-Hajjāj complaining about his brother Muhammad ibn Yūsuf. It happened that he arrived as Al-Hajjāj was on the pulpit. He got up and complained about his brother Muhammad. Thereupon, Al-Hajjāj ordered that he be imprisoned. When he descended the pulpit, he called for him feeling really angry against him. He said: 'How dare you complain about my brother!' The man replied: 'I am more honorable by Allah than your brother is by you.' Thereupon, Al-Hajjāj said: 'Set him free.'"

An honorable death is better than a life in humiliation.

The more the Muslim exalts this name in his heart and the more he acts to actualize it in his life, the greater the honor he will receive.{...And honor belongs to Allah, and to His Messenger, and to the believers...}[Surat al-Munāfiqūn: 8]

The most honorable among people are the prophets, followed by the believers.

Hence, none attains honor in this world or in the Hereafter but those who are made honorable by Allah Almighty.{Say: "O Allah, Owner of Sovereignty, You give sovereignty to whom You will and You take sovereignty away from whom You will. You honor whom You will and You humble whom You will. In Your hand is [all] good. Indeed, You are competent over all things.}[Surat Āl-'Imrān: 26]

For the seekers of honor..

Whoever seeks honor through other than Allah has actually sought it in a transient dominion and power that will soon go away.

Who could ever stand up to Allah and fight and overcome Him?!The people of Pharaoh sought honor in him:{So they cast their ropes and their sticks, and said: "By the might of Pharaoh, it is we who will certainly win."}[Surat ash-Shu'arā': 44]And what was the result?{Then Moses cast his staff, and behold, it swallowed up all that they falsely showed.}[Surat ash-Shu'arā': 45]A lot of people seek honor with the disbelievers and the enemies of religion. Those people had not estimated Allah or known Him properly.Otherwise, they would have recognized the true little worth of those people to whom they show allegiance and friendliness, for no matter how powerful they become or how many followers they may have, they are nothing compared to the might, power, and dominance of Allah.Allah Almighty has informed them that the honor and pleasure they seek cannot be reached except through Him. Indeed, they have become just like the hypocrites, whose outside differs from their inside.{Give tidings to the hypocrites that there is for them a painful punishment.Those who take disbelievers as allies instead of the believers. Do they seek with them honor? But indeed, honor belongs to Allah entirely.}[Surat an-Nisā': 138-139]

Some seek honor with their own people and tribe. Ubayy ibn Ka'b (may Allah be pleased with him) reported: "Two men bragged about their lineage during the Prophet's lifetime. One of them said: 'I am so-and-so, the son of so-and-so, the son of so-and-so. So, who are you, O you with no good mother?'

Thereupon, the Prophet (may Allah's peace and blessings be upon him) said:'Two men bragged about their lineage at the time of Moses (peace be upon him). One of them said: "I am so-and-so, the son of so-and-so - till the ninth grandfather - So, who are you, O you with no good mother?" The other one said: "I am so-and-son, the son of so-and-so, the son of Islam."

So, Allah revealed to Moses: "With regard to these two men talking about their lineage, as for you who bragged about your affiliation to the nine grandfathers, you are in Hellfire; you are the tenth of them.

And as for you who have bragged about your affiliation to two grandfathers, you are in Paradise; you are the third of them in Paradise.'"[Narrated by Ahmad; Sahīh (authentic)]

It was once said: "Let those who seek honor in their position consider what happened to Pharaoh; let those who seek honor in their wealth consider what happened to Qārūn; and let those who seek honor in their lineage consider what happened to Abu Lahab. Indeed, honor lies in piety."

Truthful was the one who said:"We are people whom Allah has honored by Islam. So, if we seek honor through something else, Allah will humiliate us."

The biggest cause of the humiliation of the Muslim Ummah today is that they do not seek honor through their Lord as they should.

He will grant you honor..

When the disbelievers began to threaten the Prophet (may Allah's peace and blessings be upon him), speak impudently with him, and show their strength, Allah Almighty revealed a verse in which He consoled His Prophet and stated that all humanity is weak. He says:{And let not their speech grieve you. Indeed, honor belongs to Allah entirely. He is the All-Hearing, the All-Knowing.}[Surat Yūnus: 65]The greater the believer's faith is, the greater the honor within his heart and the firmer his belief in victory and dominance will be. Allah Almighty says:{And Allah made it not except as [a sign of] glad tidings for you and to reassure your hearts thereby. And victory is not except from Allah, the All-Mighty, the All-Wise.}[Surat Āl-'Imrān: 126]He also says:{...And Allah will surely support those who support Him. Indeed, Allah is Powerful and All-Mighty.}[Surat al-Hajj: 40]

Whoever possesses faith attains honor, and whoever attains honor wins the love of Allah Almighty, Who says:

{...Allah will bring forth [in place of them] a people He will love and who will love Him [who are] humble towards the believers, firm against the disbelievers...}

[Surat al-Mā'idah: 54]

Ibn Kathīr said:"Whoever likes to be honorable in this world and in the Hereafter should stick to obedience to Allah. In this way, he will reach his objective, for indeed Allah Almighty is the Owner of this world and the Hereafter, and all honor belongs to Him as He says:{...Indeed, honor belongs to Allah entirely.}[Surat an-Nisā': 139]"Ibrāhīm al-Khawwās (may Allah have mercy upon him) said:"As much as the believer honors the religion of Allah, Allah grants him honor and makes him honorable in the hearts of the believers. This is the meaning of the verse that says:{...And honor belongs to Allah, and to His Messenger, and to the believers, but the hypocrites do not know.}[Surat al-Munāfiqūn: 8]"

The keys to honor:

Honor cannot be attained unless its requirements are fulfilled.

First and foremost, honor is attained by faith as Allah Almighty says:

{...And honor belongs to Allah, and to His Messenger, and to the believers, but the hypocrites do not know.}

[Surat al-Munāfiqūn: 8]

It is also attained through humility towards the believers as Allah Almighty says:{...Humble towards the believers, firm against the disbelievers...}[Surat al-Mā'idah: 54]Honor is attained through pardon as well. The Prophet (may Allah's peace and blessings be upon him) said:"Allah increases the one who pardons in honor." [narrated by Muslim]Honor can also be obtained by invoking Allah by this name as Ibrāhīm (Abraham) (peace be upon him) used to make this supplication:{Our Lord, do not make us a temptation for the disbelievers; and forgive us. Our Lord, surely You are the All-Mighty, the All-Wise.}[Surat al-Mumtahanah: 5]Also, the angels who carry the Throne used this name in their supplication for the believers:{Our Lord, and make them enter the Gardens of Eternity which You have promised them and whoever was righteous among their fathers, their spouses, and their offspring; surely You are the All-Mighty, the All-Wise.}[Surat Ghāfir: 8]Whenever the Prophet (may Allah's peace and blessings be upon him) got up from sleep suddenly during the night, he would say:"La ilāha illallāh Al-Wāhid Al-Qahhār, Rabbu as-samāwāti wa al-ard wa ma baynahuma Al-'Azīz Al-Ghaffār (There is no god except Allah, the One, the Superb Vanquisher, Lord of the heavens and the earth and what is between them, the All-Mighty, the Superb Forgiver)."[Narrated by Ibn Hibbān; Sahīh (authentic)]A man came to the Prophet (may Allah's peace and blessings be upon him) complaining of some sort of pain and the Prophet (may Allah's peace and blessings be upon him) taught him to worship Allah Almighty by His might saying:"Put your right hand upon it and say seven times: Bismillāh, a'ūdhu bi'izzatillāh wa qudratihi min sharri ma ajid wa uhādhir (In the name of Allah, I seek refuge in the honor and might of Allah from the evil that afflicts me and that I apprehend)."[Narrated by Muslim]

Contemplate!

Allah's name "Al-'Azīz" comes in association with His names: "Al-Qawiyy" (the All-Powerful), "Al-Hakīm" (the All-Wise), "Al-'Alīm" (the All-Knowing), "Al-Hamīd" (the Praiseworthy), "Al-Ghafūr" (the All-Forgiving), "Al-Wahhāb" (the Bestower), and "Al-Muqtadir" (the Supreme Determiner).

This, by Allah, stems from His boundless mercy and benevolence towards us.

It indicates the perfection of Allah's names and attributes and that they complete one another. As Allah possesses absolute might and power, He is also the All-Wise, the All-Knowing, the All-Merciful, and the All-Compassionate towards His servants, and the Praiseworthy for His words, actions, and rulings.

So, His might comprises wisdom, mercy, and justice.{...There is no god except Him, the All-Mighty, the All-Wise.}[Surat Āl-'Imrān: 6]Since His might is that of perfection and majesty, He deserves to be praised for it constantly. Allah Almighty says:{...the All-Mighty, the Praiseworthy.}[Surat Ibrāhim: 1]

O the King, Who holds the forelocks of His creation, I seek refuge in You, O the Most Generous Lord.

Your predestination is sure to come to pass. I am Your servant, seeking Your refuge and protection.

{Exalted is your Lord, the Lord of might, above what they describe.And peace be upon the Messengers.And praise be to Allah, Lord of the worlds.}[Surat as-Sāffāt: 180-182]

O Allah, the All-Mighty, grant us honor by obeying You and do not humiliate us by disobeying You.

Al-Jabbār (The Compeller)

If life turns its back on you, people leave you, everything becomes dark and tough, and you are in severe distress, then call out: O Allah, O You Who console the distressed and comfort their hearts, comfort and strengthen me. Indeed, your Lord will hear your supplication.

Allah Almighty says about Himself:{He is Allah, there is no god except Him, the King, the Most Holy, the Source of Peace, the Giver of Belief, the All-Controller, the All-Mighty, the Compeller, the Supreme. Exalted is Allah above whatever they associate with Him.}[Surat al-Hashr: 23]

Al-Jabbār is the One Who comforts broken hearts, enriches the poor, facilitates what is difficult, and provides those submissive to His majesty and magnificence with special consolation.

Al-Jabbār is also the Vanquisher of all things, to Whom everything is submissive and obedient.

Al-Jabbār is the Most High and Exalted above His creation. He has established Himself above His Throne.

All might belongs to Him alone and He is the Vanquisher of tyrants with His power. Indeed, He is far exalted above them with His greatness.

Allah Almighty praises Himself using this name as He says:{...the All-Mighty, the Compeller, the Supreme...}[Surat al-Hashr: 23]The Prophet (may Allah's peace and blessings be upon him) used to supplicate Allah in his bowing and prostration saying:"Subhān dhil-jabarūt wa al-malakūt wa al-kibriyā' wa al-'azhamah (Glory be to the Owner of might, dominion, pride, and greatness)."[Narrated by Abu Dāwūd; Sahīh (authentic)]

Do not dispute with Him!

When it comes to Allah Almighty, the name "Al-Jabbār" is that of praise and perfection. But when people are described by this name or attribute, it mostly denotes dispraise, imperfection, and defects. Do we not see that the so-called compellers among people can actually be hurt by the weakest of things, like bugs and worms, get distracted by flies, and become agitated by hunger and lazy when full?!

Hence, the messengers warned their people against the attributes of "tyranny and arrogance" without right. Allah Almighty says:{And when you strike, you strike as tyrants.}[Surat ash-Shu'arā': 130]

Whoever acts tyrannically, Allah puts a seal upon his heart:

{...Thus does Allah seal over every heart of an arrogant tyrant.}

[Surat Ghāfir: 35]

Allah Almighty threatens tyrants with punishment:

{And they requested victory from Allah, and disappointed, [therefore], was every obstinate tyrant.

Before him is Hell, and he will be given a drink of purulent water.}

[Surat Ibrāhim: 15-16]

The Prophet (may Allah's peace and blessings be upon him) said:"A neck will come out of Hellfire on the Day of Judgment. It will have two eyes which can see, two ears which can hear, and a tongue which can speak. It will say: 'I have been left in charge of three: Every obstinate tyrant, everyone who called upon a deity besides Allah, and the image makers.'"[Narrated by Al-Tirmidhi; Sahīh (authentic)]The Prophet (may Allah's peace and blessings be upon him) is also authentically reported to have said:"Hellfire and the Paradise fell into dispute; Hellfire said: 'I have been distinguished by the arrogant, tyrants...'"[Narrated by Muslim]So, where are the arrogant, where are the tyrants?

Where are kings and their sons, and those to whom

people would lower their heads in submission?

They were ruined by time and its events

and left to different homes other than their previous ones.

Knock on the door of heaven!

The Prophet (may Allah's peace and blessings be upon him) used to supplicate Allah saying:"Allāhumma ighfirli warhamni wajburni wahdini warzuqni (O Allah, forgive me, have mercy upon me, console me, guide me, and provide for me)."[Narrated by Al-Tirmidhi; Sahīh (authentic)]

In life, we go through numerous tough incidents and circumstances. Every day, we get broken by distress and trouble and so we need our Lord at all times to console our hearts and give us strength.

Everyone needs Him, young and old, rich and poor. Indeed, life and what it contains belongs to Him.

An ill person lies in his bed, weak and broken, struggling against his illness. At this point, he calls out: "O Allah!" And behold! He consoles his heart and cures him.

A destitute person, who possesses nothing at all, suffers from misery, weeps out of need, looks up to the sky and calls out: "O Allah!" And behold! He consoles his heart, fulfills his need, and removes his poverty.

A downtrodden man, who feels broken and hides his deep pain, wipes off his tears, stands at the door of his Lord and calls out: "O Allah!" And behold! Allah, the Compeller, takes revenge for him, by sending His soldiers and granting victory.

A prisoner, who languishes in prison, fettered and weak, calls out: "O Allah!" And all of a sudden, Allah comforts his heart and opens His doors for him. Relief comes and the fetters are untied.

And that a sterile man, who is gripped by sadness and loses hope, turns to prayer, in which he weeps for long and calls out: "My Lord, grant me good offspring." And behold! Comfort and relief come and Allah issues His command and sends His help. Thereupon, the unattainable becomes a reality and the smile comes back as his wife becomes pregnant.

He is the Compeller. He sends relief, comfort, and hope and He removes afflictions and distress.

Everyone calls Him: "O Allah, console us and give us strength!"{Whoever is in the heavens and earth asks Him; every day He is upon some affair.}[Surat ar-Rahmān: 29]

If you are encompassed by Allah's care, then rest assured; you are safe.

Everything hard Allah puts you through is, indeed, for your benefit even if it is painful for you.

Allah Almighty says:{And there is not a thing but with Us are their treasures. And We do not send it down except in a known measure.}[Surat al-Hijr: 21]The keys to relief are in His Hands. So, if you are in pain and distress, turn to the All-Knowing King, the Compeller, the One Who consoles hearts and sends comfort, and call out: "O Allah, the comfort of the broken, comfort my heart, give me strength, and remove my distress."{Is He [not best] Who responds to the desperate one when he calls upon Him and removes evil...}[Surat an-Naml: 62]

Indeed, for the afflictions and hardships we may face,

there is relief and a way out from our Lord.

When things get too hard and we think there is no hope,

we actually find relief coming unexpectedly.

Be kind and tender!

Remember that distress breaks hearts. So, when you see a person in anguish, be the means by which Allah consoles him. In fact, you will get the great reward on the Day of Judgment when everyone will be seeking comfort and consolation.

The Prophet (may Allah's peace and blessings be upon him) is authentically reported to have said:"Whoever removes the distress of a Muslim, Allah will remove from him one of the distresses on the Day of Judgment."[Narrated by Muslim]{...And do good as Allah has done good to you...}[Surat al-Qasas: 77]{...And Allah loves the doers of good.}[Surat Āl-'Imrān: 134]

Be gentle with people when things around them get tough.

O Allah, the One Who consoles hearts, console our hearts, strengthen us, and pardon us, O the Most Merciful of those who show mercy!

Al-Mutakabbir (The Supreme)

Superiority and pride belong to Allah Almighty alone. Allah praised Himself saying:{And to Him belongs pride in the heavens and earth, and He is the All-Mighty, the All-Wise.}[Surat al-Jāthiyah: 37]He also says:{He is Allah, there is no god except Him, the King, the Most Holy, the Source of Peace, the Giver of Belief, the All-Controller, the All-Mighty, the Compeller, the Supreme. Exalted is Allah above whatever they associate with Him.}[Surat al-Hashr: 23]

Our Lord, Exalted be He, is Supreme and Exalted above all defects and evil things and above wronging His servants.

He is Superior to the tyrants among His servants who claim grandeur.

Indeed, He is Supreme and High above anything bad or evil and above whatever does not befit His perfection and excellence.

Superiority denotes the absence of any defect, deficiency, or imperfection.

Servitude of submissiveness..

Superiority is an innate attribute of the Almighty Lord, unlike some people who pretend to be superior to others, while they are not.

Superiority and pride befit Allah Almighty alone, for He alone is the King and Owner and all others are owned; He alone is the Lord and Creator and all others are servants and created beings. Indeed, He is the sole Possessor of the attributes of perfection, beauty, majesty, and grandeur.

Therefore, Allah Almighty takes this attribute exclusively for Himself and threatens anyone assuming it with severe punishment.

The Prophet (may Allah's peace and blessings be upon him) is authentically reported to have said:

"Allah Almighty said: 'Pride is My robe, and majesty is My lower garment. If anyone disputes with Me over one of them, I will throw him in Hellfire.'"

[Narrated by Abu Dāwūd; Sahīh (authentic)]

Al-Khattābi said: "He used the robe and lower garment as an example to say - and Allah knows best -: As nobody lets others share his robe and garment with him, likewise, no created being should share pride and majesty with Me."

The status befitting a created being is that of servitude, obedience, and submission to the Great and Superior Lord, the Owner of Honor and Majesty. It is probably for this reason that we proclaim the greatness and grandeur of Allah in the position of bowing and prostration in prayer.

The Prophet (may Allah's peace and blessings be upon him) used to say during bowing and prostration in prayer:"Subhān dhil-jabarūt wa al-malakūt wa al-kibriyā' wa al-'azhamah (Glory be to the Owner of might, dominion, pride, and greatness)."[Narrated by Abu Dāwūd; Sahīh (authentic)]Allah Almighty purified His prophets and righteous servants from arrogance and pride. They used to seek refuge with Him from pride and arrogance:{But Moses said: "Indeed, I have sought refuge in my Lord and your Lord from every arrogant one who does not believe in the Day of Reckoning."}[Surat Ghāfir: 27]

Consider the consequences!

Whoever possesses this attribute of pride and arrogance, his soul will be spoiled and his heart will be stamped with a seal of rust.{...Thus does Allah seal every heart of an arrogant tyrant.} [Ghāfir: 35] {...There is not within their breasts except pride, [the extent of] which they cannot reach...}[Surat Ghāfir: 56]The leader of the arrogant is Satan,{Except Satan; he was arrogant and became among the disbelievers.}[Surat Sād: 74]Arrogance is also the trait of tyrannical kings like Pharaoh:{And he was arrogant, he and his soldiers, in the land, without right, and they thought that they would not be returned to Us.}[Surat al-Qasas: 39]Another example is a man who has great wealth and many children and who begins to feel proud because of them. Arrogance does actually sneak into his heart, driving him to reject the truth. This is like Al-Walīd ibn al-Mughīrah about whom Allah Almighty says:{Then he turned back and was arrogant.}[Surat al-Muddaththir: 23]Arrogance causes destruction to the nations that deny the truth,{As for 'Ād, they were arrogant on the earth without right...}[Surat Fussilat: 15]And about the people of Prophet Sālih (peace be upon him), Allah Almighty says:{Those who were arrogant said: "Verily, we disbelieve in what you believe in."}[Surat al-A'rāf: 76]The arrogant will end up in Hellfire; what an evil destination!{...Is there not in Hell a residence for the arrogant?}[Surat az-Zumar: 60]The Prophet (may Allah's peace and blessings be upon him) said:"The arrogant will be gathered on the Day of Judgment resembling tiny particles in the image of men. They will be covered with humiliation everywhere. They will be dragged into a prison in Hellfire called Būlas and submerged in the Fire of Fires, drinking the drippings of the people of Hellfire."[Narrated by Al-Tirmidhi; Sahīh (authentic)]May Allah keep us away from this.

The remedy:

A person who begins to feel arrogant and superior should look inside himself in a wise and deep manner and not look at his outside with a superficial and bestial look.

Let him remember the origin of his existence, where he came from, and that his end in this worldly life will be nothing but a rotten corpse.

It is related that Mutraf ibn 'Abdullah ibn al-Shikhkhīr looked at Al-Muhallab ibn Abu Safrah as he was wearing a fine garment, which he was dragging behind on the ground and walking arrogantly. Thereupon, he said: "O Abu 'Abdullah, what is this gait which Allah and His Messenger dislike?" Al-Muhallab said: "Do you not know me?" He said: "No, I know you. You began as a little drop of sperm and will end up as a dirty corpse, and inside you is urine and stool."

If only people think about what lies inside them, none of them would feel arrogant or superior.

Al-Munāwi (may Allah have mercy upon him) said: "A person should not despise anyone, for the despised one may have a purer heart, better deeds, and a more sincere intention. Despising people brings loss, humiliation, and disgrace."

Ibn Taymiyyah said: "A fearful sinner is better than an arrogant worshiper."

A wise person should act modestly, sit with the knowledgeable and the weak, visit the sick, observe those who die or suffer afflictions, and consider the stories of arrogant people to see how they rose and ultimately fell and what happened to them.

As if you did not hear about what happened to people in the past.

Neither do you see what will happen to those who live in the present.

So, if you are unaware of what happened to them, here are their dwellings;

they were ruined by the wind and the passage of time.

O Allah, we implore You by Your name "Al-Mutakabbir" to strengthen us, conceal our faults, forgive our sins, and not to make us among the arrogant, O Lord of the worlds!

Al-Khāliq Al-Khallāq (The Creator, the Sublime Creator)

Look at this nature around you and the sky high above. Glory be to the One Who created this splendid universe.

And ponder the perfect creation of the Superb Creator, and His signs and miracles.

Who created the heavens and earth? Who created grains and seeds? Who created the morning, made the night tranquil, and rendered the sun and moon a means of calculation? Who created human beings from mud? Who created the entire humankind from one soul? Who gave everything He created its due proportion and then gave it guidance?

{This is the creation of Allah. So show Me what those other than Him have created...}[Surat Luqmān: 11]

Glory be to the One Whose magnificence dazzles the minds of those who know Him!

Glory be to the One Whose miraculous signs are clear to those who reflect!

Glory be to the One Whose lights guide those walking on the path to Him!

{...So blessed is Allah, the Best of the Creators.}[Surat al-Mu'minūn: 14]

We pause here with two of the beautiful names of Allah Almighty: "Al-Khāliq" (the Creator) and "Al-Khallāq" (the Sublime Creator).

Allah Almighty says:{Indeed, your Lord – He is the Sublime Creator, the All-Knowing.}[Surat al-Hijr: 86]He also says:{He is Allah, the Creator, the Initiator, the Supreme Fashioner...}[Surat al-Hashr: 24]

It is our Lord Who brought all things into existence after they had previously been non-existent. He created them in an unprecedented manner. Indeed, the actions of Allah Almighty are in the exact measure He gave to them.

Magnificence of the Creator..

Everything that exists in the universe is His creation, pointing to His divinity and lordship. Everything that we see - and do not see - around us is a proof of the existence of Allah. He created, proportioned, fashioned everything according to His wisdom, and He continues to do so.

He covers bones with flesh and covers flesh with skin, and He clothes animals with wool and fur. He breathes life into the embryo while still in its mother's womb and then He brings it out, provides for it, and protects and teaches it. Indeed, He creates humans in the best form and gives them two eyes, a tongue, and two lips and shows them the two paths.{Who created you, proportioned you, and balanced you?In whatever form He willed has He assembled you.}[Surat al-Infitār: 7-8]{...So blessed is Allah, the Best of Creators.}[Surat al-Mu'minūn: 14]

Thus, He, Exalted be He, testifies that He is the Creator of these human bodies.

The Almighty Lord created the humans and jinn so that they would know Him and worship Him.{And I did not create the jinn and mankind except to worship Me.}[Surat adh-Dhāriyāt: 56]

The universe in harmony:

All creatures were not created for play, diversion, or for no purpose, far exalted is Allah above that! He says:{And We did not create the heavens and earth and what is between them for play.}[Surat al-Anbiyā': 16]

All existents point to the attributes and traits of the Almighty Creator and indicate His beautiful names.

If the creatures were lines to be read, you would read them and see that they clearly point to their Creator.

Through them, the Glorified King sends us messages that there is no true god except Allah, and that every creature, silent or speaking, leads to Him.

Allah Almighty says:{Indeed, We have created all things with due proportion.}[Surat al-Qamar: 49]

Doctors say that the opening of the larynx is accurately determined and designed. If it were a little wider, one's voice would disappear, and if it were a little narrower, he would find it hard to breathe. So, either easy breathing with no voice, or a clear voice with difficult breathing.

{...[It is] the work of Allah, Who perfected all things. Indeed, He is All-Aware of what you do...}[Surat an-Naml: 88]

Likewise, if our sight were stronger, our life would turn into Hell.

If you look at the glass of water you drink from, you will see it clear and pure. But if your sight were a little stronger and sharper, you would see amazing things in the glass. You would see countless living organisms and harmless germs. Certainly, you would not be able to drink then.

{Indeed, We have created all things with due proportion.}

[Surat al-Qamar: 49]

Also, if our sense of hearing were a little stronger, we would not be able to sleep at night, being disturbed by all different kinds of sounds. Even the sounds in our digestive system alone are like a large laboratory.{Indeed, We have created all things with due proportion.}[Surat al-Qamar: 49]And if our sense of touching increased a little bit, we would feel the static electricity around us, which would turn our life into an unbearable Hell.{And in yourselves. Then will you not see?}[Surat adh-Dhāriyāt: 21]{This is the creation of Allah. So show Me what those other than Him have created...}[Surat Luqmān: 11]Nonetheless, there are people with tainted dispositions and sick souls arguing regarding Allah Almighty, even though His signs exist even within their own bodies. How strange!{And they rejected them, while their [inner] selves were convinced thereof...}[Surat an-Naml: 14]{And if you ask them: "Who created the heavens and earth?" They would surely say: "Allah." Say: "Praise be to Allah"; but most of them do not know.}[Surat Luqmān: 25]

Rest assured!

The believer knows that he obtains honor and strength through the Creator. So, he feels reassured, being aware that the One Who created him will preserve him and not neglect him; and that everything, ease and hardship, poverty and opulence, will ultimately be good for him.{Indeed, the allies of Allah will have no fear, nor will they grieve.}[Surat Yūnus: 62]

O Allah, we implore You by Your name "Al-Khāliq" to make us among Your allies and close servants.

Al-Bāri' (The Initiator)

The Prophet (may Allah's peace and blessings be upon him) is authentically reported to have said:"Once Sulaymān ibn Dāwūd (Solomon) (peace be upon him and his father) said: 'Tonight I will have sexual intercourse with one hundred (or ninety-nine) women each of whom will give birth to a knight who will fight in the cause of Allah.' His companion said: 'Allah willing.' But he did not say: 'Allah willing.' Therefore, only one of those women conceived and gave birth to half a man.By the One in Whose hand Muhammad's soul is, if he had said 'Allah willing', all of them would have been knights striving in the cause of Allah."[Narrated by Al-Bukhāri and Muslim]

One cannot reach his objective or fulfill his needs except through Allah Almighty, Who is:

{...The Creator, the Initiator, the Fashioner; to Him belong the most beautiful names. Whatever is in the heavens and the earth glorifies Him, and He is the All-Mighty, the All-Wise.}

[Surat al-Hashr: 24]

O Allah, praise be to You! You have bestowed Your favor upon us as You have brought us into existence after we were nothing.{Has there come upon man a period of time when he was not a thing worth mentioning?}[Surat al-Insān: 1]Allah Almighty praises Himself as the Initiator as He says:{He is Allah, the Creator, the Initiator, the Fashioner...}[Surat al-Hashr: 24]

"Bāri'" is derived from "bar'", which has two meanings. The first is creating.

The second meaning is being away and free from something.

--

So, our Lord is the Initiator, the Maker, and the Inventor, Who brought things into existence after they had been nothing. He preferred some of His creation over others and made every race distinct from others and fashioned each in a way that fits the purpose behind its creation. So, He creates something out of nothing and gives it the traits that make it distinct from other creatures.

He created the creation free from discrepancy and disharmony.{Who created seven heavens in layers. You do not see in the creation of the Most Compassionate any inconsistency. So return [your] vision [to the sky]; do you see any flaws?}[Surat al-Mulk: 3]

Moreover, our Lord, Al-Bāri', is free from any deficiency or defect in His essence, attributes, and actions.

His name "Al-Bāri'" is witnessed in all of His creation,

and His subtle and kind acts keep descending.

Glory be to the One to Whom all creatures

prostrate themselves and proclaim His greatness and Oneness!

Allah Almighty says: {He is Allah, the Creator, the Initiator, the Fashioner...} [Surat al-Hashr: 24]

--

--

When Allah Almighty wants to create something, He first predestines it according to His knowledge and wisdom, then He initiates its existence from nothingness according to His predestination and in the form He wills, Exalted be He.

No coincidence..

A wise man was once asked: "How did you know Allah?" He said: "By reading the signs of His power that are manifest in the creatures."

{Who perfected everything which He created...}

[Surat as-Sajdah: 7]

{We did not create them both except for a true purpose...}

[Surat ad-Dukhān: 39]

Consider the plants on earth, with all its different kinds, and have a close look at all the wonderful creatures in the world,

which clearly point to the One Creator, Who has no partner.

{Say: "Observe what is in the heavens and earth"...}[Surat Yūnus: 101]There is nothing but His work, superb creation, amazing power, and the traces of His wisdom. So, who is more entitled to be the God? Indeed, He Who creates is more worthy of being worshiped and praised as the One and Only God.Indeed, most people know that they were created by Allah, but majority of them still associate partners with Him.{And most of them believe not in Allah except that they associate others with Him.}[Surat Yūsuf: 106]People fall under two categories:

The believers, who are the best among humankind.

The polytheists, who are the worst among humankind.

Let one consider his actions. If they are good, he should praise his Lord as He created him inclined to be good. Had he left his self to its own whims and vain desires and had not restrained it with fear from Allah, he would have been among the worst human beings.

Therefore, Mūsa (Moses) (peace be upon him) ordered his people to repent to Allah, the Initiator, after they had deviated from belief in Him and made an idol out of their jewelry in the form of a calf.{And [recall] when Moses said to his people: "O my people, indeed you have wronged yourselves by worshiping the calf. So, repent to your Initiator and kill yourselves. That is best for you in the sight of your Initiator." Then He accepted your repentance; indeed, He is the Accepting of repentance, the Most Merciful.}[Surat al-Baqarah: 54]

Whenever the believer knows and learns one of the beautiful names of Allah, he becomes more honorable and elevated and will have greater longing and love for Him; and he seeks closeness to his Lord by knowing that name.

He will also know that Allah has power over all things.

O Allah, the Initiator, show kindness to us and let Your mercy descend upon us.

Al-Musawwir (The Fashioner)

Ibn al-Qayyim (may Allah have mercy upon him) said:"If you consider what Allah Almighty calls His servants, in the Qur'an, to think about, you will find that He commands them to know about His Oneness and His perfect and magnificent attributes."

Verily, the book of the universe contains many lessons and signs scattered here and there

for those who have minds and intellects whereby they look and contemplate.

We will pause here with Allah's name "Al-Musawwir":

Allah Almighty says:{He is Allah, the Creator, the Initiator, the Fashioner...}[Surat al-Hashr: 24]It is our Almighty Lord Who fashioned everything He created in the way He willed and gave certain forms and distinct appearance to every created being, different, diverse, and plentiful as they are. He fashioned each form as He willed.{In whatever form He willed, He has assembled you.}[Surat al-Infitār: 8]

Our Lord, Exalted be He, is the One Who proportioned His created beings and gave them such forms and appearances that accord with His estimation, knowledge, and mercy, and which suit the interests and benefits of the creation. So, they come into existence with different and diverse forms and shapes, long and short, beautiful and ugly, male and female - each with their distinct form.

Allah Almighty says:{And We have certainly created you, then fashioned you...}[Surat al-A'rāf: 11]He also says:{...And formed you and perfected your forms; and to Him is the final destination.}[Surat at-Taghābun: 3]

O You Who know the unseen and the seen,

O You, the Lord Who created and fashioned everything,

You testified that You are One and Only,

a true testimony from You.

I turn my face to You, publicly and privately,

in praise and exaltation of You, my Lord.

Allah Almighty also says:{He is Allah, the Creator, the Initiator, the Fashioner...}[Surat al-Hashr: 24]When the three names (Al-Kāliq, Al-Bāri', Al-Musawwir) come together, each gives a distinct meaning. "Al-Khāliq" indicates estimation, "Al-Bāri'" indicates invention, and "Al-Musawwir" indicates giving everything its form. Yet, when these names are used separately, they all indicate the same meaning.Our Lord willed, predestined, then created and gave each creature its suitable form and fashion.{...Exalted is Allah far above what they describe about Him.}[Surat al-Mu'minūn: 91]The Prophet (may Allah's peace and blessings be upon him) used to say in prostration:"Allāhumma laka sajadt wa bika āmant wa laka aslamt, sajada wajhi lilladhi khalaqahu, wa sawwarahu, wa shaqqa sama'ahu wa basarah, tabārakallāhu ahsan al-khāliqīn (O Allah, to You I have prostrated and in You I have believed and to You I have submitted, and My face has prostrated to the One Who created it and formed it, and brought forth its hearing and sight. Blessed be Allah the best of creators)."[Narrated by Muslim]

The strongest signs:

The creation of man is indeed a sign for those who think and take lessons.{And in yourselves. Then will you not see?}[Surat adh-Dhāriyāt: 21]

Within human beings themselves, there are the greatest signs of their Almighty Creator.

The closest thing to a person is his own self. In fact, he contains wonders that point to the greatness of Allah Almighty that would take our whole life just to discover part of it. People turn away from this, however, and if they only pondered, they would cease to deny or disbelieve.{Cursed is man; how disbelieving is he!From what substance did He create him?From a sperm-drop He created him and proportioned him;Then He eased the way for him;Then He causes him to die and puts him in his grave.Then when He wills, He will resurrect him.}[Surat 'Abasa: 17-22]Over 7 billion people live on earth. Each one of them has his or her different form, shape, features, color, and appearance, though they all come from the same father and mother: Adam and Eve. But it is the work of Allah Almighty:{...[It is] the work of Allah, Who perfected all things. Indeed, He is All-Aware of what you do.}[Surat an-Naml: 88]Does this not require us to be thankful?! We see the favors that Allah Almighty bestows upon us since we were mere drops of sperm inside our mothers' wombs. Then, He gave us hearing and eyesight and breathed life into us. Then, He gave us food and drink and endowed us with homes and provisions, and everything we need.{Have We not made for him two eyes?And a tongue and two lips?And have shown him the two ways?}[Surat al-Balad: 8-10]

One of the greatest ways in which we can show gratitude to our Lord is to use His blessings in worshiping and obeying Him, not in sins and things displeasing to Him.

A last word..

A rational person would not mock people's forms and appearances for he knows it is Allah Who created them.{He is the One Who fashions you in the wombs as He wishes. There is no god except Him, the All-Mighty, the All-Wise.}[Surat Āl-'Imrān: 6]

Allah is the Creator, the Initiator, the Fashioner. An ugly person is not, thus, to be blamed for his ugliness. Likewise, a good-looking person has no credit or a role to play in the good look he has.

Someone once said to a wise man: "O man with the ugly face!" He replied: "It was not me who created my face to make it good. He who dispraises a product has indeed dispraised its maker."The Prophet (may Allah's peace and blessings be upon him) said:"All the creation of Allah Almighty is good."[As-Silsilah As-Sahīhah by Al-Albāni]

If you see an afflicted person, praise Allah that He has not afflicted you. As the saying goes: "Do not mock your brother because Allah may remove his affliction and afflict you."

'Abdullah ibn Mas'ūd (may Allah be pleased with him) used to say:"Affliction is linked to speech. So, if I mock a dog, I fear that I may turn into a dog."Ibrāhim al-Nakha'i (may Allah have mercy upon him) said:"I may sometimes see things with which I can find fault, yet I remain silent fearing that I may get afflicted with something similar."

O Allah, the Creator, the Initiator, the Fashioner, we implore You to make us among Your best servants and to show mercy to us on the Day when we will stand before You for reckoning.

Al-'Afuww (The Pardoner)

When sinners listen to this verse:{For those it is expected that Allah will pardon them, and Allah is ever Pardoning, All-Forgiving}[Surat an-Nisā': 99],they raise their hands in supplication to their Lord and stand humble and submissive at His door, seeking His protection and pardon. They call out: "O the Pardoner, the All-Forgiving, we have none but You to turn to."

Thereupon, the Generous and the Pardoner looks at their condition and knows their innermost thoughts, and He erases their sins and misdeeds and elevates their ranks.

Glory be to Allah, the Pardoner, the Forgiving!

If afflictions and hardships come your way and sins overburden you, call out His name and ask Him for pardon.

O Lord, no matter how great my sins are, I supplicate You as You have commanded me in humility; if only the doers of good seeks refuge in You!

then in who can the evildoer seek refuge? I know that Your pardon is far greater than my sins. If You turn down my supplication, then who would show mercy to me?

Allah Almighty says:{...Indeed, Allah is Pardoning and Forgiving.}[Surat al-Hajj: 60]

Our Lord, Exalted be He, frequently pardons His servants and forgives their sins to an infinite extent. In addition to forgiving sins, He also erases their traces altogether, thus, people will not be held accountable for them on the Day of Judgment, and He removes them from the records of the honorable scribes, i.e. the angels who write down good and bad deeds. More than that, He even causes those sinners to forget those sins so that they will not remember them and feel ashamed, replacing those evil deeds with good ones.

The Almighty Lord is ever Pardoning and Forgiving. Everyone is in need of His pardon, mercy, and bounty. He promises forgiveness and pardon to those who meet their requirements.

Allah Almighty accepts pardon on the part of His servants and facilitates for them the duties they are obligated to perform, given the shortcoming and weakness they will necessarily show. For example, Allah ordained ablution for the performance of prayer. But if a person cannot find water for ablution, He pardons that and allows him to make dry ablution, considering his helplessness.

It was said that pardon is higher than forgiveness, for the former gives a feeling of elimination while the latter gives a sense of mere concealment. Elimination is more profound than concealment.

Allah's pardon is of two types:

General pardon, which encompasses all wrongdoers from the disbelievers and others, as He removes from them punishments entailed as a result of certain actions and requiring the cessation of blessings to them. Indeed, they offend Him by reviling Him and associating partners with Him, yet He pardons and provides for them, spreads out the world for them, and gives them respite, out of His pardon and forbearance. Thus, Allah sends down the best to His servants, and evil ascends to Him from them. Indeed, Allah Almighty does not need the worship of His servants. Nonetheless, He shows affection to them through His blessings, and they incur His wrath by disobeying Him, though they stand in need of Him.

Special pardon, which is given to the repentant, the seekers of His forgiveness, and the supplicants and worshipers among the believers who get afflicted and seek His reward for their patience.

He is the Pardoner..

Out of Allah's supreme pardon, if He pardons one of His servants in this world, He does not retract it on the Day of Judgment. He is the Most Bountiful. That is the immutable rule Allah Almighty applies with His close servants.

Out of His majesty, as He pardons the repentant sinners in this world, He also pardons persistent sinners among the monotheistic believers in the Hereafter.

And out of His majesty, He pardons sins, no matter how serious they may be, even if they include transgression against His own rights, and He replaces sins with good deeds. Who could ever deal with sins like that except the Almighty Lord? If it were not for the greatness of His pardon, the earth and its inhabitants would be ruined on account of the sins committed thereon.

Out of His great pardon, He guides His servants to the means whereby they can attain His pardon, including good deeds and words and noble morals. Indeed, if a person engages in a lot of righteous acts, they prevail his sins and misdeeds.

Turn back to Him!

The Pardoner calls you from above the seven heavens saying:{And your Lord said: "Call upon Me and I will respond to you"...}[Surat Ghāfir: 60]So, what keeps you from winning His bounty?!And what keeps you from joining the caravan of the oft-repentant?

If people knock on the doors of the kings in this world and stand there in humility, you stand in humility before the King of all kings, the Bountiful and Pardoning Lord, in Whose Hand are the keys to relief, happiness, pardon, and forgiveness.

{Do they not know that it is Allah who accepts repentance from His servants...}[Surat at-Tawbah: 104]Bilāl ibn S'ad said:"You have a Lord Who does not hasten to punish anyone of you; He forgives sins, accepts repentance, draws near to those drawing near to Him, and shows compassion to those turning away from Him."The Prophet (may Allah's peace and blessings be upon him) used to supplicate Allah saying:"Allāhumma innaka 'afuwwun tuhibbu al-'afwa fa'fu 'anni (O Allah, You are Pardoning and love pardon, so pardon me)."[Narrated by Ibn Mājah; Sahīh (authentic)]Ibn al-Qayyim (may Allah have mercy upon him) said:"If He pardons you, your needs will be fulfilled without asking."Sufyān al-Thawri (may Allah have mercy upon him) said:"I would not like my reckoning to be handled by my father and mother, for I know that Allah Almighty is more merciful to me than them."

When my heart hardens and I see my sins too great, I compare them to Your pardon, and behold! They are nothing.

My hope for Your mercy is the path in which I walk to You. My Lord, Your pardon is far greater than my sins. Pardon, O the Most Generous.

The key to pardon:

Scholars said that the dearest among people in the sight of Allah Almighty are those who act in accordance with His names and attributes. Indeed, He is merciful and loves the merciful and pardoning and loves those who pardon others. Allah Almighty treats a person the way he treats other people. Allah Almighty says:{So by mercy from Allah, you were lenient with them. And if you had been rude [in speech] and harsh in heart, they would have disbanded from about you...}[Surat Āl-'Imrān: 159]Pardon from a position of strength is one of the highest levels of piety. Out of His generosity, Allah Almighty rewards pardon on people's side with greater pardon. He says:{If [instead] you show [some] good or conceal it or pardon an offense - indeed, Allah is ever Pardoning and Omnipotent.}[Surat an-Nisā': 149]When Abu Bakr al-Siddīq (may Allah be pleased with him) swore not to spend on Mistah, one of his relatives, after he slandered the Prophet's wife 'Ā'ishah (may Allah be pleased with her), as part of what came to be known as the Incident of Slander, Allah Almighty revealed:{And let not those of virtue among you and wealth swear not to give [aid] to their relatives and the needy and the emigrants for the cause of Allah, and let them pardon and overlook. Would you not like that Allah should forgive you? And Allah is All-Forgiving, Most Merciful.}[Surat an-Nūr: 22]

If a person pardons others in pursuit of reward from his Lord, Allah Almighty will give him beyond what he expects, in this world and in the Hereafter.

The Prophet (may Allah's peace and blessings be upon him) is authentically reported to have said:"Allah increases the one who pardons in honor."[Narrated by Muslim]Al-Nawawi (may Allah have mercy upon him) said:"A person who is known for his pardon and forgiveness grows in respect, prestige, and honor among people."

As the Umayyad Caliph 'Abdul-Malik ibn Marawān was delivering a profound sermon, he stopped and cried hard. Then, he said: "O Lord, my sins are great, and only a small part of Your pardon is greater than them. So, remove with a little of Your pardon my great sins."

News of this reached Al-Hasan al-Basri, who wept and said: "If there were words to be written in gold, it would be these words."

A Bedouin once supplicated: "O Allah, You commanded us to pardon those who wrong us, and we have wronged ourselves, so pardon us."

And we supplicate You:{...Our Lord, we have wronged ourselves, and if You do not forgive us and have mercy upon us, we will surely be among the losers.}[Surat al-A'rāf: 23]

O Allah, You are Pardoning and You love pardon, so pardon us, O the Most Merciful of those who show mercy!

Al-Ghafūr Al-Ghaffār (The All-Forgiving, the Superb Forgiver)

Abu Tawīl came to the Prophet (may Allah's peace and blessings be upon him) and said: "What do you think about a man who committed all sins, sparing nothing at all. Can he repent?"

He said: "Have you embraced Islam?" He replied: "As for me, I testify that there is no god except Allah, alone with no partner, and that You are the Messenger of Allah." He said: "Yes, do good deeds and give up bad ones, and Allah will turn them all into good deeds." He said: "And my serious sins and indecent acts?" He said: "Yes." Thereupon, he kept saying: "Allah is the Most Great" until he left. [Narrated by Al-Tabarāni with an authentic chain of narration]

I supplicate Allah and ask for His pardon,

and I know that He is Pardoning and Forgiving.

If sins are great in the sight of people,

they are indeed small compared to Allah's mercy.

We will talk now about one of the names of Allah, which when sinners and pious believers hear, their hearts feel attached to it and they become joyful and hopeful. It is the name "Al-Ghafūr" and "Al-Ghaffār".

Allah Almighty says:{inform My servants that I am the All-Forgiving, the Most Merciful.}[Surat al-Hijr: 49]He also says:{And said: "Ask forgiveness of your Lord. Indeed, He is ever a Superb Forgiver.}[Surat Nūh: 10]And He says:{...Indeed, your Lord is vast in forgiveness...}[Surat an-Najm: 32]

"Ghafūr" and "Ghaffār" are derived from "ghafr", which means concealment and covering.

Our Lord, Exalted be He, is the One Who covers the sins of His servants, letting no one else see them, and Who pardons their misdeeds.

Allah, Exalted be He, forgives their sins time after time, endlessly. Each time a person sins and repents, He forgives him.

The door is open..

A man came to the Prophet (may Allah's peace and blessings be upon him) and said: "O Messenger of Allah, one of us commits a sin." He said: "It is recorded against him." The man then said: "He asks forgiveness for it and repents." The Prophet (may Allah's peace and blessings be upon him) said:"He is forgiven and his repentance is accepted, and Allah does not get bored of that, but you get bored."[Narrated by Al-Tabarāni and others; Hasan (sound)]

He is the All-Forgiving. If a servant turns to Him with as many sins that could fill the earth, He will turn to him with as much forgiveness.

He is vast in forgiveness, forgiving all sins except for associating partners with Him.

Allah Almighty opens His door to all those who sin and repent. He says:{Say: "O My servants who have transgressed against themselves [by sinning], do not despair of the mercy of Allah. Indeed, Allah forgives all sins. Indeed, He is the All-Forgiving, the Most Merciful."}[Surat az-Zumar: 53]And from above the seven heavens, He addresses those who say that Allah is the third of three and calls them to repentance, so that He will forgive them. He says:{So will they not repent to Allah and seek His forgiveness? And Allah is All-Forgiving, Most Merciful.}[Surat al-Mā'idah: 74]Allah Almighty forgives all sins, except when a person dies associating partners with Him{Indeed, Allah does not forgive associating partners with Him, but He forgives what is less than that to whom He wills. And he who associates partners with Allah has indeed fabricated a tremendous sin.}[Surat an-Nisā': 48] The verses in this regard are numerous.

As for the Sunnah, here is a Qudsi Hadīth that reads:"Allah Almighty said: 'O son of Adam, so long as you call upon Me and ask of Me, I shall forgive you whatever you have done, and I shall not mind. O son of Adam, were your sins to reach the clouds of the sky and were you then to ask forgiveness of Me, I shall forgive you, and I shall not mind. O son of Adam, were you to come to Me with sins nearly as great as the earth and were you then to meet Me, ascribing no partner to Me, I shall bring you forgiveness nearly as great as it is.'"[Narrated by Al-Tirmidhi; Sahīh (authentic)]

This applies to a person who seeks forgiveness with a sincere intention and with determination not to turn back to sins. When he displays sincerity to his Lord, He even turns his sins into good deeds, out of His great generosity and grace towards His servants.

Do not despair!

Righteous deeds expiate sins as Allah, Almighty says:{...Indeed, good deeds do away with misdeeds...}[Surat Hūd: 114]The Prophet (may Allah's peace and blessings be upon him) is authentically reported to have said:"Follow the sin with a good deed which will wipe it out."[Narrated by Al-Tirmidhi; Hasan (sound)]

Moreover, the afflictions and bad things that befall a person in his own self, or in his children, or in his wealth do expiate his sins, if he shows patience and contentment in pursuit of reward from his Lord.

In fact, Allah becomes more joyful when one of His servants repents to Him than a person who lost his mount in a desert, with all his food and drink on it, and then found it.

No matter how great your sin is or how frequently you commit it, Allah's mercy is far greater as long as you keep asking for His forgiveness.{...And My mercy encompasses all things...}[Surat al-A'rāf: 156]The Prophet (may Allah's peace and blessings be upon him) authentically reported that Allah Almighty said:"A servant committed a sin and he said: 'O Allah, forgive my sin,' and Allah said: 'My servant committed a sin and then realized that he has a Lord Who forgives the sin and punishes for the sin.' He then again committed a sin and said: 'My Lord, forgive my sin,' and Allah Almighty said: 'My servant committed a sin and then realized that he has a Lord Who forgives the sin and punishes for the sin.' He again committed a sin and said: 'My Lord, forgive my sin,' and Allah Almighty said: 'My servant committed a sin and then realized that he has a Lord Who forgives the sin and punishes for the sin. Do whatever you like for I have forgiven you.'"[Narrated by Muslim]That is as long as you repent and return to Him.

Be humbly submissive to your Lord!

The door of Allah is wide open to everyone who wants to repent and return to Him. He is ever Pardoning and Forgiving, and He promises to grant pardon and forgiveness to those who fulfill their requirements. He says:{And indeed, I am the Superb Forgiver of whoever repents and believes and does righteous deeds and then follows guidance.}[Surat Taha: 82]Even if your sins are too great and too many to be counted, ask Allah Almighty to forgive them all, for He knows and counts everything.This does not mean, however, that a Muslim may freely commit sins and misdeeds and act boldly against his Lord under the pretext that Allah is All-Forgiving and Most Merciful. Indeed, Allah Almighty says:{Your Lord is most knowing of what is within yourselves. If you should be righteous, then indeed He is All-Forgiving to those who constantly turn [to Him].}[Surat al-Isrā': 25]Al-Fudayl ibn 'Iyād (may Allah have mercy upon him) said:"Asking for forgiveness without giving up the sin is the repentance of liars."

The lifeline..

Allah Almighty commands all His servants, and notably His prophets, to seek forgiveness from Him:{And said: "Ask forgiveness of your Lord. Indeed, He is ever Superb Forgiver.}[Surat Nūh: 10]And the Prophet (may Allah's peace and blessings be upon him) is authentically reported to have said:"By Allah, I ask Allah for forgiveness and repent to Him more than seventy times a day."[Narrated by Al-Bukhāri]If this is the case with the prophets, then it is more appropriate and more necessary for those less in rank to ask for forgiveness. The Prophet (may Allah's peace and blessings be upon him) said to 'Ali ibn Abu Tālib (may Allah be pleased with him):"Shall I teach you some words which if you say, Allah will forgive you, even if you were already forgiven? Say: 'La ilāha illallāh Al-'Aliyy Al-'Azhīm, la ilāha illallāh Al-

Halīm Al-Karīm, la ilāha illallāh subhānallāh Rabb al-'arsh al-'azhīm (There is no god except Allah, the High, the Magnificent. There is no god except Allah, the Forbearing, the Generous. There is no god except Allah. Glory be to Allah, the Lord of the Magnificent Throne).'"[Narrated by Al-Tirmidhi; Sahīh (authentic)]'Ali (may Allah be pleased with him) said:"It is so strange how a person might get ruined while salvation is there with him." He was asked: "What is it?" He said: "Asking Allah for forgiveness." Qatādah (may Allah have mercy upon him) said: "The Qur'an informs you of your disease and your cure. The disease is sins, and the cure is seeking forgiveness from Allah."Shaykh al-Islam (may Allah have mercy upon him) said:"Sins are a cause of trouble, and seeking forgiveness removes its causes, as Allah Almighty says:{...And Allah will not punish them while they are seeking forgiveness.}[Surat al-Anfāl: 33]"Ibn Kathīr said:"Whoever assumes this attitude - i.e. seeking forgiveness, Allah will facilitate for him his sustenance and affairs and will preserve his strength."

I complain to You about sins which I admit. Before You question me on the Day of Judgment, I hope and implore You to forgive them.

I hope that You, the Bestower of favors, will forgive and conceal them on the Day of Reckoning as You have concealed them on earth.

It is noted that the phrase "there is no god except Allah" comes in association with seeking forgiveness in the verse that says:{So know that there is no god except Allah and ask forgiveness for your sin and for the believing men and believing women...}[seeking Muhammad: 19]"This is because monotheism erases the root of polytheism and seeking forgiveness erases its branches.

The best praise of Allah is: "la ilāha illallāh" (there is no god except Allah), and the best supplication is: "astaghfirullāh" (I seek forgiveness from Allah). That is why Allah commanded the Prophet (may Allah's peace and blessings be upon him) to adhere to monotheism and to ask forgiveness for himself and his fellow believing men and women."

O Allah, forgive us, our parents, and all Muslims, O Lord of the worlds!

Al-Kabīr (The Great)

At the doorstep..

Your Lord is the Owner of might and dominion, the Great, the Exalted. Place your needs at His door and stand in humble submission before Him. He will fulfill your needs, remove your illness, repay your debt, relieve your distress, and put a smile on your face.

He is Allah, the Great, Exalted be He.

With your Lord, the Great, your wishes will turn into realities.

And your aspirations, no matter how great they may be, are too easy.

And your desires will be fulfilled, along with everything you long for.

He is the Great Lord, to Whom everyone in fear or distress turns. He is Allah, the Great,{[He is] Knower of the unseen and the seen, the Great, the Exalted.}[Surat ar-Ra'd: 9]Our Lord is the Great and the Exalted. None and nothing whatsoever is greater or more magnificent than He is.{They have not appraised Allah with true appraisal, while the earth entirely will be [within] His grip on the Day of Judgment, and the heavens will be folded in His right hand...}[Surat az-Zumar: 67]

Our Lord, Exalted be He, is great in His attributes, which comprise all perfection, majesty, and magnificence. None is like, similar, or equal to Him in terms of His perfect attributes.

Our Lord is also great in His actions. His magnificent creation attests to His magnificent actions,{The creation of the heavens and the earth is indeed greater than the creation of mankind; yet, most people do not know.}[Surat Ghāfir: 57]

Our Lord is the Great and Majestic God, the Owner of Pride, beside Whose majesty and greatness everything great becomes so insignificant.

Our Lord is Great and far Exalted above all deficiencies, imperfections, and defects.

Moreover, He is Exalted above any evil or injustice.{...The Great, the Exalted.}[Surat ar-Ra'd: 9]{...So the judgment is with Allah, the High, the Great.}[Surat Ghāfir: 12]

All praise belongs to You and all blessings and the dominion belong to You, our Lord.

None is ever more glorious than You.

Glory be to the One Who is not appraised properly by His servants,

the One and Only God, established above the Throne.

The minds are falling short in this regard.

Allah Almighty is greater than everything and too great to be encompassed in our knowledge.{...But they do not encompass it in knowledge.}[Surat Taha: 110]Allah Almighty is so great that we cannot know the nature of His essence and attributes. That is why we are forbidden from contemplating Allah, as we cannot grasp Him with our small and limited minds.The Prophet (may Allah's peace and blessings be upon him) said:"Think about the blessings of Allah, but do not think about Allah Almighty."[Narrated by Al-Tabarāni; Sahīh (authentic)]The true measure of His majesty is only known to Him and unknown to all else, including the close angels and prophets. He keeps this to Himself alone.

The most profound phrase..

Allah Almighty is greater than everything, in terms of His essence, status, might, and majesty. That is why it is said that the most profound phrase used by the Arabs for exaltation of the Almighty Lord is "Allāhu Akbar" (Allah is the Most Great). This is because it denotes a more perfect meaning than greatness. So, when we say: "Allāhu Akbar", this comprises greatness and more.

It is for this reason that this phrase "Allāhu Akbar" (Allah is the Most Great) is used in prayer and Adhān. Indeed, it is more profound than "Allāhu A'zham". The Prophet (may Allah's peace and blessings be upon him) said:"Allah Almighty said: 'Pride is My robe, and majesty is My lower garment. If anyone disputes with Me over any of them, I will throw him in Hellfire.'"[Narrated by Abu Dāwūd; Sahīh (authentic)]Imam Ibn Taymiyyah (may Allah have mercy upon him) said:"He likens His majesty to the lower garment and His pride to the robe, and it is known that the robe is higher in rank. So, this denotes that pride is more profound than majesty."

The key to approaching the King:

Hence, this phrase was prescribed for commencing prayer. In prayer, a Muslim is like a slave who enters upon the king. So, he is instructed to use the best phrase, namely "Allāhu Akbar". It is as if he is saying: Allah is the Most Great; thereby, I enter the place of my Lord, Creator, and Provider, and Allah is greater than all the worldly preoccupations.If a person says this phrase sincerely from his heart, bearing its meaning in mind, he will develop a sense of exaltation for his Lord and a feeling of modesty and submission towards Him, which will prevent him from getting preoccupied with anything apart from the Almighty Lord. Given the significance of this phrase, it is present in numerous acts of worship, aiming at winning Allah's approval.Ibn al-Qayyim (may Allah have mercy upon him) said:"{...And approval from Allah is greater...} [Surat at-Tawbah: 72]. Indeed, Allah's approval towards a servant is greater than Paradise and all that it contains, since approval is an attribute of Allah, whereas Paradise is His creation."

The honorable is the one who takes refuge in the Great Lord ..

When "Allāhu Akbar" fills a believer's heart, he takes pride in it and trusts and relies upon his Lord, and everything becomes so small in his eyes compared to the pride and majesty of Allah.

Biographers said:"After Al-Hajjāj had offered two Rak'ahs behind the Maqām, a poor man from Yemen came and performed Tawāf around the Ka'bah. During his Tawāf, a harpoon got stuck to his clothing and then fell on Al-Hajjāj's body, causing him to panic. He said: 'Hold him!' The soldiers held the poor Yemeni. He said: 'Bring him near.'Al-Hajjāj then said: 'Do you know me?' He replied: 'I do not know you.' Al-Hajjāj said: 'Who is your governor in Yemen?' He said: 'Muhammad ibn Yūsuf - the brother of Al-Hajjāj - who is unjust like him, or even worse.' He said: 'Do you not know that I am his brother?' The man wondered: 'Are you Al-Hajjāj?' He replied in the affirmative. Thereupon, the poor man said: 'How evil you are! And how evil your brother is!' He asked: 'How did you leave my brother in Yemen?' He replied: 'I left him full and fat.' Al-Hajjāj said: 'I am not asking you about his health, but about his justice.' The man said: 'I left him oppressive and unjust.' Thereupon, he said: 'Do you not know that he is my brother?' He said: 'Do you think, O Hajjāj, that your brother derives more power from you than the power I derive from the One and Only God?'"Tāwūs - the narrator - said:"By Allah, this made my hair stand on end! Then, Al-Hajjāj set this man free, and he began to perform Tawāf around the Ka'bah, fearing none but Allah."

There are people whose shrouds are dyed with the blood of sacrifice.

From the spring of "Allāhu Akbar" they drank.

--

--

No grave matter, hardship, or great distress could ever be hard for Allah, the Great.

So, the Great is Allah Almighty, and any other great one you have seen or heard about is nothing but a slave to Allah, Who is the Most Great. Hence, no distress can escape the power and will of Allah, the Owner of honor, pride, and majesty.

Allah, the Great Lord, is the One Who will turn your problems into solutions, your pains into wellbeing, your dreams into realities, and your tears into smiles.

So, hold onto the rope of Allah,

for He is the real support for you, while others will fail you.

O Allah, we implore You by Your name "Al-Kabīr" to bestow upon us the favor of entering Paradise and being saved from Hellfire.

Al-A'la Al-'Aliyy Al-Muta'āl (The Most High - the High - the Exalted)

If any disaster, distress, or serious problem hits us hard, our hearts turn to the Most High Lord, our hands are raised to the High God, and we look towards the sky waiting for relief from the High, the Most High, the Exalted Lord.

Our Lord is the High, the Most High, the Exalted. He says:{...And He is the High, the Magnificent.}[Surat al-Baqarah: 255]He also says:{Glorify the name of your Lord, the Most High.}[Surat al-A'la: 1]And He says:{[He is] Knower of the unseen and the seen, the Great, the Exalted.}[Surat ar-Ra'd: 9]

Our Lord the High, the Most High, the Exalted, is higher than all. Indeed, absolute Highness from all aspects belongs to Him.

* He is High in His essence, as He is established above His Throne, distinct from His creation, and Exalted above all beings.{The Most Compassionate rose above the Throne.}[Surat Taha: 5]* He is High in His status. Indeed, He is Exalted and possesses all attributes of perfection, beauty, and majesty. None of His creation has anything similar, equivalent, or close. His servants cannot even encompass one single attribute of His.{...And they do not encompass Him in knowledge.}[Surat Taha: 110]* He is High in His vanquishing power. He vanquished everything, and all beings are humbly submissive to Him and subject to His authority, dominance, and majesty.{And He is the Vanquisher over His servants...}[Surat al-An'ām: 18]

Above the heavens, and upon the Throne, He is High,

being separate and distinct from the whole creation.

He possesses perfect and sublime attributes.

All praise is due to Him.

Where is Allah?

The great Companion Mu'āwiyah ibn al-Hakam al-Sulami (may Allah be pleased with him) reported: "I had a bondmaid who tended my sheep by the side of Mount Uhud. One day, I happened to pass that way and found that a wolf had taken a goat from her flock. I am, after all, a man from the children of Adam and I felt sorry - angry - as they feel sorry. So, I slapped her.

I came to the Messenger of Allah (may Allah's peace and blessings be upon him) and he informed me that what I did was something grievous. I said: 'O Messenger of Allah, should I set her free?' He said: 'Bring her to me.' So, I brought her to him. He said to her: 'Where is Allah?' She said: 'In the heaven.' He said: 'Who am I?' She said: 'You are the Messenger of Allah.' Thereupon, He said:'Set her free, for she is a believer.'" [Narrated by Muslim]Saying that Allah is in the heaven means that He is Exalted above the heaven. The preposition "in" here actually means "on", like the verse that says:{...And I will crucify you in the trunks of palm trees...}[Surat Taha: 71]. "In" in this verse also means "on" - on the trunks of palm trees.We should not have the mistaken idea that the heaven encompasses Allah Almighty. Indeed, He is far exalted and greater than being encompassed by anything of His creation.

Let us pause here for a while, dear readers. Is it permissible for us to describe Allah Almighty by the opposite of what He described Himself with, like Him being present everywhere?

In Majmū' al-Fatāwa, Shaykh al-Islam Ibn Taymiyyah (may Allah have mercy upon him) said:"Allah Almighty described Himself as the High and the Most High, which is an attribute of praise and exaltation because it is an attribute of perfection; just as He praised Himself as the Magnificent, the All-Knowing, the Omnipotent, the All-Mighty, the Forbearing, the Ever-Living, the All-Sustainer, etc.

So, it is not permissible to describe Him by the opposite of these attributes. For example, we may not ascribe to Him the opposite of highness, which is lowliness, or the opposite of strength, which is weakness.

Indeed, He is far exalted above such imperfections and deficiencies that contradict the attributes of perfection established for Him."

Part of monotheism is to believe that Allah is High and Exalted above the heavens and truly established above the Throne

He is indeed above everything, and it could not be otherwise, as He is managing all the worlds.

Allah Almighty says:{Indeed, your Lord is Allah, Who created the heavens and earth in six days and then rose over the Throne...}[Surat al-A'rāf: 54]Allah Almighty mentions that Jibrīl (Gabriel) and the angels descend to earth. He says:{The angels and the Spirit descend therein by permission of their Lord for every matter.}[Surat al-Qadr: 4] Descent can only happen from a high place.He also mentions that the angels ascend to Him:{The angels and the Spirit will ascend to Him during a Day the extent of which is fifty thousand years.}[Surat al-Ma'ārij: 4]Allah Almighty also mentions that pious acts and good speech ascend to Him. He says:{...To Him ascends good speech, and righteous work raises it...}[Surat Fātir: 10]

So, to whom the deeds are raised?

If Allah Almighty Himself were everywhere, why would there be sending down, descent and the like?!

Our Lord is far exalted above having anyone similar or equal to Him.

And He is far exalted above having a wife or children.{And that exalted is the nobleness of our Lord; He has not taken a wife or a son.}[Surat al-Jinn: 3]Moreover, Allah Almighty is far exalted above having a partner in His divinity.{But when He gives them a good [child], they ascribe partners to Him concerning that which He has given them. Exalted is Allah above what they associate with Him.}[Surat al-A'rāf: 190]

The path..

Whoever knows the meanings of the three names: (Al-'Aliyy, Al-A'la, Al-Muta'āli) will realize that Allah Almighty is High by the attributes of perfection, Exalted above any defect or deficiency, and Higher than His creation.

Whoever grasps this fact, in terms of knowledge and servitude, will feel self-sufficient, honorable, and strong by his Lord.{And We raised him to a high station.}[Surat Maryam: 57]

High status, in both the worldly life and the Hereafter, can be attained by:

Faith:{But whoever comes to Him as a believer having done righteous deeds - for them there will be the highest degrees.}[Surat Taha: 75]Knowledge:{...Allah will raise those who have believed among you and those who were given knowledge, by ranks...}[Surat al-Mujādilah: 11]Humility: The Prophet (may Allah's peace and blessings be upon him) is authentically reported to have said:"None acts humbly for the sake of Allah except that Allah elevates him."[Narrated by Muslim]When one of the Companions (may Allah be pleased with them) asked companionship of the Prophet (may Allah's peace and blessings be upon him) in Paradise, he said to him:"Help me achieve this for you by frequent prostration."[Narrated by Muslim]In prostration, we say: "Subhāna rabbiya al-A'la (Glory be to my Lord, the Most High)." Allah Almighty says:{Glorify the name of your Lord, the Most High.}[Surat al-A'la: 1]

Commenting on this Dhikr in prostration, some said that it denotes the utmost submission and humility on the servant's part through the noblest part in him, namely his face, as he puts it on dust. So, when he is at the lowest level, as required by prostration, it is appropriate for him to describe his Lord as the Most High.

Hence, prostration is the position in which a person is closest to the Almighty Lord. The Prophet (may Allah's peace and blessings be upon him) said:"The closest the servant is to his Lord when his is in prostration. So, increase supplication (therein)."[Narrated by Muslim]

You have achieved your wish..

As it becomes known that the world and its affairs are managed by the Most High Lord in Whose hand the dominion of the heavens and the earth is, so you who are sick, the Healer is in the heaven; O you who are needy, the Self-Sufficient is in the heaven; O you who are sad, the One Who consoles hearts is in the heaven; O you who are sterile, the Bestower is in the heaven; O you who are in debt, the All-Provider is in the heaven; O you who are distressed, the One Who gives relief is in the heaven.

So, turn your face and heart towards the heaven and supplicate to your Lord, the Most High; and rejoice and be hopeful, for He says from above the seven heavens:{And when My servants ask you concerning Me - indeed I am near. I respond to the invocation of the supplicant when he calls upon Me. So let them respond to Me [by obedience] and believe in Me, so that they may be [rightly] guided.}[Surat al-Baqarah: 186]

Praise be to You, the Owner of bounty, glory, and highness.

Blessed are You; You give and withhold from whomever You will.

My Lord, my sins are too many and great,

but Your pardon is greater and more vast.

My Lord, You see my condition and know my need and weakness.

And You know my secret talk and innermost thoughts.

My Lord, if You leave or exclude me,

for whom would I possibly hope, and who would intercede for me?

O Allah, we implore You by Your name "Al-A'la" to elevate us in this world and in the Hereafter.

Al-Qāhir Al-Qahhār (The Vanquisher - the Superb Vanquisher)

Abu Hurayrah (may Allah be pleased with him) said:"Pharaoh fastened the hands and feet of his wife to four wedges. Whenever they were pulled away to make her suffer, the angels would cover her. Thereupon, she said:{...My Lord, build for me near You a house in Paradise and save me from Pharaoh and his deeds and save me from the wrongdoing people.}[Surat at-Tahrīm: 11]"[Narrated by Abu Ya'la; Sahīh (authentic)]

From the room of the tyrant Pharaoh, one of the world's best women did emerge; and from his palace Mūsa (Moses) (peace be upon him) came out.

That is the Pharaoh who said:{...We will kill their sons and keep their women alive; and indeed, we are dominant over them.}[Surat al-A'rāf: 127]In response, Allah, the Superb Vanquisher, vanquished this tyrant and made him a lesson and sign for the succeeding generations.{So today We will save your body, so that you may be a sign to those who succeed you. And indeed, most people are heedless of Our signs.}[Surat Yūnus: 92]Allah Almighty praises His sublime essence saying:{And He is the Vanquisher over His servants. And He is the All-Wise, the All-Aware.}[Surat al-An'ām: 18]

Our Lord is the Vanquisher by His might and power, and He is the Disposer of everything in the universe. Nothing can repel His will.

He vanquished tyrants and broke kings, and to Him everyone, all creatures, all faces, and every difficulty became humbly submissive and stood in humility before His pride and majesty.

It is our Lord, Exalted be He, to Whom all creatures yield and submit, and before Whose utmost power and might they stand in humiliation.

He is the Vanquisher of the entire universe, including the upper and the lower worlds. Nothing happens or remains still in this universe without His permission. Whatever He wills comes to pass, and whatever He does not will never happens. This is the meaning of the two names: Al-Qāhir and Al-Qahhār.

Being the Vanquisher entails being Ever-Living, All-Mighty, and Able.

The creation and creatures, on the other hand, are vanquished, dominated, and subject to Allah's power and authority.

He is the Superb Vanquisher:

Who responds to those in distress when they supplicate Him and removes the harm from them? Who gives life back to the rotten bones and repeats the creation as He made it in the first place? Who supports the oppressed and helps the weak?

Our Lord is the Vanquisher, the All-Wise. He does not create anything for no purpose, does not neglect anything, and does not accept any act or legislate any law except for a wise purpose, whether it is known or not.

To You the whole matter returns.

And from You hopes and glad tidings are received.

So, who is worthy of being worshiped as the One God? It is definitely Allah, the Superb Vanquisher, to Whom none is equal.

Prophet Yūsuf (Joseph) (peace be upon him) used this reasoning in his argument with his two fellow prisoners. He said:{O [my] two companions of prison, are separate lords better or Allah, the One, the Superb Vanquisher?}[Surat Yūsuf: 39]

Have you ever seen a vanquished person who can bring himself any good or avert from himself any harm? So, how could we ask from and rely upon weak and vanquished beings, apart from Allah, the One, the Superb Vanquisher?!

When the Prophet (may Allah's peace and blessings be upon him) got up from sleep suddenly, he would make this supplication:"La ilāha illallāh Al-Wāhid Al-Qahhār, Rabbu as-samāwāti wa al-ardi wa ma baynahuma Al-'Azīz Al-Ghaffār (There is no god but Allah, the One, the Superb Vanquisher, the Lord of the heavens and the earth and what is between them, the All-Mighty, the Superb Forgiver)."[Narrated by Ibn Hibbān; Sahīh (authentic)]

Entrust your affairs to Him..

As the believer knows that Allah is the One, the Superb Vanquisher, he declares his submission to Him, entrusts his affairs to Him, relies upon Him, and extols none and fears none but Him. He no longer fears the helpless created beings, even if they claim to possess power and might.

When faith entered the hearts of the magicians of Pharaoh and they knew that Allah is the One, the Superb Vanquisher, their response to Pharaoh's threat was:{They said: "No harm. Indeed, to our Lord we will return."}[Surat ash-Shu'arā': 50]Allah Almighty is the Vanquisher of tyrants and sinners:{And He is the Vanquisher over His servants. And He is the All-Wise, the All-Aware.}[Surat al-An'ām: 18]He Vanquished the people of Nūh (Noah) with the flood, the people of Sālih with the outcry, the people of 'Ād with the storm, the people of Lūt (Lot) with the stones, the people of Qārūn with sinking inside the earth, the people of Saba' with hunger, thirst, and extreme poverty, and He vanquished the Children of Israel with fear, dominance of their enemies, prevalent killings, and some of them were subject to transformation and plague.The vanquishing power of Allah Almighty is quite apparent.{...And We did not wrong them, but they were wronging themselves.}[Surat an-Nahl: 118]The power of Allah dominates and crushes the power of all created beings.{...To whom belongs sovereignty this Day? To Allah, the One, the Superb Vanquisher.}[Surat Ghāfir: 16]Al-Rāzi (may Allah have mercy upon him) said:"Where will the tyrants and powerful kings be when this statement will be made?

And where will the prophets, messengers, and close angels be when this reproach will be proclaimed?

Where will the people of misguidance and atheism as well as the followers of guidance and monotheism be?

Where will Adam and his progeny be?

Where will Satan and his followers be?

It is as if they will be destroyed and non-existent!

The souls depart the bodies, the bodies decay and get rotten, and all bonds are severed, and only Allah remains and will remain forever."

Not all issues are necessarily settled in worldly life. Some grievances will be dealt with again on the Day of Judgment. This truth is so hard and bitter for the unjust people.{...And indeed, our return is to Allah...}[Surat Ghāfir: 43]Al-Shāfi'i said:"There is a verse in the Qur'an that is considered as an arrow settled within the heart of the wrongdoers and a source of relief for the heart of the wronged." It was said: "What is it?" He said:"{...And never is your Lord forgetful.}[Surat Maryam: 64]"

O Allah, the Owner of power and might, keep us safe from the evil of the wicked and the cunning plots of the transgressors.

Al-Wahhāb (The Bestower)

And one of His names is the Bestower.

Look at His favors and gifts at all times.

The dwellers of the heavens and the earth never cease

to receive these blessings from Him.

Praising Himself, Allah Almighty says:{Or do they have the depositories of the mercy of your Lord, the All-Mighty, the Bestower?}[Surat Sād: 9]Our Lord, Exalted be He, is the Generous Bestower of gifts, which encompass all beings in the heavens and the earth. His giving and blessings are ceaseless. He gives without being asked and bestows favors without any means on the part of His servants.{Our Lord, let not our hearts deviate after You have guided us and grant us from Yourself mercy. Indeed, You are the Bestower.}[Surat Āl-'Imrān: 8]{Or do they have the depositories of the mercy of your Lord, the All-Mighty, the Bestower?}[Surat Sād: 9]

He is the Bestower:

Glory be to Him, a Magnificent Creator and a Generous Bestower!

Generosity and bounty are among His greatest attributes, and His giving never ceases. Could there ever be someone who is more bountiful than He is?!

His servants disobey Him but He watches over them, and He still preserves and takes care of them as they move and sleep as if they did not commit sins. He bestows His favors even upon sinners and wrongdoers.

Who supplicated Him and did not receive an answer? Who asked from Him and was not granted his request? Who stood at His door and got rejected?

Glory be to the One Who fulfills wishes lying within the heart yet not uttered by the tongue!

Glory be to Him! He guarantees the provision for all the worlds.

In fact, the favors of Allah Almighty are successively bestowed upon us since we were mere drops of sperm inside our mothers' wombs. Then, He gave us the hearing and eyesight and breathed life into us. Then, He gave us food and drink and endowed us with homes, provisions, and everything we need.

Allah Almighty says to His servant:{Have We not made for him two eyes?And a tongue and two lips?And have shown him the two ways?}[Surat al-Balad: 8-10]{O people, it is you who stand in need of Allah; as for Allah, He is the Self-Sufficient, the Praiseworthy.}[Surat Fātir: 15]

He created you and provides for you. He gave you life and causes you to die. He bestows His favors upon you. He causes you to get sick and cures you. He causes you to get hungry and satisfies your hunger. He causes you to become thirsty and quenches your thirst. He makes you laugh and cry. He teaches you what you do not know and informs you about what you are ignorant of. He prepares your provision,

answers your supplication, responds to your call, vanquishes your enemies, sends messengers to you, teaches you His book, and guides you to His path; and after all that, you disobey Him!{Cursed is man; How ungrateful he is!}[Surat 'Abasa: 17]

At His doorstep..

Do you find difficulty in life?

Do you suffer from illness?

Are you heavily in debt?

Are you crushed by poverty?

Do you wish to have a wife and children?

Do you live in perplexity and confusion?

Now, you should turn to Allah, the Bestower, the Generous Giver. Just raise your hands, stand at His door, and ask for His refuge, and behold! Your hunger, thirst, sleeplessness, and illness will disappear and the absent will come back, the misguided will be guided, the captive will be set free, and darkness will be dispelled by light.

He is the Bestower, Who turns tears into smiles, fear into security, panic into tranquility, darkness into light, and distress into unexpected relief.

The treasures of Allah Almighty are full and inexhaustible. He says:{...Call upon Me; I will respond to you...}[Surat Ghāfir: 60]Whoever supplicates Allah should ask for something big, for nothing is too big for Him.Here is Sulaymān (Solomon) (peace be upon him) asking for what is good in this world and in the Hereafter:{He said: "My Lord, forgive me and grant me a kingdom such as none other after me will deserve. Indeed, You are the Bestower."}[Surat Sād: 35]Another example is Zakariyya (Zachariah) (peace be upon him). He became an old man and his wife was barren. Nonetheless, he said:{...My Lord, grant me from Yourself a good offspring. Indeed, You are the Hearer of supplication.}[Surat Āl-'Imrān: 38]

Return to the Bestower!

The kingdom, authority, wealth, children, and good health all come from Allah, the King, the Bestower.{...And Allah gives His sovereignty to whom He wills. And Allah is All-Encompassing [in favor] and All-Knowing.}[Surat al-Baqarah: 247]{...He grants females to whom He wills, and He grants females to whom he wills.}[Surat ash-Shūra: 49]The best supplication a person can make to his Lord is the one made by learned people, who know the secrets in communicating privately with their Lord through His beautiful names, and so they ask Him for steadfastness and mercy:{Our Lord, let not our hearts deviate after You have guided us and grant us from Yourself mercy. Indeed, You are the Bestower.}[Surat Āl-'Imrān: 8]Hence, Allah Almighty made it a statement to be said in each Rak'ah of prayer, imploring Him to grant us guidance:{Guide us to the straight path.}[Surat al-Fātihah: 6]

The secret lies in the beauty of supplication!

Allah Almighty loves those who supplicate Him. Rather, if it were not for their supplication, He would not care about them. He says:{Say: "My Lord would not care for you were it not for your supplication..."}[Surat al-Furqān: 77]One of the supplications whereby we can draw close to our Lord is this one, which He teaches us in the Qur'an:{And those who say: "Our Lord, grant us from among our wives and offspring comfort to our eyes and make us an example for the righteous."}[Surat al-Furqān: 74]And after this supplication, He gives the promise of Paradise:{Those will be awarded the Chamber for what they patiently endured, and they will be received therein with greetings and [words of] peace.}[Surat al-Furqān: 75]

Whoever becomes attached to Allah Almighty, resorts to Him whenever he is in distress, and frequently knocks on His door with humble submission and sincere supplication, Allah will honor, protect, and support him throughout his life and give him beyond his wishes.

A gentle whisper..

Our Lord, Exalted be He, bestows favors in this world as a trial and test and bestows favors in the Hereafter as a reward and recompense.

So, He gives in worldly life in accordance with His will and afflicts according to His wisdom, so that one gets attached to his Lord through supplication and hope, and attains happiness through his monotheism and faith.

That is the greatest favor and gift ever, if the servant is aware of the truth of his trial.

If he knows this, he will develop a sense of love for his Lord on account of this name, extend praise and thanks to Him, and become perpetually attached to Him.

Praise be to You, our Lord, the Best Bestower.

You are the Best to fulfill our hopes and grant our wishes.

You are the Best to remove hardships and relieve distress.

And You are the Best to give and bestow favors.

O Allah, bestow Your mercy upon us; indeed You are the Bestower; and forgive us, our parents, and all Muslims, O Lord of the worlds!

Ar-Razzāq (The All-Provider)

You become hungry and thirsty and then your hunger and thirst are quenched; you become needy and then your needs are fulfilled; you suffer sleeplessness, and then you are able to sleep; you get sick and you then recover; debts are repaid; sustenance becomes abundant; prisoners get released; and darkness goes away,{...But perhaps Allah will bring conquest or a decision from Him...}[Surat al-Mā'idah: 52]

If needs, grave matters, and distressful issues, debts, and financial difficulties come to you from all directions, you have to turn to the All-Provider, Who removes grief and anguish and answers the supplication of the distressed.

Get close to the All-Provider and ponder this name, which brings a sense of tranquility and reassurance.

{Indeed, it is Allah Who is the All-Provider, the Possessor of Power, the Strong}[Surat adh-Dhāriyāt: 58]Our Lord is the All-Provider. He undertakes to provide for His servants, sustains the creation, and encompasses all in His sustenance and mercy. He does not discriminate in this regard between believers and allies and disbelievers and enemies. In fact, He sends sustenance to the weak and the strong alike, and He sends it to the embryo in its mother's womb, the bird in its nest, the snake in its burrow, and the fish in the sea.{And how many a creature carries not its [own] provision. Allah provides for it and for you. And He is the All-Hearing, the All-Knowing.}[Surat al-'Ankabūt: 60]

This name occurs in the Qur'an once in the singular form and five times in the plural form.

"Ar-Razzāq" comes in a superlative form so as to reassure us and make us know that He is a generous Lord and thus our hearts get attached to Him.

Abu Hurayrah (may Allah be pleased with him) reported: "A man became needy and he got out to the wilderness. Thereupon, his wife said: 'O Allah, provide for us so that we can make dough and bread.'

When he returned, he found the bowl full of dough, something was being roasted in the furnace, and the hand mill was operating. He asked: 'Where has this come from?' She replied: 'From the provision of Allah.' He swept what was around the hand mill.

Thereupon, the Prophet (may Allah's peace and blessings be upon him) said:'If he had left it, it would have continued to revolve - or grind - till the Day of Judgment.'"[Narrated by Al-Tabarāni in Al-Mu'jam Al-Awsat; Sahīh (authentic)]

Predestination had already been written..

If the sustenance of a person lied within a rock

stationed in the sea, hard and smooth,

it would split open

so that it could give him what is contained therein.

Or if it lied between the teeth of a predator,

Allah would cause it to come out.

Indeed, a person either goes to the sustenance predestined for him in the Preserved Tablet;

otherwise, it would come to him.

The Prophet (may Allah's peace and blessings be upon him) said:"Allah has appointed an angel in charge of the womb, and the angel says: 'O Lord, a sperm drop! O Lord, a clot! O Lord, a piece of flesh.' Then, when Allah wills to complete its creation, the angel asks: 'O Lord, a male or female? Wretched or blissful? How much will his sustenance be? How long will he live?' All that is written while the fetus is still in its mother's womb." [Narrated by Al-Bukhāri]

So, your sustenance is guaranteed. Pursuit of it does not make it more sure, neither does the hatred of anyone prevent it from coming.

In another Hadīth, the Prophet (may Allah's peace and blessings be upon him) said:"Indeed, sustenance goes after the person just as his destiny goes after him."[Narrated by Ibn Hibbān; Sahīh (authentic)]The Prophet (may Allah's peace and blessings be upon him) is also authentically reported to have said:"No soul will die without receiving its sustenance in full."[Narrated by Ibn Mājah; Sahīh (authentic)]Allah Almighty sends down the provisions in an exact measure. He is the All-Knowing of the conditions of His servants and what is best for them.{And if Allah had extended [excessively] provision for His servants, they would have committed tyranny throughout the earth. But He sends [it] down in an amount which He wills. Indeed He is All-Aware, All-Seeing of His servants.}[Surat ash-Shūra: 27]Ibn Kathīr (may Allah have mercy upon him) said:"He is All-Aware and All-Seeing as to who deserves opulence and who deserves poverty."

His treasures are full..

The sustenance of Allah Almighty is inexhaustible, and He gives it without suffering any trouble, difficulty, or hardship.

In a Qudsi Hadīth, Allah Almighty said:"O My servants, if the first of you and the last of you, and the humans of you and the jinn of you, were all to stand together in one place and ask of Me, and I were to give everyone what they requested, that would not decrease what I possess, except what is decreased of the ocean when a needle is dipped into it."[Narrated by Muslim]Although Allah Almighty provides for all His creation, He is also vast in forbearance. The Prophet (may Allah's peace and blessings be upon him) is authentically reported to have said:"No one is more patient when hearing abuse than Allah; they falsely attribute a son to Him, but He grants them safety and sustenance."[Narrated by Al-Bukhāri and Muslim]

Stop!

Abundant sustenance does not denote love from Allah Almighty. The disbelievers and the ignorant mistakenly think so, i.e. that when a person is given abundant provisions, this means Allah loves and is pleased with him. Allah Almighty says:{And they said: "We are more [than the believers] in wealth and children, and we are not to be punished."Say: "Indeed, my Lord extends provision for whom He wills or restricts it, but most people do not know."}[Surat Saba': 35-36]Conversely, little sustenance does not mean humiliation by Allah.{And as for man, when his Lord tries him and [thus] is generous to him and favors him, he says: "My Lord has honored me."But when He puts him to trial and restricts his provision, he says: "My Lord has humiliated me."No!}[Surat al-Fajr: 15-17]

The keys to provisions..

One of the best ways for attaining happiness and tranquility is to rely upon the Almighty Lord, the Provider, and trust Him with regard to sustenance, care, and protection.{Indeed, my protector is Allah, Who has sent down the Book; and He is the ally of the righteous.}[Surat al-A'rāf: 196]When Allah takes care of someone, He puts piety in his heart, which is one of the greatest means of sustenance, far better than all economic theories.{And if only the people of the cities had believed and feared Allah, We would have opened upon them blessings from the heaven and the earth; but they denied [the messengers], so We seized them for what they earned.}[Surat al-A'rāf: 96]{...And whoever fears Allah, He will make for him a way out,and will provide for him from where he does not expect...}[Surat at-Talāq: 2-3]It is an immutable law of Allah in this world that sustenance is linked to obedience to Him:{And if only they had upheld [the law of] the Torah, the Gospel, and what has been revealed to them from their Lord, they would have consumed [provision] from above them and from beneath their feet...}[Surat al-Mā'idah: 66]Conversely, sins preclude sustenance and remove the blessing:{Corruption has appeared throughout the land and sea by [reason of] what the hands of people have earned so He may let them taste part of [the consequence of] what they have done that perhaps they will return.}[Surat ar-Rūm: 41]

Forgotten provisions!

Good morals, being secure in your homeland, enjoying good health, having enough food for your day, meeting a loved one, the existence of your brother, the laughter of your child, having a righteous wife and a good friend, feeling tranquil, having eyes that can see, a tongue that can speak, and ears that can hear, sleeping tight, and greater having your parents or one of them alive.

You may be endowed with a good character, and another person endowed with wealth.

And the provision of one may be knowledge, and the provision of another could be noble morals.

A last word..

We should be on our guard against the devil's attempt to intimidate us with regard to sustenance. Allah Almighty says:{Satan threatens you with poverty and orders you to immorality, while Allah promises you forgiveness from Him and bounty. And Allah is All-Encompassing, All-Knowing.}[Surat al-Baqarah: 268]

One of the righteous predecessors said: "People have believed Satan and have belied Allah with regard to sustenance!"

People do not like poverty,

though poverty is better than opulence that makes them transgress.

Self-contentment is sufficient for a person;

yet if he does not have that, nothing will ever be sufficient for him.

O Allah, provide us with guidance, piety, chastity, and self-sufficiency; You are the Best of providers.

Al-Fattāh (The Superb Judge)

O you who are bored and tired of life and its troubles, difficulties, and anguishes! There is impending help, support, and relief. Indeed, after distress comes relief and after hardship comes ease. There is hidden care and kindness from your Lord all around you. There is a bright hope, a good future, and a true promise.{It is the promise of Allah. Allah does not fail in His promise...}[Surat ar-Rūm: 6]

With the Greatest Judge, you will have joy and relief from your distress and grief.

Allah Almighty says about Himself:{...And He is the Greatest Judge, the All-Knowing.}[Surat Saba': 26]

Our Lord, Exalted be He, opens sealed hearts through guidance, faith, and piety.

Our Lord is the One Who will open, judge, and rule between His servants in justice on the Day of Judgment. His rulings are free from any semblance of injustice. It is sheer justice and truth. Indeed, Allah is the Best of judges.{Say: "Our Lord will bring us together; then He will judge between us in truth. And He is the Greatest Judge, the All-Knowing."}[Surat Saba': 26]Our Lord removes distress, sends relief, ends hardships, bestows abundant mercy, opens the door of sustenance, and facilitates for His servants such things that reform their affairs and lives.{Whatever mercy Allah grants to people - none can withhold it; and whatever He withholds - none can release it thereafter. And He is the All-Mighty, the All-Wise.}[Surat Fātir: 2]Our Lord, Exalted be He, is the One Who opened the doors of knowledge, wisdom, and insight for His prophets and pious servants.{...And fear Allah; Allah will teach you. And Allah is All-Knowing of all things.}[Surat al-Baqarah: 282]It is our Lord Who enabled the conquest of kingdoms and countries by His pious and believing servants.{Indeed, We have given you a clear conquest.}[Surat al-Fat-h: 1]And it is our Lord Who opens the doors of many blessings for the sinners, by way of gradually drawing them to punishment.{So when they forgot that by which they had been reminded, We opened for them the doors of every [good] thing until, when they rejoiced in that which they were given, We seized them suddenly, and they were then in despair.}[Surat al-An'ām: 44]

Another meaning of "Al-Fattāh" is opening by rule, and that is the Shariah of our Lord.

And there is also opening by divine decree and predestination, which involves justice and benevolence from the Most Compassionate.

Fact..

In the comprehensive definition of Allah's name "Al-Fattāh", I cited what the scholars said in this regard. But I will pause here with the verse that says:{Whatever mercy Allah grants to people - none can withhold it; and whatever He withholds - none can release it thereafter. And He is the All-Mighty, the All-Wise.}[Surat Fātir: 2]

A fact that the believer should always bear in mind is that no one can achieve any desire or fulfill any need except through Allah Almighty, and nothing can happen except according to His will. There is no power nor strength in the entire universe except through Him, and Him alone.

No cell moves, no atom exists, no drop of water evaporates, and no leaf falls off a tree without His permission and will.

The entire world cannot cause you any harm unless Allah Almighty wills, nor can they save you from harm that Allah predestined for you.

One of the righteous predecessors wrote to his brother: "If Allah is with you, then whom would you fear? And if He is against you, then to whom would you turn?"

All keys are in His hand..

A person may get severely ill and suffer extreme pains and anguish as a result, with the doctors failing to find a remedy for his disease. All doors to cure are closed. But all of a sudden, the cure comes from the Most Compassionate, the Greatest Judge, the All-Knowing Lord, the Healer Who opens the doors of mercy and cure. He may cure him by some means, the weakest of means, or without any means at all. He is Al-Fattāh, Exalted be He.

You may get hit by tough circumstances, and all problems, crises, and pains come to you from every direction. The doors are closed and you think there is no way out of this severe distress. Yet, you suddenly find relief through the simplest of ways, from Allah, Al-Fattāh, and according to His will.

Poverty may strike you, debts surround you, and your features change and your heart gets broken when you remember your children and apprehend the creditor. You fall in confusion and loss and find all doors closed.

Yet, at this point, Allah, Al-Fattāh, sends His invisible relief, repaying your debts, ending your poverty, and comforting your soul. Indeed, it is Al-Fattāh Who has opened the doors of sustenance to you.

Your child, your father, your friend, or a loved one may travel or be away for a long while, and you feel uneasy, distressed, and perplexed and your heart trembles with longing whenever you remember this absent person. Thereupon, you stand humble at the door of your Lord, the King, the Greatest Judge, imploring Him to protect the absent one and bring him back. And behold! You receive glad tidings from above the seven heavens and the absent one turns back, the prisoner gets released, and the loved one returns to you.{Is He [not best] who responds to the desperate when he calls upon Him and removes evil...}[Surat an-Naml: 62]

Turn to Him!

He is the Greatest Judge, the All-Knowing, the Magnificent, the Most High. He is the most close and most kind to His servants.

The door of Al-Fattāh is always open. If distress gets so tough, be sure relief will soon come, and if the night becomes quite dark, that is a sign of the approaching morning. Do not lose hope in the Generous Lord, the Greatest Judge. Things never remain as they are. Trouble will soon pass. In fact, the best form of worship is to wait for relief. The future carries with it many potential changes, yet we do not know the unseen. As for our Lord, the Greatest Judge: {...Every day He is upon some affair.} [Surat ar-Rahmān: 29] and {...Perhaps Allah will bring about after that a [different] matter.} [Surat at-Talāq: 1] {For indeed, with hardship comes ease; indeed, with hardship comes ease.} [Surat ash-Sharh: 5-6]

Ask the doctor who got ill and died:

Who caused you to die with His medicine?

And ask the patient who got well and recovered

after all doctors failed to treat him: Who cured you?

Ask the healthy person who died:

Why did you die while you were in good health?

Your eyes do not cease to see these wonders

and your ears continue to hear about them.

O man, wait a little!

What has deluded you about your Lord?

Special opening..

Our provisions from Allah, Al-Fattāh, had been predestined and divided. A person may be provided with the blessing of praying for long, yet he does not fast much; another may be provided with the blessing of giving charity, but he does not possess much knowledge; someone else may be provided with the blessing of memorizing or reciting the Qur'an, yet he does not engage much in other acts of piety; and another one may be provided with the blessing of being dutiful to his parents; what an excellent privilege if one is blessed with Allah's provision!

When Allah loves one of His servants and finds him devoted and sincere,

He opens His provisions to him in an abundant way.

O Allah, open for us the blessings of the heavens and the earth as well as the doors of Your mercy and make us as means leading to goodness and blocking evil. Verily, You are Al-Fattāh, the All-Knowing!

As-Samī' (The All-Hearing)

As Allah Almighty wants you to know that He rose over the Throne, He also wants you to know that He always hears and sees you. He hears your words and sees your actions. Nothing is hidden from Him. Indeed, He hears your private talk to Him. Even your innermost thoughts and feelings are known to Him. He hears your supplication, grants your request, and accepts your repentance.

Are you squeezed by pains? Does your suffering soul yearn for its Creator?Allah Almighty hears your groaning and He is closer to you than your jugular vein. He responds to you and removes your grief and distress, for He is the All-Hearing, the All-Knowing.Praising Himself, Allah Almighty says:{...And He is the All-Hearing, the All-Knowing.}[Surat al-Baqarah: 137]Allah's name "As-Samī'" occurs 45 times in the noble Qur'an.Allah Almighty encompasses in His hearing all things that are to be heard. All voices and sounds, open and secret, in the entire universe are heard by Him, as if they were just one voice to Him. To Him, voices and sounds are not mixed and all languages are known. All voices and sounds, distant and near, open and concealed, are the same to Him. In the Qur'an, He says:{It is the same [to Him] whether any of you conceals his speech or declares it openly, whether one is hidden by night or goes forth freely by day.}[Surat ar-Ra'd: 10]The fact that created beings also have a sense of hearing does not mean that their hearing is similar to His - far Exalted be He above that! Indeed, the attributes of created beings befit their weakness, inability, and nature; whereas the attributes of the Creator befit His perfection and majesty, Exalted be He.{...There is nothing like unto Him: He is the All-Hearing, the All-Seeing.}[Surat ash-Shūra: 11]Hearing here means hearing and encompassing.{Certainly has Allah heard the speech of the one who argues with you concerning her husband and complains to Allah. And Allah hears your dialog; indeed, Allah is All-Hearing, All-Seeing.}[Surat al-Mujādilah: 1]Hearing also has the meaning of response and acceptance:{...Indeed, my Lord is the Hearer of supplication.}[Surat Ibrāhim: 39]

He is the All-Hearing; He sees and hears all that is

in the universe, open and secret.

All voices and sounds are heard by Him,

and the open and the concealed being the same to Him.

His hearing encompasses all sounds,

distant and near, and nothing is hidden from Him.

Indeed, He is All-Hearing and Near:

The Prophet (may Allah's peace and blessings be upon him) once heard the Companions (may Allah be pleased with them) supplicate Allah with loud voices. Thereupon, he said:"O people, do not trouble yourselves too much. He Whom you are invoking is not deaf or absent, but you are invoking an All-Hearing and All-Seeing (Lord)." [Narrated by Al-Bukhāri and Muslim]As soon as a person finishes his invocation and private talk with his Lord, he finds the response there, looming. This is because He is the All-Hearing, the All-Knowing.

He hears the calls of the desperate and the supplications of the needy and helps those in severe distress. He hears the praise of those who praise Him, and even the creeping of a black ant on a solid rock during a dark night is heard by Him. He hears our innermost thoughts, feelings, and obsessions.

A woman came to the Prophet (may Allah's peace and blessings be upon him) arguing about her husband. This was Khawlah (may Allah be pleased with her). 'Ā'ishah (may Allah be pleased with her), who was on the other side of the house, said she could hear some words but miss others. After this argument, Gabriel (peace be upon him) descended to Muhammad (may Allah's peace and blessings be upon him) with this verse:{Certainly has Allah heard the speech of the one who argues with you concerning her husband and complains to Allah. And Allah hears your dialog; indeed, Allah is All-Hearing, All-Seeing.}[Surat al-Mujādilah: 1]What an amazing nearness, great knowledge, and encompassing hearing!When Allah hears His close servants, this means He responds to them and protects and guides them. It is a hearing that calms their fearful hearts, like what happened with Moses (peace be upon him) when he said he was afraid of going to Pharaoh. Thereupon, Allah said:{...Fear not. Indeed, I am with you both; I hear and I see.}[Surat Taha: 46]

Allah was their Protector and He was Sufficient for them, how excellent He is as a Sufficient Protector!

The keys to relief:

If you are surrounded by fears and grave matters, implore your Lord by this great name, as the prophets (peace be upon them) used to do. Indeed, He hears the supplication, responds to those in distress, and removes harm. So, do not present your grief and distress to anyone else. Rather, fall in prostration before Allah Almighty, stand at His door, and talk and weep to Him, and then expect relief.

Zachariah (peace be upon him) called out his Lord secretly, so He gave him what his heart desired:{When he called to his Lord a private supplication.}[Surat Maryam: 3]And after he supplicated Allah by His name the All-Hearing, He gave him a righteous offspring:{...My Lord, grant me from Yourself a good offspring. Indeed, You are the All-Hearing of supplication.}[Surat Āl-'Imrān: 38]Likewise, Ibrahīm (Abraham) (peace be upon him) implored Allah by this name to accept his deed, after he and his son Isma'īl (Ishmael) finished the construction of the Ka'bah:{...Our Lord, accept from us. Indeed, You are the All-Hearing, the All-Knowing.}[Surat al-Baqarah: 127]Using this name, Abraham (peace be upon him) gave thanks to Allah for answering his supplication:{Praise to Allah, Who has granted me in old age Ishmael and Isaac. Indeed, my Lord is the All-Hearing of supplication.}[Surat Ibrāhīm: 39]Also by this name, the wife of 'Imrān sought closeness to her Lord and asked Him to accept her deed as she dedicated what was in her womb in a vow:{When the wife of 'Imrān said: "My Lord, indeed I have pledged to You what is in my womb, consecrated [for Your service], so accept this from me. Indeed, You are the All-Hearing, the All-Knowing."}[Surat Āl-'Imrān: 35]As Joseph (peace be upon him) experienced tough circumstances and evil plots, he supplicated his Lord saying:{...My Lord, prison is more liking to me than that to which they are inviting me. And if You do not avert from me their plot, I might incline toward them and [thus] be of the ignorant.So his Lord responded to him and averted from him their plan. Indeed, He is the All-Hearing, the All-Knowing.}[Surat Yūsuf: 33-34]And as Yūnus (Jonah) (peace be upon him) was in the belly of the whale, he called out:{...There is no god except You; Glorified are You. Indeed, I have been of the wrongdoers.}[Surat al-Anbiyā': 87]His feeble voice that came out of three types of darkness pierced the heaven, and behold! The All-Hearing, the All-Knowing saved him from the distress:{So We responded to him and saved him from the distress...}[Surat al-Anbiyā': 88]Allah Almighty afflicts His servants to hear their complaints and earnest imploring and supplication. He says:{He said: "I only complain of my suffering and my grief to Allah...}[Surat Yūsuf: 86]

The All-Hearing protects you..

The devils among the jinn and humans surround you and begin to whisper to you and overcome you and so you feel sad and distressed. That is why your Lord commands you to seek refuge with Him using these two names: the All-Hearing, the All-Knowing.{And if an evil suggestion comes to you from Satan, then seek refuge in Allah. Indeed, He is All-Hearing, All-Knowing.}[Surat al-A'rāf: 200]

Two men from Quraysh and one from Thaqīf - or two from Thaqīf and one from Quraysh - gathered at the Ka'bah and reviled the Companions as men with fatty bellies and poor minds. Thereupon, one of them said: "Do you think that Allah hears what we say?"

Another said: "He hears when we speak aloud and does not hear when we speak secretly."

The other said: "If He hears when we speak aloud, then He hears when we speak secretly." Thereupon, Allah Almighty revealed:{You did not bother to hide yourselves [when committing sins] from your hearing, your sight, and your skins lest they testify against you; rather you thought that Allah does not know much of what you do. And that was your assumption which you assumed about your Lord. It has brought you to ruin, and you have become among the losers.}[Surat Fussilat: 22-23]

A Reminder..

Our Prophet (may Allah's peace and blessings be upon him) used to seek refuge with Allah using these two names: the All-Hearing and the All-Knowing, when he got up for prayer during the night. He would say:"A'ūdhu billāh As-Samī' Al-'Alīm min ash-shaytān ar-rajīm, min hamzih wa nafkhih wa nafthih (I seek refuge with Allah, the All-Hearing, the All-Knowing, from the accursed devil, from his whispering, arrogance, and his poetry)."[Narrated by Abu Dāwūd; Sahīh (authentic)]He also used to seek refuge with Allah from any harm that could afflict him using these two names: the All-Hearing, the All-Knowing. He said:"Whoever says: 'Bismillāhi al-ladhi la yadurru ma'a ismihi shay'un fi al-ardi wa la fi as-samā' wa huwa As-Samī' Al-'Alīm (in the name of Allah with Whose name nothing in the earth or the heaven can cause harm, and He is the All-Hearing, the All-Knowing)' three times in the evening will not be hit by a sudden affliction till the morning, and whoever says it three times in the morning will not be hit by a sudden affliction till the evening."[Narrated by Abu Dāwūd; Sahīh (authentic)]

If you bear this name "As-Samī'" in your mind and heart, you will constantly feel close to Him, Exalted be He.

O Allah, the All-Hearing, the All-Knowing, make us among those who supplicate You and You answer their supplication and those who implore You and You show mercy to them.

Al-Basīr (The All-Seeing)

In Al-Hilyah, Abu Nu'aym said that as the Commander of the Believers, 'Umar ibn al-Khattāb (may Allah be pleased with him), was walking in the streets of Madinah by night, he heard the voice of an old woman saying to her daughter: "Mix the milk with water." But the daughter said: "Do you not know that 'Umar forbade mixing milk with water?" The old woman said: "'Umar is not here to see us." Thereupon, the daughter, confident of Allah's watchfulness over them, said: "If 'Umar cannot see us, the Lord of 'Umar sees us!"

There are people who lived in this world in a great status, permanent security, enduring happiness, and steadfastness to the truth, being pleased with their servitude to the Almighty Lord. This is for no reason but that they knew that Allah is the All-Seeing of what they do.

Allah's name "Al-Basīr" occurs 42 times in the Qur'an. Allah Almighty says:{...Indeed, Allah is All-Seeing of what you do.}[Surat al-Baqarah: 110]

Our Lord sees everything, no matter how minute it is. He sees the creeping of a black ant in a dark night on a solid rock. He sees what is below the seven earths just as He sees what is above the seven heavens.

He is the All-Seeing, the All-Knowing, and the All-Aware of all things and conditions, open and hidden.

He is the All-Seeing Who sees the creeping of ants under rocks and how food runs within their tiny bodies.

And He sees the treacherous glances of the eyes and their twinkling.

Allah Almighty established the attribute of seeing for Himself. He has two real eyes that befit His majesty. We believe in that without distortion, denial, likening, or twisted interpretation.{...There is nothing like unto Him and He is the All-Hearing, the All-Seeing.}[Surat ash-Shūra: 11]The fact that created beings also have sight does not mean that their sight is similar to His. Indeed, the attributes of created beings befit their weakness, inability, and nature; whereas the attributes of the Creator befit His perfection and majesty, Exalted be He.{...There is nothing like unto Him and He is the All-Hearing, the All-Seeing.}[Surat ash-Shūra: 11]

Out of Allah's mercy towards His servants, He addresses them gently and urges them to obey Him and be sincere to Him, though He is in no need for them and their worship. In His Noble Book, He repeats {Indeed, Allah is All-Seeing of what you do} more than forty times so as to remind the believer and alert the heedless that He is watchful over their deeds.

The pleasure of compliance..

He who knows that Allah sees him will feel too shy to commit a sin or something displeasing to Him. He who knows that Allah sees him will perfect his deeds and worship and perform them sincerely to reach the level of Ihsān (excellence), which is the highest level of obedience about which the Prophet (may Allah's peace and blessings be upon him) said:"To worship Allah as if you see Him; but if you do not see Him, He surely sees you."[Narrated by Al-Bukhāri and Muslim]If he reaches this level, he will enjoy the special company of Allah Almighty, Who said in a Qudsi Hadīth:"And My servant keeps drawing close to Me through supererogatory acts until I love him. And if I love him, I become his hearing with which he hears and his sight with which he sees."[Narrated by Al-Bukhāri]

He who knows that Allah sees him and his conditions and afflictions will feel assured and tranquil and become certain that relief is soon to come.

He who knows that Allah sees him will be too shy to be dishonest in his words and actions and deceptive towards others.

Ibn 'Umar (may Allah be pleased with him and his father) headed toward Makkah along with some of his companions. They stopped to take rest on their way. Thereupon, a shepherd descended upon them from a mountain. Ibn 'Umar said to him: "O shepherd, sell us one sheep."

The shepherd said: "I am a slave."

Ibn 'Umar said: "Tell your master that the wolf has eaten it." To this, the shepherd replied: "Where is Allah?"

Thereupon, Ibn 'Umar wept, and he bought the slave from his master and set him free.

If you become alone sometimes,

do not say I am alone, but say: Allah is watching me.

Do not think that Allah can be heedless for a while,

and nothing is hidden from Allah or unknown to Him.

Someone tried to seduce a Bedouin woman. He said to her: "No one sees us but the stars." Thereupon, she said to him: "Where is the One Who made them stars?"

It was said that whoever heeds Allah with regard to his thoughts and feelings, Allah will preserve him with regard to the actions of his body parts.

If you consider the seven types of people whom Allah will shade under His shade on the Day of Judgment, you will see that the common thing among all of them is that they firmly believe that Allah always sees them, and they worship Him as if they could see Him, thereby attaining this great status.

The good man from the people of Moses used this name as he supplicated Allah Almighty and sought refuge with Him from the evil cunning of Pharaoh and his allies:{...And I entrust my affair to Allah. Indeed, Allah is All-Seeing of His servants.}[Surat Ghāfir: 44]And what was the result?Allah answered his supplication:{So Allah protected him from the evils they plotted, and the people of Pharaoh were afflicted by the worst punishment.}[Surat Ghāfir: 45]

O Allah, Who sees the motion of the wings of gnats

during pitch-black night,

and Who sees their tiny veins

as well as the marrow of their bones.

Bestow upon me such a repentance

by which You erase my past sins.

A Reminder..

The believer should beware of the sins committed in seclusion and avoid persistence in this regard without repentance. Thawbān (may Allah be pleased with him) reported that the Prophet (may Allah's peace and blessings be upon him) said:"Indeed, I know people from my Ummah who will come on the Day of Judgment with good deeds like the mountains of Tihāmah, but Allah Almighty will make them like scattered dust."Thawbān said: "O Messenger of Allah, describe them to us and tell us more, so that we will not become of them unknowingly." He said:"They are your brothers and from your race, worshiping at night as you do, but they are people who, when they are alone, they transgress the sacred limits of Allah."[Narrated by Ibn Mājah] Those are the people who show off before others, and they remember Allah Almighty only a little.

The way you act when you are alone may raise or lower you. He who extols Allah Almighty in his seclusion, people will revere him when he is in public.

Ibn Rajab al-Hanbali (may Allah have mercy upon him) said:"Minor hypocrisy results from the difference between a person's outside and inside." He also said: "Only a person whose inside is good will end his life in a good way, as none can maintain pretence at the moment of death. Only what lies within the heart comes out then."

O Allah, the All-Seeing, pardon our weakness, shortcomings, and slips, and cause us to die as Muslims, O Lord of the worlds.

At-Tawwāb (The Accepting of Repentance)

'Umar ibn al-Khattāb (may Allah be pleased with him) said:"Sit with the oft-repentant, for they have the softest hearts."

I have done wrong, not right, and then come to You, repentant and hoping for Your forgiveness.

If You do not accept me, none would be in more loss and disappointment than me.

Let us spend some time with Allah's name "At-Tawwāb".

What an excellent name "At-Tawwāb" is! It gives the sinner hope to start anew and enter the phase of happiness and get out of the circle of frustration and darkness.{Do they not know that it is Allah Who accepts repentance from His servants and receives charities and that it is Allah Who is the Accepting of Repentance, the Most Merciful?}[Surat at-Tawbah: 104]

Our Lord is the Accepting of Repentance. He described Himself as such, in an exaggerated form, because of the large number of His servants whose repentance He accepts. Also, since His servants commit sins repeatedly, the exaggerated form indicates His vast acceptance of repentance that suits major sins.

He continues to accept the repentance and forgive the sins of those who repent and turn to Him, even if they repeat their sins and then repent endlessly.

Allah Almighty says:{But whoever repents after his wrongdoing and mends his ways, Allah will surely accept his repentance. Indeed, Allah is All-Forgiving, Most Merciful.}[Surat al-Mā'idah: 39]A man came to the Prophet (may Allah's peace and blessings be upon him) and said: "O Messenger of Allah, one of us commits a sin." He said: "It will be recorded against him." The man said: "He asks forgiveness for it and repents." He said:"He will be forgiven and his repentance will be accepted, and Allah does not get bored of that, but you get bored."[Al-Mustadrak; Hasan (sound)]

Whoever repents to Allah sincerely, Allah will accept his repentance.

What a Generous Lord!

Look at the bounty of Allah Almighty as He makes the repentance of His servant preceded and followed by acceptance from Him, Exalted be He!

He initially turns to him as He permits, guides, and inspires him to repent. That is a favor from Allah, the Generous Lord, the Most Merciful, and the Accepting of Repentance.

Then, when he actually repents to Allah, He accepts his repentance and pardons his errors and sins. Allah Almighty says:{...Then He turned to them so they could repent. Indeed, Allah is the Accepting of repentance, the Most Merciful.}[Surat at-Tawbah: 118]

There is no god except Allah. Repentance is a favor from Him, from beginning to end.

So, the Accepting of Repentance is the One Who inspires and allows His servant to repent

and then accepts his repentance, as a favor from Him.

The same holds true for good deeds. Allah inspires us and enables us to perform good deeds and then rewards us for them. So, it is all benevolence, bounty, and favor from Him.

A Reminder..

Repentance is due upon all mankind, in all stages of life, including the pious and sinful amongst them as Allah Almighty says:{...And turn to Allah in repentance, all of you, O believers, so that you might succeed.}[Surat an-Nūr: 31]Repentance falls under the perfection that Allah loves. It is not a deficiency. Allah Almighty says:{...Indeed, Allah loves those who are constantly repentant and loves those who purify themselves.}[Surat al-Baqarah: 222]He also says:{Allah has already forgiven the Prophet and the Emigrants and the Supporters...}[Surat at-Tawbah: 117]And He says about Adam (peace be upon him):{Then Adam received from his Lord [some] words, and He accepted his repentance...}[Surat al-Baqarah: 37]About Abraham and Ishmael (peace be upon both of them), He says:{...And show us our rites and accept our repentance. Indeed, You are the Accepting of repentance, the Most Merciful.}[Surat al-Baqarah: 128]And He says about Moses (peace be upon him):{...And when he awoke, he said: "Glorified are You! I have repented to You, and I am the first of the believers."}[Surat al-A'rāf: 143]

It is well known that the prophets (peace be upon them) would not persist in any sin, small or great. Repentance would serve to raise their ranks and increase their pious acts. Indeed, Allah loves those who constantly repent to Him and loves those who purify themselves.

The Prophet (may Allah's peace and blessings be upon him) said:"By Allah, I ask Allah for forgiveness and repent to Him more than seventy times a day." [Narrated by Al-Bukhāri]

Were it not that you commit sins..

Allah Almighty knows that His servants are not free from shortcomings and deficiencies. He created them this way so that His mercy, forgiveness, and acceptance of repentance can manifest amongst them. The Prophet (may Allah's peace and blessings be upon him) is authentically reported to have said:"If you were not to commit sins that Allah would forgive, Allah would replace you with people who would commit sins that He would forgive."[Narrated by Muslim]In another Hadīth, the Prophet (may Allah's peace and blessings be upon him) said:"All human beings are sinners; the best sinners are those who constantly repent."[Narrated by Al-Tirmidhi; Sahīh (authentic)]Allah Almighty praises the acceptance of His servants' repentance, as He says:{The forgiver of sin, acceptor of repentance, severe in punishment, owner of abundance. There is no deity except Him; to Him is the final return.}[Surat Ghāfir: 3]Allah Almighty wants His servants to know that He accepts repentance from them, regardless of how grave their sins may be:{...Indeed, Allah forgives all sins...}[Surat az-Zumar: 53]

In fact, Allah neither needs us nor does He need our worship. Nonetheless, He is so pleased when one of His servants repents to Him. What a Generous, Great, and Merciful Lord He is!

The Prophet (may Allah's peace and blessings be upon him) said:"Indeed, Allah is more pleased with the repentance of His believing servant than a man in a desert, who loses his mount carrying his food and drink. Then he sleeps and when he gets up, it is gone. So, he goes in search for it until he is stricken with thirst.

Then, he says to himself: 'I will go back to the place where I was and sleep there until I die.' He places his head upon his forearm waiting for death. And when he gets up, lo! There is before him his mount and his provision of food and drink on it. So, Allah is more pleased with the repentance of His believing servant than this man is pleased with his mount and provision." [Narrated by Al-Bukhāri and Muslim]

Ibn Taymiyyah (may Allah have mercy upon him) said:"Anyone who repents is loved by Allah."{...Indeed, Allah loves those who are constantly repentant and loves those who purify themselves.}[Surat al-Baqarah: 222]

So, the One Who is Merciful to His servants is worthy of receiving all the love and to be worshiped alone, without any partner. Manifestations of such love for Him should be apparent in devoting worship sincerely to Him and in drawing close to Him by obeying Him and loving whomever and whatever He loves and hating whomever and whatever He hates.

Bilāl ibn Sa'd said: "You have a Lord Who does not hasten to punish anyone of you. He forgives sins, accepts repentance, draws near those coming to Him, and shows compassion to those turning away from Him."{And it is He Who accepts repentance from His servants and pardons misdeeds, and He knows what you do.}[Surat ash-Shūra: 25]

At the doorstep..

Repentance is escaping from disobedience to obedience, from sins to good deeds, and from the loneliness of being distant from Allah to the intimacy and tranquility of being close to Him.

In repentance, one turns away from the punishment of the Almighty Lord to His vast mercy, from His wrath to His pleasure, and from Him to Him. Indeed, we cannot praise Him enough, we cannot find refuge from Him except in Him, and we cannot flee from Him but to Him.{Flee, therefore, to Allah. Surely I am a clear warner to you from Him.}[Surat adh-Dhāriyāt: 50]

O Lord, no matter how great my sins are, I supplicate You as You have commanded me.

If only the one who does good can seek refuge in You, then to whom can the wrongdoer resort?

'Ali ibn Abi Tālib (may Allah be pleased with him) said:"I wonder how one can be ruined despite having the means of salvation!" He was asked: "What is it?" He said: "Repentance and asking for Allah's forgiveness."Ibn al-Qayyim (may Allah have mercy upon him) said:"The thing that mostly prompts a Muslim to commit a sin is his reliance upon repentance. If he only knew that he may be prevented from it, he would be quite fearful."

Sincere repentance requires one to necessarily give up the sin, regret what he did, and be determined not to return to it, and he should replace his sin with a good deed. Moreover, if the sin has something to do with the rights of others, he should ask them to absolve and forgive him.

Shaqīq al-Balkhi (may Allah have mercy upon him) said:"The sign of repentance is: crying over the past sin, fearing from committing it again, abandoning evil companions, and sticking to good people."

Allah Almighty accepts sincere repentance except in two cases: when the sun rises in the west, and when the person is in the throes of death.

Wake-up shakes..

Allah Almighty may afflict His believing servant with something from which he should repent so that his servitude to Him becomes complete and he turns to his Lord and implores Him in humble submission.

Many are those who turn away from Allah Almighty and then life becomes tough for them, driving them to come back. Then when they return and taste the sweetness of being close to their Lord and the blessing of uprightness and repentance, they give thanks to Allah for the affliction and hardship that were instrumental in their salvation and success.{And We will surely let them taste the nearer punishment short of the greater punishment, so that they may return.}[Surat as-Sajdah: 21]So, if you are left to persist in your sins and deviation and enjoy blessings around, and you do not repent, you should know that you are hated and being gradually drawn to punishment. Allah Almighty says:{When they forgot the reminder that they were given, We opened for them the doors of everything – until when they rejoiced in pride for what they were given, We seized them by surprise, so they fell into utter despair.}[Surat al-An'ām: 44]When you declare your repentance, you should implore your Lord to make you steadfast. The Prophet (may Allah's peace and blessings be upon him) used to supplicate Allah saying:"Allāhumma ya muqallib al-qulūb thabbit qalbi 'ala dīnik (O Allah, Turner of the hearts, make my heart steadfast upon Your religion)."[Narrated by Al-Bukhāri in Al-Adab al-Mufrad; Sahīh (authentic)]

O Allah, pardon us, for indeed You are the Accepting of Repentance, the Most Merciful, and forgive us and our parents, verily, You are the All-Forgiving, the Most Merciful.

Al-'Alīm (The All-Knowing)

Our chests harbor thoughts, ideas, objectives, and intentions that none can hear or see except for the All-Wise, the All-Knowing.

And our consciences entertain hidden ideas that are unknown to angels, prophets, pious people, scholars, and devils. Only the Knower of the unseen knows them and everything.

The embryo is covered with layer after layer in its mother's womb, and none knows whether it is alive or dead, male or female, and will be miserable or blissful.

None knows its destiny, sustenance, and term of life except the One Who encompasses all things in His knowledge.{...And Allah is All-Knowing of everything.}[Surat al-Baqarah: 282]

Knowledge is the opposite of ignorance.

The knowledge of our Lord encompasses all things, external and internal, open and secret. His knowledge encompasses the upper and lower worlds. It encompasses the past, present, and future. Allah Almighty says:{Allah knows what is [presently] before them and what will be after them, but they do not encompass it in knowledge.}[Surat Taha: 110]He knows what lies hidden within our chests, be it belief or disbelief, truth or falsehood, good or evil.{...Indeed, Allah is All-Knowing of that within the breasts.}[Surat Āl-'Imrān: 119]{...And Allah is All-Knowing of everything.}[Surat al-Baqarah: 282]

To Him, private talk is a public one, secrets are open matters, and what is hidden is apparent and revealed to Him.

He is the All-Knowing and He encompasses all things in His knowledge, and nothing is or has ever been unknown to Him.

Nothing in the universe is hidden from or forgotten by Him.

He is the All-Knowing:

With His knowledge the leaf falls, the whisper is made, the word is uttered, the intention is made, and the drop of water descends. Indeed, everything happens with His knowledge.

He knows the living and the dead, the wet and the dry, the present and the absent, what is secret and what is public, and what is small and what is great.{He alone has the keys of the unseen; no one knows them except Him. He knows what is in the land and sea. Not a leaf falls without His knowledge, nor a grain in the darkness of the earth, nor anything moist or dry, but is [written] in a Clear Record.}[Surat al-An'ām: 59]Some of the Companions engaged in a talk that they concealed and kept to themselves.

Thereupon, Allah Almighty revealed:{...Allah knows that you used to deceive yourselves...}[Surat al-Baqarah: 187]And the Prophet (may Allah's peace and blessings be upon him) confided some discourse to one of his wives, and she revealed it. When he informed her about that, she asked him: "Who informed you about that?"{He said: "I was informed by the All-Knowing, the All-Aware."}[Surat at-Tahrīm: 3]'Umayr ibn Wahb and Safwān ibn Umayyah sat together by night at the Ka'bah, after the battle of Badr, plotting to assassinate the Prophet (may Allah's peace and blessings be upon him). Yet Allah Almighty informed him of their evil plot.{He said: "My Lord knows whatever is said in the heaven and earth, and He is the All-Hearing, the All-Knowing."}[Surat al-Anbiyā': 4]The hypocrites talked secretly amongst themselves during the battle of Tabūk and spoke critically about the Prophet (may Allah's peace and blessings be upon him), the Companions, and the religion. However, the Knower of the unseen informed His Messenger of their plot, cunning, and mockery. He says:{Did they not know that Allah knows their secrets and their private conversations and that Allah is the Knower of the unseen?}[Surat at-Tawbah: 78]

Allah's knowledge is perfect and comprehensive:

{[O people], your god is only Allah; none has the right to be worshiped except Him. He encompasses everything in knowledge."}[Surat Taha: 98]None of His creation resembles Him in terms of His perfect knowledge:{...There is nothing like unto Him, and He is the All-Hearing, the All-Seeing.}[Surat ash-Shūra: 11]{...He knew what you did not know, and He granted you prior to that an imminent conquest.}[Surat al-Fat-h: 27]When people know something, it is part of what Allah Almighty teaches them. All knowledge, related to the Sharia or destiny, does belong to Allah, the All-Mighty, the All-Wise.{They said: "Glory be to You, we have no knowledge except what You have taught us. Verily, You are the All-Knowing, the All-Wise."}[Surat al-Baqarah: 32]Allah Almighty also says:{...And He taught you what you did not know...}[Surat an-Nisā': 113]If all people were to gather all the knowledge and information they possess, it would be insignificant compared to the vast knowledge of our Lord.{And they ask you about the soul. Say: "The soul is of the affair of my Lord. And you have not been given of knowledge except a little."}[Surat al-Isrā': 85]When Al-Khidr and Mūsa (Moses) (peace be upon him) went aboard the ship and Al-Khidr saw a sparrow stand on the edge of the ship, making one or two pecks into the sea, he said to Moses:"O Moses, my and your knowledge compared to the knowledge of Allah is like the pecks of this sparrow compared to the sea."

Fact..

Our Lord keeps the knowledge of the unseen exclusively to Himself:{And with Him are the keys of the unseen; none knows them except Him...}[Surat al-An'ām: 59]He mentions five categories of the unseen:{Indeed, Allah has the knowledge of the Hour. He sends down the rain and knows what is in the wombs. No soul knows what it will do tomorrow, nor does any soul know in which land it will die. Indeed, Allah is All-Knowing, All-Aware.}[Surat Luqmān: 34]

These fives keys of the unseen are known to Allah Almighty alone:

1. Knowledge of the Hour: this is the first key to the life of the Hereafter.

2. Sending down rain: this is the key to giving life to the earth through plants.

3. Knowledge of the wombs: this is the key to life in this world.

4. Knowledge of what will happen tomorrow: this is the key to the earning in the future.

5. Knowledge of the place of death: this is the key to the life of Barzakh (Barrier) and where the particular judgment of each person will be held.

Undoubtedly, knowledge of the unseen is too great and broad to be limited to these five categories. They are merely cited as some important aspects of the unseen. In another verse, Allah Almighty says:{Say: "None in the heavens and earth knows the unseen except Allah..."}[Surat an-Naml: 65]

Whoever claims that anyone other than Allah Almighty knows the unseen has thus disbelieved in what was revealed to Muhammad (may Allah's peace and blessings be upon him).

The prophets (peace be upon them) knew nothing of the unseen except what Allah Almighty had informed them. 'Ā'ishah (may Allah be pleased with her) said:"Whoever claims that the Prophet (may Allah's peace and blessings be upon him) knew what would happen tomorrow has indeed fabricated a serious lie against Allah."{...And if I knew the unseen, I could have acquired much wealth, and no harm would have touched me...}[Surat al-A'rāf: 188]So, what about those less in rank than the prophets?!

Your share in this name..

When Allah Almighty grants someone knowledge, even if little, He has thus elevated him.{...Allah will raise those who believed among you and those who were given knowledge, by degrees...}[Surat al-Mujādilah: 11]What then if a person is knowledgeable, pious, and fearful of Allah Almighty and heedful of His rights?Such people are certain of the knowledge of Allah and so their fear and glorification of Him grow. As a consequence, Allah praises them from above seven heavens saying:{...Only those fear Allah, from among His servants, who have knowledge...}[Surat Fātir: 28]

Knowledge is the core of all noble traits. It elevates people to sublime ranks.

A person can only reach such a status through knowledge and persistently asking Allah Almighty to grant it to him, in compliance with the Prophet's supplication as taught to him by the Almighty Lord:{...And say: "My Lord, increase me in knowledge."}[Surat Taha: 114]Ibn Hazm (may Allah have mercy upon him) said:"The most sublime knowledge is what brings you closer to your Lord."Ibn al-Qayyim (may Allah have mercy upon him) said:"Were it not for the ignorance of most people of this pleasure - the pleasure of knowledge - and its great status, they would fight each other with swords to attain it. Yet, it is surrounded by difficulties and they are prevented from it with a barrier of ignorance so that Allah particularly gives it to whomever He wills, and Allah is the Owner of great bounty."

O Allah, the All-Knowing, teach us what benefits us, make us benefit from what You teach us, and increase us in knowledge.

Al-'Azhīm (The Magnificent)

Glory be to You, the Magnificent Lord!

You give sovereignty to whom You will, bring poverty after opulence, lower some people after being in a high position, and humiliate and weaken whom You will after being honorable and strong. You elevate whom You will, grant success to whom You will, decree acceptance among people for whom You will, and You give whom You will and withhold from whom You will; goodness lies in Your hand; indeed You have power over all things.

There is no god except You, the Magnificent, the Forbearing.

Your attributes are so sublime and magnificent

that we cannot extend enough praise to You.

"Al-'Azhīm" is one of the Beautiful Names of Allah Almighty. A sublime name for a Magnificent Lord. It comprises the meanings of magnificence, greatness, honor, and might.

It gives a sense of supreme strength and awe. Allah Almighty says:{...And He is the High, the Magnificent.}[Surat al-Baqarah: 255]

The Magnificent Lord possesses supreme majesty and status, and His magnificence goes beyond all limits of our minds, which cannot perceive His nature or essence.

Our Lord is the Magnificent in His essence, and none is like Him in terms of His magnificence.

As an aspect of His magnificence, the heavens and the earth are smaller than a mustard seed in His hand.{They did not revere Allah His true reverence. On the Day of Resurrection, the whole earth will be in His Grip, and the heavens will be rolled up in His Right Hand. Glorified and exalted is He above all what they associate with Him!}[Surat az-Zumar: 67]The Prophet (may Allah's peace and blessings be upon him) is authentically reported to have said:"The seven heavens compared to the Kursi (Footstool) are only like a ring thrown in a desert; and the superiority of the Throne over the Kursi is like the superiority of this desert over this ring."[Narrated by Ibn Abu Shaybah; Sahīh (authentic)]

Such is the majesty and magnificence of the Kursi and the Throne, which are part of His creation. So, what about the magnificence of Allah Almighty Himself, Who rose over the Throne high above all His creation?!

Our Lord is magnificent in His attributes for He possesses all attributes of perfection. He is magnificent in His mercy, power, giving, and beauty.

In a Qudsi Hadīth, Allah Almighty said:"Pride is My robe and magnificence is My lower garment. If anyone disputes with Me over one of them, I will throw him in Hellfire."[Narrated by Abu Dāwūd; Sahīh (authentic)]

Our Lord is magnificent also in His actions as they point to His vast wisdom, justice, grace, and will.

He is magnificent in every sense that requires us to glorify Him, and we cannot extol Him enough.

Indeed, Allah Almighty has perfect magnificence:{They did not revere Allah His true reverence. On the Day of Resurrection, the whole earth will be in His Grip, and the heavens will be rolled up in His Right Hand. Glorified and exalted is He above all what they associate with Him!}[Surat az-Zumar: 67]

Raise your hands!

Do not consider any matter as difficult for Him, regardless of how great or serious it may be. The Prophet (may Allah's peace and blessings be upon him) is authentically reported to have said:"When anyone of you supplicates, he should not say: 'O Allah, forgive me if You wish.' But he should be determined in his request and persistent in expressing his desire, for no bounty is too great for Allah to bestow (upon His slaves)."[Narrated by Al-Bukhāri and Muslim - this is the wording of Muslim]

Our Lord is magnificent in His mercy, forgiveness, forbearance, kindness, and generosity. No sin is too great for Him to forgive.

In the Hadīth about intercession, the Prophet (may Allah's peace and blessings be upon him) said:"... O Muhammad, raise your head, speak and you will be heard, ask and you will be given, and intercede and your intercession will be accepted.

I will say: 'O Lord, give me permission with regard to those who said: la ilāha illallāh (there is no god except Allah).' He will say: 'By My honor, majesty, pride, and magnificence, I will bring out of it anyone who said: la ilāha illallāh (there is no god except Allah).'" [Narrated by Al-Bukhāri and Muslim]

When my heart hardened and life became too tough for me, I considered my sins so great.

But when I compared them to Your pardon, I found Your pardon far greater.

Whoever resorts to the Magnificent Lord is safe..

It is authentically reported that whenever the Prophet (may Allah's peace and blessings be upon him) entered the mosque, he would say:"A'ūdhu billāhi Al-'Azhīm wa biwajhihi al-karīm wa sultānihi al-qadīm min ash-shaytān ar-rajīm (I seek refuge with Allah, the Magnificent, and with His honorable face, and His eternal domain from the accursed devil)." He said: "If he says so, the devil will say: 'He is granted protection against me for the rest of the day.'"[Narrated by Abu Dāwūd; Sahīh (authentic)]He who extols Allah by his tongue, i.e. engaging in Dhikr, will attain success and his scale of good deeds will be heavy on the Day of Judgment. The Prophet (may Allah's peace and blessings be upon him) is authentically reported to have said:"Two phrases are light for the tongue to utter, heavy in the Scale, and dear to the Most Compassionate: Subhānallāh wa bihamdih subhānallāh Al-'Azhīm (Glory be to Allah and His is the praise, glory be to Allah, the Magnificent)."[Narrated by Al-Bukhāri and Muslim]Allah Almighty even commanded His servants to glorify Him using this name. He says:{So glorify the name of your Lord, the

Magnificent.}[Surat al-Wāqi'ah: 74]The Prophet (may Allah's peace and blessings be upon him) commanded his Ummah to glorify Allah in prayer by this name:"As for bowing, proclaim therein the magnificence of the Lord, Exalted be He."[Narrated by Muslim]

The key to relief:

If a disaster befalls you and life becomes so hard and distressful, say:"La ilāha illallāh Al-'Azhīm Al-Halīm, la ilāha illallāh Rabbu al-'arsh al-'azhīm, la ilāha illallāh Rabbu as-samāwati wa Rabbu al-ardi wa Rabbu al-'arsh al-karīm (There is no god except Allah, the Magnificent, the Forbearing. There is no god except Allah, the Lord of the mighty Throne. There is no god except Allah, the Lord of the heavens, the earth, and the Honorable Throne)."[Narrated by Al-Bukhāri and Muslim]If you fear a person in power, indeed the power of Allah is far greater. 'Abdullah ibn Mas'ūd said:"O Allah, Lord of the seven heavens and Lord of the mighty Throne, support me against so-and-so and his allies among Your creation, lest anyone of them should oppress or transgress against me. Your support is might, all praise is due to You, and there is no god except You."The Prophet (may Allah's peace and blessings be upon him) used to seek refuge with the magnificence of Allah Almighty from being swallowed by earth in the morning and evening saying:"Allāhumma a'ūdhu bi'azhamatika min an ughtāla min tahti (O Allah, I seek refuge in Your magnificence from being swallowed up from underneath me)."[Narrated by Al-Tirmidhi; Sahīh (authentic)]Hence, whoever seeks refuge in Allah Almighty, the Magnificent Lord, and draws closer to Him and fears Him will attain security in this world and the reward in the Hereafter. Our Lord says:{...And whoever fears Allah - He will remove for him his misdeeds and make great for him his reward.}[Surat at-Talāq: 5]As for the highest degree with Allah Almighty, it is for those about whom He says:{Those who believed, emigrated, and strove in Allah's cause with their wealth and their lives are of a higher rank before Allah; it is they who will triumph.}[Surat at-Tawbah: 20]Yet, he who associates partners with Allah and does not have faith enough to proclaim His magnificence will have a recompense similar to his action, namely Hellfire - may Allah protect us from it.{"Seize him and shackle him,then make him burn in the Blazing Fire,then tie him up with chain of seventy cubits long.For he did not believe in Allah, the Most Great,}[Surat al-Hāqqah: 30-33]

How should a Muslim extol his Lord?

We extol our Lord by extolling His names and attributes, and our extolment of Him should lie within our hearts in the form of love for Him, acknowledgment of His magnificence, and being humbly submissive to Him."Whoever believes himself to be better than others and walks with a swaggering gait will meet Allah while He is angry with him."[Narrated by Ahmad; Sahīh (authentic)]Moreover, we should extol Allah Almighty by our tongues and by remembering Him frequently.{So glorify the name of your Lord, the Magnificent.}[Surat al-Wāqi'ah: 74]

And we should extol Him by our body organs, as we use them in worshiping and obeying Him. To extol Allah Almighty, we should obey Him and not disobey Him; remember Him and not forget Him; and give thanks to Him and not show ingratitude to Him.

Aspects of extolling Allah Almighty include extolling His messengers, angels, rituals, such as prayer, Zakah, fasting, Hajj, and 'Umrah.{This is so. And whoever honors the rituals of Allah, it is from the piety of the hearts.}[Surat al-Hajj: 32]Our extolment of Him also includes extolling His noble Book, which He describes as being magnificent:{We have surely given you the seven oft-repeated verses and the great Qur'an.}[Surat al-Hijr: 87]And part of extolling Him is to extol His sanctities and the sanctities of the believers.{Such [is the pilgrimage]; whoever honors the sacred rituals of Allah, it is best for him with his Lord...}[Surat al-Hajj: 30]Another aspect of extolling Him is not to give precedence to the speech of anyone, irrespective of his status, over the speech of Allah.{O you who believe, do not decide [any matter of importance] before Allah and His Messenger, and fear Allah, for Allah is All-Hearing, All-Knowing.}[Surat al-Hujurāt: 1]

O You Who created this superb creation

and guarantee sustenance for all,

Your attributes are so sublime and magnificent

that we cannot extend enough praise to You.

Here I have come to You, having nothing but my trust in You

with a regretful heart and tearful eyes.

Forgive the past sins of Your servant and enable him

to do what is pleasing to You.

Your bounty is complete, indeed.

And I very much hope You will be Bountiful to me.

I implore Allah, the Magnificent, to make us among the pious who will win the gardens of bliss.

Al-Qawiyy (The All-Powerful)

O Lord, I have turned to You in repentance

and submission, holding onto Your rope.

I do not need any powerful person, for You, my Lord,

are the Most Great, the All-Powerful.

I have tried every refuge in my life but found no refuge

more mighty and honorable than Your refuge.

Let us talk about our Almighty Lord, Who says:{Indeed, it is Allah Who is the All-Provider, Lord of Power, the Mighty.}[Surat adh-Dhāriyāt: 58]And Who says:{Allah has repelled the disbelievers in their rage without gaining any good. And Allah spared the believers from fighting, and Allah is All-Powerful, All-Mighty.}[Surat al-Ahzāb: 25]He also says:{...Indeed, Allah is All-Powerful, All-Mighty.}[Surat al-Hadīd: 25]

Our All-Powerful Lord never suffers any weakness, laxity, or fatigue.

Our Lord is the One Who is never overcome, defeated, or resisted, and Whose decree is never repelled. To Him belong the absolute power and the perfect will.

Verily, He possesses unlimited and boundless power.

Our Lord has complete power and is omnipotent. Never does He experience any inability or fatigue. His will is sure to pass at any time He wishes in His heavens or earth - Exalted be He.

He is All-Powerful in His strike and punishment.

All power belongs to Him alone.{...All power belongs to Allah...}[Surat al-Baqarah: 165]

He is the All-Powerful and power is one of His attributes; and He has complete power over those who are in power.

Power comes from Him..

How can we not be totally devoted to Him and rely upon Him for the fulfillment of our desires and needs when we are in utmost need for His power and giving?!

We cannot have any power save through His power and help, and we cannot have the strength to avoid sins and evils except through Him.

Allah Almighty grants such power to whom He wills, just like sustenance in general.

Man is weak. He is created weak, born weak, and will die weak. Allah Almighty says:{...And mankind was created weak.}[Surat an-Nisā': 28]He also says:{It is Allah Who created you in a state of weakness, then after weakness He gave you strength, then after strength He made you weak and old. He creates what He wills, and He is the All-Knowing, the Most Capable.}[Surat ar-Rūm: 54]

The days of Allah..

As many people tend to forget this truth - that humans are created weak and have no power or strength except through Allah - the devil has allured them into self-conceit and the belief that they are powerful, leading them to forget the power of Allah. Hence, they persist in their misguidance and deviation.

Take 'Ād as an example, Allah Almighty says about them:{As for 'Ād, they were arrogant in the land without right, and said, "Who is more powerful than us?" Did they not see that Allah, Who created them, is more powerful than them? Yet they continued to reject Our signs.}[Surat Fussilat: 15]When Hūd (Heber) (peace be upon him) asked them to fear Allah and worship Him alone, they said:{...Who is greater than us in strength?...}[Surat Fussilat: 15]We have vanquished other people and can defend ourselves against any punishment, thanks to our great power. They were conceited by their tall statures. Ibn 'Abbās (may Allah be pleased with him and his father) said:"The tallest among them was hundred cubits long and the shortest was sixty cubits."When their defiance and disobedience reached their peak, Allah Almighty sent upon them one of His soldiers: a ferocious wind. He says:{So We sent against them a roaring wind for several inauspicious days to make them taste a disgracing punishment in the life of this world; but the punishment of the Hereafter is far more disgracing, and they will not be helped.}[Surat Fussilat: 16]

This is one of the immutable laws of Allah, which continues throughout the ages: Those who act arrogantly and are conceited due to their power will meet the same fate as 'Ād, i.e. they will be seized by the All-Powerful Lord.

Hence, Allah Almighty says:{Say, "Travel through the land, then see how was the end of the deniers."}[Surat al-An'ām: 11]Perhaps they will learn a lesson from the terrible and deadly fates of the past nations. Scores of nations denied Allah and His messengers and acted arrogantly due to their power and advance on earth, thus, Allah seized them so powerfully.{Each of them We seized for their sin: against some of them We sent a storm of stones; some were seized by a blast; some We caused the earth to swallow; and some We drowned. It was not Allah Who wronged them, but it was they who wronged themselves.}[Surat al-'Ankabūt: 40]In the battle of the Ahzāb (allies), The polytheists besieged the Prophet (may Allah's peace and blessings be upon him) and his Companions (may Allah be pleased with them) with the intention to wipe them off the face of the earth. However, Allah Almighty sent down one of His soldiers - a wind - which made them flee from around Madinah.{Allah has repelled the disbelievers in their rage without gaining any good. And Allah spared the believers from fighting, and Allah is All-Powerful, All-Mighty.}[Surat al-Ahzāb: 25]

A boy destroyed a king; water drowned a community; a sea stamped out an army; a mosquito humiliated the tyrant Namrūd; a land swallowed Qārūn; and birds crushed the army of Abrahah.

He is the All-Powerful, Whose power amazes all.

The matter and decision entirely belong to Allah Almighty, not to His creation.

Shall I tell you?!

The more one knows the meaning of Allah's name "Al-Qawiyy", the more he will rely upon his Lord and derive all power from Him, disowning his own power and strength. The Prophet (may Allah's peace and blessings be upon him) is authentically reported to have said to one of his Companions:"Shall I inform you of a phrase which is one of the treasures of Paradise? La hawla wa la quwwata illa billāh (There is no power nor strength except through Allah)."[Narrated by Al-Bukhāri - this is his wording - and Muslim]It means: You cannot move from one state to another, or have the capacity to effect any change unless Allah helps, supports, and guides you.'Abdullah ibn Mas'ūd (may Allah be pleased with him) said:"There is no power nor strength except through Allah means you cannot turn away from disobeying Allah except through His protection, and you do not have the ability to obey Him except with His help."Ibn al-

Qayyim (may Allah have mercy upon him) said:"This phrase has an amazing effect when it comes to dealing with difficult matters, enduring hardships, meeting kings and those who are feared, and facing horrible events. It also helps in getting rid of poverty."Allah Almighty loves to see His servants humble to Him and remembering His power.{If only you had said, when you entered your garden, 'This is by Allah's Will; there is no power except with Allah.' Even though you see me inferior to you in wealth and children,}[Surat al-Kahf: 39]

Although Allah loves the humble, He also loves the strong believers. The Prophet (may Allah's peace and blessings be upon him) is authentically reported to have said: "The strong believer is better and dearer to Allah than the weak one, yet there is goodness in both of them." [Narrated by Muslim]

These two attributes occur in this verse:{...Humble towards the believers, mighty against the disbelievers...}[Surat al-Mā'idah: 54]Nations can only be strong by knowledge and work. Allah Almighty says:{Prepare against them whatever force you can and cavalry, to deter Allah's enemies and your enemies, and others besides them whom you do not know, but Allah knows them...}[Surat al-Anfāl: 60]

Do what Allah wants from you, and He will give you more than what you want.

O Allah, the All-Powerful, the All-Mighty, support us against the oppressors.

Al-Matīn (The Strong)

Abu Hurayrah (may Allah be pleased with him) reported: "A man became needy and he got out to the wilderness. Thereupon, his wife said: 'O Allah, provide for us so that we can make dough and bread.'

When he returned, he found the bowl full of dough, something was being roasted in the furnace, and the hand mill was operating. He asked: 'Where has this come from?' She replied: 'From the provision of Allah.' He then swept what was around the hand mill.

Thereupon, the Prophet (may Allah's peace and blessings be upon him) said:'If he had left it, it would have continued to revolve - or grind - till the Day of Judgment.'"[Narrated by Al-Tabarāni in Al-Mu'jam al-Awsat; Sahīh (authentic)]This is a message to anyone who has been hit by distress, weakness, difficulties, and tough living. Rejoice and expect imminent relief, clear support, ease, and strength.{[It is] the promise of Allah. Allah does not fail in His promise...}[Surat ar-Rūm: 6]

We shall pause here with one of the beautiful names of Allah, namely "Al-Matīn".

{Indeed, it is Allah Who is the All-Provider, Lord of Power, the Mighty.}[Surat adh-Dhāriyāt: 58]

Our Lord, Exalted be He, is the Strong.

He possesses unlimited power and strength. His strength is boundless and endless, and He never suffers any difficulty or fatigue in whatever He does. All might belongs to Him, He has full power over His affairs, and He is the Omnipotent Who never experiences inability.

Where are they?

Allah Almighty informs us about past nations that deviated from His commands and messengers and even claimed to be strong and dominant, and so He subjected them to a severe punishment.{As for 'Ād, they were arrogant in the land without right, and said, "Who is more powerful than us?" Did they not see that Allah, Who created them, is more powerful than them? Yet they continued to reject Our signs.}[Surat Fussilat: 15]Their end was as Allah Almighty says:{...And they became such that there was nothing left visible except [ruins of] their dwellings. This is how We recompense the wicked people.}[Surat al-Ahqāf: 25]

Where are the kings and those who used to populate the earth?

They departed and left behind what they had built and developed.

And they now lie in their graves, subject to the result of their deeds.

They have turned into rotten bones after leading a life of luxury.

Where are their soldiers? They could not help them.

And where are their wealth and fortunes?

The command of their Lord came to them unexpectedly.

So, neither their wealth nor their soldiers could support them.

Your wish comes true..

The true believer knows that Allah is powerful, strong, and that He is Competent over all things. He fulfills wishes, brings close what is distant, and turns dreams into realities.

Here is Ibrāhim (Abraham) (peace be upon him) as an example. He brought his family to a valley empty of plants and left his weak wife and little child to reside in that valley. Putting all his trust in the power of Allah Almighty, he said:{Our Lord, I have settled some of my offspring in a barren valley near Your Sacred House...}My Lord, I brought them near Your door and cut their hopes off anyone but You:{...Our Lord, so that they may establish prayer...}My Lord, so that they can serve You; indeed, You are more entitled to them than me and than themselves:{...So make hearts of the people incline toward them...}[Surat Ibrāhim: 37]My Lord, subject Your servants to help them if they needed anything; indeed, You are Capable of all things.

If you are weak, but your Lord is powerful and strong, then do not be afraid. Indeed, whoever relies upon Allah, He grants him sufficiency, and whoever presents his needs to his Lord, He fulfills them. Our Lord, Exalted be He, feels jealous when the believer's heart gets attached to anyone other than Him, when he depends on or yields to anyone other than Him, or humbles himself before anyone other than Him.

The story of Yūsuf (Joseph) (peace be upon him) is one of the best and clearest indeed. It contains different stages and shifts from one condition to another, from a crisis to a blessing, from humiliation to honor, from slavery to authority, from disunity and dispersion to reunion and harmony, from grief to joy, from opulence to famine to opulence again, and from denial to acknowledgment.

Then do not complain to the weak about the All-Powerful Lord.

If you ever complain to human beings, you are complaining about the Most Merciful to those who have no mercy.

Real strength lies in holding onto Allah Almighty alone, and not onto others, be they individuals or nations. Do you not see the bad situation in which the Muslim Ummah has fallen after they abandoned reliance upon Allah Almighty and pinned their hopes upon their enemies?They fell in the sight of Allah Almighty as well as in the eyes of their enemies. That is why they are in humiliation and loss and will not be able to restore their glory and strength unless they turn to the powerful and strong Lord, alone, with no partner.Allah Almighty says:{Allah has written: "I will surely overcome, I and My messengers." Indeed, Allah is All-Powerful, All-Mighty.}[Surat al-Mujādilah: 21]

O Allah, we ask You by Your name "Al-Matīn" to forgive us, our parents, and all Muslims.

Al-Qādir, Al-Qadīr, Al-Muqtadir (The Able - The Omnipotent - The Supreme Determiner)

Whoever establishes the commands of Allah, Allah will support him and whoever uses whatever is in his power for the sake of Allah, Allah will subject to him what is in His Hand. Indeed, the entire universe is in the Hand of Allah Almighty for He is the Able and the Omnipotent.

The Prophet (may Allah's peace and blessings be upon him) said:"While a man was walking through a barren land, he heard a voice coming out of a cloud saying: 'Irrigate the garden of so-and-so.' Thereupon, the cloud drifted in a certain direction and discharged its water over a rocky plain. The streamlets flowed into a channel. This man followed the channel until it reached a garden and he saw the owner of the garden standing in its center, working with his spade spreading the water. He asked him: 'O servant of Allah, what is your name?' He told him his name, which was the same that he heard from the cloud.

The owner of the garden then asked him: 'O servant of Allah, why did you ask about my name?' He replied: 'I heard a voice from the cloud which poured down this water saying: "Irrigate the garden of so-and-so." I would like to know what you do with it.'

He said: 'Now since you have asked me, I will tell you. I estimate the produce of the garden and give one-third of it in charity, spend one-third on myself and my family, and invest one-third back into the garden.'" [Narrated by Muslim]

{...Allah is not such that something can escape Him in the heavens or on earth. He is indeed All-Knowing, Most Capable.}[Surat Fātir: 44]{Do you not know that the dominion of the heavens and earth belongs to Allah? He punishes whom He wills and forgives whom He wills, and Allah is Most Capable of all things.}[Surat al-Mā'idah: 40]

Our Lord, Exalted be He, is competent over all things, and nothing can escape His power or will. Unlike His creation, He, Exalted be He, never experiences inability or slackness.

Our Lord possesses complete power. With His power, He brought everything into existence, and with His power, He proportioned and perfected their creation, gives life and causes death, and then resurrects His servants for the recompense, rewarding those who do good and punishing the wrongdoers.

Our Lord is the One Who {...When He intends a thing, He says to it: "Be", and it is.}[Surat Yasīn: 82]

He is the Omnipotent and nothing can ever escape His power or will.

His ability is complete..

Part of His ability is that:{...He punishes whom He wills and forgives whom He wills, and Allah is Most Capable of all things.}[Surat al-Mā'idah: 40]Allah Almighty says:{..."He is Capable to send a punishment from above you or from beneath your feet, or split you into factions, and make you suffer at the hands of one another."...}[Surat al-An'ām: 65]Another aspect of His ability is that He is able to bring and gather us together wherever we may be.{...Wherever you are, Allah will bring you all together, for Allah is Most Capable of all things..}[Surat al-Baqarah: 148]Another aspect of Allah's perfect ability, of which He informs us, is that He will grasp the earth in His Hand on the Day of Judgment and fold the heavens with His right Hand. Allah Almighty says:{They did not revere Allah His true reverence. On the Day of Resurrection, the whole earth will be in His Grip, and the heavens will be rolled up in His Right Hand. Glorified and exalted is He above all what they associate with Him!}[Surat az-Zumar: 67]

Predestination had already been written..

Our Lord, Exalted be He, predestined all determinations. He knew the measures and times of all things before creating them and then brought them into existence according to His foreknowledge.{...That is the determination of the All-Mighty, the All-Knowing.}[Surat Yasīn: 38]Allah Almighty decreed the destinies of His creatures thousands of years before He actually created them. The Prophet (may Allah's peace and blessings be upon him) is authentically reported to have said:"Allah decreed the destinies of the creatures fifty thousand years before He created the heavens and the earth, when His Throne was upon the water."[Narrated by Muslim]Hence, this is part of faith. When Jibrīl (Gabriel) (peace be upon him) asked the Messenger of Allah (may Allah's peace and blessings be upon him) about faith, he replied:"To believe in Allah, His angels, His books, His messengers, the Last Day, and to believe in destiny, the pleasant and unpleasant aspects thereof."[Narrated by Al-Bukhāri and Muslim - this is the wording of Muslim -]

Do not wonder!

Our Lord points out His ability in the Noble Qur'an, as He says:{...Allah is not such that something can escape Him in the heavens or on earth. He is indeed All-Knowing, Most Capable.}[Surat Fātir: 44]

If Allah wants to support you, He can command something, which is normally not a means of support, and make it one of the best means of support for you.

And if the Omnipotent wants to honor you, He can make those from whom you expect no good the very cause of blessings and abundance for you.

And if the Able Lord wants to remove harm from you, He can make you see no harm or cause it to fail to reach you.

Also, if the Almighty Lord wants to protect you from sin, He can make you hate it, make it hard for you to commit, or let you proceed towards it and then something occurs that prevents you from it.

So, it behooves us to knock on the door of Allah, the Omnipotent.

Prophet Abraham (peace be upon him) left his family alone, entrusting them to Allah, and said:{...So make hearts of the people incline toward them...}[Surat Ibrāhim: 37]As a result, Makkah has become a place for which the hearts yearn over the ages.Prophet Sulaymān (Solomon) (peace be upon him) supplicated:{My Lord, grant me authority and join me with the righteous.}[Surat ash-Shu'arā': 83]In response, Allah Almighty subjected the jinn to his authority.While Yūnus (Jonah) (peace be upon him) was in the darkness of the night, the sea, and the belly of the whale, he supplicated:{...There is no god except You; Glorified are You. Indeed, I have been of the wrongdoers.}[Surat al-Anbiyā': 87]Consequently, the belly of the whale became like a container for him.And Prophet Muhammad (may Allah's peace and blessings be upon him) used to supplicate Allah saying:"Allāhumma inni astakhīruka bi'ilmika wa astaqdiruka biqudratika wa as'aluka min fadlika fa'innaka taqdiru wa la aqdir (O Allah, I consult You through Your knowledge, and I seek strength through Your power, and ask of Your great bounty; for You are Able, whereas I am not)."[Narrated by Al-Bukhāri]We should seek refuge in the ability of Allah Almighty from all evils and harms, like in the supplication which the Prophet (may Allah's peace and blessings be upon him) taught us to make during illness:"A'ūdhu bi'izzatillāhi wa qudratihi min sharri ma ajidu wa uhādhir (I seek refuge in the might and ability of Allah from the evil of what I experience) seven times."[Narrated by Muslim]And Allah Almighty says:{...And Allah is Omnipotent, and Allah is All-Forgiving, Most Merciful.}[Surat al-Mumtahanah: 7]This clearly indicates that Allah's forgiveness and mercy towards His servants stem from perfect power and ability. No sin is too great for Him to forgive or conceal, and no mercy is too much for Him to bestow upon His servants.

Not all those who possess power and ability do forgive and show mercy.

And not all those who forgive and show mercy possess power and ability. Indeed, it is Allah Almighty Who has complete ability, yet He is All-Forgiving, Most-Merciful.

Everything has a measure:

Allah Almighty says:{...Whoever puts his trust in Allah, He is sufficient for him. Indeed, Allah will surely accomplish His purpose, for Allah has set a destiny for everything.}[Surat at-Talāq: 3]Whoever fears Allah and relies upon Him will find His support coming without delay and will not despair of His mercy and help. Relief is sure to come to him, for Allah Almighty is competent over all things.

However, Allah Almighty set a certain measure for everything. It has a specific time, which it cannot miss. So, when something is predestined to happen, none can delay it or bring it forward even for a single hour.

A person may sleep in despair with regard to some distress and then he wakes up to find relief.{...Allah has full power over all things.}[Surat al-Kahf: 45]

Distress lasts for a specific time and then goes away. Indeed, Allah Almighty set a measure for everything.

A tree will not bear fruit unless its specific time comes; the sun does not rise before its time; a pregnant woman only gives birth according to a specified term.{...Allah has set a destiny for everything.}[Surat at-Talāq: 3]

O Allah, forgive us and show mercy to us; indeed, You are competent over all things.

Al-Hafīzh (The All-Preserver)

It was mentioned in the two Sahīh Collections that 'Āmir ibn al-Tufayl and Arbad ibn Qays plotted against the Prophet (may Allah's peace and blessings be upon him) and sought to kill him. So, he supplicated against them.

Consequently, 'Āmir got a gland in his neck while he was in the house of a woman from Banu Salūl. Thereupon, he jumped towards his horse, took his spear, and kept saying: "A gland like the gland of camels and a death in the house of a woman from Banu Salūl!" He was still in this condition until he fell off his horse, dead.

As for Arbad ibn Qays, he went out with a camel that he intended to sell. Thereupon, Allah sent a thunderbolt upon him and his camel, burning both. Who preserved the Messenger of Allah (may Allah's peace and blessings be upon him)? He is Allah, the Preserver.

He Almighty says in His Book:{...But Allah is the best Preserver, and He is the Most Merciful of those who show mercy.}[Surat Yūsuf: 64]Our Lord, Exalted be He, preserves the heaven and the earth and what is between them. He sustains their existence by His power, hence, they neither perish nor swerve. Carrying them does not tire Him, Exalted be He, given His complete power and perfect ability. Listen to the verse that says:{Allah keeps the heavens and earth from vanishing. If they were to vanish, there is none to sustain them other than Him...}[Surat Fātir: 41]Also, our Lord preserves all deeds of His servants, good and bad, open and secret, small and great. He records all their words and knows their intentions. Nothing escapes His knowledge.{...And with Us is a preserving record.}[Surat Qāf: 4]And our Almighty Lord preserves His servants from destruction and violent deaths. He has, thus, appointed angels to preserve them as He says:{For each person there are successive angels in front of him and behind him, guarding him by the command of Allah...}[Surat ar-Ra'd: 11]

Allah's preservation of His creation falls under two categories:

General: It comprises all creatures as He facilitates their affairs and interests. Allah Almighty says: {...Surely my Lord is All-Preserver over everything.} [Surat Hūd: 57]

Special: It is a better status than the former category. It only includes the close servants of Allah as He preserves them in terms of their worldly interests, health, children, and properties. He has, thus, appointed angels to preserve them. He also preserves for them their religion from suspicions and vain inclinations and from their enemies among the humans and jinn. Then, He makes them die as believers. Allah Almighty says:{For each person there are successive angels in front of him and behind him, guarding him by the command of Allah...}[Surat ar-Ra'd: 11]Moreover, Allah Almighty undertakes to preserve His noble Book from distortion and alteration throughout the ages. He says:{It is We Who have sent down the Reminder, and it is We Who will preserve it.}[Surat al-Hijr: 9]

He preserves the Ka'bah and sustains its existence, though it was only a building made of stones and based in an uncultivated valley. He preserved it so that it remains a witness to His great preservation and to His perfect power and ability.

He defends you..

The disbelievers of Quraysh assembled around a cave which harbored two men: Muhammad (may Allah's peace and blessings be upon him) and Abu Bakr (may Allah be pleased with him). They wanted to kill both. So, Abu Bakr began to fear and looked at his great companion, who said to him:"What do you think of two (persons) the third of whom is Allah?"[Narrated by Al-Bukhāri and Muslim]

If you are encompassed by Allah's care, then rest assured for you are safe.

He is the All-Preserver!

Tyrants scheme against the pious, yet Allah Almighty preserves His close servants. Moses (peace be upon him) said:{..."Our Lord, we fear that he may hasten to punish us or transgress all bounds."Allah said: "Fear not. I am surely with you both; I hear and I see."}[Surat Taha: 45-46]Allah reassured him, preserved him, and supported him against his enemy.Who can grant victory against the enemies? He is Allah, the Preserver of His close servants, even if they are small in number.{...And if there are among you a thousand, they will overcome two thousand by the permission of Allah...}[Surat al-Anfāl: 66]{Do not lose heart nor grieve, for you have the upper hand, if you are [truly] believers.}[Surat Āl-'Imrān: 139]

A divine reward:

Allah, the All-Preserver, preserves the offspring of His close servants in their lives and after their death. An example here is Ya'qūb (Jacob) (peace be upon him) to whom Allah restored his beloved child Joseph (peace be upon him) after long years of absence and who said:{...But Allah is the best Preserver, and He is the Most Merciful of those who show mercy.}[Surat Yūsuf: 64]Another example is when Moses and Al-Khidr (peace be upon both of them) went to a village and asked its people for food, but they refused to host them. Then, Moses and Al-Khidr found a wall on the point of collapse; so, Al-Khidr rebuilt it.{As for the wall, it belonged to two orphan boys in the city, and there was a treasure under it that belonged to them. Their father was a righteous man, so your Lord willed that they should reach their maturity and retrieve their treasure, as a mercy from your Lord; I did not do it of my own accord. This is the interpretation of that which you could not bear with patience."}[Surat al-Kahf: 82]

Also, the just Caliph 'Umar ibn 'Abdul-'Azīz died and was survived by seven sons and seven daughters. He left them nothing except Allah Almighty. So, Allah preserved them. Scholars said: "His children became among the richest of people."

Valuable advice:

The Prophet (may Allah's peace and blessings be upon him) gave the following advice to Ibn 'Abbās (may Allah be pleased with him and his father):"O boy, I shall teach you some words [of advice]: Be mindful of Allah and He will protect you. Be mindful of Allah and you will find Him with you."[Narrated by Al-Tirmidhi; Sahīh (authentic)]It was said to Muhibb al-Dīn al-Tabari, a leading Shāfi'i scholar: "You jumped off the ship while you are an old man?" In response, he said a sentence that went down in history: "These are body organs which we preserved when we were young, and so Allah preserved them for us when we became old."{...But Allah is the best Preserver, and He is the Most Merciful of those who show mercy.}[Surat Yūsuf: 64]Scholars said: "Be mindful of Allah's commands by observing them, and of His prohibitions by avoiding them, and of His limits by not transgressing them, and Allah will preserve for you your life, religion, property, children, and all that He gave you in this world out of His bounty. The Prophet (may Allah's peace and blessings be upon him) said:"Be mindful of Allah and He will protect you. Be mindful of Allah and you will find Him with you."[Narrated by Al-Tirmidhi; Sahīh (authentic)]As for the Hereafter, Allah Almighty gives them glad tidings about the great win. He says:{...And those who observe the limits set by Allah. And give glad tidings to the believers.}[Surat at-Tawbah: 112]

The more you preserve the limits set by Allah Almighty, the more you will be preserved by Him. This includes the following:

Preserving monotheism and the rituals of religion, notably the prayer:{Be mindful of the prayers, especially the middle prayer; and stand before Allah in complete devotion.}[Surat al-Baqarah: 238]Preserving the hearing, sight, and heart from what is unlawful:{...Indeed, the hearing, the sight, and the heart, all of them will be called to account.}[Surat al-Isrā': 36]{...Therefore the righteous women are obedient, and protect what Allah has entrusted them with in [their husband's] absence...}[Surat an-Nisā': 34]Preserving the private parts:{And those who preserve their private parts.}[Surat al-Mu'minūn: 5]Preserving oaths:{...And preserve your oaths...}[Surat al-Mā'idah: 89]It is authentically reported that the Prophet (may Allah's peace and blessings be upon him) used to supplicate Allah saying:"Allāhumma ihfazhni min bayni yadayya wa min khalfi wa 'an yamīni wa 'an shimāli wa min fawqi wa a'ūdhu bi'azhamatika an ughtāla min tahti (O Allah, preserve me from in front of me, from behind me, on my right, on my left, and from above me, and I seek refuge in Your greatness that I should be swallowed up from underneath me)."[Narrated by Al-Tirmidhi; Sahīh (authentic)]And whenever the Prophet (may Allah's peace and blessings be upon him) went to bed, he would ask Allah Almighty to preserve him.

Glad tidings..

If the righteous person entrusts something to Allah, He preserves it for him as the Prophet (may Allah's peace and blessings be upon him) said to Abu Hurayrah (may Allah be pleased with him):"I entrust you to Allah with Whom trusts are never lost."[Narrated by Ibn Mājah; Sahīh (authentic)]In another Hadīth, the Prophet (may Allah's peace and blessings be upon him) said:"If Allah is entrusted with something, He preserves it."[Narrated by Al-Bayhaqi in Al-Sunan al-Kubra; Sahīh (authentic)]How excellent it is to seek refuge with Allah for your children! The Prophet (may Allah's peace and blessings be upon him) used to seek Allah's refuge for Al-Hasan and Al-Husayn (may Allah be pleased with both of them). When you entrust your children to Allah, you have indeed entrusted them to the All-Preserver.{...But Allah is the best Preserver, and He is the Most Merciful of those who show mercy.}[Surat Yūsuf: 64]

O Allah, we entrust to You ourselves, our parents, our children, and every blessing You have endowed us with.

Al-Ghaniyy (The Self-Sufficient)

The Prophet (may Allah's peace and blessings be upon him) said:"While Ayyūb (Job) (peace be upon him) was taking a bath naked, golden locusts began to fall on him. Job started collecting them in his clothes.

Thereupon, his Lord addressed him: 'O Job, have I not given you enough so that you are in no need of what you see now.' Job replied: 'Yes, by Your honor, but I cannot dispense with Your blessing.'" [Narrated by Al-Bukhāri]

People may be given wealth, properties, children, prestige, a high position, leadership, or authority,and a person may be surrounded by servants and soldiers at his command, and people are obedient to him and subject to his authority;nonetheless, everyone still needs Allah Almighty:{O mankind, you are those in need of Allah, while Allah is the Self-Sufficient, the Praiseworthy.}[Surat Fātir: 15]

Our Lord is the Rich and Self-Sufficient, and none is richer than Him at all. All stand in need of Him.

Allah Almighty is Self-Sufficient by His essence, attributes, and power. His self-sufficiency is so complete that He does not need anyone or anything.

It is because of His perfect self-sufficiency that He does not benefit from the worship of His obedient servants or get harmed by the sins of the disobedient ones, even if all humanity were to disbelieve in

Him. Allah Almighty says:{...But whoever disbelieves - then indeed Allah is free from need of the worlds.}[Surat Āl-'Imrān: 97]Another aspect of His perfect self-sufficiency is that He shows benevolence to His servants, intends good for them, and removes harm from them in return for nothing - only mercy and benevolence from Him.{And your Lord is the Self-Sufficient, the Possessor of mercy...}[Surat al-An'ām: 133]Another aspect of His perfect self-sufficiency is that He is far Exalted above deficiencies and defects and anything that contradicts His self-sufficiency. For example, He has taken no son or wife, there is no partner with Him in His dominion, He does not need a protector due to weakness, and there is none like or equal to Him. Allah Almighty says:{And say, "Praise be to Allah Who has not taken a son, nor does He have any partner in His dominion, nor does He need any protector out of weakness. And proclaim His greatness immensely."}[Surat al-Isrā': 111]Yet another aspect of His complete self-sufficiency is that He commands His servants to supplicate Him and promises that He will answer their supplications:{And your Lord said: "Call on Me and I will respond to you"...}[Surat Ghāfir: 60]The Prophet (may Allah's peace and blessings be upon him) is authentically reported to have said:"Nothing is more honorable in the sight of Allah Almighty than supplication."[Narrated by Al-Tirmidhi; Hasan (sound)]

The entire universe is in need of Allah Almighty..

The whole world, including humans and jinn, rich and poor, old and young, upper class and lower class, strong and weak, all stand in need of Allah Almighty in every moment.

Out of Allah's bounty, He couples His name "the Self-Sufficient" with His attribute of mercy in the verse that says:{And Your Lord is the Self-Sufficient, the Possessor of mercy...}[Surat al-An'ām: 133]He wants to inform His servants that He does not need their worship, yet He shows mercy to them in every aspect of their lives, even in the acts of worship and obligations they perform. Out of His mercy, He even accepts what is little and multiplies its reward.And out of His bounty, He couples His name "the Self-Sufficient" with His name "the Praiseworthy" in the verse that says:{And Moses said, "If you and all those who are on earth were to disbelieve, indeed Allah is Self-Sufficient, Praiseworthy."}[Surat Ibrāhim: 8]That is He greatly deserves praise, given the great blessings He bestows.

Everyone needs Him in everything, great or small, and at every hour and second.

Even the Prophet, who showed the most perfect servitude to Him, used to supplicate Him showing his humble submission and need for Him, and how he could not dispense with Him even for the blink of an eye. He used to supplicate saying:"Aslih li sha'ni kullah wa la takilni ila nafsi tarfata 'ayn (Reform all my affairs for me, and do not leave me to myself even for the blink of an eye)."[Narrated by Al-Nasā'i; Sahīh (authentic)]

You need the Self-Sufficient Lord all the time. The more you show your need for Him, the greater your reward will be.

Always remember that Allah is the Self-Sufficient and that His self-sufficiency is inherent in Him. Even if all the inhabitants of the heavens and the earth were to ask Him and He were to grant them all their requests, this would not decrease His dominion in any way.In a Qudsi Hadīth, Allah Almighty said:"O My servants, if the first and last of you, and the humans and jinn of you were all to stand together in one place and ask of Me and I were to give everyone what he requested, that would not decrease what I possess except like what is decreased of the ocean when a needle is dipped into it." [Narrated by Muslim]

The key to self-sufficiency:

How can I become self-sufficient?

Answer: As the Qudsi Hadīth says:"O son of Adam, devote yourself to My worship, and I will fill your heart with self-sufficiency and fill your hands with sustenance.O son of Adam, do not turn away from Me, or I will fill your heart with poverty and fill your hands with distractions."[Narrated by Al-Hākim in Al-Mustadrak; Sahīh (authentic)]

Once a person's heart becomes content with Allah Almighty and pleased with whatever He gives, he becomes self-sufficient, honorable, and strong through his Lord beyond any need for people. How amazing! Self-sufficiency with no great wealth, and strength and honor without authority or supporters!

The Prophet (may Allah's peace and blessings be upon him) is authentically reported to have said:"Successful is the one who embraces Islam and is provided with mere subsistence and Allah makes him content with what He has given him."[Narrated by Muslim]If a person does not have contentment within his heart, he will never feel satisfied, even if he had all the wealth in the world. The Prophet (may Allah's peace and blessings be upon him) said:"O Abu Dharr, do you think that richness is abundant wealth? Indeed, richness lies in the contentment of the heart, and poverty is the need within the heart."[Narrated by Ibn Hibbān; Sahīh (authentic)]So, a person who feels self-sufficient within his heart would not care about the hardships he may face in life. Conversely, if he has poverty within his heart, nothing in the world would satisfy him. The Prophet (may Allah's peace and blessings be upon him) is authentically reported to have said:"And be content with what Allah alloted to you, and you will become the richest among people."[Narrated by Al-Tirmidhī; Hasan (sound)]Another Hadīth reads:"He who seeks chastity, Allah will keep him chaste, and he who seeks self-sufficiency, Allah will make him self-sufficient."[Narrated by Al-Bukhāri and Muslim]

People do not like poverty,

though poverty that makes them transgress is better than opulence.

Contentment is sufficient for a person;

yet if he does not have that, nothing will ever be sufficient for him.

In Islam, a rich person is he who feels contentment within his heart and has no need for people and who stands in need of Allah Almighty. The Prophet (may Allah's peace and blessings be upon him) said:"The honor of the believer lies in his prayer at night, and his dignity lies in dispensing with people's possessions."[Narrated by Al-Hākim; Hasan (sound)]

A Bedouin was told: "The loaf of bread now costs one dinar."

He replied: "By Allah, I do not care about that, even if the grain of wheat were to cost one dinar. I worship Allah as He commanded me, and He provides for me as He promised me."

Al-Nasafi (may Allah have mercy upon him) said: "Al-Wāsiti said: 'Whoever asks from Allah alone will not be in need, and whoever seeks honor from Allah will not be humiliated.' Al-Husayn said: 'A person becomes self-sufficient as much as he stands in need before Allah.'"

A wise man once said:"Someone may keep away from me, but when I remember that I am self-sufficient by Allah and do not need him, I feel coolness within my heart."Ibn al-Sa'di (may Allah have mercy upon him) said:"Indeed, true richness lies in the contentment of the heart. There are many people who are wealthy, yet their hearts are poor and dejected."

I disown my own power and strength

and admit that I am in utmost need for my Lord.

When a person becomes self-sufficient by the Most Compassionate,

he becomes truly rich and held in awe.

O Allah, You gave us before we ask You; then what about when we actually ask You?!

O Allah, make us rich by standing in need before You, and do not make us poor by turning away from You; indeed, You are the Self-Sufficient, there is no god except You.

O Allah, grant us sufficiency with lawful things against unlawful things, and with Your bounty against being in need of others.

Al-Hakam Al-Hakīm (The Judge - The All-Wise)

Hāni' reported that when he came to the Messenger of Allah (may Allah's peace and blessings be upon him) and he heard them calling Hāni' by the nickname Abu al-Hakam, the Messenger of Allah (may Allah's peace and blessings be upon him) called him and said to him: "Allah is Al-Hakam (the Judge) and the judgment belongs to Him. Why are you known as Abu al-Hakam?" He said: "When my people differ concerning something, they come to me, and I pass judgment among them, and both sides accept it." He said: "How good this is! Do you have any children?" He said: "I have Shurayh, Muslim, and 'Abdullah." He said: "Who is the eldest of them?" He said: "Shurayh." He said: "Then, you are Abu Shurayh."[Narrated by Al-Nasā'i; Sahīh (authentic)]"Al-Hakam" and "Al-Hakīm" are from the beautiful names of Allah Almighty Who says:{...There is no god except Him, the All-Mighty, the All-Wise.}[Surat Āl 'Imrān: 6]He also says:{...Verily, His is the judgment; and He is the Swiftest of Reckoners.}[Surat al-An'ām: 62]

"Al-Hakīm has two meanings:

First: The One Who perfected all things. Allah Almighty is All-Wise because He perfected all His words and actions, all of which are right and at the peak of perfection.

An aspect of Allah's perfection, which is the climax of wisdom, is that He puts everything in its proper place. He manages His creation in the best manner and has made the creatures in the most perfect way. Neither His management nor His creation suffers any deficiency or defect. And His actions are never subject to any error or lapse. Allah Almighty says:{...The work of Allah Who perfected all things...}[Surat an-Naml: 88]Just as He perfected His creation, He also perfected the verses of His Book, the Noble Qur'an. He says:{...But Allah would abolish what Satan casts, then Allah would confirm His verses, for Allah is All-Knowing, All-Wise.}[Surat al-Hajj: 52]He describes His book as being wise:{These are verses of the wise Book.}[Surat Luqmān: 2]

Second: The Judge and Ruler among His servants as He judges between them by His Shariah.

He attributes judgment exclusively to Himself. So, it is not permissible for anyone to encroach upon this right. Allah Almighty says:{...The decision rests with Allah alone; He tells the truth and He is the Best of Judges.}[Surat al-An'ām: 57]He also says:{...Verily, His is the judgment; and He is the Swiftest of Reckoners.}[Surat al-An'ām: 62]"To take Allah Almighty as the Judge and Ruler, we should refer to His Book and His Prophet's Sunnah for judgment regarding anything we may differ about. Allah Almighty says:{Whatever is the subject of your differences, it is for Allah to judge....}[Surat ash-Shūra: 10]It is Allah Almighty alone Who is worthy of being the Judge among His servants for He is their Lord, Creator, and God.{[Say], "Should I seek a judge other than Allah when He is the One Who has sent down to you the Book explained in detail?"...}[Surat al-An'ām: 114]Our Lord is the best of judges and the All-Knowing of all things. He gives the appropriate judgment regarding any issue as Allah Almighty says:{Follow what is revealed to you, and be patient until Allah passes His judgment, for He is the Best of Judges.}[Surat Yūnus: 109]The believer is not truly a believer unless he submits to the Shariah of Allah and refers to it for judgment. Allah Almighty says:{But no, by your Lord, they will not believe until they accept you [O Prophet] as judge in their disputes, and find no discomfort within their hearts about your judgments, but accept them wholeheartedly.}[Surat an-Nisā': 65]

Any community that claims to be Muslim yet does not rule by the Shariah of Allah will not attain success.

A reward from the All-Wise..

Whoever is endowed with wisdom is indeed endowed with abundant good. And indeed Allah grants it to whomever He wills.{And certainly We gave wisdom to Luqmān...}[Surat Luqmān: 12]All prophets (peace be upon them) were given wisdom, and some of them were better than the others in this respect.The Prophet (may Allah's peace and blessings be upon him) said:"While two women were going along with their two sons, a wolf came and made away with the child of one of them. One of them said to her companion: 'It is your child that it has made away with.' And the other one said: 'Rather, it has made away with your child.'

They brought the matter to Dāwūd (David) (peace be upon him) for judgment, and he made a decision in favor of the elder one. Thereupon, they went to Sulaymān ibn Dāwūd (Solomon) (peace be upon him) and told him (the story). He said: 'Bring me a knife so that I may cut him into two parts for you.'

Thereupon, the younger one said: 'Do not do that, may Allah have mercy upon you! He belongs to her.' So, he gave a decision in favor of the younger one." [Narrated by Al-Bukhāri and Muslim]

Rest assured!

Remember that Allah possesses the utmost wisdom. He does not give except for a wise purpose and does not withhold anything except for a wise reason. Indeed, Allah's choice for you is better than your choice for your own self.{...And He has been Most Merciful to the believers.}[Surat al-Ahzāb: 43]Sufyān al-Thawri (may Allah have mercy upon him) said:"When He withholds, it is indeed giving. This is because He does not withhold due to stinginess or unavailability. Rather, He looks at what is best for the person and withholds something from him based on His choice and good judgment."A person may, in fact, pursue something that ultimately leads to untoward consequences or even to his own destruction.Ibn Mas'ūd (may Allah be pleased with him) said:"A person may pursue some matter of business or authority, and as things go easy for him, Allah looks at him and says to the angels: 'Keep it away from him. Indeed, if I facilitate this for him, it will admit him into Hellfire.' So, He makes this matter out of his reach. As a result, this person feels troubled and keeps saying: 'So-and-so went ahead of me; so-and-so caused me harm.' Yet, this matter is nothing but a favor from Allah Almighty."One of the righteous predecessors related that a man used to ask Allah to enable him to engage in conquests. Then, he heard a caller in a dream saying:"If you engage in a conquest, you will be taken captive; and if you are taken captive, you will convert to Christianity."{...And Allah Knows, while you know not.}[Surat al-Baqarah: 216]

Exalted be Allah, the All-Wise, Who decides and judges as He wills!

He is Generous, Perfect, and Forbearing. He does not hasten to inflict punishment.

Beware!

Beware of mistrusting your Lord in case you do not realize the wisdom behind something. Ascribe ignorance to yourself, for indeed our minds are incapable of realizing His wisdom. Even the angels, despite their closeness to the Almighty Lord and their knowledge of His majesty and power, did not know the wisdom behind making Adam settle on earth. They said:{..."Will You appoint on it someone who will spread corruption therein and shed blood, while we glorify You with Your praises and proclaim Your holiness?" He said, "I know that which you do not know."}[Surat al-Baqarah: 30]

So, keep silent before your Lord whenever you see His decree and actions coming so that He shows you much more of His kindness.

'Umar (may Allah be pleased with him) said:"If the veils of the unseen were lifted for us, none of us would choose for himself other than what Allah had chosen for him."

During the Hudaybiyyah Treaty, 'Umar (may Allah be pleased with him) went to the Prophet (may Allah's peace and blessings be upon him) and said: "O Messenger of Allah, are we not on the right path and they on the wrong?"

He said: "Yes."

He said: "Is it not true that our dead ones go to Paradise and theirs to Hellfire?"

He said: "Yes."

Thereupon, he remarked: "Then why should we accept a lower position with regard to our religion and return before Allah decides between us and them?"

The Prophet (may Allah's peace and blessings be upon him) said:"O Ibn al-Khattāb, I am the Messenger of Allah and He will never abandon me." Thereafter, Allah Almighty revealed Surat al-Fat-h (the Conquest). So, people came to know that the treaty was indeed a conquest.[Narrated by Al-Bukhāri and Muslim]The pens had already been lifted, the scrolls had dried up, the matter had been decided, and all decrees had been written down.{Say: "Never will we be struck except by what Allah has decreed for us; He is our protector." And upon Allah let the believers rely.}[Surat at-Tawbah: 51]

Allah is the Most Merciful of those who show mercy and the Best of Judges. So, rejoice and expect imminent relief. Tears will be followed by smiles, fear by security, and panic by tranquility. You should only adhere to piety and fear Allah.

Al-Alūsi said:"When a person fears Allah Almighty, springs of wisdom erupt from his heart and the delicate secrets get revealed to him, in accordance with his piety."{...And fear Allah so that you may be successful.}[Surat Āl 'Imrān: 130 and 200]

O Allah, the All-Wise, open for us the doors of Your wisdom and make us content with whatever You decreed for us; indeed, You are the All-Knowing, the All-Wise.

Al-Latīf (The All-Subtle/The Most Kind)

We will pause here with Allah's name "Al-Latīf", taking from its light and enjoying its shade.

Allah Almighty says:{...Indeed, my Lord is All-Subtle (Most Kind) in what He wills. Indeed, it is He Who is the All-Knowing, the All-Wise.}[Surat Yūsuf: 100]He also says:{No vision can encompass Him, but He encompasses all vision, and He is the Most Subtle, the All-Aware.}[Surat al-An'ām: 103]

In Arabic, "Latīf" is derived from "lutf", which means kindness, hospitality, generosity, gentleness, and awareness of subtle things.

So, when kindness in actions comes together with subtlety in cognizance, this conveys the meaning of Allah's name "Al-Latīf".

Our Lord, Exalted be He, is the Most Kind. None is more kind than Him. He shows kindness to His servants and does not hasten to punish them for their sins. Nothing whatsoever is hidden from Him, no matter how small or subtle it may be.

Our Lord is the One Who is good and kind to His servants and shows them benevolence in ways not apparent to them.{Allah is Most Kind to His servants, and He provides for whomever He wills...}[Surat ash-Shūra: 19]He is the One Who provides for His servants from where they do not expect.And our Lord is the One not perceived by senses and not seen by eyes:{Vision perceives Him not, but He perceives [all] vision; and He is the All-Subtle, the All-Aware.}[Surat al-An'ām: 103]Allah Almighty gives us more than what we need, charges us with duties below our capacity, and makes it easy for us to attain happiness in a short period of time:{...Indeed, my Lord is All-Subtle (Most Kind) in what He wills...}[Surat Yūsuf: 100]

He is the Most Kind to His servants, and He knows the secrets of the matters, and He reveals His might and shows His kindness.

His kindness is of two types: His kindness when He bestows blessings and His kindness when He pardons the heedlessness of His servants.

He is the Most Kind:

Your Lord, the Most Generous and the Most Kind, bestows His favors upon you in a kind and gentle manner, and He knows your situation better than you do and He is more Kind to you than your own self.

So, when the Most Kind Lord wants to show mercy to you, He sends the light of faith into your soul. As a result, your heart will radiate with its light and you will become averse to immoralities and temptations and keep away from sins.{...And He is the All-Subtle, the All-Aware.}[Surat al-An'ām: 103]When Allah wants to support you, He can command something, which is otherwise not a means of support, and make it one of the best means of support for you. Indeed, He is:{...the All-Subtle, the All-Aware.}[Surat al-An'ām: 103]And when the All-Subtle Lord wants to cure you, He causes this to happen by the most unlikely or the weakest of means. Indeed, He is: {...the All-Subtle, the All-Aware.}[Surat al-An'ām: 103]Also, when the All-Subtle wants to give you sustenance, He facilitates for you things probably unknown to you. For example, He may send a poor person to you and you give him. In return, he supplicates for you, and his supplication gets answered, after which abundant sustenance comes your way, according to His will, while you are not aware of all this. Indeed, He is: {...the All-Subtle, the All-Aware.}[Surat al-An'ām: 103]

Do you not long for Him?

If we knew what Allah keeps in store for us, we would feel an intense desire to meet Him.

How often we fall ill and He cures us!

How often we are hit by hardships and He removes them!

How often He helps us repay our debts!

And how often He sends relief after we are in distress!

This does not happen by our strength or power, but only through His grace and kindness.

If others knock on the doors of kings, you go and knock on the door of the Almighty King.

And if they stand in the court of a ruler, you stand in the court of the Most Generous Lord.

If you suffer a severe illness or a heavy debt, grieve over the absence of someone you love, fear for your children, and get tired of poverty, remember then that Allah is: {...the All-Subtle, the All-Aware.}[Surat al-An'ām: 103]The keys to relief are in His hand, His storehouses are full, and He is indeed the Most Generous.{And there is not a thing but that with Us are its stores...}[Surat al-Hijr: 21]

Happiness, security, comfort, pleasure, and cure are with Him, and in His hand is the dominion of all things, and He is over everything competent.

So, do not be distressed while you are in His company no matter how hard you suffer in this world. You should know that this is the means to you being selected by Allah Almighty, just as what happened to Yūsuf (Joseph) (peace be upon him).

And if you miss things that you think were the cause of your happiness, be certain that Allah kept them away from you before they become the cause of your misery.

The key to happiness:

If you want to be in the company of Allah, the All-Subtle, adhere to His Shariah, show gratitude for His favors, reflect upon His universe and creation, enjoy His remembrance and listen to His words, and be pleased with Him as your Lord, with His Book as a way, and with Muhammad as a Messenger.

Indeed, a person can only win the company of Allah through endeavor and hard work. And if he gets it, his heart will be filled with cheerfulness and his distress will go away, and he will forget the troubles and hardships of this world.

Be humbly submissive to the All-Subtle, the Most Kind!

Our Kind Lord loves kindness and loves that we treat each other kindly and compassionately.

The Prophet (may Allah's peace and blessings be upon him) is authentically reported to have said:"Shall I inform you of the person to whom Hellfire is forbidden, or the one who is forbidden from (entering) Hellfire? It is forbidden for everyone who is close (to people due to his modesty), lenient, and easy-going."[Narrated by Al-Tirmidhi; Sahīh (authentic)]

When you need your Lord to show you kindness and remove your distress or hardship, turn to Him in weakness and total submission and show kindness to Muslims, especially the weak amongst them.

My Lord, it befits You to be Kind and Benevolent! My Lord, my heart is in distress; so grant me Your pardon and relief!

All bounty and generosity belong to You. And my condition is indeed pitiful; and I am broken and humble.

O Allah, show us kindness, give us a sense of intimacy in closeness to You, help us worship You properly, and grant us a good ending in life.

Al-Khabīr (The All-Aware)

A Bedouin came to the Prophet (may Allah's peace and blessings be upon him) and believed in him and followed him. Then he said: "I will immigrate along with you." So, the Prophet (may Allah's peace and blessings be upon him) instructed some of his Companions to take care of him.

During the battle of Khaybar, the Prophet (may Allah's peace and blessings be upon him) got some prisoners as spoils of war, and he distributed them and gave him a share. His Companions gave him what had been allocated to him. He had been looking after some livestock for them, and when he came, they gave him his share. He said: "What is this?" They said: "A share that the Prophet (may Allah's peace and blessings be upon him) has allocated to you." He took it and brought it to the Prophet and said: "What is this?" He said: "I allocated it to you." He said: "It is not for this that I followed you. Rather, I followed you so that I might be shot here - and he pointed to his throat with an arrow - and die and enter Paradise."

The Prophet (may Allah's peace and blessings be upon him) replied: "If you are sincere with Allah, Allah will fulfill your wish." Shortly after that, they got up to fight the enemy, after which he was carried to the Prophet (may Allah's peace and blessings be upon him) after being hit with an arrow in the place he had pointed to earlier.

The Prophet (may Allah's peace and blessings be upon him) said: "Is it really him?" They replied in the affirmative. Thereupon, he said: "He was sincere with Allah and Allah fulfilled his wish." Then, the Prophet shrouded him in his own cloak, put him in front of him, and offered the funeral prayer for him. During his supplication, he said:"O Allah, this is Your servant; he went out as an immigrant in Your cause and was martyred and I am a witness to that." [Narrated by Al-Nasā'i with an authentic chain of narrators]Actions of the body organs follow actions of the heart, and salvation on the Day of Judgment lies in the soundness of the heart.{On the Day when neither wealth nor children will be of any avail,except the one who comes to Allah with a sound heart."}[Surat ash-Shu'arā': 88-89]Only Allah, the All-Knowing, the All-Aware, knows what is in the hearts. He says:{...And Allah is All-Aware of what you do.}[Surat al-Baqarah: 234]

The Almighty Lord knows the innermost thoughts and feelings of His servants. Nothing whatsoever, outward or inward, is hidden from Him, and nothing happens in His kingdom and dominion, no atom moves or stops, and no soul feels troubled or tranquil except with His knowledge.

His knowledge encompasses both the apparent and the hidden, the public and the secret. It encompasses everything: duties, impossibilities, possible things, the higher world and the lower one, the past, the present, and the future. Nothing is hidden or unknown to Him.

He informs of the consequences and outcomes of things.{It is He Who created the heavens and earth and all that is between them in six Days, then rose over the Throne. He is the Most Compassionate, so ask about Him the One Who is All-Aware.}[Surat al-Furqān: 59]

Allah is All-Knowing of outward things and All-Aware of inward ones.

He is All-Aware of the facts and the meanings and encompasses all things.

And He is the All-Knowing Lord from Whom nothing is hidden or veiled.

The status of Ihsān (perfection):

A person who knows that Allah is All-Aware of his innermost thoughts and feelings and is watching over him will feel shy that Allah should ever see him doing things displeasing to Him. Such a person will perfect his deeds and perform his worship sincerely for the sake of his Lord until he reaches the level of Ihsān, which is mentioned in this authentic Hadīth:"To worship Allah as if you see Him. But if you cannot see Him, He sees you."[Narrated by Al-Bukhāri and Muslim]Abu Hātim said:"The best act of obedience a person can do in this world is to reform his intentions and avoid spoiling consciences."

The secret lies in the heart!

Two persons may perform the same righteous deed, yet it is accepted from one of them but not form the other. For example, two men pray side by side and the prayer of one gets accepted; whereas the other one only gets a partial reward for his prayer, according to how much he focused therein. The Prophet (may Allah's peace and blessings be upon him) said:"Indeed, a man may perform a prayer and gets no reward for it except a tenth, a ninth, an eighth, a seventh, or a sixth thereof."[Narrated by Ibn Hibbān; Sahīh (authentic)]Also, a person may give charity and Allah accepts it from him and even fosters it for him, as we foster our own foal. And another person may give charity and Allah turns it down and even punishes him for it.{If you give charity publicly, it is good; but if you give it secretly to the poor, it is better for you, and He will expiate some of your sins. And Allah is All-Aware of what you do.}[Surat al-Baqarah: 271]One may pretend to lower his gaze while other people are around, yet when he is alone, he gives free rein to his eyes and violates the prohibitions set by his Lord. Only the All-Aware and All-Seeing Lord watches over what he does and knows what is in his heart.{He knows the fraud of the eyes, and all that the breasts conceal.}[Surat Ghāfir: 19]

Leading a life between obedience and disobedience carries the risk of not knowing during which of them your life will come to an end.

How you act when you are alone may raise or lower you. Whoever extols Allah Almighty in his time of seclusion, people will revere him when he is in public.

Imam Mālik (may Allah have mercy upon him) said:"Whoever likes to have relief within his heart and be saved from the throes of death and the horrors on the Day of Judgment, he should perform more good deeds in secret than in public."Ibn Rajab (may Allah have mercy upon him) said:"Only a person whose inside is good will have a good ending for his life, as none can be pretentious in the moment of death. It is only what lies within the heart that comes out then."Allah Almighty states that He is the All-Aware. He even couples His name "the All-Aware" with what people do and know more than twenty times, urging His servants to fear Him.{...Be just; that is nearer to righteousness. And fear Allah; indeed, Allah is All-Aware of what you do.}[Surat al-Mā'idah: 8]

Allah also urges us to consider our outward and inward deeds. The more one believes in the name "Al-Khabīr", the more he becomes aware of what takes place in his own world, namely his heart and body, including his innermost thoughts and secrets, like cheating, treachery, and evil intent.

Allah Almighty does not look at our forms or appearances, but He looks at our hearts and deeds.{But does he not know that when the contents of the graves are scattered.And that within the breasts is obtained.Verily, on that Day their Lord will be All-Aware of them.}[Surat al-'Ādiyāt: 9-11]

Being in the company of Allah:

When the believer takes his share in Allah's name "Al-Khabīr", he enjoys the company of his Lord and, consequently, He elevates and purifies him and makes him more preoccupied with this company than with anything else. He also makes him constantly fearful and heedful of the Almighty Creator, grants him self-sufficiency, subjects the worldly life to him, and blesses whatever He provides for him. Such a person will be safe from anxiety and distress, and the devil cannot find a way to him. Allah Almighty says:{...And whoever fears Allah, He will make for him a way out.}[Surat at-Talāq: 2]

O my Lord Who sees and hears what is within people's hearts and consciences, O You from Whom we seek relief from our hardships! I have no means but my humble submission before You and my need for You, as I knock on Your door. Exalted are You far above turning down a sinner who turns to You in repentance.

O Allah, You are the Bestower of every blessing that we expect, and to You we all resort and in You we seek refuge from every fear, need, and distress. If You reject us, we will not find another door to knock on; and You are the Owner of supreme bounty and grace.

O Allah, the All-Aware, show us kindness; indeed, You know our innermost thoughts and what lies concealed within our consciences.

Al-Halīm (The Forbearing)

Al-'Izz ibn 'Abdus-Salām said: "Knowing Allah Almighty and knowing His beautiful names and sublime attributes is the best of deeds in terms of honor, benefits, and effects."

We pause here with one of the beautiful names of Allah Almighty: "Al-Halīm".

Allah Almighty says: {...And Allah is Self-sufficient, Forbearing} [Surat al-Baqarah: 263] And He says: {...And He is ever Forbearing, All-Forgiving.} [Surat al-Isrā': 44]

Our Lord is the Owner of forbearance and tolerance. He is not provoked by the deeds of His servants, be it ignorance, disobedience, or the like. He does not hasten to punish His servants for their polytheism and disbelief in Him and for their plenty of sins.

No one is more forbearing than He is. His servants disobey Him as He watches over them, and He still preserves and takes care of them as they move and sleep as if they have not committed a sin. He bestows His favors even upon sinners and wrongdoers.

He is the Forbearing!

A sinner who is in distress stands before Him in supplication, and He responds to him and grants him his request.{When they board a ship, they supplicate Allah, devoting their faith sincerely to Him. But as soon as He rescues them to the land, they associate partners with Him,}[Surat al-'Ankabūt: 65]

There is no god except Allah. What a Forbearing Lord! He is the owner and source of bounty, generosity, and forbearance.

He is Forbearing and so He does not hasten to punish His servants for their sins and He gives them respite so that they may repent.

Abu Mūsa al-Ash'ari (may Allah be pleased with him) reported that the Prophet (may Allah's peace and blessings be upon him) said:"No one is more patient when hearing abuse than Allah Almighty. They associate rivals with Him and attribute a son to Him, but He still provides them with sustenance, grants them safety, and gives to them." [Narrated by Al-Bukhāri and Muslim]

What a Forbearing Lord!

How often Allah conceals our lapses and does not punish us for sins we commit! How often we disobey Him, and yet He calls us, although He is in no need for us, saying:{Inform My servants that I am the All-Forgiving, the Most Merciful.}[Surat al-Hijr: 49]Glory be to Allah, the All-Forbearing. He creates His servants, yet others are worshiped, and He provides for them, yet others are thanked. Goodness descends from Him to His servants, whereas evil ascends from them to Him. He shows love for them by His blessings, though He is in no need for them, and they incur His displeasure by sins, though they are in utmost need for Him.{If Allah were to take people to task for their wrongdoing, He would not leave a single living being on earth, but He gives them respite for an appointed time. When their time comes, they cannot delay it for a moment nor can they bring it forward.}[Surat an-Nahl: 61]

A whisper!

Let us beware of His wrath, because when the Forbearing Lord becomes angry, none can stand up to Him. Indeed, His forbearance comes from power and ability. He only becomes displeased with those who do not deserve mercy and are not worthy of being treated with forbearance - and that is after He gives them respite.

Allah Almighty says:{When they angered Us, We exacted Our retribution and drowned them all,}[Surat az-Zukhruf: 55]Allah Almighty may show forbearance to the disbelievers, provide for them, and not punish them in the worldly life, yet in the Hereafter, He will not pardon them or show them any clemency. Rather, the angels will drag them to Hellfire. Their entreaties will not be accepted, nor will their punishment be alleviated.{By your Lord, We will surely gather them and the devils, then We will surely bring them all around Hell on their knees.Then We will surely drag out of every group those who were most rebellious against the Most Compassionate.}[Surat Maryam: 68-69]{They urge you to hasten the punishment. And indeed, Hell will be encompassing of the disbelievers.}[Surat al-'Ankabūt: 54]

The pleasure of compliance!

One should strive to adopt this noble moral, namely forbearance. Indeed, Allah Almighty is Forbearing and Generous and loves those who are forbearing and generous among His servants.

Indeed, forbearance is one of the most noble and sublime traits.

So, show forbearance to me, my Lord, and grace from You.

Praising His Prophet Ibrāhim (Abraham) (peace be upon him), Allah Almighty says:{Surely Abraham was forbearing, tenderhearted, and oft-turning to Allah.}[Surat Hūd: 75]Forbearance was also a trait of Ismā'il (Ishmael) (peace be upon him):(So We gave him glad tidings of a forbearing boy.)[Surat as-Sāffāt: 101]

Our Prophet Muhammad (may Allah's peace and blessings be upon him) had the greatest share of this sublime moral.

Anas (may Allah be pleased with him) reported: "I was with the Messenger of Allah (may Allah's peace and blessings be upon him) and he was wearing a Najrāni cloak with a thick hem. A Bedouin approached him and pulled him violently by his cloak. I looked at the neck of the Messenger of Allah (may Allah's peace and blessings be upon) [and saw that] it was chafed by his hard tug. The Bedouin then said: 'O Muhammad, give me of Allah's wealth which is with you.' The Prophet turned to him, laughed, and ordered that he be given something." [Narrated by Al-Bukhāri and Muslim]

Also, the Prophet (may Allah's peace and blessings be upon him) praised Al-Ashajj ibn 'Abd al-Qays, saying:"Indeed, you possess two traits that Allah loves: forbearance and deliberateness."[Narrated by Muslim]

It is reported that a female slave of Maymūn ibn Mahrān came one day with a bowl of hot soup, as he was hosting some guests. She stumbled and poured the soup on him. As Maymūn was about to beat her, she said: "My master, heed Allah's verse that says: {And those who restrain anger.}" He said: "I do." She further said: "Heed the subsequent part: {And who pardon people.}" He said: "I pardon you." Then, she said: "{And Allah loves the doers of good.} [Surat Āl 'Imrān: 134]" Thereupon, he said: "I will do good to you. You are free for the sake of Allah Almighty."

Abu Hātim (may Allah have mercy upon him) said:"A wise person should remember, when he gets angry, that Allah often treats him with forbearance despite his frequent sins and violation of His prohibitions. Thereupon, he also should show forbearance and restrain his anger lest it may lead him to wrongdoing."

In conclusion..

If an affliction or a tribulation hits you, invoke Allah Almighty and include His name "Al-Halīm" in your invocation, for whenever the Prophet (may Allah's peace and blessings be upon him) was distressed, he would make this supplication:"La ilāha illallāh Al-'Azhīm Al-Halīm, la ilāha illallāh Rabbu al-'arshi al-'azhīm, la ilāha illallāh Rabbu as-samāwāti wa Rabbu al-ardi wa Rabbu al-'arshi al-karīm (There is no god except Allah, the Magnificent, the Forbearing. There is no god except Allah, the Lord of the Mighty Throne. There is no god except Allah, the Lord of the heavens, the earth, and the honorable Throne)."[Narrated by Al-Bukhāri and Muslim]

O Allah, the Forbearing, make Your forbearance a cause for our happiness in this world and in the Hereafter.

Ar-Ra'ūf (The All-Kind)

The Prophet (may Allah's peace and blessings be upon him) said:"There was a man who wronged himself greatly, and when he was dying, he said to his children: 'When I am dead, burn my body and then grind my bones and scatter me in the wind and at sea, for by Allah, if Allah gets hold of me, He will punish me in a way that He will not punish anyone else.'

So, they did that. But Allah Almighty said to the earth: 'Give back what you have taken.' Then, there he was, standing. Allah said to him: 'What made you do what you did?' He said: 'Fear from You.' So Allah forgave him." [Narrated by Al-Bukhāri and Muslim]

Praising Himself and giving glad tidings to His servants, Allah Almighty says:{...Indeed, your Lord is All-Kind, Most Merciful.}[Surat an-Nahl: 7]

"Ra'ūf" is derived from "ra'fah", which means the highest degree of mercy.

Indeed, it is good in every aspect. Allah Almighty says:{...Indeed, Allah is All-Kind and Most Merciful to mankind.}[Surat al-Baqarah: 143]

Our Lord, Exalted be He, is the One Who created us, protects us, shows mercy and kindness to us, subjects the world to us, removes harm from us, and brings all sorts of good things to us. This stems from His supreme benevolence and bounty.

Out of His kindness towards His pious servants, Allah Almighty accepts their good deeds, no matter how little they may be, and preserves their faith and does not cause it to be lost or go to waste.{...And never would Allah have caused you to lose your faith. Indeed Allah is All-Kind and Most Merciful to mankind.}[Surat al-Baqarah: 143]

The strongest signs:

Out of His supreme kindness towards His servants, He warns, encourages, intimidates, promises, and threatens them, as He wants to lead them to what is good and beneficial for them.{...And Allah warns you of Himself, and Allah is All-Kind to [His] servants.}[Surat Āl 'Imrān: 30]One of the signs of His kindness is that He revealed the Book to His Messenger so as to bring people out of darkness into light by His permission. Allah Almighty says:{It is He Who sends down upon His Servant verses of clear evidence that He may bring you out from darknesses into the light. And indeed, Allah is All-Kind and Most Merciful to you.}[Surat al-Hadīd: 9]Another sign of His kindness is that He subjected to us means of transportation, such as horses, mules, and donkeys in the past, and cars, planes, trains, etc. in modern times. Allah Almighty says:{And they carry your loads to a land you could not have reached except with difficulty to yourselves. Indeed, your Lord is All-Kind, Most Merciful.}[Surat an-Nahl: 7]Signs of His kindness also include the fact that whatever He buys from His servants - like their lives and wealth - does originally belong to Him, and He gives them abundant rewards in return. He says:{And of the people is he who sells himself, seeking means to the approval of Allah. And Allah is All-Kind to [His] servants.}[Surat al-Baqarah: 207]And as part of His supreme kindness, He answers the supplications of His close servants. Allah Almighty says:{And [there is a share for] those who came after them, saying: "Our Lord, forgive us and our brothers who preceded us in faith and put not in our hearts [any] resentment toward those who have believed. Our Lord, indeed You are All-Kind and Most Merciful."}[Surat al-Hashr: 10]Another aspect of His kindness is that He laid down certain punishments that deter people from committing crimes and drive them to adhere to piety. Indeed, it is out of kindness to reform those to whom kindness is to be shown. Kindness is a higher and more gentle form of mercy. Allah Almighty says:{And if it had not been for the favor of Allah upon you and His mercy... and because Allah is All-Kind, Most Merciful.}[Surat an-Nūr: 20]Another sign of His kindness is that He gives respite to the disbelievers and sinners instead of seizing them unexpectedly while they are not aware. And He also gives them safety, good health, and sustenance. Allah Almighty says:{Or that He would not seize them gradually [in a state of dread]? But indeed, your Lord is All-Kind and Most Merciful.}[Surat an-Nahl: 47]And one of the signs of His kindness is that He holds {...the sky from falling upon the earth, unless by His permission. Indeed Allah is All-Kind and Most Merciful to people.}[Surat al-Hajj: 65]

A message to..

Everyone who suffers poverty, distress, and a broken heart.

Everyone who is in heavy debt and, therefore, lives in loss and confusion and finds life to be narrow and tough.

Everyone who goes through severe pains, and doctors cannot find a cure for him, and there is no way.

Everyone who is in grief and distress and upon whom life has turned its back, and he is surrounded with hardships.

Everyone whose son, loved one, or friend has traveled or been away for a long while, and so he agonizes, his heart shivers in sadness, and he sees the beautiful life around him as hard and gloomy.

Remember the verse that says: {...Indeed, your Lord is All-Kind and Most Merciful.} [Surat an-Nahl: 7]. And repeat that verse that reads: {...And Allah is All-Kind to [His] servants} [Surat al-Baqarah: 207] Call out and say: My All-Kind Lord, show kindness to me, strengthen me, and remove my distress and the harm I am suffering.

Ibn al-Qayyim said:"Allah Almighty afflicts His servants to hear their complaints and earnest imploring and supplication to Him."{He said: "I only complain of my suffering and my grief to Allah..."}[Surat Yūsuf: 86]And then expect relief from your Lord, Who says:{Is He [not best] Who responds to the desperate one when he calls upon Him and removes evil and makes you inheritors of the earth? Is there a deity with Allah? Little do you remember.}[Surat an-Naml: 62]

He is the All-Kind, the Most Merciful, the Magnificent, the Most High. How close and kind He is to His servants!

When you find a hardship getting tough, know that it will soon ease; when the night getting dark, rejoice, for the morning is approaching soon.

Do not be impatient or lose hope in the All-Kind and Most Merciful Lord. Indeed, things must necessarily change. The best act of worship is to wait for relief from Allah. Days bring change and fluctuations, and the future is pregnant with many possibilities, yet they are now unseen to us. Allah Almighty says:{...Every day He is upon some affair.}[Surat ar-Rahmān: 29]He also says:{...Perhaps Allah will bring about after that a [different] matter.}[Surat at-Talāq: 1]And He says:{Verily, with every hardship comes ease,Verily, with every hardship comes ease.}[Surat ash-Sharh: 5-6]

Hearts in humble submission..

Allah Almighty describes His Prophet (may Allah's peace and blessings be upon him) as being kind, saying:{There has certainly come to you a Messenger from among yourselves. Hard to him is what you suffer; [he is] concerned over you and is kind and merciful to the believers.}[Surat at-Tawbah: 128]That means he is extremely kind and merciful towards the believers. Indeed, he is more merciful to them than their own parents.

That is why his right takes precedence over the rights of all people, and it is incumbent upon them to believe in him and respect and revere him.

The Prophet (may Allah's peace and blessings be upon him) would spend the whole night in prayer repeating one single verse:{If You should punish them - indeed they are Your servants; but if You forgive them - indeed it is You Who are the All-Mighty, the All-Wise.}[Surat al-Mā'idah: 118]Then, Allah Almighty, the All-Kind Lord, informed him that He would make him pleased with regard to his Ummah.

The believer should show kindness to himself and follow the paths of salvation and avoid those of ruin and perdition. And he should do this with other people as well.

Ibn Rajab (may Allah have mercy upon him) said:"If a person treats others generously, Allah treats him generously and graciously. Indeed, recompense is of the same type of the action."

My Lord, You see my condition and know my need and weakness.

And You hear my secret talk and innermost thoughts.

My Lord, make me taste Your pardon on a Day

when no children or wealth will be of any avail.

O Allah, the All-Kind, we implore You to admit us into Your Paradise and save us from Your Hellfire.

Al-Wadūd (The Most Affectionate)

Our Lord, as we see beautiful things around us,

this inspires love within our hearts

and encourages us to have dreams and wishes.

And indeed all our wishes and hopes come from none but You.

Our Lord, the Most Affectionate, is the One Whom the pious people love and to Whom the fearful and distressed turn for refuge and security.

He loves those who frequently repent and purify themselves. He is the Most Generous and the Most Bountiful of all those who are generous and bountiful.

Our Lord, Your giving is the most generous, Your mercy is the most vast, and Your refuge is the firmest, and You are with us when we are alone and the source of support when we are few and weak - Exalted are You!

We will talk here about Allah's name "Al-Wadūd".

Allah Almighty says:{...Indeed, my Lord is Most Merciful, Most Affectionate.}[Surat Hūd: 90]He also says:{And He is the All-Forgiving, the Most Affectionate,the Owner of the Throne, the Most Glorious.}[Surat al-Burūj: 14-15]

"Wadūd" is derived from "wudd", which means love.

Our Lord, Exalted be He, shows affection towards His close servants by making them know Him and His sublime attributes.

His affection is particularly shown to His close and pious servants. He facilitates for them the means whereby they win His love and affection. Indeed, their hearts are attracted to His affection. As He mentions to them His beautiful names and great attributes, people with sound and untainted hearts feel inclined to love Him.

My Lord, my heart was empty before I loved You.

I used to engage in play and diversion with people.

Yet when Your love called my heart, it responded.

And ever since, it never leaves Your court.

Allah is the Most Affectionate. He endears Himself to sinners among His servants and shows affections to the repentant among them, facilitating for them the means by which they can attain His forgiveness and pardon, and shows them the signs of His vast mercy.

Allah Almighty says:{Say: "O My servants who have transgressed against themselves, do not despair of the mercy of Allah. Indeed, Allah forgives all sins. Indeed, He is the All-Forgiving, the Most Merciful."}[Surat az-Zumar: 53]He also says:{...And My mercy encompasses all things...}[Surat al-A'rāf: 156]

Our Lord, Exalted be He, shows affection to His servants through His great favors and blessings, both apparent and hidden. He brought them into existence, gave them life, sustains their existence, reforms their affairs, and guides them to faith and Islam, which is the greatest of all blessings.

He is the Most Affectionate One. He loves them and they love Him. And He rewards them for their love for Him.

Indeed, this is utmost benevolence from Allah, the Bestower of favors.

Pure benevolence:

When the meaning of Allah's name "Al-Wadūd" is revealed to a person, his heart becomes attached to his Lord and he feels love and longing for Him and finds incomparable pleasure in his life.

Indeed, that is the greatest thing by which His servants worship Him and seek closeness to Him - love;{...He loves them, and they love Him...}[Surat al-Mā'idah: 54]

A person's faith in Allah is as pure as his knowledge of His names and attributes.

The believer knows that this condition can only exist through the power and will of Allah Almighty. If Allah, the Most Affectionate, loves a servant, He puts love in his heart; and when the servant loves Him, through guidance from Allah, He still rewards him with additional love, and that is utter benevolence from the Almighty Lord, as it all comes from Him.

Indeed, if a person loves his Lord truly, his love will yield sincere servitude to Him alone and will entail that he should love anyone and anything loved by Allah and hate anyone and anything that He hates. This is the essence of allegiance and dissociation.{You will not find any people who believe in Allah and the Last Day taking as allies those who oppose Allah and His Messenger, even if they were their parents, their children, their brothers, or their kindred. It is they in whose hearts Allah has instilled faith and strengthened them with a spirit from Him. He will admit them to gardens under which rivers flow, abiding therein forever. Allah is pleased with them and they are pleased with Allah. They are the party of Allah. Indeed, it is the party of Allah that will be the successful.}[Surat al-Mujādilah: 22]

Only for the lovers of Allah!

A true believer shows love for Allah by such words and deeds that win His love, the greatest of which is obeying Allah Almighty and His Messenger (may Allah's peace and blessings be upon him). Our Lord says:{Say [O Muhammad]: "If you really love Allah, then follow me, and Allah will love you..."}[Surat Āl 'Imrān: 31]A person continues to adhere to such things that are dear to his Lord and hasten to do whatever is pleasing to Him until he wins His love and closeness."If Allah Almighty loves a servant, He calls upon Jibrīl (Gabriel) and says: 'Verily, Allah loves so-and-so; so love him.' So, Gabriel loves him and calls upon the inhabitants of the heavens: 'Verily, Allah loves so-and-so; so love him.' The inhabitants of the heavens thus love him, and then he is granted acceptance on the earth."[Narrated by Al-Bukhāri]Allah Almighty says:{Those who believe and do righteous deeds, the Most Compassionate will endear them [to His creation].}[Surat Maryam: 96]When Allah Almighty loves a servant, He becomes "his hearing with which he hears, his seeing with which he sees, his hand with which he seizes, and his leg with which he walks."[Narrated by Al-Bukhāri]Ibn al-Qayyim (may Allah have mercy upon him) said:"There are ten means by which a person can win Allah's love:

1. Reciting the Qur'an and understanding and pondering its meanings and objectives.

2. Seeking closeness to Allah through supererogatory acts of worship after performing the obligatory ones.

3. Remembering Allah at all times and in all situations, by the tongue and heart, and through the deeds and in all circumstances.

4. Preferring the things He loves over the things one loves when one's personal inclinations become so intense.

5. Considering, observing, and knowing His names and attributes.

6. Observing His kindness, benevolence, and blessings, the apparent and hidden.

7. Having his heart in complete submission to the Almighty Lord.

8. Being in seclusion with Him when He descends to the heaven of this world and engaging in private talk with Him.

9. Sitting with those who love Him and are sincere to Him and picking up the good fruits from their speech.

10. Keeping away from any reason that may stand as a barrier between one's heart and the Almighty Lord."

The proof of affection:

Not all those who love are gratified by their loved ones, nor all those who are called respond.

When the lovers hear the call of their beloved Lord: "Come to prayer; come to success", they get out of their beds, push sleep away, and rise up to their feet, be it in the extreme cold or the severe heat. It is as if they are walking on silk. And when they hear: "Come to struggle", they rush to sacrifice their lives and shed their blood in the cause of their Lord.

When {...spend from what We have provided for you...} [Surat al-Baqarah: 254] is recited to them, they vie with one another in giving from their most precious and dearest possessions. They give like those who do not fear poverty.And when they hear {...and due to Allah upon the people is pilgrimage to the House...} [Surat Āl 'Imrān: 97], they come from all places and directions and cross long distances and rough terrain, weary and thirsty, saying: "Here we are, our Lord, at Your service. There is no partner with You."

Their condition is that of true lovers. A poet says it rightly:

"He whose heart is empty of intense love cannot know how love grips the heart so powerfully."

Jalāl al-Dīn al-Rūmi said:"Love turns bitterness into sweetness, dust into gold, trouble into ease, pain into recovery, prison into a spacious garden, ailment into a blessing, and oppression into mercy. It relents and softens what is hard and stiff, and it resurrects the dead and instills life into them."

My Lord, I hope to make You pleased and I do not care if all people become displeased with me.

If I obtain Your affection and love, I do not mind if my relation sours with everyone else. All that is now above dust will one day turn into dust.

Ibn al-Qayyim (may Allah have mercy upon him) said about love:"It is the secret in our deification of Allah, and its monotheism is: There is no god except Allah."While the Prophet (may Allah's peace and blessings be upon him) was delivering a speech to the people, a Bedouin stood up and said: "When will the Hour be, O Messenger of Allah?" He said: "What have you prepared for it?" He replied: "I have not prepared for it much prayer, fasting, or charity. But I love Allah and His Messenger." The Prophet (may Allah's peace and blessings be upon him) said to him: "You will be with those you love."[Narrated by Al-Bukhāri and Muslim]

I love the righteous, though I do not claim to be one of them, hoping to attain intercession because of them. And I hate those who frequently sin, even if they and I are alike in this regard.

A sign..

Harim ibn Hayyān said:"No one turns to Allah Almighty with his heart except that Allah turns to him with the hearts of the believers until He grants him their love."The believer is affectionate and friendly; he loves and is loved, and he is easy to get along with. The Prophet (may Allah's peace and blessings be upon him) said:"The believer gets along with others, and they get along with him."[Narrated by Al-Tabarāni in Al-Mu'jam al-Awsat] [Hasan (sound)]This is because he wishes good for his fellow Muslims and does not hurt or harm them in any way. It is authentically reported that the Prophet (may Allah's peace and blessings be upon him) used to supplicate saying:"Allāhumma wa as'aluka hubbaka wa hubba man yuhibbuka wa hubba 'amalin yuqarribuni ila hubbika (O Allah, I ask You Your love, the love of those who love You, and the love of an act that brings me closer to Your love)."[Narrated by Al-Tirmidhi; Sahīh (authentic)]

O Allah, our Most Affectionate Lord, we ask You for Your love, the love of those who love You, and the love of an act that brings us closer to Your love.

--

Al-Barr (The Beneficent)

O you needy servant, keep standing at the door of your Generous Lord, derive power and honor from the All-Mighty and All-Knowing Master, and implore Him by virtue of your obedience to Him; indeed, He is the Beneficent, the Most Merciful.

He will bestow His favors upon you. If you obey Him, He honors you, and if you neglect your duties, He shows mercy to you and gives you respite. If you turn to Him in repentance, He appreciates that, and if you commit sins and act wrongly, He conceals them for you.

Then, how could a person who tasted the sweetness of servitude to Him and love for Him ever be patient to get close to Him?! Or how could a person who found the pleasure of humble submission to Him not be wholly devoted to Him?!

If men's love for women is so intense

that it captivates the heart and mind,

then what could the love for the Almighty Lord

do to a lover whose heart is filled with longing?!

How truthful is the one who said: "By Allah, how desolate a path is if Allah does not secure one, and how misguiding a path is if Allah is not the one guiding him!"

Glory be to Allah, the Beneficent, the Most Merciful! His benevolence, beneficence, and blessings of every type, apparent and hidden, encompass all the inhabitants of the heavens and the earth, at every moment.

Allah Almighty says:{...and amply bestowed upon you His favors, [both] apparent and hidden...}[Surat Luqmān: 20]Praising His sublime essence, Allah Almighty says:{...Indeed, it is He Who is the Beneficent, the Most Merciful.}[Surat at-Tūr: 28]

Our Lord, Exalted be He, is Compassionate, Merciful, and Kind to His servants, and He sets aright their worldly and religious conditions and affairs.

Out of His perfect beneficence, He multiplies the reward for those who do good and pardons and forgives evildoers.

Our Lord, Who is Beneficent and Kind to His servants, intends ease for them, not hardship.

And He is Beneficent to His close servants as He has chosen them for His worship and singled them out for His protection and removal of all kinds of evils, harms, and adversities.

His vast beneficence manifests in what He has prepared for His pious servants in the Hereafter:{Indeed, we used to supplicate Him before. Indeed, it is He Who is the Beneficent, the Most Merciful.}[Surat at-Tūr: 28]

His beneficence is represented by the great blessings He bestows

upon His servants and the kindness He shows to them.

Beneficence is both an attribute in Him

and is shown in His actions.

He is a Beneficent God,

and He constantly does acts of beneficence to His servants.

Allah Almighty is Kind, Compassionate, and Beneficent to His servants and He bestows ample favors and bounties upon them and appreciates their good deeds and answers their supplications.{...and amply bestowed upon you His favors, [both] apparent and hidden...}[Surat Luqmān: 20]

They are all appointed to serve you..

The angels who carry the Throne invoke Allah's forgiveness upon you.

And the angels appointed to protect you and those charged with rain and plants do all work for your benefit and sustenance.

Planets are subject and subservient, running in their orbits, and the sun, the moon, and the stars are all subject to serve us and they move in a way that enables us to calculate our times.

Moreover, the entire lower world is subject to us. The land, the mountains, the seas, the trees, the fruits, the plants, and the animals - everything therein is for us.{And He has subjected to you all that is in the heavens and all that is on earth - all from Him. Indeed in that are signs for a people who reflect.}[Surat al-Jāthiyah: 13]

The kindness of the Beneficent Lord..

Out of His beneficence, Allah Almighty facilitated for us the path to Him. He sent down His Shariah and made it easy and free from undue restrictions or hardships. He does not charge us with things beyond our capacity.{...And He has not placed upon you in the religion any hardship...}[Surat al-Hajj: 78]{Allah does not charge a soul except with that within its capacity...}[Surat al-Baqarah: 286]{And We have certainly made the Qur'an easy for remembrance; is there anyone to take heed?}[Surat al-Qamar: 17]Out of His beneficence, Allah Almighty accepts from us what is little and gives ample rewards for it, and He forgives a lot of sins. Sufficient for us is this Hadīth in which the Prophet (may Allah's peace and blessings be upon him) said:"Indeed, Allah wrote down the good deeds and the bad ones and then made this clear:

He who intends a good deed and does not do it, Allah writes it down as a full good deed, but if he intends it and does it, Allah writes it down as ten good deeds, or up to seven hundred times or many times over.

And if he intends a sin and does not do it, Allah writes it down as a full good deed, and if he intends it and does it, Allah writes it down as one sin."[Narrated by Al-Bukhāri and Muslim]A sign of Allah's beneficence to His servants is that He becomes pleased when a servant repents to Him, and when we sin, He does not expose us. Rather, He keeps the doors of repentance wide open for us.{Say: "O My servants who have transgressed against themselves, do not despair of the mercy of Allah. Indeed, Allah forgives all sins. Indeed, He is the All-Forgiving, the Most Merciful."}[Surat az-Zumar: 53]

The Prophet (may Allah's peace and blessings be upon him) is authentically reported to have said: "Allah Almighty said: 'O son of Adam, if you supplicate Me and implore Me, I will forgive the sins you committed, and I do not mind.

O son of Adam, if your sins reach the clouds in the sky and then you ask Me for forgiveness, I will forgive you, and I do not mind.

O son of Adam, if you come to Me with sins as great as the earth and then you meet Me while not associating any partners with Me, I shall bring you forgiveness as great as it is.'" [Narrated by Al-Tirmidhi; Sahīh (authentic)]

All praise is to due to You, our Lord, though I cannot extend enough praise to You.

Due to You is praise that is good and so great that it fills the horizons. My Lord, cover me with Your mercy, You are Beneficent to all creation.

Your share in this name..

Our Lord is Beneficent and He loves beneficence and commands His servants to be beneficent.

In a comprehensive verse, Allah Almighty says:{It is not righteousness to turn your faces towards the east or the west, but righteousness is to believe in Allah, the Last Day, the angels, the Scriptures, and the prophets; and to give charity out of one's cherished wealth to relatives, orphans, the needy, the wayfarer, beggars, and to free slaves; to establish prayer and give Zakah; to fulfill the ratified pledges; to be patient at times of hardship, adversity, and during the battle. Such are the true believers, and such are the righteous.}[Surat al-Baqarah: 177]A person cannot attain the beneficence of Allah Almighty in the Hereafter except if he follows the path leading to His beneficence and pleasure. Allah Almighty says:{You will never attain righteousness until you spend in charity from what you love. Whatever you spend, Allah is All-Knowing of it.}[Surat Āl 'Imrān: 92]Al-Rāzi (may Allah have mercy upon him) said:"Whoever facilitates for people the means of welfare and comfort in this world, Allah will facilitate for him the means of welfare in this world and in the Hereafter."

O Allah, bestow Your favor upon us and save us from the punishment of Hellfire; indeed, You are the Beneficent, the Most Merciful!

Al-Qarīb (The Near)

Allah Almighty says:{When My slaves ask you concerning Me, I am indeed near. I respond to the call of the supplicant when he calls upon Me; so they should respond to Me and believe in Me, so that they may be guided.}[Surat al-Baqarah: 186]

This is a question that Allah Almighty Himself answers in a verse that pours feelings of joy, intimacy, contentment, tranquility, reassurance, and certitude in the heart of every believer.

In the atmosphere of this intimacy, affection, and closeness, let us get acquainted with Allah's name "Al-Qarīb".

Allah Almighty says:{...He is indeed All-Hearing, Near.}[Surat Saba': 50]

This is a name that abounds with amiability and many remarkable meanings and indications.

As a word, this name already says enough about its meaning, just as a clear glass shows the water therein.

Our Lord, Exalted be He, Who is Near His servants and is established over His Throne, which is above His creation. He is All-Knowing of all secrets and innermost thoughts and feelings. His companionship encompasses all.

His nearness to His creation is of two types:

First: General nearness: He is Near everyone as He knows, watches over, observes, and encompasses all things. He is above all creatures and is closer to humans than their jugular veins.

This is general nearness.{...And We are closer to him than [his] jugular vein.}[Surat Qāf: 16]

Second: Special nearness: He is Near those who worship Him, implore Him, and love Him. This kind of nearness entails that He loves and supports them in their movements and actions, answers their supplications, accepts and rewards those who worship Him.

We cannot realize this nearness in concrete terms, yet we see its effects, as they manifest in the form of kindness, care, help, success, and guidance from our Lord.{When My slaves ask you concerning Me, I am indeed near. I respond to the call of the supplicant when he calls upon Me...}[Surat al-Baqarah: 186]

Indeed, He is Near and particularly Near His devoted servants who supplicate Him.

The Prophet (may Allah's peace and blessings be upon him) is authentically reported to have said:"The One you supplicate is nearer to you than the neck of the riding camel of one of you."[Narrated by Muslim]

He hears the creeping of a black ant on a hard rock in a dark night.

In Allah's protection..

Allah Almighty is Near His pious servants. He encompasses them with His care and protection. He sends His mercy down to them and does not leave them to their own devices even for the blink of an eye. Also, He does not make their enemies dominant over them, nor does He give the devil a way against them.

They paid the price of special nearness and in return they got nearness, support, help, and protection.{...Allah said: "I am with you. If you establish prayer, give Zakah, believe in My messengers and support them, and give Allah a goodly loan...}[Surat al-Mā'idah: 12]

They felt secure with their Lord and trusted Him, and so He was with them at all times.

Consider Nūh (Noah) (peace be upon him), after 950 years of calling people to Allah, facing adversities, and suffering, he supplicated his Lord, Who responded and saved him and destroyed his foes.

Another example is Abraham (peace be upon him), he sought refuge in his Lord and so He saved him from the fire.

And He saved Yūnus (Jonah) (peace be upon him) from severe distress, brought Yūsuf (Joseph) (peace be upon him) back to his father Ya'qūb (Jacob) (peace be upon him) and reunited them and amended the relation between him and his siblings. Moreover, he restored to Jacob his sight.

And our Prophet (may Allah's peace and blessings be upon him)! He has gone through tough situations that would make people gray-haired due to great horrors and cause their hearts to jump into their mouths, to the extent that some of his Companions began to have doubts regarding Allah Almighty. At that point, the Prophet (may Allah's peace and blessings be upon him) supplicated his Lord, Exalted be He, Who fulfilled the promise, achieved the objective, and elevated the word of the truth.

Allah Almighty is Near all His believing servants. He sees and protects them.

A woman came to the Prophet (may Allah's peace and blessings be upon him) arguing about her husband. 'Ā'ishah (may Allah be pleased with her), who was in another area of the house, said that she could hear some words but not others. After this argument, Gabriel (peace be upon him) descended to Muhammad (may Allah's peace and blessings be upon him) with this verse:{Indeed, Allah has heard the words of the woman who was arguing with you [O Prophet] concerning her husband, and was complaining to Allah. Allah has heard the discussion between the two of you, for Allah is All-Hearing, All-Seeing.}[Surat al-Mujādilah: 1]Glory be to Allah Whose hearing encompasses all voices and sounds!

He is Near:

Do not raise your voice as you supplicate Him, for He is Near, hearing you.

The Prophet (may Allah's peace and blessings be upon him) heard the Companions supplicating Allah Almighty loudly. He said to them:"O people, do not trouble yourselves too much. He Whom you are invoking is not deaf or absent. But you are invoking an All-Hearing and All-Seeing (Lord)."[Narrated by

Al-Bukhāri and Muslim]Allah knows our innermost thoughts and what lies within our hearts and souls. We supplicate Him within our hearts, and He answers our supplications. He is Near.{When he called upon his Lord in private.}[Surat Maryam: 3]

We remember Him within ourselves, and He hears us and mentions us. Indeed, He is the Near Lord.

In a Qudsi Hadīth, He said:"If he remembers Me within himself, I remember him within Myself, and if he remembers Me within a group, I mention him within a better group." [Narrated by Al-Bukhāri and Muslim]

Every person does necessarily receive blessings from Allah Almighty, the Near Lord. He removes our distress, saves us from harms and dangers, and helps us obtain what we love and achieve our goals.

The door of our Near Lord is always open, and He continues to give generously. How often He fulfills our needs, accepts our supplications, and sends down His blessings and mercy!

The reward of standing in need and in humble submission before our Lord..

As you know that Allah is Near you, and He watches over your secrets and innermost thoughts, hears your supplication, sees your condition and place, and knows what is in your heart, then be a doer of good.{...Indeed, the mercy of Allah is near to the doers of good.}[Surat al-A'rāf: 56]Draw near to your Lord, for when you get closer to Him by a handspan, He gets closer to you by an arm's length. In a Qudsi Hadīth, He said:"If a servant draws closer to Me by a handspan, I shall draw closer to him by a cubit; and if he draws closer to Me by a cubit, I shall draw closer to him by the span of two outstretched arms. If he comes to Me walking, I shall come to him running."[Narrated by Al-Bukhāri and Muslim, and this is his wording]We can draw closer to our Lord by performing the obligations first and then by offering the supererogatory acts."My servant does not draw close to Me through anything dearer to Me than what I have made obligatory upon him; and My servant continues to draw close to Me through supererogatory acts until I love him."[Narrated by Al-Bukhāri]The more perfect one's servitude to Allah is, the closer he is to his Lord. As he shows more humble submission to the Creator and stands in humiliation before Him, he gets closer and closer to Him and becomes more elevated in His sight. The Prophet (may Allah's peace and blessings be upon him) is authentically reported to have said:"The nearest a servant is to his Lord is when he is prostrating, so increase (your) supplications (while in this state)."[Narrated by Muslim]

Prostration shows the highest level of extolling Allah and servitude and submission to Him, and it contains the clearest signs of love, humility, and need.

The more frequent and perfect your prostration to your Lord is, the more elevated you will be in His sight. The Prophet (may Allah's peace and blessings be upon him) said:"Make frequent prostration to Allah, for by every prostration that you make to Allah, He will raise your position a degree and will remit one of your sins."[Narrated by Muslim]Thus, you will obtain the everlasting bliss:{Those are the ones brought near [to Allah].}[Surat al-Wāqi'ah: 11]{A spring from which those near [to Allah] will drink.}[Surat al-Mutaffifīn: 28]

How blissful you are as you turn to your Lord and draw near to Him!

Even if the heaven seems to be far away, the One above the heaven is Near.

So, raise your hands and supplicate to Him; indeed, all pains will go away with your supplication.

O Lord, as long as You are Near, then we do not care if the heaven is far away.

O Allah, You said as Your speech is all true:{When My slaves ask you concerning Me, I am indeed near. I respond to the call of the supplicant when he calls upon Me; so they should respond to Me and believe in Me, so that they may be guided.}[Surat al-Baqarah: 186]

O Allah, the Near, the Responsive, answer our supplications, strengthen us, remove our distress, give us a good outcome in all our affairs, save us from disgrace in this world and punishment in the Hereafter, and forgive us, our parents, and all Muslims; indeed, You are Hearer of the supplication!

Al-Mujīb (The All-Responsive)

It gives us great hope to know that Allah Almighty hears our supplications and answers them. This indeed enlivens us

and puts our pains to rest.

'Atā' said:"Tāwūs (may Allah have mercy upon him) came to me and said: 'O 'Atā', do not ever present your needs to those who close their doors in your face. Instead, you should seek their fulfillment from the One Whose door is open to you till the Day of Judgment. He asks you to supplicate Him and promises that He will answer your supplications.'"{...So seek His forgiveness then turn to Him in repentance, for My Lord is Ever Near, All-Responsive.}[Surat Hūd: 61]Our Lord, Exalted be He, is the All-Responsive. He answers the supplications of His servants and grants their requests, and He helps the distressed and gives the fearful security. He even responds to those who disbelieve in Him and have never recognized Him!He responds to their calls and removes harm from them out of His bounty and that perhaps they may believe.Most people, however, forget the favors done to them and show ingratitude. Allah Almighty says:{When they board a ship, they supplicate Allah, devoting their faith sincerely to Him. But as soon as He rescues them to the land, they associate partners with Him.}[Surat al-'Ankabūt: 65]

At the doorstep..

When people find all doors closed and things become really hard and distressful, and they find no refuge among other created beings, they innately turn to the Almighty Creator and seek His refuge and protection. They stand humble at His door:{...Then when you are afflicted with hardship, to Him alone you cry out for help.}[Surat an-Nahl: 53]Out of His generosity, bounty, and benevolence, Allah Almighty loves to be asked at times of ease and at times of hardship. If a person knows his Lord at the time of ease, He will know him when he goes through a hardship. The Prophet (may Allah's peace and blessings be upon him) is authentically reported to have said:"Whoever likes Allah to respond to him during hardships and distress, should supplicate Him a lot during the times of ease."[Narrated by Al-Tirmidhi; Hasan (sound)]Imam Ahmad ibn Hanbal was asked: "How much is the distance between us and the Throne of the Most Compassionate?" He replied:"A sincere supplication from a sincere heart."

A Reminder..

The believer should avoid such causes that prevent his supplication from being answered. These include the following:

1. Lack of sincerity.

2. Lack of persistence and insistence in the supplication.

3. Not invoking Allah's peace and blessings upon the Prophet.

4. Expecting a quick answer.

5. Consuming unlawful food or drink or wearing unlawful clothing.

6. Abandoning the duty of enjoining what is good and forbidding what is evil.

The Sunnah specifies certain times at which supplications are most likely to be accepted. These times include the following:

1. Between the Adhān and the Iqāmah (second call to prayer).

2. In the last part of the night.

3. During prostration.

4. The hour during Friday.

5. During travel.

6. Supplication of an oppressed person.

7. Supplication of a parent against his child.

There is much room in this regard, yet when you raise your hands in supplication, remember that this is a favor from the Almighty Lord upon you; He wants to give you. So, think well of Him and be firm in your request. Allah Almighty says:{Your Lord says, "Call upon Me; I will respond to you...}[Surat Ghāfir: 60]'Ali ibn Abi Tālib (may Allah be pleased with him) said:"Lift the multitudes of afflictions by supplication."Anas ibn Mālik (may Allah be pleased with him) said:"Do not fail to supplicate, for indeed none is ruined while he supplicates."Ibn Hajar (may Allah have mercy upon him) said:"Every supplication gets answered. Yet the answers do vary. Sometimes the answer comes in the form of what one has asked for, and at other times in the form of something else in its place."

In You I seek refuge, and in whom else can I seek refuge other than You?! I am weak, my Lord; so strengthen me against my sins, which cannot be forgiven by anyone but You.

I supplicate You to forgive my sins, help me, and guide me. Indeed, no one resorts to You and ends up in disappointment.

Ibn al-Qayyim (may Allah have mercy upon him) said:"It is inappropriate for a servant to ask from other servants while he finds all what he wants with his Almighty Lord."

O Allah, the All-Responsive, answer our supplications, strengthen us, and save us and our parents from Hellfire.

Al-Majīd (The Most Glorious)

Our Lord likes to be praised..

The Prophet (may Allah's peace and blessings be upon him) is authentically reported to have said:"No one likes praise more than Allah does, and for this He promised Paradise." [Narrated by Muslim] Another narration reads: "No one likes praise more than Allah does; that is why He praised Himself."[Narrated by Al-Bukhāri]

Al-Aswad ibn Sarī' reported: "I was a poet and I went to the Prophet (may Allah's peace and blessings be upon him) and said: 'Shall I recite to you some praises that I have written for my Lord?'

He said: 'Your Lord loves praises.' And he said nothing more." [Narrated by Al-Bukhāri in Al-Adab al-Mufrad][Hasan (sound)]

No matter how much we praise You, Your greatness is far bigger.

Our glorification of Allah does not benefit Him, nor does our failure to do so ever harm Him. Indeed, He is Self-Sufficient and Praiseworthy by His very attributes, not due to praise, glorification, or gratitude on the part of His servants.

It is out of Allah's bounty towards us that He made our lives go right when we extend thanks and praise to Him, so that our souls can be purified and reassured in the company of the Almighty Creator.

These letters and this book are part of our glorification of Allah Almighty, which is a favor He has bestowed upon us. I implore Him to accept this from all of us and keep it in store for us when we meet Him on the Day of Judgment.

All praise is due to You and all blessings come from You and the dominion belongs to You. None is more glorious than You.

Allah Almighty says:{...He is Praiseworthy, Most Glorious.}[Surat Hūd: 73]

"Al-Majīd" is derived from "majd", which means complete honor, plenty, and abundance.

Our Lord, Exalted be He, possesses vast bounty and perfect glory. What could possibly be more glorious than Him?!

He is the Owner of glory, pride, majesty, and magnificence. He is Greater, more Majestic, more Exalted, and Higher than everything.

Every attribute of our Lord is perfect in every way. He is the All-Knowing, Whose knowledge is complete. He is the Most Merciful, Whose mercy encompasses all things. He is the Omnipotent, Whose power dominates everything. He is the Forbearing, Whose forbearance is complete. And He is the All-Wise, Whose wisdom is perfect.

All His names and attributes are perfect. Indeed, we cannot praise Him enough. He is as He has praised Himself.

All glory is due to You..

Allah Almighty glorified Himself for His perfection, majesty, and magnificence. In a Qudsi Hadīth, He said:"I am the Compeller, I am the Supreme, I am the King, I am the Exalted; glorifying Himself."[Narrated by Ahmad; Sahīh (authentic)]Our Lord is Praiseworthy for His greatness and glory:{...He is Praiseworthy, Most Glorious.}[Surat Hūd: 73]

He bestows a lot of blessings and favors upon His servants, and He endows His pious servants with the blessing of worshiping and glorifying Him alone.

In a Qudsi Hadīth:"When he says: {Master of the Day of Judgment}, He says: 'My servant has glorified Me.'"[Narrated by Muslim]It is authentically reported that when the Prophet (may Allah's peace and blessings be upon him) raised his head from bowing, he would say:"Rabbana laka al-hamdu mil'a as-samāwāti wa al-ard wa mil'a ma shi'ta min shay'in ba'd, ahla ath-thanā' wa al-majd (Praise be to You, our Lord, as much as what fills the heavens and the earth and what fills anything You will beyond that. You are the One worthy of being praised and glorified)."[Narrated by Muslim]

Be with Him!

From His glory all messengers and prophets derive their glory. Hence, the Companions (may Allah be pleased with them) asked the Prophet (may Allah's peace and blessings be upon him): "We know how to greet you, but how can we invoke Allah's peace upon you?"

He said:"Allāhumma salli 'ala Muhammad wa 'ala āli Muhammad kama sallayta 'ala Ibrāhim wa 'ala āli Ibrāhim innaka hamīdun majīd (O Allah, send Your peace upon Muhammad and upon the family of Muhammad, as You sent Your peace upon Abraham and the family of Abraham; indeed, You are Praiseworthy, Most Glorious)."[Narrated by Al-Bukhāri and Muslim]

The valley of success:

The Qur'an is the word of Allah. It is {...a glorious Qur'an} [Surat al-Burūj: 21], and it is noble, great, and gracious, and it abounds with goodness.

Allah Almighty glorifies Himself in His glorious Qur'an. The greatest verses therein are those that contain praise of Him and mention of His attributes. Examples include the Verse of Al-Kursi in Surat al-Baqarah, and it is the greatest verse in the Book of Allah, and Surat al-Ikhlās, which is the best surah and so meritorious to the extent that the Prophet (may Allah's peace and blessings be upon him) is authentically reported to have said about it:"It is equal to one third of the Qur'an."[Narrated by Muslim]

One of the best methods by which a person can glorify and extol his Lord is to recite His Book day and night and to hold onto it and ponder, understand, and act upon it.

The people of the Qur'an are also the people of Allah who are close to Him. The Prophet (may Allah's peace and blessings be upon him) is authentically reported to have said:"Indeed, Allah elevates some people with this Book and degrades others."[Narrated by Muslim]

'Umar ibn al-Khattāb met Nāfi' ibn al-Hārith - whom he had appointed as a governor of Makkah - in 'Asfān. He asked him: "Whom have you appointed to govern the people of the valley?" He said: "Ibn Abza." He said: "Who is Ibn Abza?" He said: "He is one of our freed slaves." He remarked: "So you have appointed a freed slave over them." He said: "He is a good reciter of the Book of Allah and knowledgeable about the laws of inheritance."

Thereupon, 'Umar (may Allah be pleased with him) said: "Our Prophet (may Allah's peace and blessings be upon him) said:'Indeed, Allah elevates some people with this Book and degrades others.'"[Narrated by Muslim]

So, glory is the share of those who adopt it and act upon it; yet those who turn away from it get nothing but humiliation.

Among the ways of glorifying Allah Almighty is to praise Him and proclaim His greatness and oneness. Whoever sticks to that shall win the good fortune in this world and in the Hereafter.

Abu Hurayrah (may Allah be pleased with him) reported that the Prophet (may Allah's peace and blessings be upon him) said:"Allah has some angels who wander around the roads and paths looking for the people of Dhikr (remembrance of Allah). When they find some people remembering Allah, they call each other saying: 'Come to the object of your pursuit.' Then, the angels encircle them with their wings up to the lowest heaven.

Their Lord asks them - though He knows better than them -: 'What do My servants say?' The angels reply: 'They exalt You, proclaim Your greatness, praise You, and glorify You.'

Allah then says: 'Did they see Me?' The angels reply: 'No, by Allah, they did not see You.'

Allah says: 'What if they saw Me?' The angels reply: 'If they saw You, they would worship You more devoutly and would exalt, glorify, and praise You more.'

Allah says: 'What do they ask Me for?' The angels reply: 'They ask You for Paradise.'

Allah says: 'Did they see it?' The angels say: 'No, by Allah, O Lord, they did not see it.'

Allah says: 'What if they saw it?' The angels say: 'If they saw it, they would be more eager for it, would seek it with greater zeal, and would have a greater desire for it.'

Allah says: 'From what do they seek refuge?' The angels reply: 'They seek refuge from Hellfire.'

Allah says: 'Did they see it?' The angels say: 'No, by Allah, O Lord, they did not see it.'

Allah says: 'What if they saw it?' The angels say: 'If they saw it, they would be more keen to turn away from it and more fearful of it.'

Thereupon, Allah says: 'I make you witnesses that I have forgiven them.'

One of the angels will say: 'There was so-and-so amongst them, and he was not one of them, but he had just come for some need.'

Allah will say: 'These are the people by virtue of whom their companion will not be miserable.'" [Narrated by Al-Bukhāri]

If their companion will not become miserable, then what about the people engaged in Dhikr themselves?!

The Throne:

Allah Almighty describes the Throne above which He established Himself as "glorious". Our Lord only chooses for Himself what is best, most perfect, and most complete. Hence, it is deservedly glorious.

All praise is due to You and all blessings and the dominion belong to You, our Lord.

None is ever more glorious than You.

You are Dominant over the Throne high above the heavens.

All faces fall prostrate and are humble before Your might.

Glory be to the One Whose servants do not appraise Him properly,

the One and Only God, Who is above the Throne.

O Allah, we ask You by Your name "Al-Majīd" to forgive us, our parents, and all Muslims.

Al-Hamīd (The Praiseworthy)

The Prophet (may Allah's peace and blessings be upon him) led his Companions in prayer one day, and as he raised his head from bowing and said: "Sami'allāhu liman hamidah (Allah hears he who praises Him)," a man behind him said: "Rabbana wa laka al-hamd hamdan kathīran tayyiban mubārakan fīh (Our Lord, praise be to You, praise that is abundant, good, and blessed)." When he finished, he asked: "Who said that?" The man said: "Me." He said: "I saw over thirty angels competing to write this down first." [Narrated by Al-Bukhāri] How could they not compete over this while Allah Almighty loves praise?!

We extend all praise to You, our Lord,

though we cannot praise You enough.

Allah Almighty praises Himself saying:{...He is the Guardian, the Praiseworthy.}[Surat ash-Shūra: 28]

Our Lord, Exalted be He, is Praiseworthy in terms of His essence, His names, attributes, and actions. He possesses the most beautiful names and the most sublime attributes, and does the best and most perfect actions.

And our Lord is Praiseworthy in terms of His Shariah, which is the best and most beneficial for all creatures.

Moreover, our Lord is Praiseworthy for His Oneness and for being Exalted above having partners, equals, or supporters due to weakness. Allah Almighty says:{And say, "Praise be to Allah Who has not taken a son, nor does He have any partner in His dominion, nor does He need any protector out of weakness. And proclaim His greatness immensely."}[Surat al-Isrā': 111]Our Lord is praised by all tongues and in every condition. All creatures constantly sing praise of Him, including inanimate objects, for His favors and blessings as well as for His perfection and majesty. Allah Almighty says:{The seven heavens and the earth, and all those in them glorify Him. There is not a single thing that does not glorify Him with His praise, but you do not understand their glorification. Indeed, He is Most Forbearing, All-Forgiving.}[Surat al-Isrā': 44]

The Almighty Lord is worthy of being praised in every form of praise. Even if His creatures did not praise Him, He is still Praiseworthy for His bounty, grace, and mercy.

No one except Him is praised for all conditions and circumstances.

Be humbly submissive to your Lord!

Allah Almighty restricted the praise exclusively to Himself, and prohibited that one should praise himself. He says:{...So do not claim purity for yourselves...}[Surat an-Najm: 32]

Our Lord praises Himself to introduce Himself to us and so that we can turn to Him through praise and hope to receive His forgiveness, bounty, and Paradise.

What a Generous Lord! He guides us to perform good deeds and then appreciates that, and rewards us for it.{...They will be called, "This is Paradise that you are made to inherit for what you used to do."}[Surat al-A'rāf: 43]When our Lord wants to make His bounty manifest upon us, He creates it and attributes it to us. For example, He gives you money, and you spend out of it in charity, and then He appreciates your charity, though the money originally belongs to Him! Out of His kindness, Allah Almighty laid down various forms of praise, so that we know how to praise Him in the best manner. He says:{All praise be to Allah, the Lord of the worlds.}[Surat al-Fātihah: 2] He also says:{All praise be to Allah Who created the heavens and earth, and made darkness and light...}[Surat al-An'ām: 1]

Praise be to You..

The greatest trait in the believers is that they praise their Lord constantly and at both good and hard times, as they know that the actions of Allah Almighty are all wise and good for them.

The Prophet (may Allah's peace and blessings be upon him) is authentically reported to have said:"If a man's child dies, Allah Almighty asks His angels: 'Have you taken the soul of My servant's child?' They reply in the affirmative.

He then asks: 'Have you taken the fruit of his heart?' They reply in the affirmative.

Then He asks: 'What did My servant say?' They say: 'He praised You and said: We belong to Allah and to Him we shall return.'

Thereupon, Allah says: 'Build a house for My servant in Paradise and name it the House of Praise.'"[Narrated by Al-Tirmidhī]Hence, one of the best forms of Dhikr is to say: Alhamdulillāh (Praise be to Allah). Allah Almighty says:{...and glorify the praise of your Lord before sunrise and before sunset.}[Surat Qāf: 39]The Prophet (may Allah's peace and blessings be upon him) is authentically reported to have said:"Whoever says: Subhānallāh wa bihamdih (Glory be to Allah and praise be to Him) one hundred times a day, his sins will be erased even if they were as much as the foam of the sea."[Narrated by Al-Bukhāri and Muslim]

The Prophet (may Allah's peace and blessings be upon him) was asked: "Which speech is the best?"

He said: "What Allah chose for His angels or His servants: Subhānallāh wa bihamdih (Glory be to Allah and praise be to Him)."[Narrated by Muslim]Praise can be expressed by the tongue, within the heart, and through the body organs.The Prophet (may Allah's peace and blessings be upon him) said:"The best servants of Allah on the Day of Judgment will be those who praise Him a lot."[Narrated by Al-Tabarāni in Al-Mu'jam al-Kabīr; Sahīh (authentic)]

Praise be to You, our Lord, praise that is good and so great that it fills the heavens

and the earth and all that it contains.

Praise be to You, eternal and blessed.

The sea has a limit, but Your praise is limitless.

Praise be to You, the Owner of glory and highness.

He who praises You with gratitude is indeed grateful.

O Allah, to You praise is due as befits the glory of Your Face and the greatness of Your might.

Ash-Shākir Ash-Shakūr (The Appreciative - The Ever-Appreciative)

The Prophet (may Allah's peace and blessings be upon him) said:"A man saw a dog eating moist earth on account of (severe) thirst. The man took his shoe (and filled it with water) and kept on pouring the water for the dog till it quenched its thirst. So, Allah appreciated his deed and admitted him into Paradise." [Narrated by Al-Bukhāri]Praising Himself, Allah Almighty says:{...Allah is Appreciative, All-Knowing.}[Surat an-Nisā': 147]He also says:{...Allah is Ever-Appreciative, Forbearing}[Surat at-

Taghābun: 17]Our Lord appreciates our little acts of obedience and gives abundant rewards for them and even multiplies the rewards many times, with no limit.{Whoever comes with a good deed will be rewarded tenfold, but whoever comes with an evil deed will only be punished with its like; and none will be wronged.}[Surat al-An'ām: 160]Our Lord even appreciates our gratitude to Him and in return increases His blessings and bounty towards us.{Whatever blessing you have, it is from Allah...}[Surat an-Nahl: 53]Our Lord also appreciates the deeds of His servants by praising them among His angels and His high company and by making them appreciated amongst other people on earth.{O descendants of those whom We carried [on board] with Noah. He was indeed a grateful slave.}[Surat al-Isrā': 3]Our Lord forgives many sins and accepts small good deeds and gives rewards for them.{...Indeed, our Lord is All-Forgiving, Ever-Appreciative}[Surat Fātir: 34]

Indeed, our Lord bestows a lot of blessings and is pleased with little gratitude.

The Prophet (may Allah's peace and blessings be upon him) said:"Allah is pleased with a person who eats some food and then praises Him for it, or who drinks some drink and then praises Him for it." [Narrated by Muslim]In another Hadīth, the Prophet (may Allah's peace and blessings be upon him) said:"Whoever says in the morning: 'Allāhumma ma asbaha bi min ni'matin faminka wahdaka la sharīka lak, falaka al-hamdu walaka ash-shukr (O Allah, whatever favor has come to me, it comes from You alone, with no partner; so to You praise and thanks are due)', he will have expressed full gratitude of the day; and if anyone says the same in the evening, he will have expressed full gratitude of the night."[Narrated by Abu Dāwūd; Hasan (sound)]

He gives and then shows appreciation!

Out of His perfect appreciation, Allah Almighty gives blessings to us and enables us to do what He appreciates. So, He gives blessings and then shows appreciation, though it all comes from Him. Allah Almighty says:{[And they will be told,] "Indeed, this is your reward, and your efforts have been appreciated."}[Surat al-Insān: 22]Glory be to the One Who bestows upon us the favor of endeavor and enables us to do it and then appreciates our deeds!Indeed, this is the utmost bounty and benevolence.All praise and thanks are due to Him.

He is the Ever-Appreciative Lord, Who does not cause our efforts to go to waste; rather, He rewards them and multiplies the reward countless times.

The greatest recompense..

When Prophet Sulaymān (Solomon) (peace be upon him) slaughtered the horses in anger because they distracted him from remembrance of his Lord, and he wanted to avoid the repetition of that distraction, Allah Almighty gave him the wind in place of the horses.

When Yūsuf (Joseph) (peace be upon him) endured the hardship of imprisonment, Allah Almighty appreciated his patience by putting him in authority.{This is how We established Joseph in the land so that he may settle wherever he wished. We extend Our mercy to whom We will, and We do not let the reward of those who do good to be lost.}[Surat Yūsuf: 56]

And when His messengers (peace be upon them) sacrificed their lives and honor in the cause of their Lord and were, thus, harmed and abused, Allah Almighty compensated them by sending His peace and blessings upon them and by making the angels invoke His peace and blessings upon them. Moreover, He made them laudable in the heavens and among people: {We chose them exclusively for the remembrance of the Final Home.} [Surat Sād: 46]

When the Companions (may Allah be pleased with them) left their homes and got out for the sake of their Lord, He compensated them by His approval and by giving them power and abundance in this world.

He is the Ever-Appreciative. He brings servants out of Hellfire on account of an atom's weight of goodness, and He does not cause this tiny amount to be lost. The Prophet (may Allah's peace and blessings be upon him) said:"While a man was on the way, he found a thorny branch of a tree there on the way and put it aside. Allah appreciated that deed and forgave him." [Narrated by Al-Bukhāri and Muslim]Then, what about those who remove moral hurdles from people's way?! What about those who make things easy for people, remove their distress, help them with their needs, and bring them joy?!It all comes from Allah Almighty and it is His favor upon us from beginning to end.

As Allah Almighty is Ever-Appreciative Himself, the dearest to Him among His servants are the grateful and the most hated to Him are the ungrateful.

Imam Ibn al-Qayyim (may Allah have mercy upon him) said:"Blessings are a trial and test from Allah, as they reveal the thankfulness of the thankful and the ingratitude of the ungrateful."

There are two forms of thankfulness:

1. By the tongue, which is praising the Bestower of favors.

2. By the body organs, which is using them in obeying Allah Almighty.

This is the attitude of all prophets and righteous people.

The Prophet (may Allah's peace and blessings be upon him) used to stand in prayer during the night for so long that his feet would get swelled. 'Ā'ishah (may Allah be pleased with her) once said to him: "Why do you do this although Allah forgave your past and future sins?" Thereupon, he said:"Should I not be a thankful servant?!" [Narrated by Al-Bukhārī]Allah Almighty praised the family of Prophet Dāwūd (David) (peace be upon him) for their gratitude. He says:{..."Do [good deeds] in gratitude, O household of David!"...}[Surat Saba': 13]

As only few of Allah's servants show proper gratitude to Him, which is an act of worship, He ordained upon us to ask Him to enable us to be thankful and to accept that from us.

The Prophet (may Allah's peace and blessings be upon him) instructed Mu'ādh to say this supplication after every prayer:"Allāhumma a'inni 'ala dhikrika wa shukrika wa husni 'ibādatik (O Allah, help me remember You, give thanks to You, and worship You properly)."[Narrated by Abu Dāwūd; Sahīh (authentic)]In another Hadīth, the Prophet (may Allah's peace and blessings be upon him) said:"Rabbi ij'alny laka shakkāran laka dhakkāran (My Lord, make me ever-grateful to You, ever-remembering of You)."[Narrated by Abu Dāwūd; Sahīh (authentic)]Then, consider this guarantee from the Lord of the worlds in case you are grateful to Him. Allah Almighty says:{Why would Allah punish you, if you are grateful and faithful? Allah is Appreciative, All-Knowing.}[Surat an-Nisā': 147]Our gratitude is, in fact, for our own benefit. Allah Almighty says:{...Whoever is grateful, it is only for his own good; and whoever is ungrateful, then Allah is Self-Sufficient, Praiseworthy.}[Surat Luqmān: 12]Whoever wants increase from his Lord should show gratitude to Him:{And [remember] when your Lord declared, "If you are grateful, I will surely give you more...}[Surat Ibrāhīm: 7]How Merciful Allah is!Beware of comparing yourself to others in terms of fortunes and blessings. This would give you nothing but grief and distress. You should rather act upon this verse:{...So hold fast to what I have given you, and be of those who are grateful.}[Surat al-A'rāf: 144]

The key to hearts:

He who is thankful to Allah Almighty should also give thanks to those through whom Allah sends His blessings, most notably his parents:{...Be grateful to Me and to your parents. To Me is the final return.}[Surat Luqmān: 14]The Prophet (may Allah's peace and blessings be upon him) said:"Whoever is not grateful to people is not grateful to Allah."[Narrated by Ahmad; Sahīh (authentic)]

Blessed be the One to Whom His servants fail to show proper gratitude,

for indeed His blessings are limitless and endless.

Those who give thanks need to give thanks for being able to give thanks.

Also, being able to give thanks for the ability to give thanks does itself entail thanks.

Indeed, every blessing and every thanks is a favor after a favor.

O Allah, make us among the thankful, O Lord of the worlds!

Al-Karīm Al-Akram (The Generous - The Most Generous)

The Prophet (may Allah's peace and blessings be upon him) is authentically reported to have said:"I know the last of the inhabitants of Paradise to enter therein and the last of the inhabitants of Hellfire to come out of it. He is a man who will be brought on the Day of Judgment and it will be said: 'Present his minor sins to him and withhold from him his major ones.' Then, the minor sins will be shown to him, and it will be said: 'On such-and-such a day you did so-and-so, and on such- and-such a day, you did so-and-so?'

He will say: 'Yes.' It will not be possible for him to deny, while he will be afraid lest his major sins should be presented before him.

It will be said to him: 'In place of every evil deed, you will have a good deed.' He will say: 'My Lord, I have done things I do not see here.'"

Abu Dharr (may Allah be pleased with him) - the narrator of the Hadīth - said: "I saw the Messenger of Allah (may Allah's peace and blessings be upon him) laugh till his premolar teeth became visible."[Narrated by Muslim]

What a Generous, Forbearing, and Great Lord!

{O mankind, what has lured you away from your Lord, the Generous?}[Surat al-Infitār: 6]{...Whoever is grateful, it is only for his own good; and whoever is ungrateful, then my Lord is Self-Sufficient, Generous.}[Surat an-Naml: 40]

Generosity is a term that comprises all good traits and acts. It does not only mean 'giving'. Scholars expressed various views with regard to the meaning of this name, all of which are right.

Our Lord is the Bestower of abundant blessings and favors. He ceaselessly brings good, and He is Great and Exalted above all deficiencies and defects. He is the Giver of favors and the Owner of grace. He gives without reason and without expecting anything in return. He gives those who are in need and those who are not in need. When He makes a promise, He fulfills it. All needs, big or small, are presented to Him. Indeed, He does not disappoint anyone who resorts to Him. He pardons sins and forgives evil deeds and even turns them into good ones. He gives us before we even ask from Him.

He endowed us with hearing, eyesight, hearts, body organs, strength, and countless talents, apparent and hidden.{...If you try to count the blessings of Allah, you cannot count them. Indeed, mankind is highly unjust and ungrateful.}[Surat Ibrāhīm: 34]He bestows His blessings upon us before we ask Him and even without asking at all, out of His bounty and generosity. He gives us and then appreciates what we do.

Our Generous Lord is the One Who pardons while possessing supreme might, and when He makes a promise, He fulfills it. He promised to give the believers various kinds of blessings, fortunes, and welfare in this world and in the Hereafter.

More than that, He even makes the punishment of the sinners subject to His will; He may punish or forgive them if He so wills.

Our Lord is the One Who does not turn down a supplicant. He is "Modest, Generous."

He gives and then shows appreciation:

He gives faith and then appreciates it:{...but Allah guides whom He wills. Whatever wealth you spend in charity, it is for your own good – as long as you do so seeking Allah's pleasure. And whatever wealth you spend in charity, you will be rewarded in full, and you will not be wronged. }[Surat al-Baqarah: 272]Al-Junayd heard a man reciting:{...We truly found him patient – an excellent and faithful slave he was. He constantly turned [to Us].}[Surat Sād: 44]Thereupon, he said: "Glory be to Allah! He gave and then praised." In other words, He endowed him with patience and then praised him for that.

To Allah I extend my praise and thanks.

All praise is due to our Lord.

I testify that other than Allah there is no god.

He is Generous, Merciful, and upon Him we pin our hopes.

Glory be to Him, Who is Most Generous!

Generosity and bounty are among His greatest attributes, and His giving never ceases. Could there ever be someone who is more bountiful than Him?!

He is the Generous Lord:

His servants disobey Him as He watches over them, and He still preserves and takes care of them as they move and sleep as if they did not commit a sin. He bestows His favors even upon sinners and wrongdoers. Who is that who supplicates Him and He does not respond to him?!Who is that who asks from Him and He does not give him?!And who is that who stands at His door and He drives him away?!He is the Owner of grace and Giver of favors. He is the Most Generous and all bounty comes from Him.

He does not need thanks..

Our Lord, Exalted be He, does not need our gratitude. Indeed, our thankfulness does not benefit Him at all, nor does ingratitude harm Him in any way. Nonetheless, He is Generous as He does not hasten to inflict punishment upon those who deserve it.{...And whoever is ungrateful, then my Lord is Self-Sufficient, Generous.}[Surat an-Naml: 40]Out of His perfect self-sufficiency and generosity, He created His servants to worship Him and undertakes to provide for all of them, humans and jinn, believers and disbelievers.{I have not created the jinn and mankind except to worship Me.I seek no provision from them, nor do I want them to feed Me.Indeed, it is Allah Who is the All-Provider, Lord of Power, the Strong.}[Surat adh-Dhāriyāt: 56-58]

He gives more than we wish..

Indeed, no request or supplication whatsoever is too great for Allah Almighty to grant and answer. He is the Magnificent, the Generous. The Prophet (may Allah's peace and blessings be upon him) is authentically reported to have said:"When anyone of you supplicates, he should not say: 'O Allah, forgive me if You will.' But he should be determined in his request and ask persistently for what he desires for no bounty is too great for Allah to bestow."[Narrated by Muslim]Another aspect of Allah's generosity is that He made supplication the most noble act of worship in His sight. The Prophet (may Allah's peace and blessings be upon him) is authentically reported to have said:"Nothing is more honorable in the sight of Allah than supplication."[Narrated by Ibn Mājah; Hasan (sound)]Think about His supreme generosity. The Prophet (may Allah's peace and blessings be upon him) said:"Verily, Allah is Modest and Generous. He is too Modest to turn down His servant empty-handed when he raises his hands (in supplication) to Him."[Narrated by Al-Tirmidhi; Sahīh (authentic)]His generosity will remain enduring and ceaseless till we meet Him. Here is the greatest favor and gift you will receive on the Day of Judgment, if you are a believer:{Such are the true believers; they will have high ranks with their Lord, and forgiveness and an honorable provision.}[Surat al-Anfāl: 4]He even gives more than we wish. In a Qudsi Hadīth, Allah Almighty said:"I have prepared for My righteous servants what no eye has ever seen, no ear has ever heard, and no human mind has ever imagined." [Narrated by Al-Bukhāri and Muslim] Indeed, what is even better than all of this is looking at His noble Face.{On that Day some faces will be bright,looking at their Lord.}[Surat al-Qiyāmah: 22-23]

Think about His supreme generosity. The Prophet (may Allah's peace and blessings be upon him) said:

"Verily, Allah is Modest and Generous. He is too Modest to turn down His servant empty-handed when he raises his hands (in supplication) to Him."

[Narrated by Al-Tirmidhi; Sahīh (authentic)]

His generosity will remain enduring and ceaseless till we meet Him. Here is the greatest favor and gift you will receive on the Day of Judgment, if you are a believer:

{Such are the true believers; they will have high ranks with their Lord, and forgiveness and an honorable provision.}

[Surat al-Anfāl: 4]

He even gives more than we wish. In a Qudsi Hadīth, Allah Almighty said:

"I have prepared for My righteous servants what no eye has ever seen, no ear has ever heard, and no human mind has ever imagined." [Narrated by Al-Bukhāri and Muslim] Indeed, what is even better than all of this is looking at His noble Face.

{On that Day some faces will be bright,

looking at their Lord.}

[Surat al-Qiyāmah: 22-23]

O Allah, make us among them, O the Most Generous of those who are generous!

The criterion:

The criterion according to which a person will be honored or humiliated on the Day of Judgment is piety.{...Indeed, the most noble of you before Allah is the most righteous among you...}[Surat al-Hujurāt: 13]The disbelievers do not deserve honor, only humiliation:{...But there are many on whom the punishment has become due. Whoever Allah disgraces, none can honor him. Allah surely does what He wills.}[Surat al-Hajj: 18]The criteria commonly used by people in this world do not matter. Allah Almighty says about them:{As for man, when he is tested by his Lord by honoring him and bestowing blessings upon him, he says, "My Lord has [deservedly] honored me!"But when he is tested by restricting his provision, he says, "My Lord has [undeservedly] humiliated me!"}[Surat al-Fajr: 15-16]Ibn al-Jawzi (may Allah have mercy upon him) said:"One of the methods by which Satan deceives ordinary people is that when they commit sins and get criticized for that, they say: Indeed, our Lord is Generous, and His pardon is vast!"

{...Indeed, the most noble of you before Allah is the most righteous among you...}

[Surat al-Hujurāt: 13]

The disbelievers do not deserve honor, only humiliation:

{...But there are many on whom the punishment has become due. Whoever Allah disgraces, none can honor him. Allah surely does what He wills.}

[Surat al-Hajj: 18]

The criteria commonly used by people in this world do not matter. Allah Almighty says about them:

{As for man, when he is tested by his Lord by honoring him and bestowing blessings upon him, he says, "My Lord has [deservedly] honored me!"

But when he is tested by restricting his provision, he says, "My Lord has [undeservedly] humiliated me!"}

[Surat al-Fajr: 15-16]

Ibn al-Jawzi (may Allah have mercy upon him) said:

"One of the methods by which Satan deceives ordinary people is that when they commit sins and get criticized for that, they say: Indeed, our Lord is Generous, and His pardon is vast!"

A Reminder..

He who gets attached to the Qur'an is given the glad tidings of being granted honor in this world and in the Hereafter. Allah Almighty says:{This is indeed a noble Qur'an.}[Surat al-Wāqi'ah: 77]It abounds with goodness and knowledge. Its memorizer gets protected and its reciter gets honored.Our Generous Lord rescues people from drowning, causes those who have been absent to return home, grants recovery to the afflicted, supports the oppressed, guides the astray, enriches the poor, cures the sick, and gives relief to the distressed. He likes to be supplicated by His names. When distressed, the Prophet (may Allah's peace and blessings be upon him) used to say:"La ilāha illallāh Al-'Azhīm Al-Halīm, la ilāha illallāh Rabbu al-'arshi al-'azhīm, la ilāha illallāh Rabbu as-samāwāti wa Rabbu al-ardi wa Rabbu al-'arshi al-Karīm (There is no god except Allah, the Magnificent, the Forbearing. There is no god except Allah, the Lord of the Mighty Throne. There is no god except Allah, the Lord of the heavens, the earth, and the Honorable Throne)."[Narrated by Al-Bukhāri and Muslim]Allah Almighty loves the generous. Ibn Rajab (may Allah have mercy upon him) said:"If a person treats others generously, Allah will treat him generously and graciously. Indeed, recompense is of the same type of the action."

{This is indeed a noble Qur'an.}

[Surat al-Wāqi'ah: 77]

It abounds with goodness and knowledge. Its memorizer gets protected and its reciter gets honored.

Our Generous Lord rescues people from drowning, causes those who have been absent to return home, grants recovery to the afflicted, supports the oppressed, guides the astray, enriches the poor, cures the sick, and gives relief to the distressed. He likes to be supplicated by His names. When distressed, the Prophet (may Allah's peace and blessings be upon him) used to say:

"La ilāha illallāh Al-'Azhīm Al-Halīm, la ilāha illallāh Rabbu al-'arshi al-'azhīm, la ilāha illallāh Rabbu as-samāwāti wa Rabbu al-ardi wa Rabbu al-'arshi al-Karīm (There is no god except Allah, the Magnificent, the Forbearing. There is no god except Allah, the Lord of the Mighty Throne. There is no god except Allah, the Lord of the heavens, the earth, and the Honorable Throne)."

[Narrated by Al-Bukhāri and Muslim]

Allah Almighty loves the generous. Ibn Rajab (may Allah have mercy upon him) said:

"If a person treats others generously, Allah will treat him generously and graciously. Indeed, recompense is of the same type of the action."

O Lord, You are All-Knowing of all things. Nothing is hidden from You. I implore You to grant us safety at times of afflictions and severe hardships. I present all my needs to You, with Whom hearts feel reassured. I have no other door but the door of my Lord, the Generous, the Bestower of favors, the Beneficent, the All-Subtle. O King of the kings, forgive my sins.

You are our Beloved One, my Lord. You cover our faults and answer our supplications. My sins kept me away from You. But I have none but You to forgive and heal me.

O Allah, the Generous, honor us by Your Paradise, pardon, and pleasure.

Al-Muqīt (The Keeper)

The Prophet (may Allah's peace and blessings be upon him) is authentically reported to have said:"Allah Almighty says: 'O son of Adam, devote yourself to My worship, and I will fill your heart with sufficiency and remove your poverty; but if you do not do that, I will fill your heart with worldly concerns and will not remove your poverty.'"[Narrated by Al-Tirmidhi; Sahīh (authentic)]In another Hadīth, the Prophet (may Allah's peace and blessings be upon him) said:"Allah's Hand is full, and this is not affected by the continuous spending day and night. Do you see what He has spent since He created the heavens and the earth? Yet all that has not decreased what is in His Hand."[Narrated by Al-Bukhāri - this is his wording - and Muslim]

"Allah Almighty says: 'O son of Adam, devote yourself to My worship, and I will fill your heart with sufficiency and remove your poverty; but if you do not do that, I will fill your heart with worldly concerns and will not remove your poverty.'"

[Narrated by Al-Tirmidhi; Sahīh (authentic)]

In another Hadīth, the Prophet (may Allah's peace and blessings be upon him) said:

"Allah's Hand is full, and this is not affected by the continuous spending day and night. Do you see what He has spent since He created the heavens and the earth? Yet all that has not decreased what is in His Hand."

[Narrated by Al-Bukhāri - this is his wording - and Muslim]

The heavens and the earth are sustained by Him, and He sets aright the affairs of this world and the Hereafter. Everything is submissive to Him and subject to His authority.

Sovereignty belongs to Him, and in His Hand are all the keys and destinies of all things, and to Him is the final destination of His servants. All glory and dominion belong to Him. None can withhold what He gives, and none can give what He withholds.

Would the Generous, All-Powerful, Most Merciful Lord, and the Keeper be unable to drive to you food and drink to sustain your life?!

It gives us pleasure to spend some time with one of Allah's beautiful names, namely "Al-Muqīt".

Allah Almighty says:{Whoever intercedes in a good cause will have a share in its reward, but whoever intercedes in an evil cause will have a share in its burden. And Allah is ever Watchful over all things.}[Surat an-Nisā': 85]

{Whoever intercedes in a good cause will have a share in its reward, but whoever intercedes in an evil cause will have a share in its burden. And Allah is ever Watchful over all things.}

[Surat an-Nisā': 85]

"Al-Muqīt" is the Supreme Determiner Who created sustenance.

"Al-Muqīt" is also the All-Preserver Who gives according to the amount needed for preservation.

Our Lord, Exalted be He, is the One Who drives to every living being its sustenance, and He directs this matter as He wills, according to His wisdom and grace.

Every created being needs a certain sustenance. Our bodies need food and drink, and our souls need knowledge. The sustenance of the angels, on the other hand, is glorification of Allah.

Allah Almighty is the Keeper and Preserver of His servants. He watches over their conditions and is All-Aware of them.

The Almighty Lord takes care of the interests of His creatures. He gives them food and provides for them.

The best provision indeed is the mind. Whoever is endowed with a good mind has been honored by his Lord.

My Lord, You are the Owner of grace that encompasses all creation.

Your supreme generosity reaches all that exists.

If another being were to own Your treasures,

which increase as You spend therefrom, he would have acted stingily.

My Lord, I seek refuge with You from our bad deeds,

and from depriving us of Your favors and blessings.

Rest assured!

Do not be concerned about what Allah Almighty has guaranteed for you for He describes Himself as the Keeper and the All-Provider.

"Al-Muqīt" is more specific than "Ar-Razzāq", for Al-Muqīt gives us food that nourishes our bodies, while Ar-Razzāq gives us all what we possess, food and everything else

As long as we are alive, sustenance and provision will surely come to us. If, out of His wisdom, He closes a certain door before you, He opens another, out of His mercy.

Think about the fetus. Its sustenance, which is blood, reaches it through one way: the navel. Then, after it comes out of its mother's womb, this way is severed and two other ways are opened for him in its place, through which better and more pleasant sustenance comes: pure and palatable milk. Then, after the phase of suckling is over, four new ways open for him, from which he gets two kinds of food and two kinds of drink. The two kinds of food come from animals and plants, whereas the two kinds of drink are water and milk.

Then, after he dies, these four ways are closed and the eight gates of Paradise are opened for the believers and they can enter from whichever gate they wish.

Be thankful!

Indeed, the blessings of Allah Almighty are countless and numberless:{...If you try to count the blessings of Allah, you cannot count them. Indeed, mankind is highly unjust and ungrateful.}[Surat Ibrāhim: 34]Our Lord bestows favors upon us even though He does not need us, fear us, or expect anything in return from us. Rather, He gives us out of benevolence, bounty, and kindness from Him.{I have not created the jinn and mankind except to worship Me.I seek no provision from them, nor do I want them to feed Me.Indeed, it is Allah Who is the All-Provider, Lord of Power, the Strong.}[Surat adh-Dhāriyāt: 56-58]Many people are ungrateful, however.{They know Allah's favors, yet they deny them, and most of them are ungrateful.}[Surat an-Nahl: 83]He gives you although you have no right upon Him, and after that you deny His rights! He bestows favors upon you without you doing Him any favor, and then you show ingratitude to Him!{Woe to man; how ungrateful he is!}[Surat 'Abasa: 17]The blessings of Allah Almighty reach you in a successive manner. When you ask from Him, He gives you; when you supplicate Him, He responds to you; and when you seek His help, He extends help to you. You cannot become self-sufficient except through Him. Hence, if you give thanks for these blessings, you still need to thank Him for another blessing; that He has enabled you to show gratitude.{And [remember] when your Lord declared, 'If you are grateful, I will surely give you more...}[Surat Ibrāhim: 7]

{...If you try to count the blessings of Allah, you cannot count them. Indeed, mankind is highly unjust and ungrateful.}

[Surat Ibrāhim: 34]

Our Lord bestows favors upon us even though He does not need us, fear us, or expect anything in return from us. Rather, He gives us out of benevolence, bounty, and kindness from Him.

{I have not created the jinn and mankind except to worship Me.

I seek no provision from them, nor do I want them to feed Me.

Indeed, it is Allah Who is the All-Provider, Lord of Power, the Strong.}

[Surat adh-Dhāriyāt: 56-58]

Many people are ungrateful, however.

{They know Allah's favors, yet they deny them, and most of them are ungrateful.}

[Surat an-Nahl: 83]

He gives you although you have no right upon Him, and after that you deny His rights! He bestows favors upon you without you doing Him any favor, and then you show ingratitude to Him!

{Woe to man; how ungrateful he is!}

[Surat 'Abasa: 17]

The blessings of Allah Almighty reach you in a successive manner. When you ask from Him, He gives you; when you supplicate Him, He responds to you; and when you seek His help, He extends help to you. You cannot become self-sufficient except through Him. Hence, if you give thanks for these blessings, you still need to thank Him for another blessing; that He has enabled you to show gratitude.

{And [remember] when your Lord declared, 'If you are grateful, I will surely give you more...}

[Surat Ibrāhim: 7]

The pillars of self-sufficiency:

If man had a valley of gold, he would wish to have two valleys.

Happiness does not lie in having abundant worldly possessions. In fact, happiness comes when a person only has food for his day, good health, and security. The Prophet (may Allah's peace and blessings be upon him) is authentically reported to have said:"Whoever among you wakes up in the morning – secure in his dwelling, healthy in his body, and has his food for the day, it is as if the whole world has been given to him."[Narrated by Al-Tirmidhi; Hasan (sound)]

"Whoever among you wakes up in the morning – secure in his dwelling, healthy in his body, and has his food for the day, it is as if the whole world has been given to him."

[Narrated by Al-Tirmidhi; Hasan (sound)]

The way of the righteous..

The believer feels reassured for he knows that Allah is the Keeper and the Provider and that his sustenance is predestined, so he will not die until he has taken it in full. Therefore, he makes his effort while relying upon his Lord and disowning his own power and ability. His heart is deeply attached to Allah, the Keeper, the All-Provider. He knows that he has no true power or strength except through Allah Almighty.

The Prophet (may Allah's peace and blessings be upon him) reported that Allah Almighty said:"O My servants, all of you are hungry except those I feed; so, ask Me for food and I will feed you." [Narrated by Muslim]Ibn Rajab (may Allah have mercy upon him) said:"One of the righteous predecessors used to ask Allah in his prayer for all his needs, even the salt for his dough and the fodder for his sheep."

"O My servants, all of you are hungry except those I feed; so, ask Me for food and I will feed you." [Narrated by Muslim]

Ibn Rajab (may Allah have mercy upon him) said:

"One of the righteous predecessors used to ask Allah in his prayer for all his needs, even the salt for his dough and the fodder for his sheep."

If a person recalls Allah's name "Al-Muqīt", feels that He is always with Him, and puts his trust in His provision, he will attain eternal bliss, which is content in this world and in the Hereafter.

Yet, the Prophet (may Allah's peace and blessings be upon him) warned us not to give the food needed by one's family to others in pursuit of Allah's reward, for this charity turns into a sin when a person neglects those under his care and upon whom he is required to spend, including his dependents and slaves. Indeed, expenditure is linked to the rights of people, and a person's dependents are more in need for his spending and their right upon him is stronger. The Prophet (may Allah's peace and blessings be upon him) is authentically reported to have said:"It is a sufficient sin for a man to neglect those he maintains."[Abu Dāwūd; Hasan (sound)]

"It is a sufficient sin for a man to neglect those he maintains."

[Abu Dāwūd; Hasan (sound)]

Out of his great concern and care for his family, the Prophet (may Allah's peace and blessings be upon him) used to store for them the food of a whole year. It is reported that the Prophet (may Allah's peace and blessings be upon him) used to sell the palm-trees of Banu al-Nadīr and store for his family their food for a whole year. [Narrated by Al-Bukhārī]

The Prophet (may Allah's peace and blessings be upon him) used to supplicate Allah Almighty saying:"Allāhumma ij'al rizqa āli Muhammad qūtan (O Allah, make the provision of the family of Muhammad sufficient for them)."[Narrated by Muslim]It means: Make their sustenance sufficient for them so that they do not get affected by poverty or humiliated by having to beg others. Also, do not give them worldly abundance lest they should incline to it, for the worldly life is transient while the Hereafter is everlasting. So, he preferred the everlasting over the transient. May Allah's peace and blessings be upon him and those who follow his guidance till the Day of Judgment.

"Allāhumma ij'al rizqa āli Muhammad qūtan (O Allah, make the provision of the family of Muhammad sufficient for them)."

[Narrated by Muslim]

It means: Make their sustenance sufficient for them so that they do not get affected by poverty or humiliated by having to beg others. Also, do not give them worldly abundance lest they should incline to it, for the worldly life is transient while the Hereafter is everlasting. So, he preferred the everlasting over the transient. May Allah's peace and blessings be upon him and those who follow his guidance till the Day of Judgment.

'O Allah, we implore You by Your name "Al-Muqīt" to provide for us from Your vast bounty and help us remember and worship You properly and be grateful servants to You.

Al-Wāsi' (The All-Encompassing)

When the believers learn about Allah's name "Al-Wāsi'", their hearts get attached to His remembrance and they long to see Him. Indeed, their hearts can only be satisfied by being humbly submissive to Him, performing Tawāf (circumambulation) around His House, standing in prayer to Him, getting out of bed for His sake, and sacrificing everything in His cause. Allah Almighty says:{...But My mercy encompasses everything...}[Surat al-A'rāf: 156]He also says:{...Allah gives kingship to whom He wills, and Allah is All-Encompassing, All-Knowing.}[Surat al-Baqarah: 247]

{...But My mercy encompasses everything...}

[Surat al-A'rāf: 156]

He also says:

{...Allah gives kingship to whom He wills, and Allah is All-Encompassing, All-Knowing.}

[Surat al-Baqarah: 247]

Our Lord is the All-Encompassing, the Self-Sufficient. His self-sufficiency and generous giving encompass all His creation.

He is the All-Encompassing in His essence, names, attributes, actions, dominion, and authority. No one can extend adequate praise to Him. He is as He has praised Himself. No matter how His servants try to describe Him, they would never be able to come close to His true nature or encompass Him in their knowledge.

Our Lord encompasses all things in His knowledge:{...Our Lord has full knowledge of everything...}[Surat al-A'rāf: 89]Nothing whatsoever is hidden from Him, Exalted be He. He hears the creeping of a black ant on a solid rock in a dark night. Everything in the heavens and the earth is known to Him.His knowledge comprises the secrets of the hearts and the good or evil intents contained therein.{He knows the sneaky glances of the eyes and what the hearts conceal.}[Surat Ghāfir: 19]{...And know that Allah knows what is in your hearts, so be cautious of Him and know that Allah is All-Forgiving, Forbearing.}[Surat al-Baqarah: 235]Our Lord, Exalted be He, is All-Encompassing in His forgiveness. He forgives all those who repent and return to Him, no matter how great their sins may be.{...Indeed, your Lord is ample in forgiveness...}[Surat an-Najm: 32]Our Lord is All-Encompassing as He provides much room for His servants with regard to the religion and does not charge them with things beyond their capacity.{To Allah belong the east and the west; wherever you turn, there is the Face of Allah. For Allah is All-Encompassing, the All-Knowing.}[Surat al-Baqarah: 115]

{...Our Lord has full knowledge of everything...}

[Surat al-A'rāf: 89]

Nothing whatsoever is hidden from Him, Exalted be He. He hears the creeping of a black ant on a solid rock in a dark night. Everything in the heavens and the earth is known to Him.

His knowledge comprises the secrets of the hearts and the good or evil intents contained therein.

{He knows the sneaky glances of the eyes and what the hearts conceal.}

[Surat Ghāfir: 19]

{...And know that Allah knows what is in your hearts, so be cautious of Him and know that Allah is All-Forgiving, Forbearing.}

[Surat al-Baqarah: 235]

Our Lord, Exalted be He, is All-Encompassing in His forgiveness. He forgives all those who repent and return to Him, no matter how great their sins may be.

{...Indeed, your Lord is ample in forgiveness...}

[Surat an-Najm: 32]

Our Lord is All-Encompassing as He provides much room for His servants with regard to the religion and does not charge them with things beyond their capacity.

{To Allah belong the east and the west; wherever you turn, there is the Face of Allah. For Allah is All-Encompassing, the All-Knowing.}

[Surat al-Baqarah: 115]

I testify that there is no god other than Allah.

He is Generous, Merciful, and upon Him we pin our hopes.

When He is asked, He gives abundantly.

And He removes harms and afflictions.

Indeed, He bestows generous favors upon His servants,

making them self-sufficient and satisfied.

No matter how much we praise Him,

He is far Greater and more Majestic.

The All-Encompassing Lord suffices you against your distress!

If we understand the meaning of Allah's name "Al-Wāsi'", our fears will go away and be replaced with tranquility and hope within our hearts.

When the farmer who finds the harvest of his crop delayed, as the water becomes scarce and his need for his fruits increases every day, knows that Allah is All-Encompassing, All-Knowing, he looks up to the sky, gets attached to his Lord, and calls out: O Allah, the All-Encompassing in giving, the All-Encompassing in mercy and generosity, give me from Your blessings and favors.

And when the barren man, who is greatly grieved and distressed due to his unfulfilled need for a child to play with and to fill his life, remembers that Allah is the All-Encompassing, the Most Generous, Who does not turn down a supplicant, a new life emerges within him and he calls out:{...My Lord, grant me by Your grace virtuous offspring...}[Surat Āl 'Imrān: 38]{..."My Lord, do not leave me childless, for You are the Best of the Inheritors."So We answered his prayer and gave him John, and made his wife fertile. They used to hasten in doing good deeds and used to call upon Us with hope and fear, and they were humble before Us.}[Surat al-Anbiyā': 89-90]And the sick person who suffers severe pains, when he remembers that Allah is the All-Encompassing Giver, the Healer, and the One Who grants His servants sufficiency, he calls out:{...I have been struck by adversity, and You are the Most Merciful of those who show mercy.}[Surat al-Anbiyā': 83]

{...My Lord, grant me by Your grace virtuous offspring...}

[Surat Āl 'Imrān: 38]

{..."My Lord, do not leave me childless, for You are the Best of the Inheritors."

So We answered his prayer and gave him John, and made his wife fertile. They used to hasten in doing good deeds and used to call upon Us with hope and fear, and they were humble before Us.}

[Surat al-Anbiyā': 89-90]

And the sick person who suffers severe pains, when he remembers that Allah is the All-Encompassing Giver, the Healer, and the One Who grants His servants sufficiency, he calls out:

{...I have been struck by adversity, and You are the Most Merciful of those who show mercy.}

[Surat al-Anbiyā': 83]

Allah Almighty, thus, removes the grief and distress and grants the remedy. Indeed, He is the All-Encompassing Lord.

The person in heavy debt feels greatly anguished and thinks that there is no way out of his tough problem. Yet behold! Allah opens up his heart and makes him resort to Him, the All-Encompassing, the Most Generous and he, thus, calls out: O You Who fulfill our needs and You are All-Encompassing in Your giving!{Is He [not better] Who responds to the distressed when he calls out to Him, and Who relieves suffering...}[Surat an-Naml: 62]In response, Allah Almighty helps him repay his debt and He provides for him from where he does not expect. Then, the smile appears on his face and he feels calm and tranquil.{Say, "Allah rescues you from it and from every distress...}[Surat al-An'ām: 64]

{Is He [not better] Who responds to the distressed when he calls out to Him, and Who relieves suffering...}

[Surat an-Naml: 62]

In response, Allah Almighty helps him repay his debt and He provides for him from where he does not expect. Then, the smile appears on his face and he feels calm and tranquil.

{Say, "Allah rescues you from it and from every distress...}

[Surat al-An'ām: 64]

The scholar may experience a tough problem and he finds the solution elusive and does not know the right thing to do. At this point, he stands in humiliation before his Lord, implores Him, and calls out: O You Who are All-Encompassing in Your giving and knowledge. O You Who taught Abraham, teach me! O You Who granted understanding to Solomon, grant me understanding!

Thereupon, help and success arrive and the problem gets solved out of the bounty of Allah, the All-Encompassing.

The husband and wife fall in dispute and get separated, destroying all bonds of love between them. Thereafter, each of them goes through a hard time after divorce. But then, they resort to their Lord, the All-Encompassing.

Thereupon, He compensates each of them by someone better than his or her previous spouse:{But if they choose to separate, Allah will compensate both out of His abundance, for Allah is All-Encompassing, All-Wise.}[Surat an-Nisā': 130]

{But if they choose to separate, Allah will compensate both out of His abundance, for Allah is All-Encompassing, All-Wise.}

[Surat an-Nisā': 130]

The deal is profitable..

Fearing poverty, a person may refrain from spending and it all goes back to the devil's whispering to him that he will be in trouble and need and calls upon him to be stingy.{Satan threatens you with poverty and orders you to commit shameful acts, but Allah promises you forgiveness and bounty from Him. And Allah is All-Encompassing, All-Knowing.}[Surat al-Baqarah: 268]And then the believer remembers that Allah, the All-Encompassing and the Generous, has made this promise:{Who is it that will lend to Allah a goodly loan, so He will multiply it for him manifold? It is Allah Who withholds and gives in abundance, and to Him you will be returned.}[Surat al-Baqarah: 245]And he remembers this verse:{Say, "All bounty is in the Hand of Allah; He grants it to whom He wills. And Allah is All-Encompassing, All-Knowing."}[Surat Āl 'Imrān: 73]Thereupon, he spends out of his money, giving a goodly loan to his Lord, being sure that Allah Almighty will compensate him in this world and in the Hereafter. As a result, he begins to receive abundant mercy and blessings from the All-Encompassing and Most Generous Lord.

{Satan threatens you with poverty and orders you to commit shameful acts, but Allah promises you forgiveness and bounty from Him. And Allah is All-Encompassing, All-Knowing.}

[Surat al-Baqarah: 268]

And then the believer remembers that Allah, the All-Encompassing and the Generous, has made this promise:

{Who is it that will lend to Allah a goodly loan, so He will multiply it for him manifold? It is Allah Who withholds and gives in abundance, and to Him you will be returned.}

[Surat al-Baqarah: 245]

And he remembers this verse:

{Say, "All bounty is in the Hand of Allah; He grants it to whom He wills. And Allah is All-Encompassing, All-Knowing."}

[Surat Āl 'Imrān: 73]

Thereupon, he spends out of his money, giving a goodly loan to his Lord, being sure that Allah Almighty will compensate him in this world and in the Hereafter. As a result, he begins to receive abundant mercy and blessings from the All-Encompassing and Most Generous Lord.

The tears of the fearful..

When the believer remembers his great sins and numerous misdeeds, he feels so sad and his eyes begin to shed tears profusely out of fear from the All-Powerful God. Yet, at this point, he recalls the verse that says:{...But My mercy encompasses everything...}[Surat al-A'rāf: 156]And the verse that says:{...Indeed, your Lord is ample in forgiveness...}[Surat an-Najm: 32]Thereupon, he declares his repentance and returns to his Lord hoping to be included in this verse where Allah Almighty says:{Except those who repent and believe, and do righteous deeds; for them Allah will change their evil deeds into good deeds, for Allah is All-Forgiving, Most Merciful.}[Surat al-Furqān: 70]Moreover, he recalls the invocation made by the angels:{...Our Lord, Your mercy and knowledge encompass everything, so forgive those who repent and follow Your way, and protect them from the punishment of the Blazing Fire.}[Surat Ghāfir: 7]So, repentance eliminates agony within his heart and the pain in his soul, and Allah makes him one of those who often repent and purify themselves and then endows him with uprightness till he passes away, after which he enters Paradise, where he will hear:{Indeed, this is Our provision [for the righteous] that will never cease.}[Surat Sād: 54]

{...But My mercy encompasses everything...}

[Surat al-A'rāf: 156]

And the verse that says:

{...Indeed, your Lord is ample in forgiveness...}

[Surat an-Najm: 32]

Thereupon, he declares his repentance and returns to his Lord hoping to be included in this verse where Allah Almighty says:

{Except those who repent and believe, and do righteous deeds; for them Allah will change their evil deeds into good deeds, for Allah is All-Forgiving, Most Merciful.}

[Surat al-Furqān: 70]

Moreover, he recalls the invocation made by the angels:

{...Our Lord, Your mercy and knowledge encompass everything, so forgive those who repent and follow Your way, and protect them from the punishment of the Blazing Fire.}

[Surat Ghāfir: 7]

So, repentance eliminates agony within his heart and the pain in his soul, and Allah makes him one of those who often repent and purify themselves and then endows him with uprightness till he passes away, after which he enters Paradise, where he will hear:

{Indeed, this is Our provision [for the righteous] that will never cease.}

[Surat Sād: 54]

Messages..

Our Lord is the All-Encompassing Whose mercy encompasses all creation.{...Your Lord is the possessor of infinite mercy...}[Surat al-An'ām: 147]Allah Almighty has made His religion easy for people and removed undue restrictions and hardships from them. He eases the duties for the sick, the travelers, the elderly, and those who have valid excuses. He does not charge them with things beyond their capacity.{...No soul is obligated beyond what it can bear...}[Surat al-Baqarah: 233]And he who finds the land restricted for him should know that Allah has made the land broad for His servants. He says:{...And Allah's earth is spacious...}[Surat az-Zumar: 10]The most encompassing favor Allah bestows upon His servants is patience. The Prophet (may Allah's peace and blessings be upon him) is authentically reported to have said:"Whoever tries to be patient, Allah will give him patience, and no one is given a better or a more encompassing gift than patience."[Narrated by Al-Bukhāri - this is his wording - and Muslim]

{...Your Lord is the possessor of infinite mercy...}

[Surat al-An'ām: 147]

Allah Almighty has made His religion easy for people and removed undue restrictions and hardships from them. He eases the duties for the sick, the travelers, the elderly, and those who have valid excuses. He does not charge them with things beyond their capacity.

{...No soul is obligated beyond what it can bear...}

[Surat al-Baqarah: 233]

And he who finds the land restricted for him should know that Allah has made the land broad for His servants. He says:

{...And Allah's earth is spacious...}

[Surat az-Zumar: 10]

The most encompassing favor Allah bestows upon His servants is patience. The Prophet (may Allah's peace and blessings be upon him) is authentically reported to have said:

"Whoever tries to be patient, Allah will give him patience, and no one is given a better or a more encompassing gift than patience."

[Narrated by Al-Bukhāri - this is his wording - and Muslim]

Patience is involved in all matters related to worship. A person needs patience to perform acts of obedience, refrain from sins, and endure the afflictions predestined for him. Indeed, our life requires patience all the way until we meet our Lord, Exalted be He.

Al-Hasan al-Basri (may Allah have mercy upon him) said:"Patience is one of the treasures of goodness, which Allah does not give except to a servant who is honorable in His sight."

"Patience is one of the treasures of goodness, which Allah does not give except to a servant who is honorable in His sight."

O Allah, You succor Your servants after they become hopeless,

show mercy to those who extend their hands to You in total need and submission.

You have accustomed them to Your generous giving without a reason,

except for a good hope in You to which they are clinging.

O Allah, the All-Encompassing Bestower, give everyone of us more than what we have asked for; indeed, You are competent over everything.

--

Ar-Raqīb (The Ever-Watchful)

Ibn al-Jawzi (may Allah have mercy upon him) said:"If one reforms his inner self, the fragrance of his benevolence will exude, and people's hearts will smell his good scent. How important our inner selves are! When an inner self is corrupt, the good outside will be of no avail."Abu Hafs al-Naysābūri (may Allah have mercy upon him) said:"If you sit to address a gathering of people, be a preacher of your own heart and self and do not get deceived by their gathering around you. They watch your outside, while Allah watches over your inside."One of the highest ranks of the believers in the sight of Allah is the constant feeling that He always watches over us. Praising His sublime essence, Allah Almighty says:{...For Allah is ever Watchful over you.}[Surat an-Nisā': 1]

"If one reforms his inner self, the fragrance of his benevolence will exude, and people's hearts will smell his good scent. How important our inner selves are! When an inner self is corrupt, the good outside will be of no avail."

Abu Hafs al-Naysābūri (may Allah have mercy upon him) said:

"If you sit to address a gathering of people, be a preacher of your own heart and self and do not get deceived by their gathering around you. They watch your outside, while Allah watches over your inside."

One of the highest ranks of the believers in the sight of Allah is the constant feeling that He always watches over us. Praising His sublime essence, Allah Almighty says:

{...For Allah is ever Watchful over you.}

[Surat an-Nisā': 1]

Our Lord watches over our innermost thoughts and feelings, and He is the Preserver from Whose knowledge nothing escapes.

He is the All-Knowing of what lies within our inner selves and consciences and watches over our glances and will hold every person accountable for what he or she does.

Our Lord is Ever-Watchful and He records the deeds of His servants.

He is Ever-Watchful and Preserving. He preserves His creation and directs its affairs in the best and most perfect manner.

Indeed, He is Ever-Watchful over our thoughts and glances; then what about our deeds and movements?!

{...Nothing is hidden from your Lord, not even an atom's weight on earth nor in heaven, nor anything smaller or greater than that, except that it is [written] in a clear Record.}[Surat Yūnus: 61]He is All-Knowing of the conditions and fluctuations of His servants day and night, and all their affairs, open and secret.

[Surat Yūnus: 61]

He is All-Knowing of the conditions and fluctuations of His servants day and night, and all their affairs, open and secret.

The Ever-Watchful Lord hears, sees, and knows everything, even our innermost thoughts before we utter or write them down.

His absolute knowledge encompasses all that exists and His absolute awareness encompasses all created beings. Nothing escapes His knowledge or awareness. All secrets and hidden things are not hidden from the Ever-Watchful. Indeed, to Him, secrets and open things are all the same.

He has succeeded..

It is reported that a man came to the Prophet (may Allah's peace and blessings be upon him) and said: "O Messenger of Allah, recite to me a comprehensive surah." The Prophet (may Allah's peace and blessings be upon him) recited to him Surat az-Zalzalah. When he finished it, the man said: "By the One Who sent you with the truth, I will never add anything to that."

Then, when the man turned his back and left, the Prophet (may Allah's peace and blessings be upon him) said: "This little man has succeeded."[Al-Mustadrak; It was graded Sahīh (authentic) by Al-Hākim and Al-Dhahabi]Sa'sa'ah ibn Mu'āwiyah came to the Prophet (may Allah's peace and blessings be upon him) and recited to him:{So whoever does an atom's weight of good will see it,and whoever does an atom's weight of evil will see it.}[Surat az-Zalzalah: 7-8]Thereupon, he said: "That is enough for me! I do not mind if I would not hear anything other than this."[Narrated by Ahmad; It was graded Hasan (sound) by Al-Arnā'ūt]One single verse could give a person a good understanding and make him close to his Lord each time he recites it and acts upon it:{...For Allah is ever Watchful over you.}[Surat an-Nisā': 1]The believer knows that Allah Almighty watches over him and sees him in all situations. He, thus, watches over his own breaths, performs his deeds sincerely for Allah's sake, and heeds Him in whatever he does. He always remembers that Allah is Ever-Watchful over him and so he reaches the level of Ihsān (excellence).{Say, "Indeed, my prayer, my sacrifice, my living and my dying are all for Allah, Lord of the worlds.}[Surat al-An'ām: 162]

[Al-Mustadrak; It was graded Sahīh (authentic) by Al-Hākim and Al-Dhahabi]

Sa'sa'ah ibn Mu'āwiyah came to the Prophet (may Allah's peace and blessings be upon him) and recited to him:

{So whoever does an atom's weight of good will see it,

and whoever does an atom's weight of evil will see it.}

[Surat az-Zalzalah: 7-8]

Thereupon, he said: "That is enough for me! I do not mind if I would not hear anything other than this."

[Narrated by Ahmad; It was graded Hasan (sound) by Al-Arnā'ūt]

One single verse could give a person a good understanding and make him close to his Lord each time he recites it and acts upon it:

{...For Allah is ever Watchful over you.}

[Surat an-Nisā': 1]

The believer knows that Allah Almighty watches over him and sees him in all situations. He, thus, watches over his own breaths, performs his deeds sincerely for Allah's sake, and heeds Him in whatever he does. He always remembers that Allah is Ever-Watchful over him and so he reaches the level of Ihsān (excellence).

{Say, "Indeed, my prayer, my sacrifice, my living and my dying are all for Allah, Lord of the worlds.}

[Surat al-An'ām: 162]

Scholars stated that one of the best acts of obedience is to constantly heed Allah Almighty, the Ever-Watchful.

The company of Allah:

The more one is heedful of Allah Almighty in his life, the more he enjoys Allah's company.

So, heed your Lord before and during worship, when you engage in permissible things, and when you commit sins.

Before worship, heed Him by considering your intention and making it sincere for Him. The Prophet (may Allah's peace and blessings be upon him) said:"And every person will get the reward according to what he has intended."[Narrated by Al-Bukhāri]

"And every person will get the reward according to what he has intended."

[Narrated by Al-Bukhāri]

During worship, continue to heed Him and be certain that you do what you do sincerely for His sake.

And when you engage in permissible things, heed Him by showing politeness and gratitude to Him for His favors.

And when you are about to commit a sin, you should heed Allah Almighty by refraining from the sin and not violating the limits set by Him. The believer quickly turns to his Lord in repentance and does not persist in sinning.{And hasten towards forgiveness from your Lord...}[Surat Āl 'Imrān: 133]

{And hasten towards forgiveness from your Lord...}

[Surat Āl 'Imrān: 133]

If you heed Allah Almighty in those four situations, this will yield relief and pleasure within your heart.

A whisper..

When Allah Almighty says:{...For Allah is Ever-Watchful over you.}[Surat an-Nisā': 1]And when He says:{...And Allah is Ever-Watchful over all things.}[Surat al-Ahzāb: 52],He actually seems to tell us the following:My servant, do you think that if you manage to conceal your sins from people, you can also manage to escape from Me?

{...For Allah is Ever-Watchful over you.}

[Surat an-Nisā': 1]

And when He says:

{...And Allah is Ever-Watchful over all things.}

[Surat al-Ahzāb: 52],

He actually seems to tell us the following:

My servant, do you think that if you manage to conceal your sins from people, you can also manage to escape from Me?

This speech becomes even more relevant in this time of ours, in which temptations are prevalent and easy to reach.

It is said that the most effective factor in building a person's character is "heedfulness of Allah Almighty" and the strongest factor in destroying a person's character is "heedfulness of people".

If you get into seclusion and become alone, do not say: I am alone.

Rather say: My Lord is Ever-Watchful over me.

O Allah, we implore You by Your name "Ar-Raqīb" to make us among Your close servants who fear You at all times, in public and in secret. O Allah, make us moderate in poverty and in richness, and make us just at times of anger and content.

Al-Hasīb (The Ever-Reckoner)

Ja'far al-Sādiq (may Allah have mercy upon him) said:"I wonder how a person may ever be fearful and not flee to the verse that says:{Allah is sufficient for us, and He is the best Disposer of affairs.}[Surat Āl-'Imrān: 173]I heard Allah say thereafter:{So they returned with favor from Allah and bounty, no harm having touched them.}[Surat Āl-'Imrān: 174]And I wonder how a person may be distressed and not flee to the verse that says:{There is no god but You; Glorified are You. Indeed, I have been of the wrongdoers.}[Surat al-Anbiyā': 87]I heard Allah say thereafter:{So We responded to him and saved him from the distress. And thus do We save the believers.}[Surat al-Anbiyā': 88]And I wonder how a person may be subject to a cunning plot and not flee to the verse that says:{And I entrust my affair to Allah. Indeed, Allah is All-Seeing of [His] slaves.}[Surat Ghāfir: 44]as I heard Allah say thereafter:{So Allah protected him from the evils they plotted.}[Surat Ghāfir: 45]"

"I wonder how a person may ever be fearful and not flee to the verse that says:

{Allah is sufficient for us, and He is the best Disposer of affairs.}

[Surat Āl-'Imrān: 173]

I heard Allah say thereafter:

{So they returned with favor from Allah and bounty, no harm having touched them.}

[Surat Āl-'Imrān: 174]

And I wonder how a person may be distressed and not flee to the verse that says:

{There is no god but You; Glorified are You. Indeed, I have been of the wrongdoers.}

[Surat al-Anbiyā': 87]

I heard Allah say thereafter:

{So We responded to him and saved him from the distress. And thus do We save the believers.}

[Surat al-Anbiyā': 88]

And I wonder how a person may be subject to a cunning plot and not flee to the verse that says:

{And I entrust my affair to Allah. Indeed, Allah is All-Seeing of [His] slaves.}

[Surat Ghāfir: 44]

as I heard Allah say thereafter:

{So Allah protected him from the evils they plotted.}

[Surat Ghāfir: 45]"

If you become helpless and find no way and no hope, having lost all the means, then say: Allah is Sufficient for me, and He is the best Disposer of affairs!

If life becomes tough and stressful for you and you fall into distress, then call out: Allah is Sufficient for me, and He is the best Disposer of affairs! Soon Allah's support, help, and relief will come to you!{So they returned with favor from Allah and bounty, no harm having touched them.}[Surat Āl-'Imrān: 174]Allah Almighty introduces Himself to His servants as the One Sufficient for them. He says:{And Allah suffices as Ever-Reckoner.}[Surat an-Nisā': 6]He also says:{Surely Allah has been Ever-Reckoner over everything.}[Surat an-Nisā': 86]

{So they returned with favor from Allah and bounty, no harm having touched them.}

[Surat Āl-'Imrān: 174]

Allah Almighty introduces Himself to His servants as the One Sufficient for them. He says:

{And Allah suffices as Ever-Reckoner.}

[Surat an-Nisā': 6]

He also says:

{Surely Allah has been Ever-Reckoner over everything.}

[Surat an-Nisā': 86]

Allah Almighty is the Ever-Reckoner.

Our Lord is Sufficient for all His servants in everything they need, be it bringing benefit or warding off harm.

His sufficiency is:

1. General sufficiency that encompasses all creatures, as He brings them into existence, gives them their sustenance, and provides them with everything needed for the purpose behind their creation.{He Who gave everything its form and then guided it.}[Surat Taha: 50]2. Special sufficiency, which is particularly given to His monotheistic servants, as He supports and empowers them and defends them against all that is unpleasant.{O Prophet, sufficient for you is Allah and for whoever follows you of the believers.}[Surat al-Anfāl: 64]Our Lord - Glorified and Exalted - is the Ever-Reckoner Who will hold all His servants accountable for their deeds on the Day of Judgment and recompense them accordingly. Nothing is hidden from Him, and even an atom's weight in the heaven or the earth does not escape His

knowledge!{And if there is [even] the weight of a mustard seed, We will bring it forth. And sufficient are We as Reckoners.}[Surat al-Anbiyā': 47]

{He Who gave everything its form and then guided it.}

[Surat Taha: 50]

2. Special sufficiency, which is particularly given to His monotheistic servants, as He supports and empowers them and defends them against all that is unpleasant.

{O Prophet, sufficient for you is Allah and for whoever follows you of the believers.}

[Surat al-Anfāl: 64]

Our Lord - Glorified and Exalted - is the Ever-Reckoner Who will hold all His servants accountable for their deeds on the Day of Judgment and recompense them accordingly. Nothing is hidden from Him, and even an atom's weight in the heaven or the earth does not escape His knowledge!

{And if there is [even] the weight of a mustard seed, We will bring it forth. And sufficient are We as Reckoners.}

[Surat al-Anbiyā': 47]

He takes care of you during adversities!

If someone is intimidated by other than Allah, then says, "Allah is Sufficient for me," He will save and support him.

Ibrāhīm (Abraham) (peace be upon him) was thrown into the fire and he said, "Allah is sufficient for us, and He is the best Disposer of affairs!" As as a result, Allah made the fire cool and peace for him.

And when our Messenger (may Allah's peace and blessings be upon him) and his Companions (may Allah be pleased with them) were threatened by the armies of disbelief and paganism, they said:{Allah is sufficient for us, and He is the best Disposer of affairs.So they returned with favor from Allah and bounty, no harm having touched them. And they pursued the pleasure of Allah, and Allah is the possessor of great bounty.}[Surat Āl-'Imrān: 173-174]

{Allah is sufficient for us, and He is the best Disposer of affairs.

So they returned with favor from Allah and bounty, no harm having touched them. And they pursued the pleasure of Allah, and Allah is the possessor of great bounty.}

[Surat Āl-'Imrān: 173-174]

Allah is the Ever-Reckoner to Whom His servants extend their hands at the latter part of the night, imploring Him to fulfill their needs, remove their distress, and guide them.

Both the strong and the weak are in His Hand, your health is in His Hand, your wife is in His Hand, those under your authority are in His Hand, your sustenance is in His Hand, kings are in His Hand, oppressors are in His Hand, and your enemy is in His Hand!

You just have to resort to Him and say: Allah is sufficient for us, and He is the best Disposer of affairs!

Stick to it!

"Allah is sufficient for us, and He is the best Disposer of affairs" is the key to relief and the door to happiness.{So they returned with favor from Allah and bounty, no harm having touched them. And they pursued the pleasure of Allah, and Allah is the possessor of great bounty.}[Surat Āl-'Imrān: 174]If you fear from illness, loss in your business, poverty, an oppressor, or an enemy, say: Allah is Sufficient for me, and He is the best Disposer of affairs!If a woman feels afraid at the time of childbirth or fears for her child or herself, let her say: Allah is Sufficient for me, and He is the best Disposer of affairs! The Prophet (may Allah's peace and blessings be upon him) said:"Whoever says in the morning and in the evening, 'Hasbiyallāhu la ilāha illa huwa 'alayhi tawakkaltu wa huwa rabb al-'arsh al-'azhīm (Allah is

Sufficient for me; there is no god but Him; I rely upon Him; and He is the Lord of the Magnificent Throne)' seven times, Allah will suffice him against whatever concerns him from the affairs of the worldly life and the Hereafter." [Ibn al-Sunni and Abu Dāwūd as Mawqūf] [Al-Arnā'ūt: authentic chain of narration]

{So they returned with favor from Allah and bounty, no harm having touched them. And they pursued the pleasure of Allah, and Allah is the possessor of great bounty.}

[Surat Āl-'Imrān: 174]

If you fear from illness, loss in your business, poverty, an oppressor, or an enemy, say: Allah is Sufficient for me, and He is the best Disposer of affairs!

If a woman feels afraid at the time of childbirth or fears for her child or herself, let her say: Allah is Sufficient for me, and He is the best Disposer of affairs! The Prophet (may Allah's peace and blessings be upon him) said:

"Whoever says in the morning and in the evening, 'Hasbiyallāhu la ilāha illa huwa 'alayhi tawakkaltu wa huwa rabb al-'arsh al-'azhīm (Allah is Sufficient for me; there is no god but Him; I rely upon Him; and He is the Lord of the Magnificent Throne)' seven times, Allah will suffice him against whatever concerns him from the affairs of the worldly life and the Hereafter." [Ibn al-Sunni and Abu Dāwūd as Mawqūf] [Al-Arnā'ūt: authentic chain of narration]

This statement means:

O Lord, I resort to You, seek Your refuge and help against what I fear from, and rely upon You; indeed, You are Sufficient for me and the source of my hope and refuge!{Is He [not best] who responds to the desperate one when he calls upon Him and removes evil.}[Surat an-Naml: 62]

{Is He [not best] who responds to the desperate one when he calls upon Him and removes evil.}

[Surat an-Naml: 62]

As you know that Allah is Sufficient for you and the Ever-Reckoner, then do not present your needs to anyone but Him!

He is the Ever-Sufficient in protection and defense for His slaves.

For the safety of the road!

As the believer knows that Allah will hold him accountable for all his actions, great and small, that nothing whatsoever is hidden from Him, and that the reckoning is not difficult for the Creator, the Ever-Reckoner, he becomes constantly prepared and heedful of his Lord in all his conditions.{Then they are returned to Allah, their true Lord. Unquestionably, to Him is the judgment, and He is the swiftest of Reckoners.}[Surat al-An'ām: 62]

{Then they are returned to Allah, their true Lord. Unquestionably, to Him is the judgment, and He is the swiftest of Reckoners.}

[Surat al-An'ām: 62]

'Ā'ishah (may Allah be pleased with her) reported: "I heard the Prophet (may Allah's peace and blessings be upon him) say in one of his prayers: 'O Allah, subject me to an easy reckoning!' I said: 'O Prophet of Allah, what is the easy reckoning?'

He said: 'That He looks into his book and pardons him. Indeed, whoever gets questioned regarding the reckoning on that Day, O 'Ā'ishah, will be ruined.'"[Narrated by Ahmad] [Sahīh (Authentic)]

[Narrated by Ahmad] [Sahīh (Authentic)]

'Umar ibn al-Khattāb (may Allah be pleased with him) said, "Hold yourself accountable before you are held accountable and weigh your deeds before they are weighed for you. Get prepared for the greatest presentation. That Day, you will be presented for judgment; nothing of you will be left hidden."

Al-Qurtubi (may Allah have mercy upon him) said,"A righteous person said, 'This is a book; your tongue is its pen; your saliva is its ink; and your organs are its papers. You are the one dictating to your angel scribes. Nothing is added thereto or omitted therefrom. If you ever deny anything therein, the witness against you regarding this matter will be from you.'"{Read your record. Sufficient is yourself against you this Day as a reckoner.}[Surat al-Isrā': 14]

"A righteous person said, 'This is a book; your tongue is its pen; your saliva is its ink; and your organs are its papers. You are the one dictating to your angel scribes. Nothing is added thereto or omitted therefrom. If you ever deny anything therein, the witness against you regarding this matter will be from you.'"

{Read your record. Sufficient is yourself against you this Day as a reckoner.}

[Surat al-Isrā': 14]

A Reminder!

In the Hereafter, there will be a tribunal in which rights will be returned to those to whom they are due. As there will be no money on that Day, good and bad deeds will be the basis of settlement. Everyone will be in desperate need even to a single good deed in his record.

The measure for any commodity is decided in line with its value. For example, iron is weighed by tonnes, fruits by kilograms, gold by grams, and diamonds by carats. But in the Hereafter deeds will be weighed by atoms.{So whoever does an atom's weight of good will see it,and whoever does an atom's weight of evil will see it.}[Surat az-Zalzalah: 7-8]Be careful about the rights of others. If you take any person's right unjustly, you will not be absolved of it. The Prophet (may Allah's peace and blessings be upon him) would even probably decide some rights in favor of those who were more skillful in presenting their arguments. So, he said:"Verily, I am only a human and the claimants bring their disputes to me; perhaps some of them are more eloquent than others. I judge according to what I hear from them.So, if I decide for anyone anything from the right of his brother, he should not take it, for indeed I thus give him a portion of fire."[Narrated by Al-Bukhāri and Muslim]

{So whoever does an atom's weight of good will see it,

and whoever does an atom's weight of evil will see it.}

[Surat az-Zalzalah: 7-8]

Be careful about the rights of others. If you take any person's right unjustly, you will not be absolved of it. The Prophet (may Allah's peace and blessings be upon him) would even probably decide some rights in favor of those who were more skillful in presenting their arguments. So, he said:

"Verily, I am only a human and the claimants bring their disputes to me; perhaps some of them are more eloquent than others. I judge according to what I hear from them.

So, if I decide for anyone anything from the right of his brother, he should not take it, for indeed I thus give him a portion of fire."

[Narrated by Al-Bukhāri and Muslim]

O Allah, You are Sufficient for us! So, be with us and do not be against us and forgive us, our parents, and all Muslims!

Al-Shahīd (The Witness) - Exalted be He

Praising His sublime Self by His Name "the Witness", Allah Almighty says:{Indeed Allah is Witness over all things.}[Surat al-Hajj: 17]

{Indeed Allah is Witness over all things.}

[Surat al-Hajj: 17]

Allah's Name "the Witness" occurs 18 times in the Book of Allah.

Our Lord, Glorified and Exalted, is the One from Whom nothing is hidden, and He is the Preserver of all things, and His knowledge encompasses everything.

Our Lord, Glorified and Exalted, gives the true testimony, supports the oppressed, and inflicts retribution upon the oppressor. He hears all sounds, low and loud, and sees all creatures, great and minute, for He encompasses all things in knowledge.

Our Almighty Lord bears witness in favor of and against His servants with regard to their deeds. His testimony is the basis and origin of all other testimonies, and it is the greatest of them all. This is because nothing is hidden from Him, and He is a Witness to all; in other words, He knows the facts and truths of everything, as He sees and watches them.

Out of His Majesty, He testifies that He is the One and Just God. He says:{Allah witnesses that there is no god but Him, and [so do] the angels and those of knowledge - [that He is] maintaining [creation] in justice.}[Surat Āl-'Imrān: 18]And He bears witness to the truthfulness of the believers who believe in His Oneness, and He gives testimony about His messengers and angels. He says:{And We have sent you [O Muhammad] to the people as a messenger, and sufficient is Allah as Witness.}[Surat an-Nisā': 79]And He gives testimony on behalf of the oppressed who has no witness or supporter against the oppressor. This testimony from Him entails help and support. Allah Almighty says:{Indeed Allah is Witness over all things.}[Surat al-Hajj: 17]His servants, on the other hand, testify to His Oneness and acknowledge their servitude to Him:{And [remember] when your Lord took from the children of Adam - from their loins - their descendants and made them testify of themselves, [saying]: "Am I not your Lord?" They said: "Yes, we have testified."}[Surat al-A'rāf: 172]

{Allah witnesses that there is no god but Him, and [so do] the angels and those of knowledge - [that He is] maintaining [creation] in justice.}

[Surat Āl-'Imrān: 18]

And He bears witness to the truthfulness of the believers who believe in His Oneness, and He gives testimony about His messengers and angels. He says:

{And We have sent you [O Muhammad] to the people as a messenger, and sufficient is Allah as Witness.}

[Surat an-Nisā': 79]

And He gives testimony on behalf of the oppressed who has no witness or supporter against the oppressor. This testimony from Him entails help and support. Allah Almighty says:

{Indeed Allah is Witness over all things.}

[Surat al-Hajj: 17]

His servants, on the other hand, testify to His Oneness and acknowledge their servitude to Him:

{And [remember] when your Lord took from the children of Adam - from their loins - their descendants and made them testify of themselves, [saying]: "Am I not your Lord?" They said: "Yes, we have testified."}

[Surat al-A'rāf: 172]

A fact:

The testimony and watchfulness of people is limited to certain times and would necessarily come to an end. People sleep, lose their senses, weaken, and then die. Allah Almighty, on the other hand, is the Ever-Living Who never dies and His watchfulness is complete and enduring.{And I was a witness over them as long as I was among them; but when You took me up, You were the Observer over them, and You are Witness over all things.}[Surat al-Mā'idah: 117]The testimony of Allah Almighty is the greatest ever. It is a testimony of a Lord Who is Omnipresent and sees all things, and no aspect of the truth is hidden from Him - unlike people. So, if Allah testifies for someone, that is enough for him, and he does not need the testimony of anyone else.{Say: "What thing is greatest in testimony?" Say: " Allah is witness between me and you. And this Qur'an was revealed to me so that I may warn you thereby and whomever it reaches. Do you [truly] testify that there are other gods with Allah?" Say: "I will not testify [with you]." Say: "Indeed, He is but one God, and I am free of what you associate [with Him]."}[Surat al-An'ām: 19]This testimony is one of the best means whereby we can confront the falsehood of our opponents:{And those who disbelieve say: "You are not a messenger." Say: "Sufficient is Allah as Witness between me and you, and [the witness of] whoever has knowledge of the Scripture."}[Surat ar-Ra'd: 43]

{And I was a witness over them as long as I was among them; but when You took me up, You were the Observer over them, and You are Witness over all things.}

[Surat al-Mā'idah: 117]

The testimony of Allah Almighty is the greatest ever. It is a testimony of a Lord Who is Omnipresent and sees all things, and no aspect of the truth is hidden from Him - unlike people. So, if Allah testifies for someone, that is enough for him, and he does not need the testimony of anyone else.

{Say: "What thing is greatest in testimony?" Say: " Allah is witness between me and you. And this Qur'an was revealed to me so that I may warn you thereby and whomever it reaches. Do you [truly] testify that there are other gods with Allah?" Say: "I will not testify [with you]." Say: "Indeed, He is but one God, and I am free of what you associate [with Him]."}

[Surat al-An'ām: 19]

This testimony is one of the best means whereby we can confront the falsehood of our opponents:

{And those who disbelieve say: "You are not a messenger." Say: "Sufficient is Allah as Witness between me and you, and [the witness of] whoever has knowledge of the Scripture."}

[Surat ar-Ra'd: 43]

The Day of Presentation!

When the servants stand before their Lord on the Day of Judgment, He will hold them accountable as a Lord Who knows them and is Aware of their secrets and a Preserver of their words and deeds.{Indeed Allah is Witness over all things.}[Surat al-Hajj: 17]The believer knows that his deeds will not be lost with Allah Almighty.{Say: "Whatever reward I might have asked of you, it is yours. My reward is only from Allah, and He is Witness over all things."}[Surat Saba': 47]As for the disbeliever, nothing of his deeds will be lost. Even if he forgets any of them, Allah Almighty has recorded them:{Allah had recorded it, while they forgot it; and Allah is Witness over all things.}[Surat al-Mujādilah: 6]

{Indeed Allah is Witness over all things.}

[Surat al-Hajj: 17]

The believer knows that his deeds will not be lost with Allah Almighty.

{Say: "Whatever reward I might have asked of you, it is yours. My reward is only from Allah, and He is Witness over all things."}

[Surat Saba': 47]

As for the disbeliever, nothing of his deeds will be lost. Even if he forgets any of them, Allah Almighty has recorded them:

{Allah had recorded it, while they forgot it; and Allah is Witness over all things.}

[Surat al-Mujādilah: 6]

Your duty!

He who knows that Allah is a Witness over him inwardly and outwardly will feel shy that He should see him commit a sin or something not pleasing to Him. He who knows that Allah sees him will perfect his deeds and worship and perform them sincerely in order to reach Ihsān, and that is the highest level of worship, about which the Prophet (may Allah's peace and blessings be upon him) said:"To worship Allah as if you see Him. If you cannot see Him, He sees you."[Narrated by Al-Bukhāri and Muslim]

"To worship Allah as if you see Him. If you cannot see Him, He sees you."

[Narrated by Al-Bukhāri and Muslim]

If you become alone sometimes,

do not say I am alone! But say: Allah is watching over me!

Do not ever think that there is something

hidden from Allah or unknown to Him!

The believers are always aware that Allah is Ever-Watchful over them and sees everything they do, great or small. He says:{There is nothing absent from your Lord [even] an atom's weight on the earth or in the heaven or [anything] smaller than that or greater but it is in a clear record.}[Surat Yūnus: 61]As the Prophet (may Allah's peace and blessings be upon him) was sending Mu'ādh to Yemen, he said, "O Messenger of Allah, give me advice." He said:"Fear Allah as much as you can, and remember Allah at every stone and tree."[Narrated by Ahmad] [Sahīh (Authentic)]Ibn al-Qayyim (may Allah have mercy upon him) said:"When a person engages in Dhikr a lot on the way, at home, on journeys, and in different locations, this increases the witnesses in his favor on the Day of Judgment."{That Day, it will report its news.}[Surat az-Zalzalah: 4]{And Allah is sufficient as Witness.}[Surat an-Nisā': 79]

{There is nothing absent from your Lord [even] an atom's weight on the earth or in the heaven or [anything] smaller than that or greater but it is in a clear record.}

[Surat Yūnus: 61]

As the Prophet (may Allah's peace and blessings be upon him) was sending Mu'ādh to Yemen, he said, "O Messenger of Allah, give me advice." He said:

"Fear Allah as much as you can, and remember Allah at every stone and tree."

[Narrated by Ahmad] [Sahīh (Authentic)]

Ibn al-Qayyim (may Allah have mercy upon him) said:

"When a person engages in Dhikr a lot on the way, at home, on journeys, and in different locations, this increases the witnesses in his favor on the Day of Judgment."

{That Day, it will report its news.}

[Surat az-Zalzalah: 4]

{And Allah is sufficient as Witness.}

[Surat an-Nisā': 79]

It was said: He who heeds Allah with regard to his thoughts and feelings, He will preserve him with regard to the actions of his body organs.

If we consider the seven types of people whom Allah will cover under His shade on the Day of Judgment, we will find out that the common feature among them is that they all believe that Allah is Witness over them and so they worship Him as if they could see Him, thereby attaining this great status.

O Allah, the Witness, we implore You to forgive us, show mercy to us, and pardon us, O the Most Merciful of those who show mercy!

Al-Haqq (The Truth) - Exalted be He

He has made His evidences clear to those who behold and think, and made His signs clear to the worlds. He has rebutted the excuses of the obstinate and the arguments of the deniers, thus brightly revealing the proofs of His Lordship and Divinity and dispelling doubts and their darkness.{For that is Allah, your Lord, the Truth.}[Surat Yūnus: 32]{So high exalted is Allah, the King, the Truth}[Surat Taha: 114]{Thereafter they are returned to Allah, their Lord, the Truth.}[Surat al-An'ām: 62]

{For that is Allah, your Lord, the Truth.}

[Surat Yūnus: 32]

{So high exalted is Allah, the King, the Truth}

[Surat Taha: 114]

{Thereafter they are returned to Allah, their Lord, the Truth.}

[Surat al-An'ām: 62]

Our Lord is the Truth in His Self, names, attributes, and actions. There is no doubt or suspicion regarding Him. He is the true deity worthy of being worshiped, and there is no other true god worthy of worship.

He is the Truth, Exalted be He, and all else are untruth and misguidance. Whoever takes other than Allah as a god has indeed adopted a falsehood, a fabrication, and untruth.{That is because Allah is the Truth, and that which they call upon besides Him is falsehood, and that Allah is the High, the Great.}[Surat al-Hajj: 62]Our Lord is the Truth, His speech is true, His actions are true, meeting with Him is true, His messengers are true, His books are true, His religion is true, and worshiping Him alone with no partner is the truth; and everything that is rightly attributed to Him is the truth.{So high exalted is Allah, the King, the Truth}[Surat Taha: 114]'Abdullāh ibn 'Abbās (may Allah be pleased with him) reported that whenever the Prophet (may Allah's peace and blessings be upon him) got up for prayer late in the night, he would say:"O Allah, You are the Truth, Your promise is true, the meeting with You is true, Your speech is true, Paradise is true, Hellfire is true, Muhammad is true, and the Hour is true." [Narrated by Al-Bukhāri and Muslim]

{That is because Allah is the Truth, and that which they call upon besides Him is falsehood, and that Allah is the High, the Great.}

[Surat al-Hajj: 62]

Our Lord is the Truth, His speech is true, His actions are true, meeting with Him is true, His messengers are true, His books are true, His religion is true, and worshiping Him alone with no partner is the truth; and everything that is rightly attributed to Him is the truth.

{So high exalted is Allah, the King, the Truth}

[Surat Taha: 114]

'Abdullāh ibn 'Abbās (may Allah be pleased with him) reported that whenever the Prophet (may Allah's peace and blessings be upon him) got up for prayer late in the night, he would say:

"O Allah, You are the Truth, Your promise is true, the meeting with You is true, Your speech is true, Paradise is true, Hellfire is true, Muhammad is true, and the Hour is true." [Narrated by Al-Bukhāri and Muslim]

The conflict!

There is an permanent conflict between the truth and falsehood. Whoever is with Allah is indeed upon the clear truth and will win in this world and in the Hereafter.{It is He who has sent His Messenger with guidance and the religion of truth to manifest it over all religions, although they who associate partners with Allah dislike it.}[Surat at-Tawbah: 33]The believers follow the truth.{That is because those who disbelieve follow falsehood, and those who believe follow the truth from their Lord. Thus does Allah present to the people their comparisons.}[Surat Muhammad: 3]And they urge and advise one another to hold fast to the truth:{By the time,Indeed, mankind is in loss,Except for those who believe, do righteous deeds, and advise one another to truth and advise one another to patience.}[Surat al-'Asr]He who rejects the truth after it became apparent to him is indeed arrogant and wrongful to himself. The Prophet (may Allah's peace and blessings be upon him) said:"Arrogance is to reject the truth and despise people."[Narrated by Muslim]

{It is He who has sent His Messenger with guidance and the religion of truth to manifest it over all religions, although they who associate partners with Allah dislike it.}

[Surat at-Tawbah: 33]

The believers follow the truth.

{That is because those who disbelieve follow falsehood, and those who believe follow the truth from their Lord. Thus does Allah present to the people their comparisons.}

[Surat Muhammad: 3]

And they urge and advise one another to hold fast to the truth:

{By the time,

Indeed, mankind is in loss,

Except for those who believe, do righteous deeds, and advise one another to truth and advise one another to patience.}

[Surat al-'Asr]

He who rejects the truth after it became apparent to him is indeed arrogant and wrongful to himself. The Prophet (may Allah's peace and blessings be upon him) said:

"Arrogance is to reject the truth and despise people."

[Narrated by Muslim]

Where is the way?

Many people still search for the truth so as to be guided to the True God.

Some rely upon the call of natural disposition within them.{The natural disposition that Allah has created people upon.}[Surat ar-Rūm: 30]

{The natural disposition that Allah has created people upon.}

[Surat ar-Rūm: 30]

While others turn to the principle of causality, which establishes that every made thing must have a maker, every incident must have an agent that causes it to happen, and every system must have an organizer.

Some others deal with this issue on the basis of calculation. They are the people of doubt and suspicion. They ultimately reach the conclusion that the safer choice for them in terms of their worldly life and that of the Hereafter is to believe in Allah, the Hereafter, resurrection, and reckoning. As the poet says,

"Both the diviner and physician say the bodies will not be resurrected! To them I say: If you are right, I will lose nothing!

But if you are wrong, then you both will be losers!"

Doubt does not lead to salvation. Allah Almighty says:{Can there be doubt about Allah, the Creator of the heavens and earth?}[Surat Ibrāhīm: 10]There are some among them who are still in confusion and polytheism. We seek refuge with Allah from misguidance after bring guided!{Then is he who knows that what has been revealed to you from your Lord is the truth like one who is blind? Only the people of understanding will take heed.}[Surat ar-Ra'd: 19]The truth is: Everything that is proved to draw us closer to Allah Almighty is true, and everything that keeps us away from Him is false and wrong.{Say: "If you really love Allah, then follow me, Allah will love you."}[Surat Āl-'Imrān: 31]Ibn Taymiyyah (may Allah have mercy upon him) said,"A person is not righteous by merely knowing the truth without loving, wanting, and following it."

{Can there be doubt about Allah, the Creator of the heavens and earth?}

[Surat Ibrāhīm: 10]

There are some among them who are still in confusion and polytheism. We seek refuge with Allah from misguidance after bring guided!

{Then is he who knows that what has been revealed to you from your Lord is the truth like one who is blind? Only the people of understanding will take heed.}

[Surat ar-Ra'd: 19]

The truth is: Everything that is proved to draw us closer to Allah Almighty is true, and everything that keeps us away from Him is false and wrong.

{Say: "If you really love Allah, then follow me, Allah will love you."}

[Surat Āl-'Imrān: 31]

Ibn Taymiyyah (may Allah have mercy upon him) said,

"A person is not righteous by merely knowing the truth without loving, wanting, and following it."

Indeed, the real disaster for a person is not affliction in himself or his wealth or children, but in his religion. That is the biggest disaster and irreparable loss. Doubt replaces certainty, and thus he sees the truth as untruth and the untruth as truth and sees the right as wrong and the wrong as right.

Settle at the valley of salvation!

Could there ever be a great distress or hardship that is not easy to Allah Almighty? Indeed, Allah is the Truth, His speech is true, and His promise is true.

So, it behooves us to trust our Lord, rely upon Him, expect bounty and benevolence from Him, and be attached to His promises. He alone brings benefit and removes harm. His kindness engulfs all, and there is wisdom in whatever He does. With every hardship and distress, He puts ease and relief. After the night, morning comes, and after famine comes rain.

Allah Almighty does not turn down the supplication of a true believer, for He is the Truth and His promise is true. In the Qur'an, He says:{And your Lord says: "Call upon Me; I will respond to you." Indeed, those who disdain My worship will enter Hell humiliated.}[Surat Ghāfir: 60]

{And your Lord says: "Call upon Me; I will respond to you." Indeed, those who disdain My worship will enter Hell humiliated.}

[Surat Ghāfir: 60]

Hence, all your problems will be solved, all your pains will come to an end, all your dreams will be real, and all your tears will turn into smiles. So, rest assured!

Your poverty will end, your thirst will be quenched, and after separation and severance of ties, there will be reunion and connection. Allah Almighty says:{So rely upon Allah; indeed, you are upon the clear truth.}[Surat an-Naml: 79]

{So rely upon Allah; indeed, you are upon the clear truth.}

[Surat an-Naml: 79]

O Allah, show us what is true as true and help us follow it, and show us what is false as false and help us keep away from it!

Al-Mubīn (The Evident) - Exalted be He

Stick to the door of your Lord, the Evident, seek honor and power from the Ever-Mighty and All-Knowing God, and implore Him by worshiping Him, and He will bestow His grace upon you.

If you obey Him, He honors you and bestows His favors upon you; and if you neglect your duties, He shows mercy to you and gives you respite. And if you turn to Him in repentance, He accepts your repentance. And if you commit sins and act wrongly, He conceals them for you!

Our hearts are only alive by virtue of closeness to Him, and the tears only flow out of fear of being away from Him, or in hope for being connected with Him.

Someone rightly said,"By Allah, how desolate a path is if Allah did not secure it, and how misguided a path is if Allah is not your guide!"

"By Allah, how desolate a path is if Allah did not secure it, and how misguided a path is if Allah is not your guide!"

We are in dire need to reach the door of Allah, the Evident, so as to make our way clear.

Let us approach the lights of one of the names of Allah Almighty, namely Al-Mubīn (the Evident).

Praising Himself, Allah Almighty says:{That Day, Allah will pay them in full their deserved recompense, and they will know that it is Allah Who is the Truth, the Evident.}[Surat al-Nūr: 25]

{That Day, Allah will pay them in full their deserved recompense, and they will know that it is Allah Who is the Truth, the Evident.}

[Surat al-Nūr: 25]

Evident means clear and apparent.

Our Lord, Exalted be He, is the Evident to all creatures and Whose existence and oneness is evident, and so is the fact that there is no partner to Him in His lordship, divinity, names, or attributes.

And it is our Almighty Lord Who shows to His servants the path of guidance and makes clear to them the deeds that entail reward and those that entail punishment. On the Day of Judgment, the doubts of the hypocrites who used to argue about Allah's promises in the worldly life, will go away.

Being evident is one of the greatest Attributes of Allah Almighty.

He is Evident in two ways:

First: Allah is Evident through His books and revelations which He sent down to His prophets and messengers:{There has come to you from Allah a light and an evident Book.}[Surat al-Mā'idah: 15]Second: He is Evident through the signs He created which are indicating to their Creator.{Indeed, in the creation of the heavens and earth and the alternation of the night and day are signs for those who understand.}[Surat Āl-'Imrān: 190]

{There has come to you from Allah a light and an evident Book.}

[Surat al-Mā'idah: 15]

Second: He is Evident through the signs He created which are indicating to their Creator.

{Indeed, in the creation of the heavens and earth and the alternation of the night and day are signs for those who understand.}

[Surat Āl-'Imrān: 190]

In everything there is a sign proving that He is the One God.

As the Qur'an is evident, so were the messengers of Allah (peace be upon them). Prophet Nūh is quoted in the Qur'an as saying:{I am only an evident warner.}[Surat ash-Shu'arā': 115]Allah Almighty commanded Prophet Muhammad (may Allah's peace and blessings be upon him) to say:{It has only been revealed to me that I am a clear warner.}[Sād: 70]Moreover, Allah Almighty informs His servants in His books and by the tongues of His messengers that, on the Day of Judgment, He will clarify the things about which they differ in the worldly life. He says:{And He will surely make evident to you on the Day of Resurrection that over which you used to differ.}[Surat an-Nahl: 92]If the truth is made evident to someone and he still turns away from it, his recompense will be a painful punishment. Allah Almighty says:{But if you deviate after evident proofs have come to you, then know that Allah is All-Mighty, All-Wise.}[Surat al-Baqarah: 209]Likewise, he who conceals the truth subjects himself to curse. Allah Almighty says:{Indeed, those who conceal what We sent down of clear proofs and guidance after We made it clear for the people in the Scripture - those are cursed by Allah and cursed by those who curse.}[Surat al-Baqarah: 159]

{I am only an evident warner.}

[Surat ash-Shu'arā': 115]

Allah Almighty commanded Prophet Muhammad (may Allah's peace and blessings be upon him) to say:

{It has only been revealed to me that I am a clear warner.}

[Sād: 70]

Moreover, Allah Almighty informs His servants in His books and by the tongues of His messengers that, on the Day of Judgment, He will clarify the things about which they differ in the worldly life. He says:

{And He will surely make evident to you on the Day of Resurrection that over which you used to differ.}

[Surat an-Nahl: 92]

If the truth is made evident to someone and he still turns away from it, his recompense will be a painful punishment. Allah Almighty says:

{But if you deviate after evident proofs have come to you, then know that Allah is All-Mighty, All-Wise.}

[Surat al-Baqarah: 209]

Likewise, he who conceals the truth subjects himself to curse. Allah Almighty says:

{Indeed, those who conceal what We sent down of clear proofs and guidance after We made it clear for the people in the Scripture - those are cursed by Allah and cursed by those who curse.}

[Surat al-Baqarah: 159]

The people of intellects!

Allah, the Evident, made His signs clear to those who think and observe [1].

Showing His signs for the whole creation and rebutting the excuses of those who are obstinate, Allah Almighty says:{Is He [not best] who made the earth a stable ground and placed within it rivers and made for it firm mountains and placed between the two seas a barrier? Is there a deity with Allah? [No], but most of them do not know.Is He [not best] who responds to the desperate one when he calls upon Him and removes evil and makes you inheritors of the earth? Is there a deity with Allah? Little do you remember.Is He [not best] who guides you through the darknesses of the land and sea and who sends the winds as glad tidings before His mercy? Is there a deity with Allah? High exalted is Allah above whatever they associate with Him.Is He [not best] who begins creation and then repeats it and who provides for you from the heaven and earth? Is there a deity with Allah? Say: "Produce your proof, if you should be truthful."}[Surat an-Naml: 61-64]Glory be to the One Whose magnificence and clear signs dazzle the minds and eyes of those who know Him and walk on the path to Him!

{Is He [not best] who made the earth a stable ground and placed within it rivers and made for it firm mountains and placed between the two seas a barrier? Is there a deity with Allah? [No], but most of them do not know.

Is He [not best] who responds to the desperate one when he calls upon Him and removes evil and makes you inheritors of the earth? Is there a deity with Allah? Little do you remember.

Is He [not best] who guides you through the darknesses of the land and sea and who sends the winds as glad tidings before His mercy? Is there a deity with Allah? High exalted is Allah above whatever they associate with Him.

Is He [not best] who begins creation and then repeats it and who provides for you from the heaven and earth? Is there a deity with Allah? Say: "Produce your proof, if you should be truthful."}

[Surat an-Naml: 61-64]

Glory be to the One Whose magnificence and clear signs dazzle the minds and eyes of those who know Him and walk on the path to Him!

---

[1] The author of the book "Allah Ahl al-Thanā' Wa al-Majd" says: "The believer does not need anyone to affirm to him the existence of Allah Almighty or explain to him the necessity of faith. But I will cite here some excerpts, words, testimonies, and admissions by a number of scientists, intellectuals, and philosophers. Dr. Henry Link, the well-known psychiatrist, who had disbelieved in religion, opposed faith, and denied the existence of God, returned after a long and unique journey and said, 'Religion is the belief in some power as the source of life. This power is: the power of God, the One Who directs the universe, and is the Creator of the heavens.' Mr. Hush said, 'As the scope of science widens, we get strong increasing proofs of the existence of a more intelligent creator whose power is unlimited and endless. Geologists, mathematicians, astronomers, and physicists have all cooperated to construct the edifice of science, which is: the edifice of the greatness of God alone.' For his part, Herbert Spencer elaborated in his treatise 'Education' on this issue. He said, 'Science disproves superstitions, yet it does not contradict religion itself.' Then, he mentioned a number of examples, saying, 'When a scientist looks into a drop of water and knows that it is composed of oxygen and hydrogen in a particular percentage, which, if significantly changed, would turn the water into something else, he believes in the greatness, power, and wisdom of the Creator more than non-physicists, who see nothing in the drop of water except that it is merely a drop of water!' Sir John Arthur Thomson, the well-known Scottish physicist and author, in the series of books titled 'Science and Religion', said, 'We decide on the basis of insight that the greatest service done by science is that it led man to an idea about God that is nobler and more sublime.' As for William James, the famous psychologist, he said, 'There is an inseparable bond between God and us. If we subject ourselves to His guidance, all our wishes and hopes will be accomplished.'"

Consider the plants on earth, with all its different kinds, and have a close look at all the wonderful creatures in the world,

which clearly point to the One Creator, Who has no partner.

In the concluding verses of Surat Āl-'Imrān, Allah Almighty praises people of intellects as they open their insights to receiving His signs in the universe and turn to Him with their hearts while standing, sitting, and lying on their sides. Their hearts are filled with faith, and their hands are raised up to Allah in sincere supplication, asking Him for guidance. So, the response comes as follows:{And their Lord responded to them: "Never will I allow the work of [any] worker among you to be lost, whether male or female; you are of one another. So those who emigrated or were evicted from their homes or were harmed in My cause or fought or were killed - I will surely expiate for them their misdeeds, and I will surely admit them to gardens under which rivers flow, as reward from Allah, and with Allah is the best reward."}[Surat Āl-'Imrān: 195]

{And their Lord responded to them: "Never will I allow the work of [any] worker among you to be lost, whether male or female; you are of one another. So those who emigrated or were evicted from their homes or were harmed in My cause or fought or were killed - I will surely expiate for them their misdeeds, and I will surely admit them to gardens under which rivers flow, as reward from Allah, and with Allah is the best reward."}

[Surat Āl-'Imrān: 195]

O Allah, we implore You by Your name "the Evident" to admit us into the Gardens of Bliss and save us from Hellfire, O Lord of the worlds!

Al-Muhīt (The Encompassing) - Exalted be He

Ibn Hajar (may Allah have mercy upon him) said,"The more a person is knowledgeable of Allah and His names, attributes, actions, and rulings, the more fearful and heedful of Him he becomes. Indeed, fear of Allah decreases as much as knowledge of Him decreases.

"The more a person is knowledgeable of Allah and His names, attributes, actions, and rulings, the more fearful and heedful of Him he becomes. Indeed, fear of Allah decreases as much as knowledge of Him decreases.

When a person knows that Allah is the Encompassing, he feels reassured, his grief goes away, and his heart gets attached to his Encompassing Lord."

Allah Almighty informs His servants that He is the Encompassing. He says:{And to Allah belongs whatever is in the heavens and whatever is on the earth. And Allah is ever Encompassing of all things.}[Surat an-Nisā': 126]Nothing whatsoever escapes the knowledge of our Lord, Exalted and Glorified be He, be it great or small, outward or inward. He describes Himself saying:{Surely He is Encompassing of all things.}[Surat Fussilat: 54]

{And to Allah belongs whatever is in the heavens and whatever is on the earth. And Allah is ever Encompassing of all things.}

[Surat an-Nisā': 126]

Nothing whatsoever escapes the knowledge of our Lord, Exalted and Glorified be He, be it great or small, outward or inward. He describes Himself saying:

{Surely He is Encompassing of all things.}

[Surat Fussilat: 54]

His encompassing includes His knowledge and His watchfulness of all things, as it includes His power and the fact that nothing can escape Him. He also encompasses things by His authority and judgment.

It is stated in Sharh Al-Tahāwiyyah, "As for Him being Encompassing, Allah Almighty says:{And Allah encompasses them from all sides.}[Surat al-Burūj: 20]{Surely He is Encompassing of all things.}[Surat Fussilat: 54]This, however, does not mean that the creatures are inside the Holy Self of Allah - far Exalted is He above that saying!

{And Allah encompasses them from all sides.}

[Surat al-Burūj: 20]

{Surely He is Encompassing of all things.}

[Surat Fussilat: 54]

This, however, does not mean that the creatures are inside the Holy Self of Allah - far Exalted is He above that saying!

Yet, it means that He encompasses everything by His greatness, knowledge, and power. Ibn 'Abbās (may Allah be pleased with him) said, 'The seven heavens and the seven earths and what exists therein and between them are in the Hand of the Most Merciful, like a mustard seed in the hand of anyone of you.'"

He is the Encompassing!

He encompasses His servants in a complete and perfect manner. None can escape His knowledge or power. He encompasses their selves, words, and deeds. In the Qur'an, He says:{And that Allah has encompassed all things in knowledge.}[Surat at-Talāq: 12]

{And that Allah has encompassed all things in knowledge.}

[Surat at-Talāq: 12]

This is the general encompassing of the inhabitants of the heavens and the earth, which is the encompassing of mercy.

As for His specific encompassing, that is of power and vanquishing, which includes His threat to the sinful and obstinate people.

This name more often comes along with threats to the disbelievers and hypocrites. Allah Almighty knows their cunning plots and their lies, and He encompasses them from all sides, and is Ever-Watchful over them. To Him they will all return ultimately, and none of them can escape!

About the disbelievers, Allah Almighty says:{But Allah is Encompassing of the disbelievers.}[Surat al-Baqarah: 19]And about people who show off and act boastfully, He says:{And do not be like those who came forth from their homes boastfully and to be seen by people and avert [them] from the way of Allah. And Allah is All-Encompassing of what they do.}[Surat al-Anfāl: 47]And Allah Almighty says about the people who gloat and devise evil plots from among the disbelievers and the hypocrites:{If good touches you, it distresses them; but if harm strikes you, they rejoice at it. And if you are patient and fear Allah, their plot will not harm you at all. Indeed, Allah is All-Encompassing of what they do.}[Surat Āl-'Imrān: 120]When the punishment of Allah descends upon some people, it encompasses them:{Verily I fear for you the torment of an encompassing Day.}[Surat Hūd: 84]On the Day of Judgment, Hellfire will encompass the disbelievers:{Indeed, We have prepared for the wrongdoers a fire whose walls will encompass them.}[Surat al-Kahf: 29]

{But Allah is Encompassing of the disbelievers.}

[Surat al-Baqarah: 19]

And about people who show off and act boastfully, He says:

{And do not be like those who came forth from their homes boastfully and to be seen by people and avert [them] from the way of Allah. And Allah is All-Encompassing of what they do.}

[Surat al-Anfāl: 47]

And Allah Almighty says about the people who gloat and devise evil plots from among the disbelievers and the hypocrites:

{If good touches you, it distresses them; but if harm strikes you, they rejoice at it. And if you are patient and fear Allah, their plot will not harm you at all. Indeed, Allah is All-Encompassing of what they do.}

[Surat Āl-'Imrān: 120]

When the punishment of Allah descends upon some people, it encompasses them:

{Verily I fear for you the torment of an encompassing Day.}

[Surat Hūd: 84]

On the Day of Judgment, Hellfire will encompass the disbelievers:

{Indeed, We have prepared for the wrongdoers a fire whose walls will encompass them.}

[Surat al-Kahf: 29]

Rest assured!

As the believer knows that Allah Almighty is the Encompassing, he feels reassured and relies upon his Lord and fears Him. He does not think that Allah's support will come late, nor does he despair of His mercy or lose hope for relief. Indeed, relief will come to him without any doubt!

He knows that the scuttling of the ship is an act of complete kindness, the killing of the boy is an act of perfect mercy, and the concealment of the treasure of the two orphans is an act of utmost loyalty.{And how can you have patience in something about which you have no knowledge?}[Surat al-Kahf: 68]Yet all matters are predestined and happen at certain times, not before or after. Indeed, everything with Allah has a determined term:{And if you are patient and fear Allah, their plot will not harm you at all. Indeed, Allah is Encompassing of what they do.}[Surat Āl-'Imrān: 120]

{And how can you have patience in something about which you have no knowledge?}

[Surat al-Kahf: 68]

Yet all matters are predestined and happen at certain times, not before or after. Indeed, everything with Allah has a determined term:

{And if you are patient and fear Allah, their plot will not harm you at all. Indeed, Allah is Encompassing of what they do.}

[Surat Āl-'Imrān: 120]

However, Allah Almighty set a certain measure for everything. It has a specific time, which it cannot miss. So, when something is predestined to happen, none can delay it or bring it forward even for a single hour.

Any distress has its specific term after which it goes away. So, we should not be in rush to get what we want and get rid of unpleasant things. This is not our decision or responsibility. What we are required to do is to pursue the proper means and display patience. Indeed, help and relief from Allah Almighty reach those who seek it everywhere!

Ibrāhīm (Abraham) (peace be upon him) was surrounded and thrown into the fire. And then it was nothing but coolness and peace for him!

Likewise, Yūsuf (Joseph) (peace be upon him) was surrounded by his siblings, who threw him into the well. And he was surrounded another time by the governor's wife and other women with her. And he was put in jail. But Allah, the Encompassing, dispelled the plots of the enemies and granted victory and support to Yūsuf, putting him in charge of the treasures of the country at the time.

The household of the mother of Mūsa (Moses) (peace be upon him) was surrounded, and she had to throw him into the river. Yet, this turned out favorably for her and him, and he returned to her while she was reassured.

Pharaoh surrounded Moses (peace be upon him) and his followers, yet this ended up in destruction for Pharaoh and victory for Moses!

The disbelievers surrounded the Prophet's house, and he left Makkah, expelled and sorrowful. Then, Allah Almighty encompassed his enemies and he later came back to the city, victorious!

As the believer recalls that Allah is the Encompassing, he increases in faith and pleasure about his Lord and he flees to Him, being humbly submissive to His greatness and commands, in line with the verse that says:{Therefore flee to Allah. Surely I am a clear warner to you from Him.}[Surat adh-Dhāriyāt: 50]

{Therefore flee to Allah. Surely I am a clear warner to you from Him.}

[Surat adh-Dhāriyāt: 50]

To You I seek refuge, and who else can grant refuge!

Give refuge to a weak servant who needs Your protection!

I have tried every refuge in my life but found no refuge

more mighty and honorable than Your refuge!

So, answer my supplication and respond to my earnest request.

Indeed, whoever supplicates You and turns to You in hope is never disappointed!

O Allah, we implore You by Your Name "the Encompassing" to encompass our enemies with punishment and give us relief from every distress and a way out from every hardship!

Al-Awwal - Al-Ākhir - Al-Zhāhir - Al-Bātin (The First - The Last - The Outward - The Inward) - Exalted be He

Allah Almighty praises His Sublime Self, saying:{He is the First and the Last, and the Manifest and the Hidden; and He is All-Knowing of everything.}[Surat al-Hadīd: 3]The Prophet (may Allah's peace and blessings be upon him) said:"Allāhumma rabb as-samāwāti wa rabb al-ard wa rabb al-'arsh al-'azhīm rabbana wa rabba kulli shay' fāliq al-habbi wa an-nawa wa munzil al-tawrāh wa al-injil wa al-furqān a'udhu bika min sharri kulli shay'in anta ākhidhun binasiyatih (O Allah, the Lord of the seven heavens and the Lord of the Magnificent Throne. Our Lord and the Lord of everything, the Splitter of the grain and the date-stone, the Revealer of the Torah, the Gospel, and the Furqān (the Qur'an), I seek refuge in You from the evil of everything that You seize by the forelock.)Allāhumma anta al-awwalu fa laysa qablaka shay' wa anta al-ākhiru fa laysa ba'daka shay' wa anta al-zhāhiru fa laysa fawqaka shay' wa anta al-bātinu fa laysa dūnaka shay' iqdi 'anna ad-dayn wa aghnina min al-faqr (O Allah, You are the First; nothing was before you. You are the Last; nothing will be after You. You are the Outward; nothing is above You. You are the Inward; nothing is below You. Remove our debts from us and enrich us against poverty!)"[Narrated by Muslim]

{He is the First and the Last, and the Manifest and the Hidden; and He is All-Knowing of everything.}

[Surat al-Hadīd: 3]

The Prophet (may Allah's peace and blessings be upon him) said:

"Allāhumma rabb as-samāwāti wa rabb al-ard wa rabb al-'arsh al-'azhīm rabbana wa rabba kulli shay' fāliq al-habbi wa an-nawa wa munzil at-tawrāh wa al-injil wa al-furqān a'udhu bika min sharri kulli shay'in anta ākhidhun binasiyatih (O Allah, the Lord of the seven heavens and the Lord of the Magnificent Throne. Our Lord and the Lord of everything, the Splitter of the grain and the date-stone, the Revealer of the Torah, the Gospel, and the Furqān (the Qur'an), I seek refuge in You from the evil of everything that You seize by the forelock.)

Allāhumma anta al-awwalu fa laysa qablaka shay' wa anta al-ākhiru fa laysa ba'daka shay' wa anta al-zhāhiru fa laysa fawqaka shay' wa anta al-bātinu fa laysa dūnaka shay' iqdi 'anna ad-dayn wa aghnina min al-faqr (O Allah, You are the First; nothing was before you. You are the Last; nothing will be after You. You are the Outward; nothing is above You. You are the Inward; nothing is below You. Remove our debts from us and enrich us against poverty!)"

[Narrated by Muslim]

He is the First, before Whom there was nothing.

He is the Last, after Whom there will be nothing.

He is the Manifest, above Whom there is nothing.

He is the Hidden, below Whom there is nothing.

All these names revolve around the meaning that Allah Almighty encompasses His creation in terms of time and place.

The Names "the First and the Last" indicate that He is Encompassing in time, for there is nothing before Him; all things came into existence after Him, and He preceded them all.

And there is nothing after Him. He is the Ever-Lasting and will remain after all His creation perish.

Allah's Names "the Outward and the Inward" indicate that He encompasses His creation in terms of place. He is above everything, and nothing is higher than Him. He is High above the Throne, and the Throne is the highest among created things. And Allah Almighty is High and Exalted in terms of His Self, status, attributes, and vanquishing power.

And nothing is below Allah Almighty, the Inward. This means that He encompasses all things and is nearer to them than their own selves. He watches over all consciences and knows the innermost thoughts and feelings.

Although He is Exalted and High above the Throne and over the heavens, He is near to His servants and watchful over their outward and inward aspects.{And We have already created man and know what his soul whispers to him, and We are closer to him than [his] jugular vein.}[Surat Qāf: 16]{Say: "Whether you conceal what is in your hearts or reveal it, Allah knows it."}[Surat Āl-'Imrān: 29]

{And We have already created man and know what his soul whispers to him, and We are closer to him than [his] jugular vein.}

[Surat Qāf: 16]

{Say: "Whether you conceal what is in your hearts or reveal it, Allah knows it."}

[Surat Āl-'Imrān: 29]

He is close to you!

He hears your speech and sees your deeds. Nothing of your secrets is hidden from Him.

One day the Prophet (may Allah's peace and blessings be upon him) heard his Companions supplicate to Allah Almighty loudly. Thereupon, he said:"O people, do not trouble yourselves too much. He Whom you are invoking is not deaf or absent, rather you are invoking an All-Hearing and All-Seeing (Lord)."[Narrated by Al-Bukhāri and Muslim]

"O people, do not trouble yourselves too much. He Whom you are invoking is not deaf or absent, rather you are invoking an All-Hearing and All-Seeing (Lord)."

[Narrated by Al-Bukhāri and Muslim]

You whisper in your prostration: "Subhāna rabbi al-A'la (Glory be to my Lord, the Most High!)" And behold! The heavens open their doors to your supplication and the Lord hears you. Do not ever think that He is distant or that any secret of yours could be hidden from Him!

He hears the creeping of a black ant on a hard rock in a dark night!{Not a leaf falls but that He knows it.}[Surat al-An'ām: 59]

{Not a leaf falls but that He knows it.}

[Surat al-An'ām: 59]

Out of His wisdom and grace, He reminds us that He initiated the creation of all created beings and that they are all slaves to Him. So, as He alone brought us into existence, we should also worship and love Him alone as the One and Only God.

Do not get bored of standing!

If you become helpless and surrounded by fears, remember that He is the First and the Last, that He is close to you, and that He is Able to do all things and is Vanquisher over His servants, and He directs every matter from the heaven to the earth and then it ascends to Him. And remember that He is Watchful over your innermost thoughts and feelings.

Thus, your heart has a Lord to turn to, a God to worship, and an Eternal Refuge to rely upon for the fulfillment of needs and relief from distress. If this settles in you, your heart will be joyful, your soul will calm down, your conscience will be at ease, and relief will be at hand, as you know that Allah is the First and the Last, and the Manifest and the Hidden, and that He is Able to do all things.

The fire did not burn Ibrāhīm (peace be upon him) on account of divine care and protection.{We said: "O fire, be cool and safety for Abraham."}[Surat al-Anbiyā': 69]Also, Mūsa (peace be upon him) did not drown at the sea, because he said with a confident voice while believing in the power of Allah,{He said: "No, indeed, with me is my Lord; He will guide me."}[Surat ash-Shu'arā': 62]And as Yūnus (peace be upon him) was in the belly of the whale, he called out,{There is no god but You; Glorified are You. Indeed, I have been of the wrongdoers.}[Surat al-Anbiyā': 87]A weak voice that was released from the three layers of darkness: the darkness of the night, the darkness of the sea, and the darkness in the belly of the whale. It pierced these layers and headed towards the heaven. Thereupon, relief came.

{We said: "O fire, be cool and safety for Abraham."} [Surat al-Anbiyā': 69]

Also, Mūsa (peace be upon him) did not drown at the sea, because he said with a confident voice while believing in the power of Allah,

{He said: "No, indeed, with me is my Lord; He will guide me."}

[Surat ash-Shu'arā': 62]

And as Yūnus (peace be upon him) was in the belly of the whale, he called out,

{There is no god but You; Glorified are You. Indeed, I have been of the wrongdoers.}

[Surat al-Anbiyā': 87]

A weak voice that was released from the three layers of darkness: the darkness of the night, the darkness of the sea, and the darkness in the belly of the whale. It pierced these layers and headed towards the heaven. Thereupon, relief came.

And for the helpless person there are subtle and kind acts in the unseen!

They had already been predestined for him!

A turning point!

A person cannot confront events alone, nor can he deal with disasters and grave matters. This is because he is created weak and powerless, unless he relies upon his Lord, as he knows that He is the First Who had preceded everything, and the Last Who will remain after everything, and that He is the Manifest Who is above everything and the Hidden Who is closer to everything.

No heaven can hide another heaven from Him, nor can an earth hide another earth. Manifest cannot cover hidden things from Him because hidden things are manifest to Him, the unseen is seen, the distant is near, and the secret is overt for Him.

How blissful he is who gets attached to Allah Almighty, learns the names of his Lord, reforms his own inner self, performs his deeds with sincerity, clings to patience, and places his trust in the Creator! That is devotion along with pure love and affection.

Longing for Him grips and shakes me!

Ibn al-Qayyim (may Allah have mercy upon him) said,"Learning these four names - the First, the Last, the Manifest, the Hidden - is the pillar of knowledge. It behooves a person to know them as much as his ability and understanding can take him."

"Learning these four names - the First, the Last, the Manifest, the Hidden - is the pillar of knowledge. It behooves a person to know them as much as his ability and understanding can take him."

He is the First and the Last!

Nothing had preceded Him, and nothing will come after Him!

Knowing these four names and their meanings have profound impact in warding off Satan's whisperings.

A man called Abu Zumayl came to the prominent scholar of the Ummah, 'Abdullāh ibn 'Abbās (may Allah be pleased with him) and asked him, "O Ibn 'Abbās, I find something within my heart."He said, "What is it?" He said, "By Allah, I will not reveal it." He said, "Is it something of doubt?" Then he laughed and added, "No one could be safe from that, until Allah Almighty revealed:{So if you are in doubt [O Muhammad] about what We have revealed to you, then ask those who have been reading the Scripture before you. The truth has certainly come to you from your Lord; so never be among those who doubt.}[Surat Yūnus: 94]"Then, he said to me, "If you find something within your heart, say,{He is the First and the Last, the Manifest and the Hidden; and He is All-Knowing of everything.}[Surat al-Hadīd: 3]"

{So if you are in doubt [O Muhammad] about what We have revealed to you, then ask those who have been reading the Scripture before you. The truth has certainly come to you from your Lord; so never be among those who doubt.}

[Surat Yūnus: 94]"

Then, he said to me, "If you find something within your heart, say,

{He is the First and the Last, the Manifest and the Hidden; and He is All-Knowing of everything.}

[Surat al-Hadīd: 3]"

O Allah, the First and the Last and the Manifest and the Hidden, reform our innermost selves, grant us a good end in all affairs, and save us from disgrace in this world and in the Hereafter!

Al-Wakīl (The Disposer of affairs) - Exalted be He

Let us pause a little and ponder the verse that says:{And rely upon the Ever-Living Who does not die, and glorify Him with His praise. Sufficient is He with the sins of His servants, All-Aware.}[Surat al-Furqān: 58]

{And rely upon the Ever-Living Who does not die, and glorify Him with His praise. Sufficient is He with the sins of His servants, All-Aware.}

[Surat al-Furqān: 58]

This is a call from the King, the Vanquisher, to every believing man and woman. A call to everyone who is sick, distressed, or under debt. A call to everyone who is fearful or hesitant!

He informs us that He is the Disposer of affairs and the One Able to do all things. He can turn all your problems into solutions, your pains into wellness and soundness, your dreams into reality, your fears into security, and your tears into smiles!

I disown my power and strength, and stand before my Lord with utmost humility!

Rid your soul of its weakness, anxiety, and reluctance and let it relish comfort under the shades of Allah, the Disposer of affairs, in the those lines as we reflect upon this noble name.

Allah Almighty says:{And He is Disposer of all things.}[Surat al-An'ām: 102]

{And He is Disposer of all things.}

[Surat al-An'ām: 102]

The scholars said: The Disposer of affairs is the One in charge of managing the affairs of His creation by His knowledge, perfect power, and all-inclusive wisdom.

He is the One Who undertakes to provide for His servants, take care of their interests, manage their affairs, and guide them to what is beneficial and what is harmful to them in this life and the in Hereafter.

This is the general meaning of managing of affairs, which applies to all creation.{Allah is the Creator of all things, and He is Disposer of all affairs.}[Surat az-Zumar: 62]

{Allah is the Creator of all things, and He is Disposer of all affairs.}

[Surat az-Zumar: 62]

But there is a special meaning for Disposer, which specifically applies to the pious servants of Allah who obey and love Him. He facilitates ease for them, keeps them away from hardships, and take charge of their affairs.

Hence, Allah Almighty commanded His Prophet (may Allah's peace and blessings be upon him) and the whole Ummah to rely upon Him. He says:{And rely upon the Ever-Living who does not die.}[Surat al-Furqān: 58]He singles them out with His love, in this verse:{Indeed, Allah loves those who rely [upon Him].}[Surat Āl-'Imrān: 159]

{And rely upon the Ever-Living who does not die.}

[Surat al-Furqān: 58]

He singles them out with His love, in this verse:

{Indeed, Allah loves those who rely [upon Him].}

[Surat Āl-'Imrān: 159]

Reliance upon Allah is a sign of belief and piety and a trait of the believers. It is one of the best degrees of attachment to the most beautiful names of our Lord.

To the truthful!

Ibn al-Qayyim (may Allah have mercy upon him) said,"Reliance upon Allah is half the religion, and the other half is turning to Him. Indeed, religion is seeking the help of Allah and worshiping Him."

"Reliance upon Allah is half the religion, and the other half is turning to Him. Indeed, religion is seeking the help of Allah and worshiping Him."

Reliance upon Allah: is seeking help from Him, and turning to Him: is the worship.

Reliance upon Allah increases with the increase of faith and decreases with its decrease. He who does not rely upon his Lord has no faith.{And upon Allah rely, if you should be believers.}[Surat al-Mā'idah: 23]Allah Almighty provides sufficiency for us as long as we rely upon Him.{And whoever relies upon Allah, then He is sufficient for him.}[Surat at-Talāq: 3]Be sincere in your reliance upon Allah and you will get what you want, even if it was something great. The Prophet (may Allah's peace and blessings be upon him) said:"If only you rely on Allah the way you should, He will provide for you as He provides for birds; they set out hungry in the morning and return with full bellies in the evening."[Narrated by At-Tirmidhi] [Sahīh (Authentic)]We all wish to attain a high rank in the sight of Allah Almighty in this world and in the Hereafter. This does not actually happen except to those who sincerely rely upon their Lord. Their hearts entertain such reliance, while their tongues utters the following words at the time of adversities,{Allah is sufficient for us, and He is the best Disposer of affairs.}[Surat Āl-'Imrān: 173]So, the greatness, miracles, and protection of Allah Almighty appear for His close servants.{Allah is sufficient for us, and He is the best Disposer of affairs.}[Surat Āl-'Imrān: 173]Abraham (peace be upon him) said it when he was thrown into the fire. Then, what was the result?{We said: "O fire, be cool and safety upon Abraham."}[Surat al-Anbiyā': 69]And our Prophet (may Allah's peace and blessings be upon him) and his Companions (may Allah be pleased with them) said it when it was said to them:{"Indeed, the people have gathered against you, so fear them." But it [merely] increased them in faith, and they said: "Allah is sufficient for us, and He is the best Disposer of affairs."}[Surat Āl-'Imrān: 173]And what was the result?{So they returned with favor from Allah and bounty, no harm having touched them.}[Surat Āl-'Imrān: 174]If you reach this rank, then you have attained His love, Glorified and Exalted be He.{And when you decide, then rely upon Allah. Indeed, Allah loves those who rely [upon Him].}[Surat Āl-'Imrān: 159]In addition to this love, He gives you a great reward:{So whatever thing you have been given, it is but [for] enjoyment of the worldly life. But what is with Allah is better and more lasting for those who believe and rely upon their Lord.}[Surat ash-Shūra: 36]

{And upon Allah rely, if you should be believers.}

[Surat al-Mā'idah: 23]

Allah Almighty provides sufficiency for us as long as we rely upon Him.

{And whoever relies upon Allah, then He is sufficient for him.}

[Surat at-Talāq: 3]

Be sincere in your reliance upon Allah and you will get what you want, even if it was something great. The Prophet (may Allah's peace and blessings be upon him) said:

"If only you rely on Allah the way you should, He will provide for you as He provides for birds; they set out hungry in the morning and return with full bellies in the evening."

[Narrated by At-Tirmidhi] [Sahīh (Authentic)]

We all wish to attain a high rank in the sight of Allah Almighty in this world and in the Hereafter. This does not actually happen except to those who sincerely rely upon their Lord. Their hearts entertain such reliance, while their tongues utters the following words at the time of adversities,

{Allah is sufficient for us, and He is the best Disposer of affairs.}

[Surat Āl-'Imrān: 173]

So, the greatness, miracles, and protection of Allah Almighty appear for His close servants.

{Allah is sufficient for us, and He is the best Disposer of affairs.}

[Surat Āl-'Imrān: 173]

Abraham (peace be upon him) said it when he was thrown into the fire. Then, what was the result?

{We said: "O fire, be cool and safety upon Abraham."}

[Surat al-Anbiyā': 69]

And our Prophet (may Allah's peace and blessings be upon him) and his Companions (may Allah be pleased with them) said it when it was said to them:

{"Indeed, the people have gathered against you, so fear them." But it [merely] increased them in faith, and they said: "Allah is sufficient for us, and He is the best Disposer of affairs."}

[Surat Āl-'Imrān: 173]

And what was the result?

{So they returned with favor from Allah and bounty, no harm having touched them.}

[Surat Āl-'Imrān: 174]

If you reach this rank, then you have attained His love, Glorified and Exalted be He.

{And when you decide, then rely upon Allah. Indeed, Allah loves those who rely [upon Him].}

[Surat Āl-'Imrān: 159]

In addition to this love, He gives you a great reward:

{So whatever thing you have been given, it is but [for] enjoyment of the worldly life. But what is with Allah is better and more lasting for those who believe and rely upon their Lord.}

[Surat ash-Shūra: 36]

To those who rely upon their Lord!

Be sincere in your reliance upon Allah, and He will protect you from Satan.{Indeed, he has no authority over those who believe and rely upon their Lord.}[Surat an-Nahl: 99]If the enemies set traps of cunning plots against you, set for them the wall of reliance upon Allah.{And recite to them the news of Noah, when he said to his people, "O my people, if my residence and my reminding of the signs of Allah has become burdensome upon you, then I rely upon Allah. So resolve upon your plan and [call upon] your associates. Then let not your plan be obscure to you. Then carry it out upon me and do not give me respite."}[Surat Yūnus: 71]Whoever wants victory against the enemies and relief from distress should rely upon Allah Almighty.{If Allah should aid you, no one can overcome you; but if He should forsake you, who is there that can aid you after Him? And upon Allah let the believers rely.}[Surat Āl-'Imrān: 160]And if people abandon you, turn to the Disposer of affairs and rely upon Him.{But if they turn away, say, "Allah is Sufficient for me; there is no god but Him. On Him I rely, and He is the Lord of the Great Throne."}[Surat at-Tawbah: 129]If you are required to engage in reconciliation and reform, engage through reliance upon Allah:{And if they incline to peace, then incline to it [also] and rely upon Allah. Indeed, it is He who is the All-Hearing, the All-Knowing.}[Surat al-Anfāl: 61]If faith settles in your heart and you know that your matter lies in the Hands of the Almighty Lord, do not rely then upon anyone but Him:{Say: "He is my Lord; there is no god but Him. Upon Him I rely, and to Him is my return."}[Surat ar-Ra'd: 30]Whoever persistently relies upon his Lord in all situations, He will be sufficient for him:{And rely upon Allah. And Allah is sufficient as Disposer of affairs.}[Surat al-Ahzāb: 3]

{Indeed, he has no authority over those who believe and rely upon their Lord.} [Surat an-Nahl: 99]

If the enemies set traps of cunning plots against you, set for them the wall of reliance upon Allah.

{And recite to them the news of Noah, when he said to his people, "O my people, if my residence and my reminding of the signs of Allah has become burdensome upon you, then I rely upon Allah. So resolve upon your plan and [call upon] your associates. Then let not your plan be obscure to you. Then carry it out upon me and do not give me respite."}

[Surat Yūnus: 71]

Whoever wants victory against the enemies and relief from distress should rely upon Allah Almighty.

{If Allah should aid you, no one can overcome you; but if He should forsake you, who is there that can aid you after Him? And upon Allah let the believers rely.}

[Surat Āl-'Imrān: 160]

And if people abandon you, turn to the Disposer of affairs and rely upon Him.

{But if they turn away, say, "Allah is Sufficient for me; there is no god but Him. On Him I rely, and He is the Lord of the Great Throne."}

[Surat at-Tawbah: 129]

If you are required to engage in reconciliation and reform, engage through reliance upon Allah:

{And if they incline to peace, then incline to it [also] and rely upon Allah. Indeed, it is He who is the All-Hearing, the All-Knowing.}

[Surat al-Anfāl: 61]

If faith settles in your heart and you know that your matter lies in the Hands of the Almighty Lord, do not rely then upon anyone but Him:

{Say: "He is my Lord; there is no god but Him. Upon Him I rely, and to Him is my return."}

[Surat ar-Ra'd: 30]

Whoever persistently relies upon his Lord in all situations, He will be sufficient for him:

{And rely upon Allah. And Allah is sufficient as Disposer of affairs.}

[Surat al-Ahzāb: 3]

Before going out!

Excellent man is he who goes out of his house while relying upon his Lord, and so Allah is sufficient for him and the Disposer of his affairs. The Prophet (may Allah's peace and blessings be upon him) said:"When a man goes out of his house and says, 'In the name of Allah, I rely upon Allah; there is no power nor strength except through Allah,' the following will be said to him at that time: 'You are guided, defended, and protected.'The devils will go far from him and another devil will say: 'How can you deal with a man who has been guided, defended, and protected?'"[Narrated by Abu Dāwūd] [Sahīh (Authentic)]The Prophet's Companions felt sad and troubled when they heard the Prophet (may Allah's peace and blessings be upon him) say:"How can I be at ease when the one with the Trumpet has put his lips to the Trumpet waiting to hear the order to blow it?"When he perceived that they felt sad and troubled, he said to them:"Say: Allah is sufficient for us, and He is the best Disposer of affairs; upon Allah we rely."[Narrated by Al-Tirmidhi] [Sahīh (Authentic)]

"When a man goes out of his house and says, 'In the name of Allah, I rely upon Allah; there is no power nor strength except through Allah,' the following will be said to him at that time: 'You are guided, defended, and protected.'

The devils will go far from him and another devil will say: 'How can you deal with a man who has been guided, defended, and protected?'"

[Narrated by Abu Dāwūd] [Saḥīḥ (Authentic)]

The Prophet's Companions felt sad and troubled when they heard the Prophet (may Allah's peace and blessings be upon him) say:

"How can I be at ease when the one with the Trumpet has put his lips to the Trumpet waiting to hear the order to blow it?"

When he perceived that they felt sad and troubled, he said to them:

"Say: Allah is sufficient for us, and He is the best Disposer of affairs; upon Allah we rely."

[Narrated by Al-Tirmidhī] [Saḥīḥ (Authentic)]

A Reminder!

The concept of reliance upon Allah has disappeared from the lives of many people. They forgot Allah, Glorified and Exalted, and so He forgot them, and they abandoned reliance upon their Lord, and so He left them to their own selves.

A person falls ill and he pins his hopes upon physicians and medicines, which are mere means, and he forgets the Lord of the heavens and the earth in Whose Hand cure lies.

Another person gets in trouble and suffers hardships and tribulations and becomes sad and distressed. So, he turns to his friends and loved ones for help, and forgets the Almighty Lord!

The enemies plot against him and his foes besiege him, and so he remains in severe anguish and distress, being heedless of the One Who is closer to him than his jugular vein - Glorified and Exalted be He.

Ibn Al-Jawzi (may Allah have mercy upon him) said,"A pious person should know that Allah Almighty is sufficient for him, and so he should not attach his heart to the means. Allah Almighty says:{And whoever relies upon Allah, then He is sufficient for him.}[Surat at-Talāq: 3]"Others understand reliance upon Allah to mean passive reliance with no effort or pursuit of the proper means. For example, a group of the people from Yemen set out for Hajj without taking the required provisions for the journey, saying, "We rely upon our Lord!" Then, they began to beg food from people. Thereupon, Allah Almighty revealed:{And take provisions, indeed, the best provision is fear of Allah.}[Surat al-Baqarah: 197]In other words: take such provisions that save your faces and protect you from the humiliation of begging.

"A pious person should know that Allah Almighty is sufficient for him, and so he should not attach his heart to the means. Allah Almighty says:

{And whoever relies upon Allah, then He is sufficient for him.}

[Surat at-Talāq: 3]"

Others understand reliance upon Allah to mean passive reliance with no effort or pursuit of the proper means. For example, a group of the people from Yemen set out for Hajj without taking the required provisions for the journey, saying, "We rely upon our Lord!" Then, they began to beg food from people. Thereupon, Allah Almighty revealed:

{And take provisions, indeed, the best provision is fear of Allah.}

[Surat al-Baqarah: 197]

In other words: take such provisions that save your faces and protect you from the humiliation of begging.

Some people say, "My sustenance had already been predestined; so, why should I make effort?!"

A man asked the Prophet (may Allah's peace and blessings be upon him), "O Messenger of Allah, should I tie it and rely upon Allah or release it and rely upon Him?" He (may Allah's peace and blessings be upon him) said: "Tie it and rely upon Allah."[Narrated by At-Tirmidhī] [Hasan (Sound)]Allah Almighty says:{It is He who made the earth subservient to you - so walk among its slopes and eat of His provision

- and to Him is the resurrection.}[Surat al-Mulk: 15]So, taking the proper means does not contradict reliance upon Allah. In fact, reliance upon Him is not valid without pursuing the proper means; otherwise, this would be nothing but idleness and false reliance!{Our Lord, upon You we have relied, and to You we have returned, and to You is the destination.}[Surat Al-Mumtahanah: 4]

[Narrated by At-Tirmidhi] [Hasan (Sound)]

Allah Almighty says:

{It is He who made the earth subservient to you - so walk among its slopes and eat of His provision - and to Him is the resurrection.}

[Surat al-Mulk: 15]

So, taking the proper means does not contradict reliance upon Allah. In fact, reliance upon Him is not valid without pursuing the proper means; otherwise, this would be nothing but idleness and false reliance!

{Our Lord, upon You we have relied, and to You we have returned, and to You is the destination.}

[Surat Al-Mumtahanah: 4]

The path is from here!

How can I rely upon Allah Almighty in my life?

First: You should know His Beautiful Names and Attributes. The more Allah is revered and extolled within your heart, the closer you get to Him.

Second: Trust Him and think positively of Him."I am as My servant thinks of Me."[Narrated by Ibn Mājah] [Sahīh (Authentic)]This person who spends in charity does so only because he trusts Allah Almighty and knows that He will give him better compensation. Likewise, he who gets out of bed and stands before Allah in prayer does so only because he thinks positively of his Lord. The same holds true for those who perform Hajj, 'Umrah, and other acts of worship and piety.Third: Renounce your own power and admit your weakness before your Lord. Show your need to Him and supplicate Him to not leave you to your own devices or to any of His servants. An authentic Hadīth contains this supplication:"Allāhumma rahmataka arju fa la takilni ila nafsu tarfata 'ayn (O Allah, I hope for Your mercy. So, do not leave me to my own devices even for the blink of an eye!"[Narrated by Ahmad] [Sahīh (Authentic)]

"I am as My servant thinks of Me."

[Narrated by Ibn Mājah] [Sahīh (Authentic)]

This person who spends in charity does so only because he trusts Allah Almighty and knows that He will give him better compensation. Likewise, he who gets out of bed and stands before Allah in prayer does so only because he thinks positively of his Lord. The same holds true for those who perform Hajj, 'Umrah, and other acts of worship and piety.

Third: Renounce your own power and admit your weakness before your Lord. Show your need to Him and supplicate Him to not leave you to your own devices or to any of His servants. An authentic Hadīth contains this supplication:

"Allāhumma rahmataka arju fa la takilni ila nafsu tarfata 'ayn (O Allah, I hope for Your mercy. So, do not leave me to my own devices even for the blink of an eye!"

[Narrated by Ahmad] [Sahīh (Authentic)]

Fourth: Pursue the means to fulfill your needs, which include supplication to Allah.

Fifth: Remember the power of Allah and His ability to transform conditions and that in His Hand is the dominion of the heavens and the earth, and He is Able to do all things. Always remember that treasures of everything lie in the Hand of Allah. So, you can only entrust your affairs to Him as a weak and helpless child who depends upon his father - and for Allah is the highest attribute!{And I entrust my affair to Allah. Indeed, Allah is All-Seeing of [His] servants.}[Surat Ghāfir: 44]Sixth: Be content with what Allah has decreed for you and know that it is in your best interest. If you do not show contentment, then you are as what Bishr al-Hāfi said:"Someone says, 'I rely upon Allah' while he tells a lie against Allah, for if he truly relied upon Him, he would be content with whatever Allah did to him."

{And I entrust my affair to Allah. Indeed, Allah is All-Seeing of [His] servants.}

[Surat Ghāfir: 44]

Sixth: Be content with what Allah has decreed for you and know that it is in your best interest. If you do not show contentment, then you are as what Bishr al-Hāfi said:

"Someone says, 'I rely upon Allah' while he tells a lie against Allah, for if he truly relied upon Him, he would be content with whatever Allah did to him."

Ibn Hamdūn related that a strong wind blew and destroyed the plants of an old woman in the desert. Thereupon, she got her head out of the tent, looked at the burnt plants, raised her head towards the sky, and said, "Do whatever You want, for my sustenance is upon You!"

If a person properly relies upon the Ever-Living Lord Who does not die, Allah will reform, complete, and perfect all his affairs.{And rely upon the Ever-Living Who does not die, and exalt [Allah] with His praise. And sufficient is He with the sins of His servants, All-Aware.}[Surat al-Furqān: 58]

{And rely upon the Ever-Living Who does not die, and exalt [Allah] with His praise. And sufficient is He with the sins of His servants, All-Aware.}

[Surat al-Furqān: 58]

O Allah, the Disposer of affairs, do not leave us to our own devices, even for the blink of an eye, strengthen us for we are weak and powerless, and console us; indeed, You are Able to do all things!

Al-Nūr (The Light) - Glorified be He

Praising Himself, Allah Almighty says:

{Allah is the Light of the heavens and the earth. The example of His light is like a niche within which is a lamp, the lamp is within a glass, the glass is as if it were a pearly [white] star lit from [the oil of] a blessed olive tree, neither of the east nor of the west, whose oil would almost glow even if untouched by fire. Light upon light. Allah guides to His light whom He wills. And Allah presents examples for the people, and Allah is All-Knowing of all things.}[Surat an-Nūr: 35]The Prophet (may Allah's peace and blessings be upon him) used to make this supplication:"Allāhumma ij'al fi qalbi nūran, wa fi basari nūran, wa fi sam'i nūran, wa 'an yamīni nūran, wa 'an yasāri nūran, wa fawqi nūran, wa tahti nūran, wa amāmi nūran, wa khalfi nūran, waj'al li nūra (O Allah, place light in my heart, light in my sight, light in my hearing, light on my right, light on my left, light above me, light below me, light in front of me, light behind me, and make light for me.)" [Narrated by Al-Bukhāri and Muslim]

[Surat an-Nūr: 35]

The Prophet (may Allah's peace and blessings be upon him) used to make this supplication:

"Allāhumma ij'al fi qalbi nūran, wa fi basari nūran, wa fi sam'i nūran, wa 'an yamīni nūran, wa 'an yasāri nūran, wa fawqi nūran, wa tahti nūran, wa amāmi nūran, wa khalfi nūran, waj'al li nūra (O Allah, place light in my heart, light in my sight, light in my hearing, light on my right, light on my left, light above me, light below me, light in front of me, light behind me, and make light for me.)" [Narrated by Al-Bukhāri and Muslim]

By Allah, this is the most precious thing Allah Almighty may ever give to a servant: His light and guidance.

We are talking here about the provision of hearts and the pleasure of souls. Indeed, this is the greatest, most beneficial, and best provision ever. As a poet says,

Your remembrance keeps it too preoccupied

to eat or drink!

Your light illuminates the path for it,

and Your speech is like the pleasant singing of the camel driver,

who reminds the camels of the sweet destination,

and so they do not feel bored or tired of the journey!

In His light!

Allah Almighty says:{Allah is the Light of the heavens and the earth.}[Surat an-Nūr: 35]

{Allah is the Light of the heavens and the earth.}

[Surat an-Nūr: 35]

The texts of the Qur'an and Sunnah in which Allah Almighty calls Himself as Light come in three ways, as Ibn Taymiyyah (may Allah have mercy upon him) said,

First: He possesses the attribute of light. In the Qur'an, He says:{And the earth will shine with the light of its Lord.}[Surat az-Zumar: 69]And in a Hadīth:"And He cast some of His light upon them."[Narrated by Ibn Hibbān] [Sahīh (Authentic)]Second: He, Glorified and Exalted, is light:{Allah is the Light of the heavens and the earth.}[Surat an-Nūr: 35]And in a Hadīth:"You are the Light of the heavens and the earth."[Narrated by Al-Bukhāri and Muslim]Third: His Veil is light, as related in an authentic Hadīth:"His Veil is light, and if He were to remove it, the glow of His Face would burn everything of His creation, as far as His gaze reaches."[Narrated by Muslim]--The light of Allah Almighty is not like the created lights:{There is nothing like unto Him, and He is the All-Hearing, the All-Seeing.}[Surat ash-Shūra: 11]

{And the earth will shine with the light of its Lord.}

[Surat az-Zumar: 69]

And in a Hadīth:

"And He cast some of His light upon them."

[Narrated by Ibn Hibbān] [Sahīh (Authentic)]

Second: He, Glorified and Exalted, is light:

{Allah is the Light of the heavens and the earth.}

[Surat an-Nūr: 35]

And in a Hadīth:

"You are the Light of the heavens and the earth."

[Narrated by Al-Bukhāri and Muslim]

Third: His Veil is light, as related in an authentic Hadīth:

"His Veil is light, and if He were to remove it, the glow of His Face would burn everything of His creation, as far as His gaze reaches."

[Narrated by Muslim]

--

The light of Allah Almighty is not like the created lights:

{There is nothing like unto Him, and He is the All-Hearing, the All-Seeing.}

[Surat ash-Shūra: 11]

Light is one of His Names

and also one of His Attributes. Glory be to Him!

Take these words as a gift from me!

The erudite scholar 'Abd al-Rahmān al-Sa'di (may Allah have mercy upon him) said,"One of the Names and Attributes of Allah is An-Nūr (Light). He is the Owner of majesty, honor, and glory. If the veil were to be lifted off His noble Face, the glow of His Face would burn everything of His creation, as far as His gaze reaches."

"One of the Names and Attributes of Allah is An-Nūr (Light). He is the Owner of majesty, honor, and glory. If the veil were to be lifted off His noble Face, the glow of His Face would burn everything of His creation, as far as His gaze reaches."

He is the source of light for all the worlds. His Light dispels darkness and illuminates the Throne, the Kursi, the seven heavens, and the entire universe. This is an actual light.

As for the moral light, this is the light that illuminated the hearts of the prophets, pious people, and the angels. This includes the lights of knowing and loving Him. Indeed, His servants' knowledge of Him brings to their hearts lights, as much as they know of His Attributes of Majesty and Beauty.

The sweetness of His guidance!

If you know Allah Almighty, you thus possess the greatest and most sublime of all areas of knowledge. Useful knowledge brings lights to the heart. So, what about this knowledge which is the best, most sublime, and the root of all other knowledge!

Thereupon, this verse truly applies to your heart:{Allah is the Light of the heavens and the earth. The example of His light is like a niche within which is a lamp, the lamp is within a glass, the glass is as if it were a pearly [white] star lit from [the oil of] a blessed olive tree, neither of the east nor of the west, whose oil would almost glow even if untouched by fire. Light upon light. Allah guides to His light whom He wills. And Allah presents examples for the people, and Allah is All-Knowing of all things.}[Surat an-Nūr: 35]

{Allah is the Light of the heavens and the earth. The example of His light is like a niche within which is a lamp, the lamp is within a glass, the glass is as if it were a pearly [white] star lit from [the oil of] a blessed olive tree, neither of the east nor of the west, whose oil would almost glow even if untouched by fire. Light upon light. Allah guides to His light whom He wills. And Allah presents examples for the people, and Allah is All-Knowing of all things.}

[Surat an-Nūr: 35]

This is the light of belief in Allah Almighty and His Attributes and signs. It is in the hearts of the believers like that light which combines all good traits.

The Prophet (may Allah's peace and blessings be upon him) used to say in his supplication:"Allahumma ij'al fi qalbi nūran, wa fi basari nūran, wa fi sam'i nūran, wa 'an yamīni nūran, wa 'an yasāri nūran, wa fawqi nūran, wa tahti nūran, wa amāmi nūran, wa khalfi nūran, waj'al li nūra (O Allah, place light in my heart, light in my sight, light in my hearing, light on my right, light on my left, light above me, light below me, light in front of me, light behind me, and make light for me)."[Narrated by Al-Bukhāri and Muslim]Once the heart becomes full of this light, it manifests on the face, which shines as a result. Then, the body organs comply and become submissive and obedient. Allah Almighty says:{Allah guides to His light whom He wills.}[Surat an-Nūr: 35]Ibn Sa'di (may Allah have mercy upon him) said, "When their inside gets illuminated by prayer, their outside becomes radiant.{Their mark is on their faces from the trace of prostration.}"This light prevents a person from committing immoral acts. The Prophet (may

Allah's peace and blessings be upon him) said:"An adulterer is not a believer at the time of committing adultery, a drinker of alcoholic drink is not a believer at the time of drinking, and a thief is not a believer at the time of committing theft."[Narrated by Al-Bukhāri and Muslim]

"Allahumma ij'al fi qalbi nūran, wa fi basari nūran, wa fi sam'i nūran, wa 'an yamīni nūran, wa 'an yasāri nūran, wa fawqi nūran, wa tahti nūran, wa amāmi nūran, wa khalfi nūran, waj'al li nūra (O Allah, place light in my heart, light in my sight, light in my hearing, light on my right, light on my left, light above me, light below me, light in front of me, light behind me, and make light for me)."

[Narrated by Al-Bukhāri and Muslim]

Once the heart becomes full of this light, it manifests on the face, which shines as a result. Then, the body organs comply and become submissive and obedient. Allah Almighty says:

{Allah guides to His light whom He wills.}

[Surat an-Nūr: 35]

Ibn Sa'di (may Allah have mercy upon him) said, "When their inside gets illuminated by prayer, their outside becomes radiant.

{Their mark is on their faces from the trace of prostration.}"

This light prevents a person from committing immoral acts. The Prophet (may Allah's peace and blessings be upon him) said:

"An adulterer is not a believer at the time of committing adultery, a drinker of alcoholic drink is not a believer at the time of drinking, and a thief is not a believer at the time of committing theft."

[Narrated by Al-Bukhāri and Muslim]

His Book is light!

Allah Almighty informs us that the Books He revealed are light from Him that illuminates the hearts of His servants. He says:{Indeed, We sent down the Torah, in which was guidance and light.}[Surat al-Mā'idah: 44]Allah Almighty also says:{And We gave him the Gospel, in which was guidance and light.}[Surat al-Mā'idah: 46]And the greatest light sent down is the Book revealed to Muhammad (may Allah's peace and blessings be upon him). Allah Almighty says:{There has come to you from Allah a light and an evident Book.}[Surat al-Mā'idah: 15]Through it, Allah Almighty brings those who believe out of darkness into light:{Alif Lām Ra. This is a Book which We have sent down to you [O Prophet], so that you may bring people out of the depths of darkness into light – with their Lord's permission – to the path of the All-Mighty, the Praiseworthy.}[Surat Ibrāhīm: 1]Therefore, when the disbelievers realize the great impact of this light upon this Ummah, they try hard to extinguish it. Yet Allah Almighty is preserving His Book.{They want to extinguish the light of Allah with their mouths, but Allah will perfect His light, although the disbelievers dislike it.}[Surat as-Saff: 8]And the Almighty Lord will always preserve this Ummah as long as they hold onto His Book.

{Indeed, We sent down the Torah, in which was guidance and light.}

[Surat al-Mā'idah: 44]

Allah Almighty also says:

{And We gave him the Gospel, in which was guidance and light.}

[Surat al-Mā'idah: 46]

And the greatest light sent down is the Book revealed to Muhammad (may Allah's peace and blessings be upon him). Allah Almighty says:

{There has come to you from Allah a light and an evident Book.}

[Surat al-Mā'idah: 15]

Through it, Allah Almighty brings those who believe out of darkness into light:

{Alif Lām Ra. This is a Book which We have sent down to you [O Prophet], so that you may bring people out of the depths of darkness into light – with their Lord's permission – to the path of the All-Mighty, the Praiseworthy.}

[Surat Ibrāhīm: 1]

Therefore, when the disbelievers realize the great impact of this light upon this Ummah, they try hard to extinguish it. Yet Allah Almighty is preserving His Book.

{They want to extinguish the light of Allah with their mouths, but Allah will perfect His light, although the disbelievers dislike it.}

[Surat as-Saff: 8]

And the Almighty Lord will always preserve this Ummah as long as they hold onto His Book.

In a word!

As "The Light" is one of the Names and Attributes of Allah, His religion is light, His Messenger is light, His speech is light, and the abode of honor for His servants is a glittering light. This light is shining within the hearts of the believers and manifesting on their tongues and body organs. In addition, Allah Almighty will complete this light for them on the Day of Judgment. He says:{Their light will proceed before them and on their right; they will say: "Our Lord, perfect for us our light and forgive us. Indeed, You are Capable of all things"}[Surat at-Tahrīm: 8]

{Their light will proceed before them and on their right; they will say: "Our Lord, perfect for us our light and forgive us. Indeed, You are Capable of all things"}

[Surat at-Tahrīm: 8]

O Allah, the Light of the heavens and the earth, perfect for us our light and forgive us. Indeed, You are Able to do all things!

Al-Kāfi (The All-Sufficient)

Jābir (may Allah be pleased with him) reported: "We took part in the Battle of Najd along with the Messenger of Allah (may Allah's peace and blessings be upon him) and when the time for the afternoon rest approached while he was in a valley with plenty of thorny trees, he dismounted under a tree and rested in its shade and hung his sword (on it). The people dispersed amongst the trees seeking shade. While we were in that state, the Messenger of Allah (may Allah's peace and blessings be upon him) called us and we came and found a Bedouin sitting in front of him. The Prophet (may Allah's peace and blessings be upon him) said: 'This one came to me while I was asleep, and he took my sword stealthily. I woke up while he was standing at my head, holding my sword unsheathed. He said: "Who will save you from me?" I replied: "Allah." So, he sheathed it and sat down, and here he is.' The Prophet (may Allah's peace and blessings be upon him) did not punish him." [Narrated by Al-Bukhāri and Muslim]

Allah Almighty says:{Is Allah not sufficient for His slave?...}[Surat az-Zumar: 36]

{Is Allah not sufficient for His slave?...}

[Surat az-Zumar: 36]

Our Lord, Exalted be He, is sufficient for His servants as He provides for them, protects them, and sets aright their affairs. So, He grants them sufficiency, which is general sufficiency that applies to all creation.

As for His special sufficiency, He gives it to those who rely upon Him and turn to Him in belief and repentance.

This sufficiency is broad as Allah Almighty says:{Is Allah not sufficient for His slave? Yet they frighten you with those [whom they worship] besides Him. Whoever Allah causes to stray, there is none to guide him.}[Surat az-Zumar: 36]He also says:{...Whoever puts his trust in Allah, He is sufficient for him...}[Surat at-Talāq: 3]That means He grants him sufficiency in all his worldly and religious affairs.An aspect of His sufficiency that He granted His Messenger (may Allah's peace and blessings be upon him) and the believers is that He supported them with angels and granted them victory:{...To Allah belong the soldiers of the heavens and earth...}[Surat al-Fat-h: 4]And He says:{Yes, if you stay patient and fear Allah, and the enemy should launch a surprise attack on you, your Lord will help you with five thousand marked angels.}[Surat Āl 'Imrān: 125]

{Is Allah not sufficient for His slave? Yet they frighten you with those [whom they worship] besides Him. Whoever Allah causes to stray, there is none to guide him.}

[Surat az-Zumar: 36]

He also says:

{...Whoever puts his trust in Allah, He is sufficient for him...}

[Surat at-Talāq: 3]

That means He grants him sufficiency in all his worldly and religious affairs.

An aspect of His sufficiency that He granted His Messenger (may Allah's peace and blessings be upon him) and the believers is that He supported them with angels and granted them victory:

{...To Allah belong the soldiers of the heavens and earth...}

[Surat al-Fat-h: 4]

And He says:

{Yes, if you stay patient and fear Allah, and the enemy should launch a surprise attack on you, your Lord will help you with five thousand marked angels.}

[Surat Āl 'Imrān: 125]

He is the All-Sufficient:

We cannot dispense with our Lord in terms of all our affairs, even for the blink of an eye. We need Him to protect us and grant us sufficiency and success. In one of the greatest Hadīths the Prophet (may Allah's peace and blessings be upon him) said about sufficiency given by our Lord:"When a man goes out of his house and says: 'Bismillāh tawakkaltu 'alallāh wa la hawla wa la quwwata illa billāh (In the Name of Allah, I rely upon Allah; there is no power nor strength except through Allah)', thereupon it will be said to him: 'You are guided, defended, and protected.'The devils will go far from him and another devil will say: 'How can you deal with a man who has been guided, defended, and protected?'"[Narrated by Abu Dāwūd; Sahīh (authentic)]The believer often implores his Lord and invokes Him by His beautiful names asking Him for protection and steadfastness. He alone can grant us sufficiency and protection. Whenever the Prophet (may Allah's peace and blessings be upon him) went to bed, he would say:"Al-hamdulillāhi alladhi at'amana wa saqāna wa kafāna wa āwāna fa kam mimman la kāfiya lahu wa la mu'wi (Praise be to Allah Who gave us food and drink, provided for us sufficiency, and gave us shelter, for there are many who have none to provide for them or to give them shelter)." [Narrated by Muslim]

"When a man goes out of his house and says: 'Bismillāh tawakkaltu 'alallāh wa la hawla wa la quwwata illa billāh (In the Name of Allah, I rely upon Allah; there is no power nor strength except through Allah)', thereupon it will be said to him: 'You are guided, defended, and protected.'

The devils will go far from him and another devil will say: 'How can you deal with a man who has been guided, defended, and protected?'"

[Narrated by Abu Dāwūd; Sahīh (authentic)]

The believer often implores his Lord and invokes Him by His beautiful names asking Him for protection and steadfastness. He alone can grant us sufficiency and protection. Whenever the Prophet (may Allah's peace and blessings be upon him) went to bed, he would say:

"Al-hamdulillāhi alladhi at'amana wa saqāna wa kafāna wa āwāna fa kam mimman la kāfiya lahu wa la mu'wi (Praise be to Allah Who gave us food and drink, provided for us sufficiency, and gave us shelter, for there are many who have none to provide for them or to give them shelter)." [Narrated by Muslim]

Stay at His door!

When the believer trusts his Lord, relies upon Him sincerely, and pins great hopes upon Him, Allah will not disappoint him for He says:{...Whoever puts his trust in Allah, He is sufficient for him...}[Surat at-Talāq: 3]Here is a connection between the means and the Owner of those means. The Prophet (may Allah's peace and blessings be upon him) is authentically reported to have said:"Allah says: 'I am as My servant thinks of Me. If he thinks well of Me, he gets it; and if he thinks ill of Me, he gets it.'"[Narrated by Ahmad; Sahīh (authentic)]

{...Whoever puts his trust in Allah, He is sufficient for him...}

[Surat at-Talāq: 3]

Here is a connection between the means and the Owner of those means. The Prophet (may Allah's peace and blessings be upon him) is authentically reported to have said:

"Allah says: 'I am as My servant thinks of Me. If he thinks well of Me, he gets it; and if he thinks ill of Me, he gets it.'"

[Narrated by Ahmad; Sahīh (authentic)]

Allah Almighty took charge of Yūsuf's affairs. He made the caravan traveling in the desert in need of water so that they could get Yūsuf (Joseph) (peace be upon him) out of the well. Then, He made the ruler of Egypt in need of children so as to adopt him. Then, He made the king in need of someone to interpret his dream so he would be released from prison. Thereafter, He made all of Egypt in need of food so that he could become the ruler of Egypt. When Allah takes charge of your affairs, He facilitates for you all means of success and bliss while you are not aware. Just rely upon Him, for He is sufficient for you, and say from your heart: I entrust my affairs to Allah.

A test..

Ibn al-Qayyim (may Allah have mercy upon him) said: "As He mentions His sufficiency for those who rely upon Him, this may lead some to mistakenly believe that His sufficiency should come promptly at the time of reliance. So, He follows that with His saying:{...for Allah has set a destiny for everything.}[Surat at-Talāq: 3]That means there is a specific time for this, and it cannot come before or after it.So, a person should not be hasty and say: I have relied upon Allah and supplicated Him, yet I have seen nothing as a result and have not received sufficiency.Indeed, Allah will surely accomplish His purpose at the time He had set for it."

{...for Allah has set a destiny for everything.}

[Surat at-Talāq: 3]

That means there is a specific time for this, and it cannot come before or after it.

So, a person should not be hasty and say: I have relied upon Allah and supplicated Him, yet I have seen nothing as a result and have not received sufficiency.

Indeed, Allah will surely accomplish His purpose at the time He had set for it."

Hence, Allah Almighty tests some of His servants with regard to the sincerity of their reliance upon Him by delaying His response. When this gets too long for some, they abandon reliance upon their Lord and turn to other people in need and humiliation, even if it were at the expense of their religion and the pleasure of their Creator.

The Prophet (may Allah's peace and blessings be upon him) is authentically reported to have said:"Whoever seeks Allah's pleasure by people's wrath, Allah will grant him sufficiency and spare him people's wrath. And whoever seeks people's pleasure by Allah's wrath, Allah will entrust him to people."[Narrated by Al-Tirmidhi; Sahīh (authentic)]

"Whoever seeks Allah's pleasure by people's wrath, Allah will grant him sufficiency and spare him people's wrath. And whoever seeks people's pleasure by Allah's wrath, Allah will entrust him to people."

[Narrated by Al-Tirmidhi; Sahīh (authentic)]

The adequate answer..

A person cannot reach this goal unless he makes the Hereafter his chief concern. The Prophet (may Allah's peace and blessings be upon him) is authentically reported to have said:"Whoever makes the Hereafter his only concern, aside from all other concerns, Allah will spare him the concerns of his worldly life. But whoever has so many concerns about worldly affairs, Allah will not care in which one of its valleys he would be ruined."[Narrated by Ibn Mājah; Sahīh (authentic)]Ibn al-Qayyim (may Allah have mercy upon him) said:"Whoever gets preoccupied with Allah and forgets himself, Allah gives him sufficiency in terms of himself; whoever gets preoccupied with Allah and forgets people, Allah gives him sufficiency in terms of people; whoever gets preoccupied with himself and forgets Allah, Allah leaves him to his own devices; and whoever gets preoccupied with people and forgets Allah, Allah leaves him to them."

"Whoever makes the Hereafter his only concern, aside from all other concerns, Allah will spare him the concerns of his worldly life. But whoever has so many concerns about worldly affairs, Allah will not care in which one of its valleys he would be ruined."

[Narrated by Ibn Mājah; Sahīh (authentic)]

Ibn al-Qayyim (may Allah have mercy upon him) said:

"Whoever gets preoccupied with Allah and forgets himself, Allah gives him sufficiency in terms of himself; whoever gets preoccupied with Allah and forgets people, Allah gives him sufficiency in terms of people; whoever gets preoccupied with himself and forgets Allah, Allah leaves him to his own devices; and whoever gets preoccupied with people and forgets Allah, Allah leaves him to them."

He Whose mercy encompasses all creation will grant you sufficiency. Sufficient for you is a Lord Whose kindness is ceaseless and Who continues to protect you, conceal your faults, and bestow His favors upon you.

Sufficiency from the Bestower of grace and favors comes to you in merciful and affectionate ways, though He sees you when you commit sins and engage in disobedience.

O Allah, the All-Sufficient, grant us sufficiency with what You have made lawful beyond need for what You have made unlawful, and make us with Your bounty in no need of others.

Al-Mawla Al-Waliyy (The Protector - The Guardian)

You are in need of support and care and someone to refer to and rely upon. You need a protector. You need someone to keep you reassured. You need someone strong enough to protect you against the evils of your enemies. You are in need of Allah, Your Protector.

I have come to You, the Owner of majesty, so remove my distress.

To whom a servant would complain, if not to You, O the Master of all masters.

Allah Almighty says:{...He is the Guardian, the Praiseworthy.}[Surat ash-Shūra: 28]He also says:{Allah is the Protector of those who believe; He brings them out of the depths of darkness into the light...}[Surat al-Baqarah: 257]

{...He is the Guardian, the Praiseworthy.}

[Surat ash-Shūra: 28]

He also says:

{Allah is the Protector of those who believe; He brings them out of the depths of darkness into the light...}

[Surat al-Baqarah: 257]

Our Almighty Lord is the Guardian and Protector of all His creation. He created them and manages their affairs and disposes of everything in the heavens and the earth constantly. No one but Allah can bring about benefit or remove harm and evil. The forelocks of all of us are in His Hand, Exalted be He.

This is general support and protection. It comprises all creatures and servants, pious and impious, believers and disbelievers.

As for Allah's special support and protection, this is for His pious servants as He brings them out of the darkness of ignorance, disbelief, and sins into the light of knowledge, belief, and obedience. He supports them against their enemies and sets aright their worldly and religious affairs.

This support entails compassion, mercy, reform, protection, and love. Allah Almighty says:{Allah is the Protector of those who believe; He brings them out of the depths of darkness into the light...}[Surat al-Baqarah: 257]

{Allah is the Protector of those who believe; He brings them out of the depths of darkness into the light...}

[Surat al-Baqarah: 257]

He protects you as much as you obey Him:

Allah Almighty protects and supports the believer insomuch as he loves Him. Ibn al-Qayyim (may Allah have mercy upon him) said: "The basis of protection is love. Without love, there is no protection. Likewise, hostility is based on hatred.

Allah is the Guardian of the believers and they are His supporters. They show loyalty to Him by their love for Him, and He grants them protection by His love for them. Indeed, Allah protects His believing servant insomuch as he loves Him."

The protection of Allah Almighty is unlike any other.{...There is nothing like unto Him, and He is the All-Hearing, the All-Seeing.}[Surat ash-Shūra: 11]Allah Almighty bestows His support and protection upon His servants by way of benevolence, mercy, and consolation for them.{Allah is the Protector of those who believe...}[Surat al-Baqarah: 257]By contrast, when people show loyalty to one another, they do so because of their need for help, support, and protection, given their weakness and need.However, the All-Mighty and the Self-Sufficient Lord does not give support or enter into alliance due to need or weakness. In the Qur'an, He says:{And say, "All praise be to Allah Who has not taken a son, nor does He have any partner in His dominion, nor does He need any protector out of weakness. And proclaim His greatness immensely."}[Surat al-Isrā': 111]

{...There is nothing like unto Him, and He is the All-Hearing, the All-Seeing.}

[Surat ash-Shūra: 11]

Allah Almighty bestows His support and protection upon His servants by way of benevolence, mercy, and consolation for them.

{Allah is the Protector of those who believe...}

[Surat al-Baqarah: 257]

By contrast, when people show loyalty to one another, they do so because of their need for help, support, and protection, given their weakness and need.

However, the All-Mighty and the Self-Sufficient Lord does not give support or enter into alliance due to need or weakness. In the Qur'an, He says:

{And say, "All praise be to Allah Who has not taken a son, nor does He have any partner in His dominion, nor does He need any protector out of weakness. And proclaim His greatness immensely."}

[Surat al-Isrā': 111]

They are the people..

The supporters of Allah among His servants refer to those who love Him and love His Messenger (may Allah's peace and blessings be upon him) and love anyone who loves Allah and His Messenger and hate anyone who hates Allah and His Messenger; and they show loyalty to those who show loyalty to Allah and His Messenger and show hostility to those who are hostile to Allah and His Messenger; and they obey Allah and avoid disobeying Him.{Whoever takes Allah, His Messenger, and the believers as their allies, then it is the party of Allah that will certainly prevail.}[Surat al-Mā'idah: 56]{You will not find any people who believe in Allah and the Last Day taking as allies those who oppose Allah and His Messenger...}[Surat al-Mujādilah: 22]

{Whoever takes Allah, His Messenger, and the believers as their allies, then it is the party of Allah that will certainly prevail.}

[Surat al-Mā'idah: 56]

{You will not find any people who believe in Allah and the Last Day taking as allies those who oppose Allah and His Messenger...}

[Surat al-Mujādilah: 22]

The path:

Allah's protection can only be attained through two things: faith and piety. Allah Almighty says:{Indeed, the allies of Allah will have no fear, nor will they grieve.Those who believe and fear Allah.For them are glad tidings in the life of this world and in the Hereafter; there is no change in Allah's words. That is the supreme triumph.}[Surat Yūnus: 62-64]Allah's protection is to be acquired by certain causes and actions by the heart and body organs as Allah Almighty says:{As for those who strive in Our cause, We will surely guide them to Our ways, for Allah is certainly with those who do good.}[Surat al-'Ankabūt: 69]{...and He will be their Protector because of what they used to do.}[Surat al-An'ām: 127]

{Indeed, the allies of Allah will have no fear, nor will they grieve.

Those who believe and fear Allah.

For them are glad tidings in the life of this world and in the Hereafter; there is no change in Allah's words. That is the supreme triumph.}

[Surat Yūnus: 62-64]

Allah's protection is to be acquired by certain causes and actions by the heart and body organs as Allah Almighty says:

{As for those who strive in Our cause, We will surely guide them to Our ways, for Allah is certainly with those who do good.}

[Surat al-'Ankabūt: 69]

{...and He will be their Protector because of what they used to do.}

[Surat al-An'ām: 127]

People enjoy different levels of Allah's protection and support in accordance with their varying degrees of faith and piety.

The keys to acceptance:

The more one pleases Allah Almighty by observing the obligations and doing the recommended acts of piety, the more he loves his Lord and draws closer to Him.

The Prophet (may Allah's peace and blessings be upon him) is authentically reported to have said:"Allah Almighty says: 'I will declare war against he who shows hostility to a pious worshiper of Mine. And the most beloved thing with which My slave comes nearer to Me is what I have enjoined upon him; and My slave keeps on coming closer to Me through performing supererogatory acts of worship till I love him. When I love him, I become his hearing with which he hears, his seeing with which he sees, his hand with which he seizes, and his leg with which he walks; and if he asks (something) from Me, I give him, and if he asks for My refuge, I protect him.and I do not hesitate to do anything as I hesitate to take the soul of the believer; as he hates death, and I hate to hurt him.'"[Narrated by Al-Bukhāri]Shaykh al-Islam Ibn Taymiyyah (may Allah have mercy upon him) said:"A person does not become a pious servant of Allah unless he follows the Prophet (may Allah's peace and blessings be upon him) inwardly and outwardly. The more he follows the Prophet, the more he becomes a pious servant of Allah."

"Allah Almighty says: 'I will declare war against he who shows hostility to a pious worshiper of Mine. And the most beloved thing with which My slave comes nearer to Me is what I have enjoined upon him; and My slave keeps on coming closer to Me through performing supererogatory acts of worship till I love him. When I love him, I become his hearing with which he hears, his seeing with which he sees, his hand with which he seizes, and his leg with which he walks; and if he asks (something) from Me, I give him, and if he asks for My refuge, I protect him.

and I do not hesitate to do anything as I hesitate to take the soul of the believer; as he hates death, and I hate to hurt him.'"

[Narrated by Al-Bukhāri]

Shaykh al-Islam Ibn Taymiyyah (may Allah have mercy upon him) said:

"A person does not become a pious servant of Allah unless he follows the Prophet (may Allah's peace and blessings be upon him) inwardly and outwardly. The more he follows the Prophet, the more he becomes a pious servant of Allah."

If He grants you His protection, He will surprise you!

This special protection entails kindness and help to His servants:{Allah is the Protector of those who believe; He brings them out of the depths of darkness into the light...}[Surat al-Baqarah: 257]This also entails mercy and forgiveness of sins:{...You are our Guardian, so forgive us and have mercy upon us, for You are the Best of the Forgivers.}[Surat al-A'rāf: 155]And it entails help and support against the enemies:{...You are our Protector, so give us victory over the disbelieving people.}[Surat al-Baqarah: 286]Allah Almighty says:{But Allah is your Protector, and He is the Best of helpers.}[Surat Āl 'Imrān: 150]Also, Allah's protection entails admission into Paradise and salvation from Hellfire. Allah Almighty says:{They will have the Home of Peace with their Lord, and He will be their Protector because of what they used to do.}[Surat al-An'ām: 127]It is a great favor from Allah that He becomes your Protector. In the Qur'an, He says:{...What an excellent Protector and an excellent Helper!}[Surat al-Anfāl: 40]If Allah is your protector, you have attained security in this world and in the Hereafter:{...They are the ones who will be secure, and it is they who are rightly guided.}[Surat al-An'ām: 82]You feel reassured because Allah Almighty is with you. You constantly say:{Say, "Nothing will ever befall us except that which Allah has decreed for us; He is our Protector." And in Allah alone let the believers put their trust.}[Surat at-Tawbah: 51]He may harden your circumstances and make it difficult for you with the aim of selecting you:{But We wanted to bestow favor upon those who were oppressed in the land, and make them leaders and inheritors [of the land].}[Surat al-Qasas: 5]

{Allah is the Protector of those who believe; He brings them out of the depths of darkness into the light...}

[Surat al-Baqarah: 257]

This also entails mercy and forgiveness of sins:

{...You are our Guardian, so forgive us and have mercy upon us, for You are the Best of the Forgivers.}

[Surat al-A'rāf: 155]

And it entails help and support against the enemies:

{...You are our Protector, so give us victory over the disbelieving people.}

[Surat al-Baqarah: 286]

Allah Almighty says:

{But Allah is your Protector, and He is the Best of helpers.}

[Surat Āl 'Imrān: 150]

Also, Allah's protection entails admission into Paradise and salvation from Hellfire. Allah Almighty says:

{They will have the Home of Peace with their Lord, and He will be their Protector because of what they used to do.}

[Surat al-An'ām: 127]

It is a great favor from Allah that He becomes your Protector. In the Qur'an, He says:

{...What an excellent Protector and an excellent Helper!}

[Surat al-Anfāl: 40]

If Allah is your protector, you have attained security in this world and in the Hereafter:

{...They are the ones who will be secure, and it is they who are rightly guided.}

[Surat al-An'ām: 82]

You feel reassured because Allah Almighty is with you. You constantly say:

{Say, "Nothing will ever befall us except that which Allah has decreed for us; He is our Protector." And in Allah alone let the believers put their trust.}

[Surat at-Tawbah: 51]

He may harden your circumstances and make it difficult for you with the aim of selecting you:

{But We wanted to bestow favor upon those who were oppressed in the land, and make them leaders and inheritors [of the land].}

[Surat al-Qasas: 5]

If your Lord grants you His protection, then you are under great care and enjoying a grand blessing; you err and He punishes you; you act extravagantly and He withholds things from you; and you behave arrogantly and He disciplines you. This is only because He is your protector, and what an excellent Protector and an excellent Helper!

You know with certain knowledge that this is a punishment from a loving Lord, not a punishment, for Allah does not punish His beloved servants.{The Jews and Christians say, "We are Allah's children and

His beloved ones." Say, "Why then does He punish you for your sins? Rather, you are humans just like anyone else He created...}[Surat al-Mā'idah: 18]

{The Jews and Christians say, "We are Allah's children and His beloved ones." Say, "Why then does He punish you for your sins? Rather, you are humans just like anyone else He created...}

[Surat al-Mā'idah: 18]

My Lord, You are worthy of showing benevolence, and to You belong great grace and abundant bounty.

So pardon me, for I am at Your door, broken and humiliated.

O Allah, we implore You by Your name "Al-Mawla" to confer Your favor upon us and admit us into Paradise and to make us among Your pious servants and allies, in public and in secret.

Al-Hādi (The Guide)

I went astray for long, not knowing guidance.

This brought darkness into my heart.

And when Allah wanted to drive me towards guidance,

He showed me the path of the truth and guided me.

So, I threw away the darkness of misguidance and ruin,

and turned to the bright light of guidance.

I proceeded towards the religion of Prophet Muhammad,

rightly guided, and became, after the misguidance, a caller to guidance.

Out of Allah's mercy towards His servants, He rendered guidance in His Hand and He called Himself "Al-Hādi".

We pause here with this name as we implore Allah Almighty to guide us to the truth and to the straight path.

Allah Almighty says:{...Allah surely guides those who believe to the straight path.}[Surat al-Hajj: 54]He also says:{...but your Lord is sufficient as a Guide and Helper.}[Surat al-Furqān: 31]

{...Allah surely guides those who believe to the straight path.}

[Surat al-Hajj: 54]

He also says:

{...but your Lord is sufficient as a Guide and Helper.}

[Surat al-Furqān: 31]

Our Lord, Exalted be He, is the One Who guides His servants to bring about benefits and ward off harms and evils and He teaches them what they do not know. He guides them to success, inspires them to be pious, and makes their hearts relenting and submissive to Him.

Allah's guidance to people

falls under four categories:

First: General guidance: All beings are guided to their interests in terms of their living and subsistence. Such guidance encompasses all that lives: humans, jinn, animals, birds, etc.

Second: Guidance in which accountable servants are shown the way and things are made clear for them. It is the argument of Allah Almighty against His servants, none will be punished except after it has been established against him.

Allah Almighty says:{As for Thamūd, We showed them guidance, but they preferred blindness over the guidance...}[Surat Fussilat: 17]Third: Guidance of help, inspiration, and making the heart inclined to accept the truth and be pleased with it. Allah Almighty says:{Whoever Allah guides is truly guided...}[Surat al-Isrā': 97]{...Whoever believes in Allah, He will guide his heart...}[Surat at-Taghābun: 11]Hence, Allah Almighty commands His servants to ask Him for guidance. He even instructs them to do so in every Rak'ah (unit of prayer):{Guide us to the straight path.}[Surat al-Fātihah: 6]Fourth: Guidance to Paradise and to Hellfire on the Day of Judgment. Allah Almighty says:{He will guide them, and will set their condition right.}[Surat Muhammad: 5]{...They will say, "All praise be to Allah Who has guided us to this, for We would not have been guided to this if Allah had not guided us...}[Surat al-A'rāf: 43]As for guidance to Hellfire, Allah Almighty says:{[The angels will be told], "Gather all those who did wrong and their fellows, and whatever they used to worshipbesides Allah, and lead them to the way of Hell.}[Surat as-Sāffāt: 22-23]

{As for Thamūd, We showed them guidance, but they preferred blindness over the guidance...}

[Surat Fussilat: 17]

Third: Guidance of help, inspiration, and making the heart inclined to accept the truth and be pleased with it. Allah Almighty says:

{Whoever Allah guides is truly guided...}

[Surat al-Isrā': 97]

{...Whoever believes in Allah, He will guide his heart...}

[Surat at-Taghābun: 11]

Hence, Allah Almighty commands His servants to ask Him for guidance. He even instructs them to do so in every Rak'ah (unit of prayer):

{Guide us to the straight path.}

[Surat al-Fātihah: 6]

Fourth: Guidance to Paradise and to Hellfire on the Day of Judgment. Allah Almighty says:

{He will guide them, and will set their condition right.}

[Surat Muhammad: 5]

{...They will say, "All praise be to Allah Who has guided us to this, for We would not have been guided to this if Allah had not guided us...}

[Surat al-A'rāf: 43]

As for guidance to Hellfire, Allah Almighty says:

{[The angels will be told], "Gather all those who did wrong and their fellows, and whatever they used to worship

besides Allah, and lead them to the way of Hell.}

[Surat as-Sāffāt: 22-23]

The more you are guided, the higher you get elevated..

Guidance is the greatest blessing bestowed by Allah, the Guide, upon His servants. All other blessings are transient.

Those versed in knowledge are the most keen on maintaining this blessing, and they supplicate Allah to not let it go away:{Our Lord, do not let our hearts deviate after You have guided us...}[Surat Āl 'Imrān: 8]Guidance has no maximum limit. No matter how well a person may be guided, there is more and greater guidance. The more a person is heedful of his Lord, the higher he gets to another guidance. He grows in guidance as long as he grows in piety. Allah Almighty says:{Allah increases in guidance those who are guided...}[Surat Maryam: 76]If he misses a share of piety, he also misses a similar share of guidance. He who attains guidance has obtained eternal bliss. Allah Almighty says:{Guide us to the straight path,the path of those whom You have blessed...}[Surat al-Fātihah: 6-7]The sign of guidance is relief in the heart. Allah Almighty says:{Whoever Allah wills to guide, He opens his heart to Islam...}[Surat al-An'ām: 125]When Allah guides someone, no one can lead him astray, and the opposite is also true. Allah Almighty says:{...Whoever Allah causes to stray, there is none to guide him.And whoever Allah guides, none can lead him astray...}[Surat az-Zumar: 36-37]The Prophet (may Allah's peace and blessings be upon him) would often supplicate:"Allāhumma inni as'aluka al-huda wa at-tuqa wa al-'afāf wa al-ghina (O Allah, I ask You for guidance, piety, chastity, and richness)."[Narrated by Muslim]Teaching 'Ali (may Allah be pleased with him), the Prophet (may Allah's peace and blessings be upon him) said:"Say: Allāhumma ihdini wa saddidni (O Allah, guide me and keep me steadfast on the right path)."[Narrated by Muslim]He also taught Al-Hasan ibn 'Ali (may Allah be pleased with him and his father) to say during the supplication of Witr:"Allāhumma ihdini fīman hadayt (O Allah, guide me among those You have guided)."[Narrated by Abu Dāwūd; Sahīh (authentic)]

{Our Lord, do not let our hearts deviate after You have guided us...}

[Surat Āl 'Imrān: 8]

Guidance has no maximum limit. No matter how well a person may be guided, there is more and greater guidance. The more a person is heedful of his Lord, the higher he gets to another guidance. He grows in guidance as long as he grows in piety. Allah Almighty says:

{Allah increases in guidance those who are guided...}

[Surat Maryam: 76]

If he misses a share of piety, he also misses a similar share of guidance. He who attains guidance has obtained eternal bliss. Allah Almighty says:

{Guide us to the straight path,

the path of those whom You have blessed...}

[Surat al-Fātihah: 6-7]

The sign of guidance is relief in the heart. Allah Almighty says:

{Whoever Allah wills to guide, He opens his heart to Islam...}

[Surat al-An'ām: 125]

When Allah guides someone, no one can lead him astray, and the opposite is also true. Allah Almighty says:

{...Whoever Allah causes to stray, there is none to guide him.

And whoever Allah guides, none can lead him astray...}

[Surat az-Zumar: 36-37]

The Prophet (may Allah's peace and blessings be upon him) would often supplicate:

"Allāhumma inni as'aluka al-huda wa at-tuqa wa al-'afāf wa al-ghina (O Allah, I ask You for guidance, piety, chastity, and richness)."

[Narrated by Muslim]

Teaching 'Ali (may Allah be pleased with him), the Prophet (may Allah's peace and blessings be upon him) said:

"Say: Allāhumma ihdini wa saddidni (O Allah, guide me and keep me steadfast on the right path)."

[Narrated by Muslim]

He also taught Al-Hasan ibn 'Ali (may Allah be pleased with him and his father) to say during the supplication of Witr:

"Allāhumma ihdini fīman hadayt (O Allah, guide me among those You have guided)."

[Narrated by Abu Dāwūd; Sahīh (authentic)]

Leading a life between worship and sins carries the risk of ending your life in sins.

Shaykh al-Islam Ibn Taymiyyah (may Allah have mercy upon him) said:"Sins do always accompany man. So, he needs guidance in every moment. In fact, he needs guidance more than he needs food and drink."

"Sins do always accompany man. So, he needs guidance in every moment. In fact, he needs guidance more than he needs food and drink."

Knock on the door of the heaven!

About Ibrāhim (Abraham) (peace be upon him), Allah Almighty says:{He said, "I am going to my Lord; He will guide me...}[Surat as-Sāffāt: 99]

{He said, "I am going to my Lord; He will guide me...}

[Surat as-Sāffāt: 99]

Turn to Allah with your weakness, He will turn to you with His power. Go to Him with your humiliation, He will give you honor.

Go to Allah in loneliness, and He will give you company.

Go to Allah in need, and He will make you self-sufficient.

Go to Allah with your distress, and He will give you relief.

Go to Allah with your grief, and He will grant you joy.

My Lord, save me from Your punishment; I am humbly submissive to You and fearful of You.

Make me taste Your pardon on a Day no children or wealth will be of any avail.

A last word..

Al-Shīrāzi (may Allah have mercy upon him) said:"One day I stayed up at night with my father and the people around us were asleep. I said: 'None of those has got up to offer two Rak'ahs!' He said: 'Son, if you remained asleep, it would be better for you than talking ill of people.'"Your righteousness does not give you the right to mock the misguidance of others. Indeed, hearts are between the two Fingers of Allah and He overturns them as He wishes. So, do not be deluded by your worship and pious acts for these are only favors from your Lord. Implore Him to make you steadfast on guidance and to guide others. Addressing His Prophet (may Allah's peace and blessings be upon him), Allah Almighty says:{Had We not made you stand firm, you would nearly have inclined to them a little.}[Surat al-Isrā': 74]So, what about us?!

"One day I stayed up at night with my father and the people around us were asleep. I said: 'None of those has got up to offer two Rak'ahs!' He said: 'Son, if you remained asleep, it would be better for you than talking ill of people.'"

Your righteousness does not give you the right to mock the misguidance of others. Indeed, hearts are between the two Fingers of Allah and He overturns them as He wishes. So, do not be deluded by your worship and pious acts for these are only favors from your Lord. Implore Him to make you steadfast on guidance and to guide others. Addressing His Prophet (may Allah's peace and blessings be upon him), Allah Almighty says:

{Had We not made you stand firm, you would nearly have inclined to them a little.}

[Surat al-Isrā': 74]

So, what about us?!

O Allah, guide us to the truth over which there was disagreement, by Your permission; indeed, You guide whom You will to a straight path.

An-Nasīr (the Helper)

The Prophet's Companions (may Allah be pleased with them) did not like the terms of the Hudaybiyah Treaty.

'Umar ibn al-Khattāb (may Allah be pleased with him) reported: "I came to the Prophet (may Allah's peace and blessings be upon him) and said: 'Are you not the Prophet of Allah?' He said: 'Yes.' I said: 'Are we not on the path of truth and our enemy on the path of falsehood?' He said: 'Yes.' I said: 'So, why would we act humbly with regard to our religion?'

Thereupon, he (may Allah's peace and blessings be upon him) said:'I am the Messenger of Allah; I do not disobey Him and He shall grant me victory.'"[Narrated by Al-Bukhāri - this is his wording - and Muslim]

'I am the Messenger of Allah; I do not disobey Him and He shall grant me victory.'"

[Narrated by Al-Bukhāri - this is his wording - and Muslim]

Exalted are You Who make the truth victorious over widespread evil.

You give the rights to those to whom they are due, and Your help is the strongest and closest.

About Himself, Allah Almighty says:{...then know that Allah is your Protector. What an excellent Protector and an excellent Helper!}[Surat al-Anfāl: 40]It is the Almighty Lord Who helps His messengers, prophets, and pious servants and supports them against their enemies in this world and on the Day of Judgment. Allah Almighty says:{We will surely help Our messengers and those who believe in the life of this world and on the Day when the witnesses will come forward.}[Surat Ghāfir: 51]

{...then know that Allah is your Protector. What an excellent Protector and an excellent Helper!}

[Surat al-Anfāl: 40]

It is the Almighty Lord Who helps His messengers, prophets, and pious servants and supports them against their enemies in this world and on the Day of Judgment. Allah Almighty says:

{We will surely help Our messengers and those who believe in the life of this world and on the Day when the witnesses will come forward.}

[Surat Ghāfir: 51]

Our Lord is the One Who helps the vulnerable and saves the oppressed from oppression, even if they are disbelievers. Indeed, there is no true helper for them but Allah.

Allah Almighty helps the believers against their enemies, including the outside enemies such as the disbelievers and oppressors, and the inside enemies like one's self and the devil, which are more dangerous than one's external enemies.{As for those who strive in Our cause, We will surely guide them to Our ways, for Allah is certainly with those who do good.}[Surat al-'Ankabūt: 69]If help comes from Allah to anyone, he cannot be defeated; and if Allah fails someone, no one can help him.{If Allah helps you, none can overcome you...}[Surat Āl 'Imrān: 160]

{As for those who strive in Our cause, We will surely guide them to Our ways, for Allah is certainly with those who do good.}

[Surat al-'Ankabūt: 69]

If help comes from Allah to anyone, he cannot be defeated; and if Allah fails someone, no one can help him.

{If Allah helps you, none can overcome you...}

[Surat Āl 'Imrān: 160]

Forms of help:

Allah Almighty bestows His help upon His servants in various and limitless forms and types that they do not expect.

It may take the form of sending supporting angels as Allah helped His Prophet (may Allah's peace and blessings be upon him) and his Companions during the Battle of Badr. It may also come in the form of wind like the case of 'Ād and the Battle of Ahzāb; or by sending birds in flocks like the case of the companions of the elephant; or by the outcry like the case of Thamūd; or by sinking into earth like the case of Qārūn; or by throwing from a high place as happened to the people of Lūt (Lot); or by the flood like the case of the people of Nūh (Noah).

The soldiers of Allah Almighty are numberless, and He shall certainly fulfill His purpose, and He is Able to do all things.

Help may sometimes come in the form of victory over the enemies, such as the victory of Sulaymān (Solomon) and Dāwūd (David) (peace be upon both of them) and the victory of Prophet Muhammad (may Allah's peace and blessings be upon him).

And it may also come in the form of revenge against the deniers during the prophets' lifetime, like the people of Noah, the people of Lot, and Pharaoh; or after their death, like enabling Bukhtanasar (Nebuchadnezzar) to overcome the killers of Prophet Yahya (John the Baptist) (peace be upon him) and enabling the Romans to overpower those who had wanted to kill 'Isa (Jesus) (peace be upon him).

Allah Almighty says:{We will surely help Our messengers and those who believe in the life of this world and on the Day when the witnesses will come forward.}[Surat Ghāfir: 51]

{We will surely help Our messengers and those who believe in the life of this world and on the Day when the witnesses will come forward.}

[Surat Ghāfir: 51]

The adequate answer..

Al-Suddi said:"The prophets and the believers would be killed in worldly life although they were helped (by Allah). The people who did this to the prophets and the believers would not die until Allah send other people through whom He would take revenge for those who had been killed. Thus, the obscurity in this verse is cleared."There is another obscurity cited by some people regarding the verse that says:{...And Allah will never give the disbelievers a way over the believers.}[Surat an-Nisā': 141]

"The prophets and the believers would be killed in worldly life although they were helped (by Allah). The people who did this to the prophets and the believers would not die until Allah send other people through whom He would take revenge for those who had been killed. Thus, the obscurity in this verse is cleared."

There is another obscurity cited by some people regarding the verse that says:

{...And Allah will never give the disbelievers a way over the believers.}

[Surat an-Nisā': 141]

There is no obscurity in this regard as far as the Hereafter is concerned.

But with regard to worldly life, the answer is as Ibn al-Qayyim (may Allah have mercy upon him) said:"If their faith weakens, their enemies get a way against them in proportion to the decrease in their faith."Indeed, the believer is endowed with honor, dominance, help, and victory:{We will surely help Our messengers and those who believe in the life of this world and on the Day when the witnesses will come forward.}[Surat Ghāfir: 51]What we see today, as the disbelievers are stronger and dominant over the believers, is due to what the Muslims did to their religion by way of adding thereto or omitting therefrom. If they repent, their faith will be complete and help will come to them from their Lord:{This is the promise of Allah. Allah never breaks His promise...}[Surat ar-Rūm: 6]The price for help is faith, preparation, and patience. Allah Almighty says:{...For it is incumbent upon Us to help the believers.}[Surat ar-Rūm: 47]He also says:{Prepare against them whatever force you can...}[Surat al-Anfāl: 60]And He says:{...But if you keep patient and fear Allah, their schemes will not harm you in the least...}[Surat Āl 'Imrān: 120]And the Prophet (may Allah's peace and blessings be upon him) said:"... And victory comes with patience."[Narrated by Ahmad; Sahīh (authentic)]Thereupon, help comes down from Allah, the Supporter, the Helper, Who says:{...Victory only comes from Allah, the All-Mighty, the All-Wise.}[Surat Āl 'Imrān: 126]He also says:{If Allah helps you, none can overcome you...}[Surat Āl 'Imrān: 160]

"If their faith weakens, their enemies get a way against them in proportion to the decrease in their faith."

Indeed, the believer is endowed with honor, dominance, help, and victory:

{We will surely help Our messengers and those who believe in the life of this world and on the Day when the witnesses will come forward.}

[Surat Ghāfir: 51]

What we see today, as the disbelievers are stronger and dominant over the believers, is due to what the Muslims did to their religion by way of adding thereto or omitting therefrom. If they repent, their faith will be complete and help will come to them from their Lord:

{This is the promise of Allah. Allah never breaks His promise...}

[Surat ar-Rūm: 6]

The price for help is faith, preparation, and patience. Allah Almighty says:

{...For it is incumbent upon Us to help the believers.}

[Surat ar-Rūm: 47]

He also says:

{Prepare against them whatever force you can...}

[Surat al-Anfāl: 60]

And He says:

{...But if you keep patient and fear Allah, their schemes will not harm you in the least...}

[Surat Āl 'Imrān: 120]

And the Prophet (may Allah's peace and blessings be upon him) said:

"... And victory comes with patience."

[Narrated by Ahmad; Sahīh (authentic)]

Thereupon, help comes down from Allah, the Supporter, the Helper, Who says:

{...Victory only comes from Allah, the All-Mighty, the All-Wise.}

[Surat Āl 'Imrān: 126]

He also says:

{If Allah helps you, none can overcome you...}

[Surat Āl 'Imrān: 160]

If Allah is with you, who could stand against you?!

And if He is against you, who could help you?!

Whoever resorts to Allah Almighty, He will give him sufficiency and elevate his status:{...And hold fast to Allah, for He is your Protector; what an excellent Protector and an excellent Helper!}[Surat al-Hajj: 78]

{...And hold fast to Allah, for He is your Protector; what an excellent Protector and an excellent Helper!}

[Surat al-Hajj: 78]

Moreover, the believer loves his fellow believers and supports them even when they are distant from him in terms of place or time.

O Allah, the Helper, help us against the disbelievers.

Al-Wārith (The Inheritor)

It was said to a wise man: Why do you always hold a stick even though you are not old or sick? He replied: So as to remember that I am on a journey.

I hold the stick not due to weakness

or old age.

But I obliged myself to hold it to remind myself

that the resident is in fact traveling.

Travelers are notified that they have no permanent stay in this life, hence, they should not feel settled therein. Allah Almighty says:{It is We Who will inherit the earth and all those who are on it, and to Us they will be returned.}[Surat Maryam: 40]

{It is We Who will inherit the earth and all those who are on it, and to Us they will be returned.}

[Surat Maryam: 40]

In fact, Allah is the Inheritor - Exalted be He.

We pause here with Allah's name "Al-Wārith". This is a reminder for ourselves; hopefully Allah will show mercy to us.

Allah Almighty says:{Indeed, it is We Who give life and cause death, and We are the Inheritors [of all things].}[Surat al-Hijr: 23]

{Indeed, it is We Who give life and cause death, and We are the Inheritors [of all things].}

[Surat al-Hijr: 23]

Our Lord, Exalted be He, will remain after all creatures perish, and He will inherit everything after all those in the heavens and the earth will cease to exist.

Our Lord is the Inheritor Who has no testator and the Ever-Lasting Lord Whose kingdom has no bounds.{It is We Who will inherit the earth and all those who are on it, and to Us they will be returned.}[Surat Maryam: 40]Allah Almighty is the original possessor of all things, and He bequeathes whatever He wills to whomever He wills. In the Qur'an, He says:{The earth belongs to Allah; He gives it as an inheritance to whom He wills of His slaves, but the outcome is for those who fear Allah.}[Surat al-A'rāf: 128]

{It is We Who will inherit the earth and all those who are on it, and to Us they will be returned.}

[Surat Maryam: 40]

Allah Almighty is the original possessor of all things, and He bequeathes whatever He wills to whomever He wills. In the Qur'an, He says:

{The earth belongs to Allah; He gives it as an inheritance to whom He wills of His slaves, but the outcome is for those who fear Allah.}

[Surat al-A'rāf: 128]

The Almighty Lord will bequeath to the believers the dwellings of the disbelievers in this world and in the Hereafter.

Regarding their dwellings in worldly life, Allah Almighty says:{He also made you inherit their land, their homes and their wealth, and a land on which you have not yet set foot...}[Surat al-Ahzāb: 27]And regarding their dwellings in the Hereafter, He says:{Such is the Paradise which We will give as an inheritance to those of Our slaves who feared Allah.}[Surat Maryam: 63]He also says:{We will remove all ill feelings from their hearts and rivers will flow beneath them. They will say, "All praise be to Allah Who has guided us to this, for We would not have been guided to this if Allah had not guided us. The messengers of our Lord came with the truth." They will be called, "This is Paradise that you are made to inherit for what you used to do."}[Surat al-A'rāf: 43]Moreover, the Qur'an is a book of guidance, honor, and success, which Allah gives as inheritance to those whom He chooses. He says:{Then We made to inherit the Book those whom We have chosen from among Our slaves. But among them are some who wrong themselves, some follow a middle course, and some are foremost in good deeds with Allah's permission. That is the great bounty.}[Surat Fātir: 32]

{He also made you inherit their land, their homes and their wealth, and a land on which you have not yet set foot...}

[Surat al-Ahzāb: 27]

And regarding their dwellings in the Hereafter, He says:

{Such is the Paradise which We will give as an inheritance to those of Our slaves who feared Allah.}

[Surat Maryam: 63]

He also says:

{We will remove all ill feelings from their hearts and rivers will flow beneath them. They will say, "All praise be to Allah Who has guided us to this, for We would not have been guided to this if Allah had not guided us. The messengers of our Lord came with the truth." They will be called, "This is Paradise that you are made to inherit for what you used to do."}

[Surat al-A'rāf: 43]

Moreover, the Qur'an is a book of guidance, honor, and success, which Allah gives as inheritance to those whom He chooses. He says:

{Then We made to inherit the Book those whom We have chosen from among Our slaves. But among them are some who wrong themselves, some follow a middle course, and some are foremost in good deeds with Allah's permission. That is the great bounty.}

[Surat Fātir: 32]

The real ownership..

As the believers are made successors on earth and they will ultimately return to their Lord, Allah, out of His bounty, commands them to spend out of what He has bestowed upon them, though all entirely belongs to Him, and He promises to give them abundant rewards for that. Allah Almighty says:{Believe in Allah and His Messenger, and spend [in Allah's cause] out of what He has entrusted you with. For those among you who believe and spend, there will be a great reward.}[Surat al-Hadīd: 7]He also says:{Why is it that you do not spend in the cause of Allah, when Allah alone will inherit the heavens and earth?...}[Surat al-Hadīd: 10]So, the real ownership is what one keeps in store for the Day of Judgment.Mutarrif reported that his father 'Abdullah ibn al-Shikhkhīr (may Allah be pleased with him) said: "I came to the Messenger of Allah (may Allah's peace and blessings be upon him) as he was reciting: {Competition for worldly gains distracts you [from Allah]} [Surat at-Takāthur: 1] Thereupon, he said:'The son of Adam says: "My wealth, my wealth." O son of Adam, do you own of your wealth other than what you eat and consume, or what you wear and wear out, or what you give in charity and send forward?'" [Narrated by Muslim]

{Believe in Allah and His Messenger, and spend [in Allah's cause] out of what He has entrusted you with. For those among you who believe and spend, there will be a great reward.}

[Surat al-Hadīd: 7]

He also says:

{Why is it that you do not spend in the cause of Allah, when Allah alone will inherit the heavens and earth?...}

[Surat al-Hadīd: 10]

So, the real ownership is what one keeps in store for the Day of Judgment.

Mutarrif reported that his father 'Abdullah ibn al-Shikhkhīr (may Allah be pleased with him) said: "I came to the Messenger of Allah (may Allah's peace and blessings be upon him) as he was reciting: {Competition for worldly gains distracts you [from Allah]} [Surat at-Takāthur: 1] Thereupon, he said:

'The son of Adam says: "My wealth, my wealth." O son of Adam, do you own of your wealth other than what you eat and consume, or what you wear and wear out, or what you give in charity and send forward?'" [Narrated by Muslim]

The believer knows that what he possesses is only a trust given to him, and Allah Almighty looks to see how he will act.

The wealth and family are nothing but a trust;

and trusts will surely be returned one day.

In supplications..

You should know that invoking Allah Almighty by this name falls under the general meaning of the verse that says:{Allah has the Most Beautiful Names, so call upon Him by them...}[Surat al-A'rāf:180]This is specially so when we are keen to use the name suitable for the situation and the object of invocation. An example is the supplication by Zakariyya (Zachariah) (peace be upon him):{And [remember] Zachariah, when he cried out to his Lord, "My Lord, do not leave me childless, for You are the Best of Inheritors."}[Surat al-Anbiyā': 89]Another verse reads:{And I fear my kinsmen after me, and my wife is barren; so grant me from Yourself an heir,who will inherit [prophethood] from me and from the house of Jacob, and make him, O Lord, well pleasing to You.}[Surat Maryam: 5-6]The inheritance referred to in the verses is that of knowledge, prophethood, and the call to Allah. It is not an inheritance of wealth. Another example of such blessed inheritance occurs in the verse that says:{And Solomon inherited David...}[Surat an-Naml: 16]The Prophet (may Allah's peace and blessings be upon him) is authentically reported to have said in supplication:"Allāhumma amti'ni bisam'i wa basari waj'alhuma al-wāritha minni (O Allah, make me enjoy my hearing and my sight and leave them to inherit me)."[Narrated by Al-Hākim in Al-Mustadrak; Sahīh (authentic)]

{Allah has the Most Beautiful Names, so call upon Him by them...}

[Surat al-A'rāf:180]

This is specially so when we are keen to use the name suitable for the situation and the object of invocation. An example is the supplication by Zakariyya (Zachariah) (peace be upon him):

{And [remember] Zachariah, when he cried out to his Lord, "My Lord, do not leave me childless, for You are the Best of Inheritors."}

[Surat al-Anbiyā': 89]

Another verse reads:

{And I fear my kinsmen after me, and my wife is barren; so grant me from Yourself an heir,

who will inherit [prophethood] from me and from the house of Jacob, and make him, O Lord, well pleasing to You.}

[Surat Maryam: 5-6]

The inheritance referred to in the verses is that of knowledge, prophethood, and the call to Allah. It is not an inheritance of wealth. Another example of such blessed inheritance occurs in the verse that says:

{And Solomon inherited David...}

[Surat an-Naml: 16]

The Prophet (may Allah's peace and blessings be upon him) is authentically reported to have said in supplication:

"Allāhumma amti'ni bisam'i wa basari waj'alhuma al-wāritha minni (O Allah, make me enjoy my hearing and my sight and leave them to inherit me)."

[Narrated by Al-Hākim in Al-Mustadrak; Sahīh (authentic)]

In connection with this name, scholars noted that a person should fear Allah Almighty with regard to the rights of inheritance and refrain from being unjust to any rightful heir.

O Allah, we implore You by Your name "Al-Wārith" to maintain our hearing and sight and keep them sound till we die.

Ash-Shāfi (The Healer)

The Prophet (may Allah's peace and blessings be upon him) went to visit a sick Bedouin who was suffering severe pain. Encouraging and consoling him, the Prophet (may Allah's peace and blessings be upon him) said: "It is a purification."

The Bedouin said: "Rather, it is a fever that boils in an old man and leads him to the grave."

Thereupon, the Prophet (may Allah's peace and blessings be upon him) said: "Then, it is so." [Narrated by Al-Bukhāri and Muslim]

In most cases, a person recovers or continues to be ill due to himself. If we have joyful thoughts, we become happy. So, when we entertain hopeful thoughts about recovery and put our trust in Allah Almighty, we get actually cured, by Allah's permission. On the contrary, if obsessions about illness overcome us, we will mostly remain sick.

Our Lord has opened the door of hope to every sick person. He says:{...Call upon Me; I will respond to you...}[Surat Ghāfir: 60]He also says:{Allah has the Most Beautiful Names, so call upon Him by them...}[Surat al-A'rāf:180]

{...Call upon Me; I will respond to you...}

[Surat Ghāfir: 60]

He also says:

{Allah has the Most Beautiful Names, so call upon Him by them...}

[Surat al-A'rāf:180]

One of Allah's beautiful names is "Ash-Shāfi". So, let us seek closeness to Allah Almighty by this name so that we can draw close to our purpose and fulfill our needs.

Whenever the Prophet (may Allah's peace and blessings be upon him) visited a sick person, or a sick person was brought to him, he would say:"Adh-hib al-bās Rabba an-nās, ishfi wa anta Ash-Shāfi la shifā'a illa shifā'uka shifā'an la yughādiru saqama (O Allah, the Lord of the people, remove the trouble and heal, for You are the Healer. No healing is of any avail but Yours; healing that leaves no ailment)."[Narrated by Al-Bukhāri and Muslim]

"Adh-hib al-bās Rabba an-nās, ishfi wa anta Ash-Shāfi la shifā'a illa shifā'uka shifā'an la yughādiru saqama (O Allah, the Lord of the people, remove the trouble and heal, for You are the Healer. No healing is of any avail but Yours; healing that leaves no ailment)."

[Narrated by Al-Bukhāri and Muslim]

Healing is cure and recovery from illness.

Our Lord, Exalted be He, is the One Who removes trouble and sickness, and cures the ill through the proper means as well as through hope. An ill person may recover without medicine, or he may recover by undergoing medical treatment, which leads to cure. Both are the same as far as the ability of Allah is concerned.

As Allah Almighty cures sick bodies, He also heals hearts, chests, and souls and purifies them from their sickness and discomfort. In the Qur'an, He says:{O mankind, there has come to you an exhortation from your Lord, a cure for [illness] of the hearts, a guidance and mercy for the believers.}[Surat Yūnus: 57]

{O mankind, there has come to you an exhortation from your Lord, a cure for [illness] of the hearts, a guidance and mercy for the believers.}

[Surat Yūnus: 57]

Allah Almighty heals whomever He wills, and He may keep the methods of remedy out of the doctors' reach, if He so decides.

He alone can bring about healing. He has no partner and there is no true healing but His. Abraham (peace be upon him) is quoted in the Qur'an as saying:{And when I am ill He heals me.}[Surat ash-Shu'arā': 80]Also, the Prophet (may Allah's peace and blessings be upon him) said:"... There is no healer but You."[Narrated by Al-Bukhāri]Out of Allah's bounty, He does not send down a disease except with its remedy. The Prophet (may Allah's peace and blessings be upon him) is authentically reported to have said:"O servants of Allah, make use of medical treatment for Allah has not created a disease without making a remedy for it, with the exception of one disease: old age."[Narrated by Al-Tirmidhi; Sahīh (authentic)]

{And when I am ill He heals me.}

[Surat ash-Shu'arā': 80]

Also, the Prophet (may Allah's peace and blessings be upon him) said:

"... There is no healer but You."

[Narrated by Al-Bukhāri]

Out of Allah's bounty, He does not send down a disease except with its remedy. The Prophet (may Allah's peace and blessings be upon him) is authentically reported to have said:

"O servants of Allah, make use of medical treatment for Allah has not created a disease without making a remedy for it, with the exception of one disease: old age."

[Narrated by Al-Tirmidhi; Sahīh (authentic)]

Your refuge..

A person may fall ill and all means of cure get blocked, and hope begins to vanish and distress hardens, with no refuge in sight among created beings. In a situation like this, he seems to say:

> It has destroyed me, though it is something hidden.

I would not be weakened by the vicissitudes of life.

But now, if I even rest my head upon my hand,

I get attacked by what weakens my hand.

If the night becomes tougher than the day,

One would wish that the day were dark as night.

Under such circumstances, one, driven by his innate disposition, resorts to his Lord in bad need and submissiveness.{...Then when you are afflicted with hardship, to Him alone you cry out for help.}[Surat an-Nahl: 53]The believer invokes Allah by His name "the Healer", saying: O Allah, cure me; O the Healer, heal me.Likewise, the disbeliever resorts to Allah and stands submissive and weak at His door hoping to be cured.{When adversity befalls man, he cries out to Us. Then when We grant him a favor from Us, he says, "I have been granted this only because of my knowledge." It is rather a test, but most of them do not know.}[Surat az-Zumar: 49]After such persistence and patience, relief comes, and the Healer gives His permission for healing.{Is He [not better] Who responds to the distressed when he calls out to Him, and Who relieves suffering...}[Surat an-Naml: 62]

{...Then when you are afflicted with hardship, to Him alone you cry out for help.}

[Surat an-Nahl: 53]

The believer invokes Allah by His name "the Healer", saying: O Allah, cure me; O the Healer, heal me.

Likewise, the disbeliever resorts to Allah and stands submissive and weak at His door hoping to be cured.

{When adversity befalls man, he cries out to Us. Then when We grant him a favor from Us, he says, "I have been granted this only because of my knowledge." It is rather a test, but most of them do not know.}

[Surat az-Zumar: 49]

After such persistence and patience, relief comes, and the Healer gives His permission for healing.

{Is He [not better] Who responds to the distressed when he calls out to Him, and Who relieves suffering...}

[Surat an-Naml: 62]

His bounty is great and His giving is ceaseless. At a certain point, you find that the needs are fulfilled, the supplications are answered, mercy descends, the tribulation comes to an end, and the cure arrives.

How often a doctor tells a patient that he will die, and he leaves in sadness and distress;

yet it is the doctor who dies, and the patient lives on.

Ibn al-Qayyim (may Allah have mercy upon him) said:"Allah Almighty does not afflict His servants to ruin them, but to test their patience and servitude to Him. Allah has the right of the servitude of hardship upon His servants."

"Allah Almighty does not afflict His servants to ruin them, but to test their patience and servitude to Him. Allah has the right of the servitude of hardship upon His servants."

The way of the righteous..

The difference between the believers and others is that the believers know that everything is in the Hand of Allah Almighty and that He is the Healer and the Most Merciful of those who show mercy, and that the disease has only been sent for a good purpose only known to Allah, the Most Merciful.{...But it maybe that you dislike something which is good for you...}[Surat al-Baqarah: 216]No matter how things become hard and turbulent, they are all subject to Allah's will.{...Allah's decree always prevails, but most people do not know.}[Surat Yūsuf: 21]So, the believer meets his illness with contentment and submission to Allah's will, seeking divine reward.The believer also knows that "whatever had befallen him would not have missed him; and whatever had missed him would not have befallen him." Allah Almighty says:{Say, "Nothing will ever befall us except that which Allah has decreed for us..."}[Surat at-Tawbah: 51]And the Prophet (may Allah's peace and blessings be upon him) said:"If you spend the like of Uhud of gold in the cause of Allah, Allah will not accept it from you until you believe in destiny, and until you know that what had befallen you would not have missed you and what had missed you would not have befallen you. If you die believing in other than this, you will enter Hellfire."[Narrated by Abu Dāwūd; Sahīh (authentic)]

{...But it maybe that you dislike something which is good for you...}

[Surat al-Baqarah: 216]

No matter how things become hard and turbulent, they are all subject to Allah's will.

{...Allah's decree always prevails, but most people do not know.}

[Surat Yūsuf: 21]

So, the believer meets his illness with contentment and submission to Allah's will, seeking divine reward.

The believer also knows that "whatever had befallen him would not have missed him; and whatever had missed him would not have befallen him." Allah Almighty says:

{Say, "Nothing will ever befall us except that which Allah has decreed for us..."}

[Surat at-Tawbah: 51]

And the Prophet (may Allah's peace and blessings be upon him) said:

"If you spend the like of Uhud of gold in the cause of Allah, Allah will not accept it from you until you believe in destiny, and until you know that what had befallen you would not have missed you and what had missed you would not have befallen you. If you die believing in other than this, you will enter Hellfire."

[Narrated by Abu Dāwūd; Sahīh (authentic)]

'Ali ibn Abi Tālib passed by 'Adiyy ibn Hātim (may Allah be pleased with both of them) and found him sad and dejected. He asked him: "O 'Adiyy, why are you sad and dejected?"

He said: "Why should I not be so, whereas my children were killed and my eye was gouged out?"

Thereupon, 'Ali said: "O 'Adiyy, if a person accepts the predestination of Allah, it happens to him and he gets rewarded; and if he does not accept the predestination of Allah, it still happens to him, and his deeds are rendered worthless."

Scholars said: The more a person stands in need of Allah and in humble submission to Him, the more readily his supplications get answered and relief comes.

Everyone of us has necessarily experienced illness and seen how it exposes our weakness and that there is no power nor strength except through Allah. Yet, when the cure comes and the illness and trouble go away, our condition changes, as the poet says:

We invoke our Lord in every distress and then forget Him after the relief.

How could we hope that our invocations be answered, whereas we have blocked the way by sins?!

Amazing indeed is our attitude towards Allah Almighty!

Do not be sad!

If you are afflicted with a disease, you should know that Allah is the Healer and nothing escapes His power. If you think that your illness is incurable, you thus distrust your Lord. Just turn to Him, place your trust in Him, show patience in pursuit of reward from Him, give charity, and implore Him pressingly: O Allah, the Healer! Indeed, He is the Truth, His speech is true, and He is Able to do all things. He says:{Your Lord says, "Call upon Me; I will respond to you...}[Surat Ghāfir: 60]The Prophet (may Allah's peace and blessings be upon him) said:"Verily, Allah is Modest, Generous. He is too Modest to turn down His servant empty-handed when he raises his hands (in supplication) to Him."[Narrated by Al-Tirmidhi; Sahīh (authentic)]Allah Almighty says:{Is He [not better] Who responds to the distressed when he calls out to Him, and Who relieves suffering...}[Surat an-Naml: 62]If you go through such a situation, Allah, out of His bounty, bestows upon you His great reward. The Prophet (may Allah's peace and blessings be upon him) said:"No affliction hits a Muslim except that Allah expiates his sins on account of it, even if it is the prick of a thorn."[Narrated by Al-Bukhāri - this is his wording - and Muslim]Ibn Taymiyyah (may Allah have mercy upon him) said:"Allah has such high ranks in His Abode of Honor - i.e. Paradise - that will only be attained by the afflicted."

{Your Lord says, "Call upon Me; I will respond to you...}

[Surat Ghāfir: 60]

The Prophet (may Allah's peace and blessings be upon him) said:

"Verily, Allah is Modest, Generous. He is too Modest to turn down His servant empty-handed when he raises his hands (in supplication) to Him."

[Narrated by Al-Tirmidhi; Sahīh (authentic)]

Allah Almighty says:

{Is He [not better] Who responds to the distressed when he calls out to Him, and Who relieves suffering...}

[Surat an-Naml: 62]

If you go through such a situation, Allah, out of His bounty, bestows upon you His great reward. The Prophet (may Allah's peace and blessings be upon him) said:

"No affliction hits a Muslim except that Allah expiates his sins on account of it, even if it is the prick of a thorn."

[Narrated by Al-Bukhāri - this is his wording - and Muslim]

Ibn Taymiyyah (may Allah have mercy upon him) said:

"Allah has such high ranks in His Abode of Honor - i.e. Paradise - that will only be attained by the afflicted."

Moreover, an afflicted person can derive some consolation from others who are also afflicted. Indeed, afflictions and sadness are common among people.

Many are the afflictions and many are those who have to endure them patiently!

You are not alone in tribulation; your hardship may be less compared to the hardships of others.

Many are those who have been ill and confined to their beds for years. They turn to the right and the left in severe pain and suffering. Remember that this life is the prison for the believers and an abode of sadness and afflictions. As houses are alive with their inhabitants in the morning, they may suddenly become ruined and empty in the evening. {We have created man in hardship.}[Surat al-Balad: 4]

They turn to the right and the left in severe pain and suffering.

Remember that this life is the prison for the believers and an abode of sadness and afflictions. As houses are alive with their inhabitants in the morning, they may suddenly become ruined and empty in the evening.

{We have created man in hardship.}

[Surat al-Balad: 4]

Accept your life as it is and adapt to it. Indeed, it is innately hard and perfection is not part of its nature.

Were it not for the bitterness of illness, one would not know the taste of good health.

We have a good example in Ayyūb (Job) (peace be upon him).

A believer should constantly ask Allah for safety and good health. 'Abdullah al-Taymiyy (may Allah have mercy upon him) used to say: "Ask Allah for safety and soundness constantly, for the afflicted person, even if his affliction is severe, is not more entitled to supplication than a sound and healthy one, who is not safe from afflictions.

"Ask Allah for safety and soundness constantly, for the afflicted person, even if his affliction is severe, is not more entitled to supplication than a sound and healthy one, who is not safe from afflictions.

Indeed, those who are afflicted today were sound and safe only a short while ago, and those who will be afflicted tomorrow are sound and safe today."

Ibn al-Qayyim (may Allah have mercy upon him) said: "Among the most effective ways of curing an illness is doing good, charity, Dhikr (remembrance of Allah), supplication, and repentance."

"Among the most effective ways of curing an illness is doing good, charity, Dhikr (remembrance of Allah), supplication, and repentance."

Ask the doctor who fell severely ill: How did you fall ill despite your medicine?!

And ask a sick person who recovered despite the failure of doctors to treat him: Who restored good health to you?!

Indeed, He is the Most Merciful Lord, the Healer. {And when I am ill He heals me.}[Surat ash-Shu'arā': 80]

{And when I am ill He heals me.}

[Surat ash-Shu'arā': 80]

O Allah, the Healer, cure us and cure all sick Muslims, O Lord of the worlds!

Al-Jamīl (The Beautiful)

Sohaib (may Allah be pleased with him) reported that the Prophet (may Allah's peace and blessings be upon him) said: "When the dwellers of Paradise enter Paradise, Allah Almighty will ask: 'Do you want Me to give you anything more?' They will say: 'Have You not brightened our faces? Have You not made us enter Paradise and saved us from Hellfire?' He will then lift the veil, and of all the things they were given, nothing will be dearer to them than looking at their Lord." [Narrated by Muslim]

"When the dwellers of Paradise enter Paradise, Allah Almighty will ask: 'Do you want Me to give you anything more?' They will say: 'Have You not brightened our faces? Have You not made us enter Paradise and saved us from Hellfire?' He will then lift the veil, and of all the things they were given, nothing will be dearer to them than looking at their Lord." [Narrated by Muslim]

Glory be to the One about Whose beauty minds get perplexed!

Glory be to the One about Whose greatness minds get boggled!

And glory be to the One Whose lights dazzle the minds!

Allah is Beautiful and He loves beauty. Rather, He is all beauty, and all beauty comes from Him. He acts beautifully and gives reward for beautiful acts.

He is the Beautiful indeed. How could He not be?!

The beauty of all creation

is only a trace of the Beautiful Lord,

Whose beauty is far greater

and too magnificent to be expressed in words!

The Prophet (may Allah's peace and blessings be upon him) said:"Indeed, Allah is Beautiful and loves beauty." [Narrated by Muslim]Commenting on Ibn al-Qayyim's Nūniyyah poem, Shaykh Al-Sa'di (may Allah have mercy upon him) said:"The Beautiful is the One Who possesses the traits of beauty and excellence. He is Beautiful in His essence, names, attributes, and actions. No one can describe even part of His beauty. In spite of all the enduring bliss, pleasures, and inestimable joys in which they will live, when the dwellers of Paradise see their Lord and enjoy His beauty, they will forget the bliss they have been in and their previous joys will vanish, and they will wish that the current situation will endure so that His beauty and light will cover them and add to their beauty. Indeed, their hearts were in permanent longing for seeing their Lord, and on 'the Day of Increase', they will be joyful beyond measure.He is also Beautiful in His names. All of them are beautiful; rather, they are the best and most beautiful ever.{Allah has the Most Beautiful Names, so call upon Him by them...}[Surat al-A'rāf:180]

"Indeed, Allah is Beautiful and loves beauty." [Narrated by Muslim]

Commenting on Ibn al-Qayyim's Nūniyyah poem, Shaykh Al-Sa'di (may Allah have mercy upon him) said:

"The Beautiful is the One Who possesses the traits of beauty and excellence. He is Beautiful in His essence, names, attributes, and actions. No one can describe even part of His beauty. In spite of all the enduring bliss, pleasures, and inestimable joys in which they will live, when the dwellers of Paradise see their Lord and enjoy His beauty, they will forget the bliss they have been in and their previous joys will vanish, and they will wish that the current situation will endure so that His beauty and light will cover them and add to their beauty. Indeed, their hearts were in permanent longing for seeing their Lord, and on 'the Day of Increase', they will be joyful beyond measure.

He is also Beautiful in His names. All of them are beautiful; rather, they are the best and most beautiful ever.

{Allah has the Most Beautiful Names, so call upon Him by them...}

[Surat al-A'rāf:180]

They all point to the supreme praise, glory, and perfection. None of His names has partial perfection - it is complete perfection.

And He is Beautiful in His attributes, all of which comprise perfection, commendation, and praise.

Moreover, His actions are all beautiful. They are acts of kindness and benevolence for which He is worthy of praise and gratitude."

If the trees were pens, the seas were ink, and the heavens were tablets, and all creatures kept praising Allah and writing down their praise of His beauty, they would fall short in giving Him His due and fail to show proper gratitude to Him.

Minds do not encompass His beauty, nor do eyes grasp it. The Prophet (may Allah's peace and blessings be upon him) said:"I cannot enumerate praise of You. You are as You have praised Yourself."[Narrated by Muslim]

"I cannot enumerate praise of You. You are as You have praised Yourself."

[Narrated by Muslim]

The beauty of the worlds..

All that the world contains - the land, seas, plants, the sun, the moon, the stars, and the animals - points to the beauty of Allah Almighty. He is the giver of beauty, and the giver of beauty must be far more beautiful.{...So Blessed is Allah, the Best of the Creators.}[Surat al-Mu'minūn: 14]

{...So Blessed is Allah, the Best of the Creators.}

[Surat al-Mu'minūn: 14]

Only those whose hearts are illuminated by the light of faith could see this beauty, and they see beyond it the beauty, magnificence, and perfection of Allah.

Yet, if a person turns away from remembrance of Allah, denies His light, and revolts against His guidance, he will be deprived of seeing His magnificent beauty. This is because he has lost his insight and has become spiritually blind.

O you who complain while having no disease, what would you do then if you became sick?!

I wonder how you can see thorns in the flowers but fail to see above the dew the flowers. Indeed, he who has no beauty within his soul sees no beauty in the world around him.

Longing..

Belief in this name increases a person in faith and longing to see the Beautiful Lord. The Prophet (may Allah's peace and blessings be upon him) used to supplicate saying:"Wa as'aluka ladhdhat an-nazhari ila wajhika wa ash-shawqa ila liqā'ika (And I ask You for the delight of looking at Your Face and the joy of meeting You)."[Narrated by Al-Tirmidhi; Sahīh (authentic)]Then, he becomes tranquil and content with whatever Allah predestined for him, for He only does what is wise and good for His believing servants. All His actions are beautiful, and beautiful actions only lead to what is beautiful. This is how we should trust our Lord. In a Qudsi Hadīth, Allah Almighty said:"I am as My servant thinks of Me. If he thinks well of Me, he gets it; and if he thinks ill of Me, he gets it."[Narrated by Ahmad; Sahīh (authentic)]

"Wa as'aluka ladhdhat an-nazhari ila wajhika wa ash-shawqa ila liqā'ika (And I ask You for the delight of looking at Your Face and the joy of meeting You)."

[Narrated by Al-Tirmidhi; Sahīh (authentic)]

Then, he becomes tranquil and content with whatever Allah predestined for him, for He only does what is wise and good for His believing servants. All His actions are beautiful, and beautiful actions only lead to what is beautiful. This is how we should trust our Lord. In a Qudsi Hadīth, Allah Almighty said:

"I am as My servant thinks of Me. If he thinks well of Me, he gets it; and if he thinks ill of Me, he gets it."

[Narrated by Ahmad; Sahīh (authentic)]

I supplicate Allah and trust Him as much as if

I see what He will do.

Do not be ungrateful!

The believer is beautiful, inwardly and outwardly, as he seeks closeness to Allah through his beauty. Also, Allah Almighty loves beautiful words, manners, and deeds, as He loves His servants to beautify their tongues with truthfulness, their hearts with sincerity, repentance, and reliance upon Him, their body organs with obedience and worship, and to beautify their bodies by showing Allah's favors upon them in terms of fine clothing and cleanliness and purification.

The believer knows his Lord through His beauty and worships Him according to the magnificence existing in His Shariah and religion.

When the Prophet (may Allah's peace and blessings be upon him) said to his Companions:"Anyone who has an atom's weight of arrogance in his heart will not enter Paradise."A man said: "One likes his clothes to be fine and his shoes to be fine."Thereupon, he (may Allah's peace and blessings be upon him) said:"Indeed, Allah is beautiful and He loves beauty. Arrogance is to reject the truth and despise people."[Narrated by Muslim]

"Anyone who has an atom's weight of arrogance in his heart will not enter Paradise."

A man said: "One likes his clothes to be fine and his shoes to be fine."

Thereupon, he (may Allah's peace and blessings be upon him) said:

"Indeed, Allah is beautiful and He loves beauty. Arrogance is to reject the truth and despise people."

[Narrated by Muslim]

O Allah, endow us with beauty in this world and in the Hereafter, give us inward and outward beauty, and make our words and deeds beautiful, O Lord of the worlds!

Al-Qābid - Al-Bāsit (The Constrictor - The Expander)

A word before starting..

To one who pursued all paths but found them blocked and knocked on all doors and found them closed..

To one who explored his inner self and the secrets of his being and found life constricted, despite its vastness..

To one who felt the bitterness of humiliation, and the shackles of helplessness trod on him and battered his being..

To one who was forsaken by his relatives and friends, and his foes gloated over him and he lost his self-confidence..

To one who was hit hard by disasters and surrounded by difficulties and unpleasant things, and relief was too slow in coming to him..

To one whose heart hardened and became hopeless and tired of life..

To one who suffered severe illness, a heavy debt, or abject poverty..

I say to them all: Do not be sad, for Allah Almighty is the Constrictor and the Expander. He will remove your distress and protect you at times of hardships and disasters. He will make you strong without your folks and self-sufficient without wealth, and He will grant you more if you show gratitude to Him, mention you if you mention Him, and give you if you ask from Him.

So, turn to Him and seek closeness to Him through His two names: (Al-Qābid - Al-Bāsit). These two names are closely connected and should always be used together. We may not praise Allah by one of them without the other.

If you want to obtain tranquility and relief within your heart, say as the Prophet (may Allah's peace and blessings be upon him) used to say:"O Allah, all praise is due to You.

"O Allah, all praise is due to You.

O Allah, none can constrict what You expand nor expand what You constrict, nor bring near what You put far away or put far away what You bring near. No one can give what You withhold nor withhold what You give.

O Allah, expand for us some of Your blessings, mercy, favor, and sustenance."[Narrated by Al-Bukhāri in Al-Adab al-Mufrad; Sahīh (authentic)]

[Narrated by Al-Bukhāri in Al-Adab al-Mufrad; Sahīh (authentic)]

In the shades of His two names: Al-Qābid and Al-Bāsit:

Our Lord, Exalted be He, is the One Who expands the provision for whomever He wills, ending poverty altogether, and Who constricts it to whomever He wills, until he possesses nothing. He does that by His perfect ability and justice, in line with His wisdom, and in ways that suit the conditions of His servants.If He gives him abundance, this does not stem from extravagance or ignorance, and if He constricts His sustenance, this is not due to insufficiency or stinginess. Allah Almighty says:{If Allah were to give abundant provision to [all] His slaves, they would transgress on earth; but He sends down what He wills in due measure. Indeed, He is All-Aware and All-Seeing of His slaves.}[Surat ash-Shūra: 27]When the prices went up during the Prophet's lifetime, the Companions (may Allah be pleased with them) asked the Prophet (may Allah's peace and blessings be upon him) to fix the prices. They said: "O Messenger of Allah, the prices have gone up. So, fix the prices for us." He said:"Allah is the One Who fixes prices, the constrictor, the Expander, the Provider."[Narrated by Ibn Mājah; Sahīh (authentic)]

If He gives him abundance, this does not stem from extravagance or ignorance, and if He constricts His sustenance, this is not due to insufficiency or stinginess. Allah Almighty says:

{If Allah were to give abundant provision to [all] His slaves, they would transgress on earth; but He sends down what He wills in due measure. Indeed, He is All-Aware and All-Seeing of His slaves.}

[Surat ash-Shūra: 27]

When the prices went up during the Prophet's lifetime, the Companions (may Allah be pleased with them) asked the Prophet (may Allah's peace and blessings be upon him) to fix the prices. They said: "O Messenger of Allah, the prices have gone up. So, fix the prices for us." He said:

"Allah is the One Who fixes prices, the constrictor, the Expander, the Provider."

[Narrated by Ibn Mājah; Sahīh (authentic)]

Our Lord, Exalted be He, takes charity from the wealthy and expands the provision for the weak. He takes charity, grows it, and expands His blessings.

And our Lord is the One Who takes the souls out of the bodies at the time of death and expands the souls in them at the beginning of life.

Also, Allah Almighty constricts the hearts of people and makes them so narrow as if they were climbing into the sky, and He expands them beyond capacity out of His benevolence, kindness, and beauty, thus putting joy and relief into them. In the Qur'an, He says:{Whoever Allah wills to guide, He opens his heart to Islam; and whoever He wills to lead astray, He makes his heart tight and constricted, as if he were climbing up into the sky. This is how Allah punishes those who do not believe.}[Surat al-An'ām: 125]

{Whoever Allah wills to guide, He opens his heart to Islam; and whoever He wills to lead astray, He makes his heart tight and constricted, as if he were climbing up into the sky. This is how Allah punishes those who do not believe.}

[Surat al-An'ām: 125]

Our Lord constricts and expands by His two honorable Hands, in a real manner and in a way that befits His majesty and magnificence, for whomever He wills among His servants. This includes the heavens and the earth.

Allah Almighty says:{They did not revere Allah His true reverence. On the Day of Resurrection, the whole earth will be in His Grip, and the heavens will be rolled up in His Right Hand. Glorified and exalted is He above all what they associate with Him!}[Surat az-Zumar: 67]The Prophet (may Allah's peace and blessings be upon him) is authentically reported to have said:"Allah Almighty will take hold of His heavens and earth with His two Hands and say: 'I am Allah - constricting and expanding His Fingers - I am the King.'"[Narrated by Muslim]And our Lord expands His Hand to accept the repentance of those who do wrong. The Prophet (may Allah's peace and blessings be upon him) is authentically reported to have said:"Allah expands His Hand during the night so the sinners of the day may repent, and expands His Hand during the day so the sinners of the night may repent. He keeps doing so until the sun rises from the west."[Narrated by Muslim]

{They did not revere Allah His true reverence. On the Day of Resurrection, the whole earth will be in His Grip, and the heavens will be rolled up in His Right Hand. Glorified and exalted is He above all what they associate with Him!}

[Surat az-Zumar: 67]

The Prophet (may Allah's peace and blessings be upon him) is authentically reported to have said:

"Allah Almighty will take hold of His heavens and earth with His two Hands and say: 'I am Allah - constricting and expanding His Fingers - I am the King.'"

[Narrated by Muslim]

And our Lord expands His Hand to accept the repentance of those who do wrong. The Prophet (may Allah's peace and blessings be upon him) is authentically reported to have said:

"Allah expands His Hand during the night so the sinners of the day may repent, and expands His Hand during the day so the sinners of the night may repent. He keeps doing so until the sun rises from the west."

[Narrated by Muslim]

Our Lord also gives respite to the sinners, making them live between hope and fear.

Our Lord expands His Hand every night to those who ask and supplicate Him. The Prophet (may Allah's peace and blessings be upon him) is authentically reported to have said:"...Then He expands His Hands and says: 'Who will lend One Who is neither indigent nor tyrant?'"[Narrated by Muslim]Also, our Lord gives expanse in knowledge and stature to whomever He wills. In the Qur'an, He says:{...And has increased him abundantly in knowledge and physique...}[Surat al-Baqarah: 247]Our Lord will take a handful of Hellfire, with His honorable Hand, and bring out people who have never done any good. In a lengthy Hadīth, the Prophet (may Allah's peace and blessings be upon him) said:"And He will take a handful of Hellfire, bringing out of it some people who never did good."[Narrated by Muslim]

"...Then He expands His Hands and says: 'Who will lend One Who is neither indigent nor tyrant?'"

[Narrated by Muslim]

Also, our Lord gives expanse in knowledge and stature to whomever He wills. In the Qur'an, He says:

{...And has increased him abundantly in knowledge and physique...}

[Surat al-Baqarah: 247]

Our Lord will take a handful of Hellfire, with His honorable Hand, and bring out people who have never done any good. In a lengthy Hadīth, the Prophet (may Allah's peace and blessings be upon him) said:

"And He will take a handful of Hellfire, bringing out of it some people who never did good."

[Narrated by Muslim]

Also, our Lord constricts and expands light and darkness, leading to the alternation of night and day.

And He constricts things by prohibition and expands others by permission.

He also constricts and expands the hearts of His servants, and thus the believers live between hope and fear.

He constricts and expands,

and He elevates and lowers, by justice and measure.

The measure:

When a servant walks on the path to his Lord, worshiping Him and performing obligatory and supererogatory acts, with his heart being in deep attachment to Allah, you find him in relief and joy, with this good condition being expanded for him by the Almighty Lord. On the other hand, when a servants commits sins, he becomes uneasy and dispirited.

This feeling of unease is the constriction by Allah Almighty. It is a fleeting tribulation that leads to His grace.{[And Allah also turned in mercy to] the three who stayed behind, until the earth became constrained to them, despite its vastness, and their souls became a burden to them, and they realized that there was no refuge from Allah except in Him. Then He turned to them in mercy, so that they might repent, for Allah is the Accepter of Repentance, the Most Merciful.}[Surat at-Tawbah: 118]

{[And Allah also turned in mercy to] the three who stayed behind, until the earth became constrained to them, despite its vastness, and their souls became a burden to them, and they realized that there was no refuge from Allah except in Him. Then He turned to them in mercy, so that they might repent, for Allah is the Accepter of Repentance, the Most Merciful.}

[Surat at-Tawbah: 118]

On the other hand, the feeling of relief and joy and the inclination towards Allah fall under the expanding by our Lord.

Also, the feeling of unease, backtracking from worship, or lack of pleasure in worship falls under constriction. Indeed, a person could be constricted by sins, be they outward or inward, like the diseases of the heart.

Thereupon, the Prophet (may Allah's peace and blessings be upon him) said:"Verily, when a person commits a sin, his heart is marked with a black spot. When he repents, his heart is polished clean. But if he returns, it increases until it covers his entire heart. And that is the 'Rān' which Allah mentions:{No indeed! Their hearts have been stained by what they used to commit!}[Surat al-Mutaffifīn: 14]"[Narrated by Ibn Hibbān; Classified as Sahīh (authentic) by Al-Arnā'ūt]The believer oscillates between expanding and constricting. Hence, he constantly implores his Lord to make him steadfast and grant him a good ending. The Prophet (may Allah's peace and blessings be upon him) used to supplicate saying:"Ya muqallib al-qulūb thabbit qalby 'ala dīnik (O Turner of the hearts, keep my heart firm upon Your religion)."[Narrated by Al-Tirmidhi; Sahīh (authentic)]If this is the case of the believer, then what about one who persists in sins and disobedience?!

"Verily, when a person commits a sin, his heart is marked with a black spot. When he repents, his heart is polished clean. But if he returns, it increases until it covers his entire heart. And that is the 'Rān' which Allah mentions:

{No indeed! Their hearts have been stained by what they used to commit!}

[Surat al-Mutaffifīn: 14]"

[Narrated by Ibn Hibbān; Classified as Sahīh (authentic) by Al-Arnā'ūt]

The believer oscillates between expanding and constricting. Hence, he constantly implores his Lord to make him steadfast and grant him a good ending. The Prophet (may Allah's peace and blessings be upon him) used to supplicate saying:

"Ya muqallib al-qulūb thabbit qalby 'ala dīnik (O Turner of the hearts, keep my heart firm upon Your religion)."

[Narrated by Al-Tirmidhi; Sahīh (authentic)]

If this is the case of the believer, then what about one who persists in sins and disobedience?!

The greatest type of expanding:

Therefore, scholars said: The greatest act of expanding by Allah is expanding mercy within the hearts, illuminating them and bringing them out of the darkness of sins.{Is one whose heart Allah has opened to Islam, so he is enlightened by his Lord [like a disbeliever]?...}[Surat az-Zumar: 22]{Whoever Allah wills to guide, He opens his heart to Islam...}[Surat al-An'ām: 125]And its opposite occurs in the verse that says:{And whoever He wills to lead astray, He makes his heart tight and constricted, as if he were climbing up into the sky}[Surat al-An'ām: 125]In another verse, Allah Almighty says:{Say, "My Lord extends provision to whom He wills or restricts it, but most people do not know".}[Surat Saba': 36]He also says:{Your Lord extends provision to whom He wills or restricts it. He is All-Aware and All-Seeing of His slaves.}[Surat al-Isrā': 30]He informs us that expanding and constricting lie in His Hand and are subject to His will and predestination. He expands for whomever He wills his wealth, good health, lifespan, or knowledge - or constricts it. He is the All-Wise, the All-Aware. The abundance you see the enemies of Allah enjoying is not an act of expanding, but in fact a plot to gradually drag them to their ruin.The believer may be deprived of something, yet this is in fact a gift for him; and he may be given something, and this is not but a trial for him.{But it maybe that you dislike something which is good for you, and you like something which is bad for you.}[Surat al-Baqarah: 216]

{Is one whose heart Allah has opened to Islam, so he is enlightened by his Lord [like a disbeliever]?...}

[Surat az-Zumar: 22]

{Whoever Allah wills to guide, He opens his heart to Islam...}

[Surat al-An'ām: 125]

And its opposite occurs in the verse that says:

{And whoever He wills to lead astray, He makes his heart tight and constricted, as if he were climbing up into the sky}

[Surat al-An'ām: 125]

In another verse, Allah Almighty says:

{Say, "My Lord extends provision to whom He wills or restricts it, but most people do not know".}

[Surat Saba': 36]

He also says:

{Your Lord extends provision to whom He wills or restricts it. He is All-Aware and All-Seeing of His slaves.}

[Surat al-Isrā': 30]

He informs us that expanding and constricting lie in His Hand and are subject to His will and predestination. He expands for whomever He wills his wealth, good health, lifespan, or knowledge - or constricts it. He is the All-Wise, the All-Aware. The abundance you see the enemies of Allah enjoying is not an act of expanding, but in fact a plot to gradually drag them to their ruin.

The believer may be deprived of something, yet this is in fact a gift for him; and he may be given something, and this is not but a trial for him.

{But it maybe that you dislike something which is good for you, and you like something which is bad for you.}

[Surat al-Baqarah: 216]

A Reminder..

Allah Almighty is the One Who expands and constricts and Who elevates and lowers, according to His predestination. This does not mean, however, that such things do not happen due to the people themselves and their acts. They do certain things and find their consequences. The Prophet (may Allah's peace and blessings be upon him) combined these two meanings in the Hadīth that reads:"Whoever loves to have his sustenance expanded and his term of life prolonged should maintain ties of kinship."[Narrated by Al-Bukhāri and Muslim]

"Whoever loves to have his sustenance expanded and his term of life prolonged should maintain ties of kinship."

[Narrated by Al-Bukhāri and Muslim]

So, the expansion of sustenance lies in the Hand of Allah; whereas maintaining ties of kinship is a cause to be fulfilled by the person himself.

A whisper..

When Allah expands a person's wealth, knowledge, stature, or status, he should draw close to his Lord by showing benevolence to His servants as Allah has shown him benevolence. This is a way of expressing gratitude for Allah's favors by which the favors continue to exist. However, if he cannot afford to give people, then let him treat them kindly.{For Allah loves those who do good.}[Surat Āl 'Imrān: 134]

{For Allah loves those who do good.}

[Surat Āl 'Imrān: 134]

O Allah, the One Who constricts and expands, expand for us Your mercy and protect us from the evil of Your creatures.

O Allah, expand for us Your blessings, mercy, favor, and sustenance.

Al-Muqaddim - Al-Mu'akhkhir (The Advancer - the Delayer)

Ibn al-Qayyim (may Allah have mercy upon him) said:"A person is moving, not standing still. He is either going up or down, moving forward or backwards.

"A person is moving, not standing still. He is either going up or down, moving forward or backwards.

There is nothing standstill at all, neither in nature nor in the Shariah. There are only stages that pass by so quickly and lead to Paradise or Hellfire. One may go fast or slowly and may advance or lag behind.

No one ever remains standing on this path. People may only go in different directions and move at varying speeds.{Hellfire is indeed one of the greatest matters,a warning to mankind,to whoever among you chooses to advance or regress.}[Surat al-Muddaththir: 35-37]He does not mention anyone standing still, for there will be no abode other than Paradise and Hellfire and no path whatsoever that leads to other than them.

{Hellfire is indeed one of the greatest matters, a warning to mankind,

to whoever among you chooses to advance or regress.} [Surat al-Muddaththir: 35-37]

He does not mention anyone standing still, for there will be no abode other than Paradise and Hellfire and no path whatsoever that leads to other than them.

So, he who is not advancing towards this one by good deeds is necessarily lagging behind toward that one on account of evil deeds."

Advancing and delaying are in the Hand of Allah Almighty. That is why His beautiful names include: The Advancer and the Delayer.

Ibn 'Abbās (may Allah be pleased with him and his father) reported: "When the Prophet (may Allah's peace and blessings be upon him) got up to perform prayer during the night, he would supplicate saying:'Faghfir li mā qaddamtu wa mā akhkhartu wa mā asrartu wa mā a'lantu anta Al-Muqaddim wa anta Al-Mu'akhkhir lā ilāha illā anta - or lā ilāha ghayruk (So, forgive me my future and past faults and those faults I commit secretly or openly. Indeed, You are the Advancer and You are the Delayer. There is no god but You - or there is no god other than You)." [Narrated by Al-Bukhāri and Muslim]

'Faghfir li mā qaddamtu wa mā akhkhartu wa mā asrartu wa mā a'lantu anta Al-Muqaddim wa anta Al-Mu'akhkhir lā ilāha illā anta - or lā ilāha ghayruk (So, forgive me my future and past faults and those faults I commit secretly or openly. Indeed, You are the Advancer and You are the Delayer. There is no god but You - or there is no god other than You)." [Narrated by Al-Bukhāri and Muslim]

Our Lord is the Advancer and the Delayer. He puts things in their proper place and position, advancing some and delaying others, as He wishes.

He had predestined measures before He created the creation.

And He prefers whomever He wishes among His pious servants to others and puts His servants in varying ranks and degrees, some above others.

He also advances those He wills to the ranks of the forerunners and delays those He wills and prevents them from reaching them. And He may delay things beyond their expected time for His knowledge and wisdom about the good consequences resulting from that. Indeed, no one can advance what He delays or delay what He advances.

Our Lord, Exalted be He, advances whomever He wills among His servants to His mercy by helping him, and delays whomever He wills and holds him from reaching that by way of disappointment.

As dictated by politeness and courtesy, we should use both names together, not separately, because perfection lies in using them together.

Our Lord is the Advancer and the Delayer, and these two names

describe His essence as well as His actions.

Advance and delay

are both universal and Shariah-related:

As an example of the universal advance and delay, Allah Almighty puts some of His creatures ahead of others in terms of creation and existence. In a Hadīth, the Prophet (may Allah's peace and blessings be upon him) said:"The first thing Allah created was the pen."[Narrated by Abu Dāwūd; Sahīh (authentic)]He created the heavens and the earth in six days, put the creation of the angels ahead of the creation of the jinn and humans, and put the creation of the jinn ahead of the creation of humans. He says:{And the jinn We created before that, from smokeless fire.}[Surat al-Hijr: 27]Adam (peace be upon him) was the first human created and then his children followed him in terms of creation and existence. They come in succession - some earlier and some later.It does not follow that those who were created earlier are superior to those who were created later. In fact, Adam was created at the end of the six days. Nonetheless, he and his children are given preference over many of those created before them.{We have honored the children of Adam, carried them on land and sea, provided for them good things and favored them above many of those whom We have created.}[Surat al-Isrā': 70]

"The first thing Allah created was the pen."

[Narrated by Abu Dāwūd; Sahīh (authentic)]

He created the heavens and the earth in six days, put the creation of the angels ahead of the creation of the jinn and humans, and put the creation of the jinn ahead of the creation of humans. He says:

{And the jinn We created before that, from smokeless fire.}

[Surat al-Hijr: 27]

Adam (peace be upon him) was the first human created and then his children followed him in terms of creation and existence. They come in succession - some earlier and some later.

It does not follow that those who were created earlier are superior to those who were created later. In fact, Adam was created at the end of the six days. Nonetheless, he and his children are given preference over many of those created before them.

{We have honored the children of Adam, carried them on land and sea, provided for them good things and favored them above many of those whom We have created.}

[Surat al-Isrā': 70]

Moreover, Muhammad (may Allah's peace and blessings be upon him) is the Seal of all prophets and he is the best of them; and his Ummah is the last nation and the best of all nations.

On the other hand, those who come earlier may be superior to those who come later. An example is Prophet Ibrāhīm (Abraham) (peace be upon him). He is the father of prophets and better than all prophets and messengers who came after him, except for Prophet Muhammad (may Allah's peace and blessings be upon him).

As for the Shariah-related advance and delay, the Adhān (call to prayer), for example, comes ahead of prayer, and the Friday sermon is before the Friday prayer. Acts of worship have a specific order in terms of their requirements and duties, without which they may be invalid.

The Shariah-related advance also includes giving precedence to some acts of worship and persons over others. Obligations, for instance, are dearer to Allah than the supererogatory acts. Moreover, the best among people are the prophets and messengers, who also enjoy varying degrees of excellence and merit, which also applies to ordinary people, some of whom are better than others.

When the believer knows that Allah is the Advancer and the Delayer, he will get deeply attached to Him alone and implore Him to grant him faith and steadfastness, and he will rely upon Him, for none can advance what He delays or delay what He advances.

The true advance:

The true beneficial advance is the one a person makes towards the obedience of Allah Almighty and His pleasure and Paradise. The delay in doing so is the dispraised delay indeed. Allah Almighty says:{And hasten towards forgiveness from your Lord and a Paradise as wide as the heavens and earth, prepared for the righteous.}[Surat Āl 'Imrān: 133]He also says:{Race one another towards forgiveness from your Lord and Paradise the width of which is like the width of the heaven and earth}[Surat al-Hadīd: 21]And the Prophet (may Allah's peace and blessings be upon him) is authentically reported to have said:"Come forward and be close to me and let those who come after you follow your lead. If people continue to fall behind, Allah puts them behind."[Narrated by Muslim]

{And hasten towards forgiveness from your Lord and a Paradise as wide as the heavens and earth, prepared for the righteous.}

[Surat Āl 'Imrān: 133]

He also says:

{Race one another towards forgiveness from your Lord and Paradise the width of which is like the width of the heaven and earth}

[Surat al-Hadīd: 21]

And the Prophet (may Allah's peace and blessings be upon him) is authentically reported to have said:

"Come forward and be close to me and let those who come after you follow your lead. If people continue to fall behind, Allah puts them behind."

[Narrated by Muslim]

As for worldly advance and delay, it is not what matters in the sight of Allah Almighty, and so it has no benefit.

Furthermore, it is a sign of faith to advance those advanced by Allah Almighty and delay those delayed by Him. Thus, the criterion according to which we advance or delay, love or hate, and show loyalty or disavowal to anyone is the criterion established by our Lord, Exalted be He, Who says:{Do those who commit evil deeds think that We will make them equal to those who believe and do righteous deeds, in this life and after their death? How poorly they judge!}[Surat al-Jāthiyah: 21]

{Do those who commit evil deeds think that We will make them equal to those who believe and do righteous deeds, in this life and after their death? How poorly they judge!}

[Surat al-Jāthiyah: 21]

O Allah, the Advancer and the Delayer, we implore You to forgive us, admit us into Your Paradise, and save us from Your Hellfire.

Al-Hayiyy (The Modest)

The Messenger of Allah (may Allah's peace and blessings be upon him) saw a man taking a bath in the open area without a waist-wrapper. Disapproving of this act, he ascended the pulpit and, after praising Allah, said:"Verily Allah is Modest and Concealing, and He loves modesty and concealment. So, when any of you bathes, let him cover himself."[Narrated by Abu Dāwūd; Sahīh (authentic)]

"Verily Allah is Modest and Concealing, and He loves modesty and concealment. So, when any of you bathes, let him cover himself."

[Narrated by Abu Dāwūd; Sahīh (authentic)]

Our Lord is the Modest. He possesses complete modesty that befits His perfection, majesty, and exaltedness. This is not like the modesty of people, which denotes weakness.

The modesty of the Almighty Lord is of a different kind that can not be grasped by our minds. It is modesty that is based on generosity, kindness, and majesty.

Out of Allah's majesty, His modesty is to refrain from such things that do not befit His vast mercy, complete bounty, and great pardon and forbearance. For example, He is so Modest that He does not turn down a servant who raises his hands to Him in supplication.

The Prophet (may Allah's peace and blessings be upon him) said:"Verily, Allah is Modest, Generous. He is too Modest to turn down His servant empty-handed when he raises his hands (in supplication) to Him."[Narrated by Al-Tirmidhī; Sahīh (authentic)]

"Verily, Allah is Modest, Generous. He is too Modest to turn down His servant empty-handed when he raises his hands (in supplication) to Him."

[Narrated by Al-Tirmidhī; Sahīh (authentic)]

Out of Allah's majesty, despite His complete self-sufficiency and ability, He is too Modest to expose His servants and cause their concealment to unravel.

Allah is the Modest and He does not expose His servants when they engage in sins.

Rather, He conceals their faults for He is the Concealing and the Forgiver.

Out of His Justice, Allah Almighty is not shy about the truth. In the Qur'an, He says:{...But Allah is not shy of [telling] the truth...}[Surat al-Ahzāb: 53]The more a believer heeds Allah Almighty, the greater his sense of modesty will be.

{...But Allah is not shy of [telling] the truth...}

[Surat al-Ahzāb: 53]

The more a believer heeds Allah Almighty, the greater his sense of modesty will be.

A fact:

The greater a person's faith is, the greater his modesty will be. Hence, the prophets were the most modest among people. Prophet Muhammad (may Allah's peace and blessings be upon him) was described as "more modest than a virgin in her private place".

Modesty is part of faith. The Prophet (may Allah's peace and blessings be upon him) said:"Faith has over seventy branches, and modesty is a branch of faith."[Narrated by Al-Bukhāri and Muslim]

"Faith has over seventy branches, and modesty is a branch of faith."

[Narrated by Al-Bukhāri and Muslim]

The greatest and dearest modesty is modesty towards Allah Almighty.

When the Prophet (may Allah's peace and blessings be upon him) said to his Companions (may Allah be pleased with them): "Show proper modesty towards Allah," they said: "O Messenger of Allah, we indeed show modesty, praise be to Allah."

Thereupon, he said:"That is not what I mean; but he who shows proper modesty towards Allah should guard the head and what it retains, guard the belly and what it contains, and remember death and decay; and he who desires the Hereafter should abandon the adornment of this world. Whoever does that has shown proper modesty towards Allah."[Narrated by Al-Tirmidhi; Hasan (sound)]Ibn al-Qayyim (may Allah have mercy upon him) said:"If a person feels modest and shy upon committing a sin, Allah will be too Modest to punish him on the Day of Judgment; and if a person does not feel shy to commit a sin, Allah will not be too Modest to punish him."

"That is not what I mean; but he who shows proper modesty towards Allah should guard the head and what it retains, guard the belly and what it contains, and remember death and decay; and he who desires the Hereafter should abandon the adornment of this world. Whoever does that has shown proper modesty towards Allah."

[Narrated by Al-Tirmidhi; Hasan (sound)]

Ibn al-Qayyim (may Allah have mercy upon him) said:

"If a person feels modest and shy upon committing a sin, Allah will be too Modest to punish him on the Day of Judgment; and if a person does not feel shy to commit a sin, Allah will not be too Modest to punish him."

How beautiful modesty is!

Modesty brings nothing but goodness. One day the Prophet (may Allah's peace and blessings be upon him) passed by someone who was censuring another on account of his modesty and he seemed to say that modesty did harm to him. Thereupon, the Prophet (may Allah's peace and blessings be upon him) said to him:"Leave him, for indeed modesty is part of faith."[Narrated by Al-Bukhāri and Muslim]

"Leave him, for indeed modesty is part of faith."

[Narrated by Al-Bukhāri and Muslim]

Modesty is a sign of chivalry, magnanimity, and good manners.

A modest person has a sense of the greatness and magnificence of Allah Almighty and he always heeds Him.

One of the righteous predecessors once said: "I knew that Allah is Watchful over me so I felt shy to let Him see me committing a sin."

If you privately engage in a suspicious matter in darkness, and your self prods you into sinning,

be modest towards Allah and tell it: He Who has created the darkness sees me.

'Umar ibn al-Khattāb (may Allah be pleased with him) said:"If a person's modesty decreases, his piety decreases; and he whose piety decreases, his heart dies."Ibn Daqīq al-'Īd (may Allah have mercy upon him) said:"Modesty continues to be praiseworthy, commendable, and required. It was not abrogated in the laws brought by the previous prophets."

"If a person's modesty decreases, his piety decreases; and he whose piety decreases, his heart dies."

Ibn Daqīq al-'Īd (may Allah have mercy upon him) said:

"Modesty continues to be praiseworthy, commendable, and required. It was not abrogated in the laws brought by the previous prophets."

A last word..

Describing the women of Paradise, Allah Almighty says:{In them there will be maidens of restrained gaze...}[Surat ar-Rahmān: 56]In other words, they only look at their husbands. Then, He describes their charm and beauty saying:{As if they were rubies and pearls.}[Surat ar-Rahmān: 58]He mentions their chastity and modesty ahead of beauty and charm, since the beauty of a woman has no value without her chastity and modesty.It is said that one of the punishments for sins is being deprived of modesty and brightness of face. The Prophet (may Allah's peace and blessings be upon him) said:"Indeed, some of what people learned from the words of the early prophets: If you feel no shame, then do whatever you wish."[Narrated by Al-Bukhāri]

{In them there will be maidens of restrained gaze...}

[Surat ar-Rahmān: 56]

In other words, they only look at their husbands. Then, He describes their charm and beauty saying:

{As if they were rubies and pearls.}

[Surat ar-Rahmān: 58]

He mentions their chastity and modesty ahead of beauty and charm, since the beauty of a woman has no value without her chastity and modesty.

It is said that one of the punishments for sins is being deprived of modesty and brightness of face. The Prophet (may Allah's peace and blessings be upon him) said:

"Indeed, some of what people learned from the words of the early prophets: If you feel no shame, then do whatever you wish."

[Narrated by Al-Bukhāri]

If you do not fear the future consequences for your actions or have a sense of modesty, then do whatever you want.

Indeed, a person is good as long as he adheres to modesty.

Remember that the most hated person in the sight of Allah is the one who passes the night in sins while Allah conceals him and then in the morning, he removes the cover put over him by Allah.

O Allah, endow us with modesty and help us be fearful of You in public and in secret.

Ad-Dayyān (The Recompenser)

A man came and sat in front of the Messenger of Allah (may Allah's peace and blessings be upon him) and said: "O Messenger of Allah, I have two slaves who lie to me, deceive me, and disobey me, and I scold them and hit them. So, what is my case because of them?"

He said: "The extent to which they betrayed you, disobeyed you, and lied to you will be measured against how much you punish them. If your punishing them is equal to their sins, then the two will be the same, nothing for you and nothing against you. But if your punishment exceeds their sins, some of your rewards will be taken from you and given to them." So, the man left and began weeping and crying aloud.

Thereupon, the Prophet (may Allah's peace and blessings be upon him) said:"Do you not read in the Book of Allah:{We will place the scales of justice on the Day of Resurrection, and no soul will be wronged in the least. Even if a deed is the weight of a mustard seed, We will bring it forth. Sufficient are We as Reckoners.}[Surat al-Anbiyā': 47]?"The man said: "By Allah, O Messenger of Allah, I see nothing better for myself and them than me parting with them. Bear witness that they are all free."[Narrated by Al-Tirmidhī; Sahīh (authentic)]

"Do you not read in the Book of Allah:

{We will place the scales of justice on the Day of Resurrection, and no soul will be wronged in the least. Even if a deed is the weight of a mustard seed, We will bring it forth. Sufficient are We as Reckoners.}

[Surat al-Anbiyā': 47]?"

The man said: "By Allah, O Messenger of Allah, I see nothing better for myself and them than me parting with them. Bear witness that they are all free."

[Narrated by Al-Tirmidhī; Sahīh (authentic)]

Indeed, if people were to know the purpose of their creation, they would not be heedless and indifferent.

Rather, they would be concerned with nothing but pleasing their Lord.

Jābir (may Allah be pleased with him) reported that the Prophet (may Allah's peace and blessings be upon him) said:"Allah will resurrect people and call out with a voice that will be heard by those distant as well as those near saying: 'I am the King, I am the Recompenser. None of the people of Hellfire should enter Hellfire while being entitled to some right with anyone of the people of Paradise until I take it from him in retribution; and none of the people of Paradise should enter Paradise while anyone of the people of Hellfire is entitled to some right with him until I take it from him in retribution, even if it were a slap on the face.'"[Narrated by Ahmad; Sahīh (authentic)]

"Allah will resurrect people and call out with a voice that will be heard by those distant as well as those near saying: 'I am the King, I am the Recompenser. None of the people of Hellfire should enter Hellfire while being entitled to some right with anyone of the people of Paradise until I take it from him in retribution; and none of the people of Paradise should enter Paradise while anyone of the people of Hellfire is entitled to some right with him until I take it from him in retribution, even if it were a slap on the face.'"

[Narrated by Ahmad; Sahīh (authentic)]

Our Lord, Exalted be He, rose over the Throne above all His dominion. The entire creation, including kings and tyrants and all beings, is subject to His power and authority and all faces are submissive and humble to Him. Our forelocks are in His Hand, and so are all the matters and affairs and the dominion of the universe. There is no true judge, lord, or god but Him.

Our Lord is the Recompenser. He will take His servants to account and recompense, and judge them on the Day of Resurrection. In the Qur'an, He says:{Master of the Day of Judgment.}[Surat al-Fātihah: 4]{We will place the scales of justice on the Day of Resurrection, and no soul will be wronged in the least. Even if a deed is the weight of a mustard seed, We will bring it forth. Sufficient are We as Reckoners.}[Surat al-Anbiyā': 47]He who finds good therein should praise Allah, and he who finds otherwise should blame none but himself.{On the Day when every soul will find itself faced with whatever good it has done, and whatever evil it has done – it will wish that there were a great distance between it and its evil. And Allah warns you of Himself, and Allah is All-Kind to His slaves.}[Surat Āl 'Imrān: 30]

{Master of the Day of Judgment.}

[Surat al-Fātihah: 4]

{We will place the scales of justice on the Day of Resurrection, and no soul will be wronged in the least. Even if a deed is the weight of a mustard seed, We will bring it forth. Sufficient are We as Reckoners.}

[Surat al-Anbiyā': 47]

He who finds good therein should praise Allah, and he who finds otherwise should blame none but himself.

{On the Day when every soul will find itself faced with whatever good it has done, and whatever evil it has done – it will wish that there were a great distance between it and its evil. And Allah warns you of Himself, and Allah is All-Kind to His slaves.}

[Surat Āl 'Imrān: 30]

Consider the consequences!

Allah, the Just Lord, inflicts retribution upon the wrongful on behalf of the wronged and upon the master on behalf of the slave, and the same holds true for animals as well. The Prophet (may Allah's peace and blessings be upon him) said:"All creatures will be gathered on the Day of Judgment - animals, birds, and everything - and Allah's justice will reach such an extent that He will take the right of the hornless animals from the horned ones."[Narrated by Al-Hākim in Al-Mustadrak; Sahīh (authentic)]Another wording reads:"And even the right of an atom from another atom."[Narrated by Ahmad; Sahīh (authentic)]

"All creatures will be gathered on the Day of Judgment - animals, birds, and everything - and Allah's justice will reach such an extent that He will take the right of the hornless animals from the horned ones."

[Narrated by Al-Hākim in Al-Mustadrak; Sahīh (authentic)]

Another wording reads:

"And even the right of an atom from another atom."

[Narrated by Ahmad; Sahīh (authentic)]

If you know that you will meet your Lord, the Recompenser, on the Day of Judgment; that Allah does not wrong anyone even for the weight of an atom; that the relationship among people is based upon competition while it is based on tolerance between Allah and His servants; and that the reckoning will be conducted on the basis of good and bad deeds, then how could you give away your good deeds and take from the bad deeds of others, despite your knowledge that you will surely be held accountable?!

So, be smart and hold yourself accountable before you are brought to account. As the saying goes: "A wise person would hold himself accountable and prepare for what comes after death; and a helpless person would follow his vain desires and then engage in wishful thinking about Allah."

The Prophet (may Allah's peace and blessings be upon him) asked his Companions (may Allah be pleased with them): "Do you know who the bankrupt is?" They said: "The bankrupt among us is the one who has neither money nor property." Thereupon, he said:"The bankrupt in my Ummah is the one who will come on the Day of Judgment with prayer, fasting, and Zakah, but since he hurled abuse at others, accused others of committing adultery without evidence, unlawfully consumed the wealth of others, shed the blood of others, and beat others, his good deeds will be credited to the accounts of others, and if his good deeds fall short to clear his account, others' sins will be cast on him and he will be thrown in Hellfire."[Narrated by Muslim]'Umar ibn al-Khattāb (may Allah be pleased with him) said:"Hold yourselves accountable before you are brought to account and weigh your deeds before they are weighed on your behalf. Indeed, the reckoning tomorrow will be easier for you if you hold yourselves accountable today, and be prepared for the great gathering."{On that day, you will be brought forth [before Allah], and none of your secrets will remain hidden.}[Surat al-Hāqqah: 18]

"The bankrupt in my Ummah is the one who will come on the Day of Judgment with prayer, fasting, and Zakah, but since he hurled abuse at others, accused others of committing adultery without evidence, unlawfully consumed the wealth of others, shed the blood of others, and beat others, his good deeds will be credited to the accounts of others, and if his good deeds fall short to clear his account, others' sins will be cast on him and he will be thrown in Hellfire."

[Narrated by Muslim]

'Umar ibn al-Khattāb (may Allah be pleased with him) said:

"Hold yourselves accountable before you are brought to account and weigh your deeds before they are weighed on your behalf. Indeed, the reckoning tomorrow will be easier for you if you hold yourselves accountable today, and be prepared for the great gathering."

{On that day, you will be brought forth [before Allah], and none of your secrets will remain hidden.}

[Surat al-Hāqqah: 18]

Remember when you will come to Allah alone, as the scales of judgment will be in place,

and the veils will be lifted and all sins will be exposed.

Remember also the statement of Abu al-Dardā' (may Allah be pleased with him): "Righteousness does not go to waste, sins are not forgotten, the Recompenser does not sleep. So, be as you wish to be; you will reap what you sow."

If you suffer injustice and oppression, rejoice and derive hope and comfort from Allah's name "Ad-Dayyān".

By Allah, oppression has evil consequences, and oppressors are those who do wrong.

To the Recompenser we shall return, and there all disputes will be settled.

O Allah, the Recompenser, we implore You to bestow Your forgiveness and mercy upon us the Day we will be resurrected and gathered for reckoning.

Al-Mannān (The Bestower of favors)

The favors of Allah Almighty are countless and numberless. How often He removes our afflictions and cures our diseases! And how often He brings us relief from our grief and distress!

The greatest favor a person hopes to attain in the Hereafter is the forgiveness of his sins. This is to be achieved through faith and righteous deeds, even if little.

A case in point is 'Amr ibn Thābit. He embraced Islam during the Battle of Uhud and got killed in it, without even offering a single prayer. They mentioned him to the Prophet (may Allah's peace and blessings be upon him), who said:"He is among the people of Paradise."[Narrated by Ahmad; Sahīh (authentic); Al-Haythami said in Al-Majma': Its narrators are reliable]

"He is among the people of Paradise."

[Narrated by Ahmad; Sahīh (authentic); Al-Haythami said in Al-Majma': Its narrators are reliable]

Another example is the man who killed a hundred persons. Allah Almighty saw his sincere repentance and forgave him.

The greatest favor to be bestowed upon any person in this life is guidance.{...Rather, it is Allah Who has done you a favor by guiding you to faith, if you are truthful.}[Surat al-Hujurāt: 17]

{...Rather, it is Allah Who has done you a favor by guiding you to faith, if you are truthful.}

[Surat al-Hujurāt: 17]

One of the names by which Allah praised Himself is "Al-Mannān".

Anas (may Allah be pleased with him) reported that he was sitting with the Prophet (may Allah's peace and blessings be upon him) while a man was praying and then made this supplication: "Allāhumma inni as'aluka bi'anna laka al-hamd, lā ilāha illa ant Al-Mannān, Badī' as-samāwāti wa al-ard, yā Dhal-Jalāl wa al-Ikrām, yā Hayy yā Qayyūm (O Allah, I implore You by virtue of the fact that all praise is due to You, there is no god but You, You are the Bestower of Favors, the Originator of the heavens and earth, the Owner of majesty and honor, the Ever-Living, the All-Sustainer)."

Thereupon, the Prophet (may Allah's peace and blessings be upon him) said:"He has implored Allah by His greatest name by which when supplicated, He answers, and by which when asked, He gives."[Narrated by Al-Nasā'i, Al-Tirmidhi, Abu Dāwūd, and Ibn Mājah; Sahīh (authentic)]

"He has implored Allah by His greatest name by which when supplicated, He answers, and by which when asked, He gives."

[Narrated by Al-Nasā'i, Al-Tirmidhi, Abu Dāwūd, and Ibn Mājah; Sahīh (authentic)]

Our Lord, Exalted be He, is the Generous Bestower of gifts, blessings, and favors. He gives before being asked and grants us more than we hope and wish.

Since He bestows all favors upon His servants, He has the right to remind them of His favors, but they do Him no favor. Among His greatest favors is that He gives us life, the mind, the tongue, the shape, and everything we possess. His giving is indeed generous.

One of His best favors upon His servants is that He sent them the messengers as bringers of glad tidings and warners, saving the believers from Hellfire and guiding them to the straight path.

{Allah has conferred favor on the believers when He sent them a messenger from among themselves, reciting to them His verses, purifying them, and teaching them the Book and Wisdom, although before that they were clearly misguided.}[Surat Āl 'Imrān: 164]{...Rather, it is Allah Who has done you a favor by guiding you to faith, if you are truthful.}[Surat al-Hujurāt: 17]Among His favors is that He saves the weak and vulnerable in all times from tyrants and wicked people and grants them security and power:{But We wanted to bestow favor upon those who were oppressed in the land, and make them leaders and inheritors [of the land].}[Surat al-Qasas: 5]

[Surat Āl 'Imrān: 164]

{...Rather, it is Allah Who has done you a favor by guiding you to faith, if you are truthful.}

[Surat al-Hujurāt: 17]

Among His favors is that He saves the weak and vulnerable in all times from tyrants and wicked people and grants them security and power:

{But We wanted to bestow favor upon those who were oppressed in the land, and make them leaders and inheritors [of the land].} [Surat al-Qasas: 5]

The blissful:

Allah Almighty is the most worthy of being praised, thanked, and worshiped. His favors upon the believers continue incessantly until they enter Paradise. His favors upon them in the worldly life are guidance and protection; whereas in the Hereafter, they are salvation from Hellfire, entering Paradise, and looking at His noble Face. Allah Almighty says:{They will say, "Before this, we used to be in awe [of Allah] when we were living among our people.Therefore Allah conferred favor upon us and protected us from the punishment of the Scorching Fire.Indeed, we used to call upon Him before. He is indeed the Most Kind, Most Merciful."}[Surat at-Tūr: 26-28]

{They will say, "Before this, we used to be in awe [of Allah] when we were living among our people.

Therefore Allah conferred favor upon us and protected us from the punishment of the Scorching Fire.

Indeed, we used to call upon Him before. He is indeed the Most Kind, Most Merciful."}

[Surat at-Tūr: 26-28]

The course of the believers..

When the believer recognizes the favors of Allah Almighty upon him, he gets amazed and feels at ease, and he stands in need before his Creator praising Him alone. This is the greatest door through which a person can go to his Lord, namely the door of humbleness and total helplessness before Allah. He invokes and implores Him, calling out: O Allah, the Bestower of Favors!

At this point, wishes are fulfilled, requests are granted, sins are forgiven, grief and distress come to an end, the captives get released, the sick get cured, those who have been away and absent come back, and the calls of those in bad need for help are answered:{Is He [not better] Who responds to the distressed when he calls out to Him, and Who relieves suffering, and Who makes you successors on earth? Is there any god besides Allah? Little is it that you take heed!}[Surat an-Naml: 62]

{Is He [not better] Who responds to the distressed when he calls out to Him, and Who relieves suffering, and Who makes you successors on earth? Is there any god besides Allah? Little is it that you take heed!}

[Surat an-Naml: 62]

And if you missed things that you thought were the cause of your happiness, be certain that Allah kept them away from you before they become the cause of your misery.

Do not consider what you do as favors!

Allah Almighty praises Himself by the favors He bestows upon His servants. Yet, He dispraises those who consider themselves to be conferring favors upon Allah or people on account of their charitable spending or pious acts. In the Qur'an, Allah Almighty says:{They think that they have done you a favor by embracing Islam. Say, "Do not consider your Islam as a favor to me. Rather, it is Allah Who has done you a favor by guiding you to faith, if you are truthful.}[Surat al-Hujurāt: 17]Our Lord warns us not to remind others of our favors because this renders our charities worthless:{O you who believe, do not nullify your charities with reminders and hurtful words...}[Surat al-Baqarah: 264]The Prophet (may Allah's peace and blessings be upon him) also warned us against reminding others of our favors. He said:"There are three to whom Allah will not speak on the Day of Judgment: the bestower of favors who does not give anything without reminding others of his favors, the seller of goods who sells them by taking a false oath, and one who lets his lower garment hang low."[Narrated by Muslim]In another Hadīth, the Prophet (may Allah's peace and blessings be upon him) is authentically reported to have said:"He who reminds others of his favors, he who is undutiful to his parents, and he who is a drunkard will not enter Paradise."[Narrated by Al-Nasā'i; Sahīh (authentic)]

{They think that they have done you a favor by embracing Islam. Say, "Do not consider your Islam as a favor to me. Rather, it is Allah Who has done you a favor by guiding you to faith, if you are truthful.}

[Surat al-Hujurāt: 17]

Our Lord warns us not to remind others of our favors because this renders our charities worthless:

{O you who believe, do not nullify your charities with reminders and hurtful words...}

[Surat al-Baqarah: 264]

The Prophet (may Allah's peace and blessings be upon him) also warned us against reminding others of our favors. He said:

"There are three to whom Allah will not speak on the Day of Judgment: the bestower of favors who does not give anything without reminding others of his favors, the seller of goods who sells them by taking a false oath, and one who lets his lower garment hang low."

[Narrated by Muslim]

In another Hadīth, the Prophet (may Allah's peace and blessings be upon him) is authentically reported to have said:

"He who reminds others of his favors, he who is undutiful to his parents, and he who is a drunkard will not enter Paradise."

[Narrated by Al-Nasā'i; Sahīh (authentic)]

Do not spoil your favors by reminding others of them. Indeed, the generous one does not remind others of his generosity.

Hence, righteous people used to advise one another saying: If you give something to someone and then perceive that your greeting embarrasses him, refrain from greeting him.

When magnanimous people do someone a favor, they subsequently forget them, and when anyone does them a favor, they never forget it.

Generosity is never kept unknown wherever it happens,

neither are the generous wherever they are.

O Allah, the Bestower of Favors, bestow upon us the favor of reforming our affairs and children and giving us a good end in this life.

Al-Jawād (The Bountiful)

If needs, grave matters, and distressful things, debts, and financial difficulties come to you from all directions, you have to turn to the Bountiful Lord, Who removes grief and anguish and answers the supplication of the distressed.

The Prophet (may Allah's peace and blessings be upon him) said:"Indeed, Allah is Bountiful and loves bounty."[Narrated by Al-Tirmidhi; Sahīh (authentic)]Shaykh Al-Sa'di (may Allah have mercy upon him) said:"The Bountiful means that He, Exalted be He, is the possessor of absolute bounty, Whose generosity and various favors and blessings encompass all beings.And He bestows special bounty upon those who ask for it, either by their very condition or by actual requests, whether they are pious or impious, Muslims or disbelievers. If anyone asks Allah for something, He grants it to him. Indeed, He is Beneficent and Most Merciful.{Whatever blessing you have, it is from Allah. Then when you are afflicted with hardship, to Him alone you cry out for help.}[Surat an-Nahl: 53]"

"Indeed, Allah is Bountiful and loves bounty."

[Narrated by Al-Tirmidhi; Sahīh (authentic)]

Shaykh Al-Sa'di (may Allah have mercy upon him) said:

"The Bountiful means that He, Exalted be He, is the possessor of absolute bounty, Whose generosity and various favors and blessings encompass all beings.

And He bestows special bounty upon those who ask for it, either by their very condition or by actual requests, whether they are pious or impious, Muslims or disbelievers. If anyone asks Allah for something, He grants it to him. Indeed, He is Beneficent and Most Merciful.

{Whatever blessing you have, it is from Allah. Then when you are afflicted with hardship, to Him alone you cry out for help.}

[Surat an-Nahl: 53]"

Who could ever be more generous and bountiful than our Lord?

His servants disobey Him, and yet He cares for them as they sleep in their beds as if they did not show disobedience to Him. He preserves them as if they committed no sin. He treats sinners with bounty and gives them respite and shows mercy to those who repent to Him.

He is the Self-Sufficient beyond any need for His servants. Nonetheless, He shows love towards them through His favors, bounty, and respite.

The treasuries of Allah Almighty are full. His spending does not decrease them at all. The Prophet (may Allah's peace and blessings be upon him) is authentically reported to have said:"Allah's Hand is full and this is not affected by the continuous spending day and night. Do you see what He has spent since He created the heavens and the earth? Yet all that has not decreased what is in His Hand."[Narrated by Al-Bukhāri - this is his wording - and Muslim]

"Allah's Hand is full and this is not affected by the continuous spending day and night. Do you see what He has spent since He created the heavens and the earth? Yet all that has not decreased what is in His Hand."

[Narrated by Al-Bukhāri - this is his wording - and Muslim]

--

--

He loves those of His servants who ask from Him and pin their hopes upon Him, so that He will give them even more of His bounty and favors. He is so Bountiful that He even gets angry at those who do not ask from Him. The Prophet (may Allah's peace and blessings be upon him) said:"Whoever does not ask from Allah incurs His wrath."[Narrated by Al-Tirmidhi; Hasan (sound)]In another Hadīth, the Prophet (may Allah's peace and blessings be upon him) said:"Nothing is more honorable in the sight of Allah than supplication."[Narrated by Al-Tirmidhi; Hasan (sound)]

"Whoever does not ask from Allah incurs His wrath."

[Narrated by Al-Tirmidhi; Hasan (sound)]

In another Hadīth, the Prophet (may Allah's peace and blessings be upon him) said:

"Nothing is more honorable in the sight of Allah than supplication."

[Narrated by Al-Tirmidhi; Hasan (sound)]

He is the Bountiful Whose bounty and favors encompass the entire universe.

He is the Bountiful Who does not turn down a supplicant, even if he was a disbeliever.

The believer who trusts his Lord is bountiful and aspires to Allah's bounty and generosity. He knows that Allah, the Bountiful, will bestow upon him many times more from His bounty, blessings, and benevolence.{Who is there to lend Allah a goodly loan, so He will multiply it for him, and for him there will be a generous reward?}[Surat al-Hadīd: 11]{This is the promise of Allah. Allah never breaks His promise...}[Surat ar-Rūm: 6]So, he gives and spends in order to draw close to his Lord.

{Who is there to lend Allah a goodly loan, so He will multiply it for him, and for him there will be a generous reward?}

[Surat al-Hadīd: 11]

{This is the promise of Allah. Allah never breaks His promise...}

[Surat ar-Rūm: 6]

So, he gives and spends in order to draw close to his Lord.

Our Prophet (may Allah's peace and blessings be upon him) was the most generous and bountiful among all people. His generosity was like fast winds, and he was even more generous during Ramadān.

The Messenger of Allah (may Allah's peace and blessings be upon him) was never asked for something except that he would give it. A man once went to him and he gave him a herd of sheep that filled the space between two mountains. So, the man returned to his people and said: "O people, embrace Islam for indeed Muhammad gives so generously that he does not seem to fear poverty." [Narrated by Muslim] He was never asked for something and he said: No!

When anyone went to ask from him, he would find him smiling as if he was to be given something, rather than be asked to give.

It is said:

Bounty covers up any defect as the poet says:

Be covered by generosity, for generosity conceals any defect.

A generous person occupies a leading position among people owing to his generosity.

Were it not for the difficulty, everyone would be prominent. Yet, generosity yields poverty and bravery brings death.

O Allah, the Bountiful, bestow upon us from Your bounty and blessings.

Ar-Rafīq (The Kind)

'Ā'ishah (may Allah be pleased with her) reported: "A group of Jews went to the Messenger of Allah (may Allah's peace and blessings be upon him). As they entered, they said: 'As-sām (death) be upon you.' I grasped it and said: 'May As-sām and curse be upon you!'

Thereupon, the Prophet (may Allah's peace and blessings be upon him) said: 'Take it easy, O 'Ā'ishah! Indeed, Allah loves kindness in all affairs.' I said: 'O Messenger of Allah, have you not heard what they said?'

He said: 'I have replied: And upon you.'"[Narrated by Al-Bukhāri - this is his wording - and Muslim]

[Narrated by Al-Bukhāri - this is his wording - and Muslim]

He used to pardon wrongdoing so much

as if he did not see any evil from people.

It is Allah Almighty, the Kind, Who endowed the Prophet (may Allah's peace and blessings be upon him) with such great kindness. Our Lord removes grief and distress, cures the sick, restores freedom to captives, returns the absent, and consoles the broken-hearted.

The Prophet (may Allah's peace and blessings be upon him) is authentically reported to have said:"Indeed, Allah is Kind and loves kindness."[Narrated by Al-Bukhāri and Muslim]

"Indeed, Allah is Kind and loves kindness."

[Narrated by Al-Bukhāri and Muslim]

Our Lord, Exalted be He, is Kind in His decrees, predestination, and actions.

He is Kind in His commands, rulings, religion, and Shariah.

Out of His kindness and wisdom in His actions, He created all creatures in a gradual manner, even though He is Able to create them all at once in one instant.

Our Lord is Kind in His Shariah and in His commands and prohibitions. He does not charge His servants with things beyond their capacity, nor does He impose difficult obligations on them; rather, He gives them dispensations, out of kindness and mercy towards them. Also, He did not prescribe the duties on them all at once. Rather, He prescribed them gradually from one condition to another, so that people could get familiar with and accustomed to these obligations.

Out of His kindness, He gives respite to sinners and does not hasten to punish them so that they can repent and return to Him.

Another aspect of Allah's kindness is that He facilitates all means to goodness, most notably making it easy to memorize and understand His Book.{We have certainly made the Qur'an easy to understand and remember; is there anyone to take heed?}[Surat al-Qamar: 17]

{We have certainly made the Qur'an easy to understand and remember; is there anyone to take heed?}

[Surat al-Qamar: 17]

He is the Kind and He loves His kind servants,

and He gives them security on account of their kindness.

The kind ones:

He who knows that Allah is Kind will grow in love, exaltation, and gratitude towards Him. Allah Almighty loves His names and those who adopt them, except those names He dislikes for His servants to assume. He is Merciful and loves those who are merciful; Generous and loves those who are generous; and Kind and loves those who are kind.

The most worthy among people of this trait are the prophets, led by Prophet Muhammad (may Allah's peace and blessings be upon him). His treatment of people was full of kindness. He would never get angry for personal reasons or feel troubled due to people's human weaknesses and defects. Moreover, he would not keep for himself anything of the worldly vanities. Rather, he would give all what he possessed, lovingly. His forbearance, benevolence, compassion, and affection encompassed people. No one associated with him except that his heart became full of love for him, due to his kindness and generosity.

One day a Bedouin urinated in a corner of the mosque. Having seen him, the Companions rushed to him while expressing their disapproval at his act. Thereupon, the Prophet (may Allah's peace and blessings be upon him) said:"Do not interrupt him. Leave him."When the Bedouin was over, the Prophet (may Allah's peace and blessings be upon him) called him and said:"It is not appropriate to use mosques for urinating or filth. Indeed, they are built for the remembrance of Allah Almighty, prayer, and the recitation of the Qur'an."[Narrated by Muslim]Indeed, Allah Almighty is Kind and loves those who are kind. The Prophet (may Allah's peace and blessings be upon him) is authentically reported to have said:"Allah is Kind and loves kindness. He gives for kindness what He does not give for harshness."[Narrated by Muslim]

"Do not interrupt him. Leave him."

When the Bedouin was over, the Prophet (may Allah's peace and blessings be upon him) called him and said:

"It is not appropriate to use mosques for urinating or filth. Indeed, they are built for the remembrance of Allah Almighty, prayer, and the recitation of the Qur'an."

[Narrated by Muslim]

Indeed, Allah Almighty is Kind and loves those who are kind. The Prophet (may Allah's peace and blessings be upon him) is authentically reported to have said:

"Allah is Kind and loves kindness. He gives for kindness what He does not give for harshness."

[Narrated by Muslim]

The most worthy of this trait among people, after the prophets, are kings and rulers, and the callers to Allah from the preachers and scholars, as well as parents. People have enough grief and concerns and they are in need for someone to console them, not someone who treats them harshly. They need mercy, compassion, care, cheerfulness, and affection.

People are in greater need for kindness than for receiving something along with harsh treatment. Those who are more entitled to your kindness are yourself, your parents, your spouse, your children, your subjects, and your co-workers and friends.

Your share in this name..

The Prophet (may Allah's peace and blessings be upon him) is authentically reported to have said: "Whoever is given his share of kindness has been given his share of goodness in this world and in the Hereafter. Upholding kinship ties, good manners, and good neighborliness maintain houses and prolong lifespans."[Narrated by Ahmad; Sahīh (authentic)]In another Hadīth, the Prophet (may Allah's peace and blessings be upon him) is authentically reported to have said:"When Allah wills good for a household, He gives them kindness."[Narrated by Ahmad; Sahīh (authentic)]The Prophet (may Allah's peace and blessings be upon him) also said:"Verily, kindness does not exist in anything but it adorns it, and it is not removed from anything except that it makes it defective."[Narrated by Muslim]Hence, the most hateful among people are those who are rough and harsh. Allah Almighty says:{...If you had been harsh and hard-hearted, they would have dispersed from you...}[Surat Āl 'Imrān: 159]The Prophet (may Allah's peace and blessings be upon him) also said:"Whoever is deprived of kindness is deprived of goodness."[Narrated by Muslim]

[Narrated by Ahmad; Sahīh (authentic)]

In another Hadīth, the Prophet (may Allah's peace and blessings be upon him) is authentically reported to have said:

"When Allah wills good for a household, He gives them kindness."

[Narrated by Ahmad; Sahīh (authentic)]

The Prophet (may Allah's peace and blessings be upon him) also said:

"Verily, kindness does not exist in anything but it adorns it, and it is not removed from anything except that it makes it defective."

[Narrated by Muslim]

Hence, the most hateful among people are those who are rough and harsh. Allah Almighty says:

{...If you had been harsh and hard-hearted, they would have dispersed from you...}

[Surat Āl 'Imrān: 159]

The Prophet (may Allah's peace and blessings be upon him) also said:

"Whoever is deprived of kindness is deprived of goodness."

[Narrated by Muslim]

O Allah, we implore You by Your name "Ar-Rafīq" to show kindness to us and facilitate for us all ways of goodness.

As-Sayyid (The Master)

'Abdullah ibn al-Shikhkhīr (may Allah be pleased with him) reported: "I went in the delegation of Banu 'Āmir to the Prophet (may Allah's peace and blessings be upon him). We said: 'You are our master.' He said: 'The Master is Allah Almighty.'

We said: 'The best of us in excellence and the greatest of us in generosity.' He said:'Say what you like, or some of what you like, but do not let the devil overcome you.'"[Narrated by Abu Dāwūd; Sahīh (authentic)]

'Say what you like, or some of what you like, but do not let the devil overcome you.'"

[Narrated by Abu Dāwūd; Sahīh (authentic)]

--

Linguistically, "As-Sayyid" means one who surpasses others by his forbearance, wealth, status, and usefulness, and who gives his money to right causes.

It is also used to refer to a person who is not overcome by his anger. And it refers to the noble, the king, and the chief.

The master of a slave is his owner, and the master of a woman is her husband. Allah Almighty says:{...And they found her master (husband) at the door...}[Surat Yūsuf: 25]

{...And they found her master (husband) at the door...}

[Surat Yūsuf: 25]

The master of something is the best and most distinguished in it.

And none possesses perfect mastery and sovereignty but our Lord.

In the shades of Allah's name "As-Sayyid":

Our Lord, Exalted be He, is the Master with perfect mastery, glory, honor, majesty, forbearance, self-sufficiency, vanquishing power, knowledge, and wisdom. He possesses every attribute of these in a perfect and complete manner.

Allah Almighty is the Master Who possesses all perfect kinds of honor and sovereignty.

These are His attributes and none shares them with Him or competes with Him over any of them.

He is the God, the Master, the Eternal Refuge,

upon Whom all creatures rely and to Whom they submit.

He possesses perfect attributes from all aspects.

His perfection is marred by no deficiency whatsoever.

All creatures are slaves to Him and in need of Him. The angels, humans, and jinn cannot dispense with Him. They stand in need for His bounty, kindness, and care. So, it befits Him to be the Master, and it befits them to call Him as such.

Our Lord, Exalted be He, is the Master and the Disposer of the universe, and there is no partner with Him or equal to Him.

He is the Master to Whom alone obedience should be devoted and humiliation and submission should be displayed. He has no partner with Him.

He is the Master worthy of being worshiped - without any partner.{Say [O Prophet], "Should I seek a lord other than Allah, when He is the Lord of everything?"}[Surat al-An'ām: 164]

{Say [O Prophet], "Should I seek a lord other than Allah, when He is the Lord of everything?"}

[Surat al-An'ām: 164]

Ibn 'Abbās (may Allah be pleased with him and his father) said: "A God, a Master."

Wrong thinking!

A person may be given wealth, children, prestige, a high position, authority, or leadership. He may be surrounded by servants and soldiers and guarded by armies, with people revering him and yielding submissively to his authority and power. Thus, he attains such massive power and dominance. Yet, his dominance is still incomplete and transient.

Some are deceived by their dreams during sleep.

How deceptive their dreams are and how wrong their interpretation thereof is!

If a person believes that Allah Almighty is the real Master, his heart will get attached to Him alone, fearing and relying upon Him, seeking His help, and hoping for His mercy and reward. This is because He is the Disposer of the affairs of His creation, and we are all weak and in need of Him.{O people, it is you who are in need of Allah, whereas Allah is the Self-Sufficient, the Praiseworthy.}[Surat Fātir: 15]So, he does not humbly submit except to Allah Almighty alone, the One, the Superb Vanquisher, the Master, the Eternal Refuge.

{O people, it is you who are in need of Allah, whereas Allah is the Self-Sufficient, the Praiseworthy.}

[Surat Fātir: 15]

So, he does not humbly submit except to Allah Almighty alone, the One, the Superb Vanquisher, the Master, the Eternal Refuge.

O masters!

Sovereignty among people is based upon dignity, honor, high status, and good reputation, and these things can only be attained by obedience to our Lord. That is why the prophets and pious people prevailed and attained such a high status among people.

As for those who disbelieve in Allah and turn away from Him, for them there is no dignity or dominance; even if they attain worldly dominance, it is false and fleeting.

Hence, it is prohibited to address a hypocrite by the title: master. The Prophet (may Allah's peace and blessings be upon him) said:"Do not call a hypocrite: master, for if he is a master, you will have angered your Almighty Lord."[Narrated by Abu Dāwūd; Sahīh (authentic)]

"Do not call a hypocrite: master, for if he is a master, you will have angered your Almighty Lord."

[Narrated by Abu Dāwūd; Sahīh (authentic)]

The sanctuary of the Master:

Calling someone "master" is permissible for Allah Almighty describes Yahya (John the Baptist) (peace be upon him) as {a master} [Surat Āl 'Imrān: 39]. And the Prophet (may Allah's peace and blessings be upon him) also said:"I am the master of the children of Adam, and I am not bragging."[Narrated by Muslim]In another Hadīth, the Prophet (may Allah's peace and blessings be upon him) said about Sa'd ibn Mu'ādh:"Stand for your master."[Narrated by Al-Bukhāri]There is no contradiction between this and the Hadīth that says: "The master is Allah."[Narrated by Abu Dāwūd; Sahīh (authentic)]The believers take "the master of people" to mean their leader and Imam.

"I am the master of the children of Adam, and I am not bragging."

[Narrated by Muslim]

In another Hadīth, the Prophet (may Allah's peace and blessings be upon him) said about Sa'd ibn Mu'ādh:

"Stand for your master."

[Narrated by Al-Bukhāri]

There is no contradiction between this and the Hadīth that says: "The master is Allah."

[Narrated by Abu Dāwūd; Sahīh (authentic)]

The believers take "the master of people" to mean their leader and Imam.

When the Arabs say "so-and-so is our master", they mean: He is our leader whom we respect and revere.

As for describing Allah as the Master, this means that He is the Lord of all creatures, and they are all slaves to Him.

The Prophet (may Allah's peace and blessings be upon him) forbade it when it was said to him: "You are our master." He said:"The Master is Allah. Say what you like, or some of what you like, but do not let the devil overcome you."[Narrated by Abu Dāwūd; Sahīh (authentic)]This points out how the Prophet (may Allah's peace and blessings be upon him) was so keen to protect monotheism and block the means to polytheism.He also disliked that people should praise him to his face, though they would only say what is true. In a Hadīth, he (may Allah's peace and blessings be upon him) said:"I am the master of the children of Adam."[Narrated by Muslim]He feared that they might be deeply attached and submissive to any created being in a way that can only be devoted to Allah, the One God, the Superb Vanquisher.

"The Master is Allah. Say what you like, or some of what you like, but do not let the devil overcome you."

[Narrated by Abu Dāwūd; Sahīh (authentic)]

This points out how the Prophet (may Allah's peace and blessings be upon him) was so keen to protect monotheism and block the means to polytheism.

He also disliked that people should praise him to his face, though they would only say what is true. In a Hadīth, he (may Allah's peace and blessings be upon him) said:

"I am the master of the children of Adam."

[Narrated by Muslim]

He feared that they might be deeply attached and submissive to any created being in a way that can only be devoted to Allah, the One God, the Superb Vanquisher.

O Allah, we implore You by Your name "As-Sayyid" to elevate our rank and remove our burdens; indeed You are Able to do all things.

Badī' as-Samāwāt wa al-Ard (The Originator of the heavens and earth)

"I am so touched by the discovery of the truth in the Noble Qur'an!

This Noble Qur'an describes the universe from the highest point therein.

As we have seen, it could not have come from a human source. After reading the Noble Qur'an, I have come to know my future. I will plan my research upon this comprehensive outlook."[Professor Youchidi Couzan]

[Professor Youchidi Couzan]

This is nature. O you who are moving on earth, stop here and let me show you the superb creation of the Almighty Creator.

The land around you and the heavens do offer great signs that point to His existence and magnificent creation.

if we ponder the creation of the heavens and the earth, we see signs of Allah, the Originator of the universe, Who says about Himself:{The Originator of the heavens and earth. When He decrees a matter, He only says to it, "Be," and it is.}[Surat al-Baqarah: 117]

{The Originator of the heavens and earth. When He decrees a matter, He only says to it, "Be," and it is.}

[Surat al-Baqarah: 117]

Ibn Kathīr (may Allah have mercy upon him) said: "He is the Originator, Creator, and Innovator of the heavens and the earth in an unprecedented manner."

Shaykh Al-Sa'di (may Allah have mercy upon him) said: "{The Originator of the heavens and the earth} is their Creator and Innovator in a way of utmost beauty, perfection, and excellence."

A call to the people of intellects!

Since He is like this, then it is not proper to ascribe to Him anything in the heavens or the earth as His son, far Exalted be He far above that. In fact, all that exists therein is created and brought to existence by Him and is submissive to Him and subject to His authority. In the Qur'an, He says:{They say, "Allah has taken a son." Glory be to Him! Rather, to Him belongs all that is in the heavens and earth – all are devoutly obedient to Him.The Originator of the heavens and earth. When He decrees a matter, He only says to it, "Be," and it is.}[Surat al-Baqarah: 116-117]

{They say, "Allah has taken a son." Glory be to Him! Rather, to Him belongs all that is in the heavens and earth – all are devoutly obedient to Him.

The Originator of the heavens and earth. When He decrees a matter, He only says to it, "Be," and it is.}

[Surat al-Baqarah: 116-117]

If it is established that everything in the heavens and the earth was created and originated by Him, it follows then that they are all among His servants and part of His dominion; so, it is impossible for Him to have a son.

If this is the case, then it is incumbent upon the people to comply with His commands and prohibitions and not ascribe to Him a son or a wife.

Our Lord commands us to contemplate the universe and His magnificent creation. He says:{Indeed, in the creation of the heavens and earth and the alternation of the night and day are signs for people of understanding.}[Surat Āl 'Imrān: 190]The entire universe offers signs pointing to its Creator, the All-Hearing, the All-Seeing Lord and supporting belief in Him.

{Indeed, in the creation of the heavens and earth and the alternation of the night and day are signs for people of understanding.}

[Surat Āl 'Imrān: 190]

The entire universe offers signs pointing to its Creator, the All-Hearing, the All-Seeing Lord and supporting belief in Him.

If created beings were lines to be read, you would read them and see that they clearly point to their Creator.

Through them, the Glorified King sends us messages that there is no true god but Allah, and that every creature, mute or speaking, leads to Him.

Contemplate the universe!

Bilāl (may Allah be pleased with him) once went to the Prophet (may Allah's peace and blessings be upon him) to notify him of the Fajr prayer, and he found him lying down and weeping. He said: "O Messenger of Allah, why are you weeping whereas Allah forgave your past and future sins?"

He (may Allah's peace and blessings be upon him) said: "Woe to you, Bilāl! Why should I not weep while Allah has revealed this to me tonight:{Indeed, in the creation of the heavens and earth and the alternation of the night and day are signs for people of understanding.}[Surat Āl 'Imrān: 190]?"He recited the verses to the end of the Surah.Then, he (may Allah's peace and blessings be upon him) said: "Woe to anyone who recites them and does not contemplate them!"[Narrated by Ibn Hibbān; Sahīh (authentic)]The view of the heavens and what they contain - stars, planets, the sun, and the moon - and the earth and what it contains - the mountains, rivers, seas, animals, plants, inanimate objects, and living and dead beings - point to the Originator of the heavens and the earth.{Blessed is He Who placed in the sky constellations, and placed therein a radiant lamp and a luminous moon.It is He Who made the night and the day to follow each other so that everyone who wishes may reflect or become grateful.}[Surat al-Furqān: 61-62]In a conference of the Muslim Youth, held in Riyadh in 1979, US Professor Palmer stood up when he heard the verse that says:{Are the disbelievers not aware that the heavens and earth were joined together and then We split them apart?...}[Surat al-Anbiyā': 30]He remarked: "Yes, indeed, the universe was in its beginning a massive contiguous cloud of smoke and gas, and thereafter gradually transformed into millions and millions of stars filling the sky. This, by no means, can be attributed to a man who died 1400 years ago, for he did not possess telescopes or spacecrafts to help him discover these facts. So, the one who informed Muhammad of this must have been Allah." Professor Palmer, then, declared his conversion to Islam at the end of the conference.In the 8th medical conference held in Riyadh, 1404 AH, Professor Tejatat Tejasen, the head of Anatomy and Embryology section, Mai University, Thailand, stood up and said:"Since Prophet Muhammad could not read or write, then he must have been a messenger who brought this fact. This was given to him through revelation from a creator who knows everything. This creator must be Allah.

{Indeed, in the creation of the heavens and earth and the alternation of the night and day are signs for people of understanding.}

[Surat Āl 'Imrān: 190]?"

He recited the verses to the end of the Surah.

Then, he (may Allah's peace and blessings be upon him) said: "Woe to anyone who recites them and does not contemplate them!"

[Narrated by Ibn Hibbān; Sahīh (authentic)]

The view of the heavens and what they contain - stars, planets, the sun, and the moon - and the earth and what it contains - the mountains, rivers, seas, animals, plants, inanimate objects, and living and dead beings - point to the Originator of the heavens and the earth.

{Blessed is He Who placed in the sky constellations, and placed therein a radiant lamp and a luminous moon.

It is He Who made the night and the day to follow each other so that everyone who wishes may reflect or become grateful.}

[Surat al-Furqān: 61-62]

In a conference of the Muslim Youth, held in Riyadh in 1979, US Professor Palmer stood up when he heard the verse that says:

{Are the disbelievers not aware that the heavens and earth were joined together and then We split them apart?...}

[Surat al-Anbiyā': 30]

He remarked: "Yes, indeed, the universe was in its beginning a massive contiguous cloud of smoke and gas, and thereafter gradually transformed into millions and millions of stars filling the sky. This, by no means, can be attributed to a man who died 1400 years ago, for he did not possess telescopes or spacecrafts to help him discover these facts. So, the one who informed Muhammad of this must have been Allah." Professor Palmer, then, declared his conversion to Islam at the end of the conference.

In the 8th medical conference held in Riyadh, 1404 AH, Professor Tejatat Tejasen, the head of Anatomy and Embryology section, Mai University, Thailand, stood up and said:

"Since Prophet Muhammad could not read or write, then he must have been a messenger who brought this fact. This was given to him through revelation from a creator who knows everything. This creator must be Allah.

Therefore, I think it is high time to say: 'I testify that there is no god but Allah and that Muhammad is the Messenger of Allah.'"

A remedy..

The name of Allah "Al-Badī'" is of great significance; whoever uses it in supplication gets his supplication answered.

Anas (may Allah be pleased with him) reported: "The Prophet (may Allah's peace and blessings be upon him) entered the mosque while a man had prayed and was saying in supplication: 'Allāhumma la ilāha illa ant Al-Mannān, Badī' as-samāwāt wa al-ard, yā Dhal-Jalāl wa al-Ikrām (O Allah, there is no god but You, the Bestower of Favors, the Originator of the heavens and the earth, the Owner of majesty and honor)!'

Thereupon, the Prophet (may Allah's peace and blessings be upon him) said:'Do you know that by which he supplicated Allah? He supplicated Allah by His greatest name by which when supplicated, He answers, and by which when asked, He gives.'"[Narrated by Al-Tirmidhi; Sahīh (authentic)]

'Do you know that by which he supplicated Allah? He supplicated Allah by His greatest name by which when supplicated, He answers, and by which when asked, He gives.'"

[Narrated by Al-Tirmidhi; Sahīh (authentic)]

O Allah, forgive us and bestow Your mercy upon us, O the Most Merciful of those who show mercy!

O the Originator of the heavens and the earth, forgive and pardon us and show mercy to us; indeed You are Able to do all things.

Al-Mu'ti (The Giver)

Giving is one of His greatest gifts,

generosity is one of His attributes,

and bounty is among His greatest traits. Who could ever be greater than Him in generosity and giving?!

One of the beautiful names of Allah is "Al-Mu'ti".

The Prophet (may Allah's peace and blessings be upon him) is authentically reported to have said:"When Allah wills good for someone, He gives him proper understanding of the religion. Indeed, I am only a distributer, and Allah gives."[Narrated by Al-Bukhāri and Muslim]

"When Allah wills good for someone, He gives him proper understanding of the religion. Indeed, I am only a distributer, and Allah gives."

[Narrated by Al-Bukhāri and Muslim]

Our Lord, Exalted be He, is the One Who actually gives to all creatures. No one can withhold what He gives or give what He withholds.

His giving encompasses all that exists. It has no limits or bounds. This is the perfect generosity and bounty.

When our Lord gives, that is benevolence from Him and reform for us; and if He withholds, that stems from His wisdom.

He gives and withholds. These are His favors, and He mercifully gives whomever He wishes and wisely withholds from whomever He wishes.

And His withholding is just and fair.

Allah's giving falls under two categories:

1. General giving in worldly life:

It encompasses all people, believers and disbelievers, as Allah Almighty sets aright their worldly affairs. In the Qur'an, He says:{We give both – the latter and the former – from the bounty of your Lord, and Your Lord's bounty is not restricted.}[Surat al-Isrā': 20]

{We give both – the latter and the former – from the bounty of your Lord, and Your Lord's bounty is not restricted.}

[Surat al-Isrā': 20]

2. Special giving in worldly life and in the Hereafter:

It encompasses the prophets, the messengers, and righteous people. Allah Almighty provides them in this life with lawful sustenance, good children, faith, piety, certitude, and clear guidance. These are the best gifts in worldly life. The Messenger of Allah (may Allah's peace and blessings be upon him) said:"Allah Almighty gives worldly opulence to those He loves and those He does not love; but He only gives the religion to those He loves." [Narrated by Al-Hākim in Al-Mustadrak; Classified as Sahīh (authentic) by Al-Dhahabi]And in the Hereafter, He gives them the greatest gift in His Paradise, which is more magnificent and perfect than all else. Allah Almighty says:{A reward and a generous gift from your Lord.}[Surat an-Naba': 36]

"Allah Almighty gives worldly opulence to those He loves and those He does not love; but He only gives the religion to those He loves." [Narrated by Al-Hākim in Al-Mustadrak; Classified as Sahīh (authentic) by Al-Dhahabi]

And in the Hereafter, He gives them the greatest gift in His Paradise, which is more magnificent and perfect than all else. Allah Almighty says:

{A reward and a generous gift from your Lord.}

[Surat an-Naba': 36]

The greatest gift in Paradise will be the pleasure of the Lord of all the worlds and looking at His noble Face.

The keys of giving:

Our Lord is Generous and Giving and He loves those who give generously. That is why generous givers occupy such high status among people. The Prophet (may Allah's peace and blessings be upon him) said:"Hands are of three types: Allah's Hand is the upper one; the hand of the giver is next to it; and the beggar's hand is the lowest. So, give what is surplus, and do not submit yourself to the demand of your soul."[Narrated by Abu Dāwūd; Sahīh (authentic)]Generous people will be greatly rewarded by the King of all kings.{...And spend [in Allah's cause] out of what He has entrusted you with. For those among you who believe and spend, there will be a great reward.}[Surat al-Hadīd: 7]Allah Almighty promised His Prophet (may Allah's peace and blessings be upon him) to give him until he becomes satisfied:{And your Lord will certainly give you so much that you will be well pleased.}[Surat ad-Duha: 5]Among the things Allah Almighty will give His Prophet (may Allah's peace and blessings be upon him) in the Hereafter is the Kawthar River:{We have surely given you [O Prophet] the Kawthar.}[Surat al-Kawthar: 1]About the Kawthar, the Prophet (may Allah's peace and blessings be upon him) said:"It is a river which my Lord has promised me. It has abundance of good and upon it there is a basin to which my Ummah will come on the Day of Judgment. Its vessels are as numerous as the stars."[Narrated by Muslim]

"Hands are of three types: Allah's Hand is the upper one; the hand of the giver is next to it; and the beggar's hand is the lowest. So, give what is surplus, and do not submit yourself to the demand of your soul."

[Narrated by Abu Dāwūd; Sahīh (authentic)]

Generous people will be greatly rewarded by the King of all kings.

{...And spend [in Allah's cause] out of what He has entrusted you with. For those among you who believe and spend, there will be a great reward.}

[Surat al-Hadīd: 7]

Allah Almighty promised His Prophet (may Allah's peace and blessings be upon him) to give him until he becomes satisfied:

{And your Lord will certainly give you so much that you will be well pleased.}

[Surat ad-Duha: 5]

Among the things Allah Almighty will give His Prophet (may Allah's peace and blessings be upon him) in the Hereafter is the Kawthar River:

{We have surely given you [O Prophet] the Kawthar.}

[Surat al-Kawthar: 1]

About the Kawthar, the Prophet (may Allah's peace and blessings be upon him) said:

"It is a river which my Lord has promised me. It has abundance of good and upon it there is a basin to which my Ummah will come on the Day of Judgment. Its vessels are as numerous as the stars."

[Narrated by Muslim]

As Allah Almighty looks at you and sees that you rely upon Him and consider Him to be your refuge, presenting all your needs to Him alone, He will give you better than what you ask for and honor you beyond what you wish.

Glory be to the One Who grants wishes lying within the heart yet not uttered by the tongue!

Glory be to Him! He guarantees the provision for all the worlds and nothing escapes His knowledge.

O Allah, bestow Your favors upon us and give us generously and do not deprive us and turn us down empty-handed, O Lord of the worlds!

Al-Muhsin (The Benevolent)

The Prophet (may Allah's peace and blessings be upon him) is authentically reported to have said:"If you judge, judge justly, and if you kill, kill benevolently; indeed, Allah is Benevolent and He loves benevolence."[Narrated by Al-Tabarāni in Al-Mu'jam al-Awsat; Hasan (sound)]In another Hadīth, Shaddād ibn Aws (may Allah be pleased with him) reported that the Prophet (may Allah's peace and blessings be upon him) said:"Indeed, Allah Almighty is Benevolent and He loves benevolence."[Al-Jāmi' al-Saghīr; Sahīh (authentic)]Our Lord, Exalted be He, is Perfect in His essence, attributes, and actions.{Allah has the Most Beautiful Names, so call upon Him by them...}[Surat al-A'rāf: 180]No one is more excellent or perfect than He is!It is our Lord:{Who perfected everything He created...}[Surat as-Sajdah: 7]

"If you judge, judge justly, and if you kill, kill benevolently; indeed, Allah is Benevolent and He loves benevolence."

[Narrated by Al-Tabarāni in Al-Mu'jam al-Awsat; Hasan (sound)]

In another Hadīth, Shaddād ibn Aws (may Allah be pleased with him) reported that the Prophet (may Allah's peace and blessings be upon him) said:

"Indeed, Allah Almighty is Benevolent and He loves benevolence."

[Al-Jāmi' al-Saghīr; Sahīh (authentic)]

Our Lord, Exalted be He, is Perfect in His essence, attributes, and actions.

{Allah has the Most Beautiful Names, so call upon Him by them...}

[Surat al-A'rāf: 180]

No one is more excellent or perfect than He is!

It is our Lord:

{Who perfected everything He created...}

[Surat as-Sajdah: 7]

Benevolence is an inseparable attribute of Him. Nothing in existence is spared of His benevolence for a while. Indeed, He encompasses all creatures in His benevolence and bounty, including the pious and the wicked, the believers and the disbelievers. They cannot exist or continue to live without His bounty and favors.

Allah's benevolence towards His servants first manifests as He brought them out of nothing into existence.{Was there not a period of time when man was not a thing [even] mentioned?} [Surat al-Insān: 1] {...And initiated the creation of man from clay.}[Surat as-Sajdah: 7]Then, He fashioned them in the best form:{...He shaped you and perfected your form...}[Surat Ghāfir: 64]Then, He gave them minds that distinguish between the truth and falsehood:{And shown him the two ways [of right and wrong]?}[Surat al-Balad: 10]And He subjected to them the heavens and the earth and what is between them:{Do you not see that Allah has made subservient to you all that is in the heavens and on earth, and has abundantly bestowed upon you His favors, both apparent and hidden?...}[Surat Luqmān: 20]And He bestowed His countless favors upon them:{...If you try to count the blessings of Allah, you cannot count them. Indeed, mankind is highly unjust and ungrateful.}[Surat Ibrāhīm: 34]

{Was there not a period of time when man was not a thing [even] mentioned?} [Surat al-Insān: 1] {...And initiated the creation of man from clay.}

[Surat as-Sajdah: 7]

Then, He fashioned them in the best form:

{...He shaped you and perfected your form...}

[Surat Ghāfir: 64]

Then, He gave them minds that distinguish between the truth and falsehood:

{And shown him the two ways [of right and wrong]?}

[Surat al-Balad: 10]

And He subjected to them the heavens and the earth and what is between them:

{Do you not see that Allah has made subservient to you all that is in the heavens and on earth, and has abundantly bestowed upon you His favors, both apparent and hidden?...}

[Surat Luqmān: 20]

And He bestowed His countless favors upon them:

{...If you try to count the blessings of Allah, you cannot count them. Indeed, mankind is highly unjust and ungrateful.}

[Surat Ibrāhīm: 34]

Complete benevolence:

The greatest benevolence Allah bestows upon His servants is guiding them to this religion and making them inclined and steadfast on it till death.{Indeed, Allah is with those who fear Him and those who do good.}[Surat an-Nahl: 128]Leading His close servants to a good and safe life:{Whoever does righteous deeds, male or female, while being a believer, We will surely grant him a good life, and We will surely reward them according to the best of their deeds.}[Surat an-Nahl: 97]Removing the distress of His close servants and saving them from adversities. Yūsuf (Joseph) (peace be upon him) is quoted in the Qur'an as saying:{...My Lord is gracious to whom He wills...}[Surat Yūsuf: 100]Then, His perfect benevolence towards His close servants will be displayed in the Hereafter. That is the highest benevolence, and even more. Allah Almighty says:{For those who do good there will be the best reward and more...}[Surat Yūnus: 26]

{Indeed, Allah is with those who fear Him and those who do good.}

[Surat an-Nahl: 128]

Leading His close servants to a good and safe life:

{Whoever does righteous deeds, male or female, while being a believer, We will surely grant him a good life, and We will surely reward them according to the best of their deeds.}

[Surat an-Nahl: 97]

Removing the distress of His close servants and saving them from adversities. Yūsuf (Joseph) (peace be upon him) is quoted in the Qur'an as saying:

{...My Lord is gracious to whom He wills...}

[Surat Yūsuf: 100]

Then, His perfect benevolence towards His close servants will be displayed in the Hereafter. That is the highest benevolence, and even more. Allah Almighty says:

{For those who do good there will be the best reward and more...}

[Surat Yūnus: 26]

The best reward for them is Paradise.

And what is more: is looking at the Face of their Exalted Lord. Indeed, there is nothing better, more beautiful, more perfect, or more sublime than His noble Face.

Moreover, He combines for them the two kinds of reward, of this world and of the Hereafter. He says:{So Allah gave them the reward of this world and the best reward of the Hereafter, for Allah loves those who do good.}[Surat Āl 'Imrān: 148]Our Lord, Exalted be He, is the Owner of great benevolence and perfection. Hence, He perfected His Shariah and included in it the good outcomes and lofty objectives, which are beneficial for all humanity.{...Who could be better than Allah in judgment for people who are certain in faith?}[Surat al-Mā'idah: 50]

{So Allah gave them the reward of this world and the best reward of the Hereafter, for Allah loves those who do good.}

[Surat Āl 'Imrān: 148]

Our Lord, Exalted be He, is the Owner of great benevolence and perfection. Hence, He perfected His Shariah and included in it the good outcomes and lofty objectives, which are beneficial for all humanity.

{...Who could be better than Allah in judgment for people who are certain in faith?}

[Surat al-Mā'idah: 50]

Ihsān (perfection/benevolence) is of two kinds:

1. Ihsān in worshiping Allah Almighty:

This is the highest and most sublime position as mentioned in the well-known long Hadīth involving Jibrīl (Gabriel), where the Prophet (may Allah's peace and blessings be upon him) interpreted Ihsān as follows:"It is to worship Allah as if you could see Him; if you do not see Him, He sees you."[Narrated by Al-Bukhāri and Muslim]

"It is to worship Allah as if you could see Him; if you do not see Him, He sees you."

[Narrated by Al-Bukhāri and Muslim]

2. Ihsān towards the servants of Allah Almighty:

This is to bring to them all kinds of goodness and refrain from harming them. Allah Almighty says:{...Allah does not allow the reward of those who do good to go to waste.}[Surat at-Tawbah: 120]Our Lord, Exalted be He, loves His names and loves that His servants draw close to Him by actions entailed by the meanings of His names. He is Merciful and loves those who are merciful, Generous and loves those who are generous, and Benevolent and loves those who act benevolently. In the Qur'an, He says:{...For Allah loves those who do good.}[Surat al-Baqarah: 195]The most entitled to one's benevolence and kindness are his parents, as Allah Almighty says:{We have enjoined upon man kindness to his parents...}[Surat al-Ahqāf: 15]He also says:{...And do good as Allah has done good to you...}[Surat al-Qasas: 77]

{...Allah does not allow the reward of those who do good to go to waste.}

[Surat at-Tawbah: 120]

Our Lord, Exalted be He, loves His names and loves that His servants draw close to Him by actions entailed by the meanings of His names. He is Merciful and loves those who are merciful, Generous and loves those who are generous, and Benevolent and loves those who act benevolently. In the Qur'an, He says:

{...For Allah loves those who do good.}

[Surat al-Baqarah: 195]

The most entitled to one's benevolence and kindness are his parents, as Allah Almighty says:

{We have enjoined upon man kindness to his parents...}

[Surat al-Ahqāf: 15]

He also says:

{...And do good as Allah has done good to you...}

[Surat al-Qasas: 77]

To You, Lord of the Throne, I complain.

And I supplicate You during hardships.

My Lord, fulfill our wishes

and be Merciful to us and answer our supplications.

O You Who always show benevolence,

O You Who always show forgiveness,

we seek refuge in You, our Lord, from our evil actions.

We hope for Your forgiveness and pardon.

Help us, help us, and remove our hardships

and save us from trouble and harm.

Bestow Your bounty, benevolence, forgiveness, and pardon.

Indeed, You are worthy of doing that.

O Allah, make us among the benevolent and show benevolence to us and accept from us, from our parents, and from all Muslims.

Pauses of reflection upon the beautiful names of Allah

1. The believer should make his best effort to know Allah Almighty and His names, attributes, and actions, without negating, likening, distorting, or asking about their nature or manner.

His knowledge should be derived from the Qur'an and Sunnah and the authentic reports from the Companions (may Allah be pleased with them) and those who followed them with righteousness.

2. The names of Allah Almighty should be taken as they are reported, and not to be subject to our personal reasoning. Hence, we should take them as they are mentioned in the Qur'an and Sunnah, without addition or omission.

3. The beautiful names of Allah Almighty should not be regarded as limited or numbered, for there are other names and attributes which He, Exalted be He, keeps to Himself as part of the unseen, and they are not known to anyone, including angels and prophets. A Hadīth reads in part of it:"... I ask You by every name that belongs to You, which You have named Yourself with, revealed in Your Book, taught any one of Your creation, or kept to Yourself in the knowledge of the unseen with You..."[Narrated by Al-Tabarāni in Al-Mu'jam al-Kabīr; Sahīh (authentic)]

"... I ask You by every name that belongs to You, which You have named Yourself with, revealed in Your Book, taught any one of Your creation, or kept to Yourself in the knowledge of the unseen with You..."

[Narrated by Al-Tabarāni in Al-Mu'jam al-Kabīr; Sahīh (authentic)]

With regard to the Prophet's Hadīth: "Allah has ninety nine names, one hundred minus one, and whoever memorizes them will enter Paradise," [Narrated by Al-Bukhāri and Muslim] this is a one complete statement, which indicates that whoever memorizes the ninety nine names will enter Paradise. Yet, this does not necessarily mean that they are only ninety nine and not more.

For example, we may say "so-and-so has a hundred slaves that he has prepared for Jihad." This does not mean that he does not possess other slaves prepared for other purposes than Jihad. There is no disagreement among scholars on this point.

Moreover, the Prophet's statement "and whoever memorizes them will enter Paradise" means: Whoever memorizes and understands them and praises Allah Almighty thereby. These are three degrees. Whoever does any of them, along with sincere intention, and acts accordingly has indeed memorized them, as stated by Al-Qurtubi, Al-Khattābi, and Ibn al-Qayyim (may Allah have mercy upon them).

4. All the names of Allah Almighty are beautiful, and they fall under four categories:

First: Names of beauty:

They inspire within people's souls a sense of intimacy, love for Allah and meeting Him, and feelings of comfort and tranquility. They open the door of hope for people so they do not despair of Allah's mercy. Examples of these names include: Ar-Rahmān (the Most Compassionate), Ar-Rahīm (the Most Merciful), Al-Karīm (the Generous), Al-'Afuww (the Pardoner), Al-Halīm (the Forbearing), Al-Ghafūr (the All-Forgiving), At-Tawwāb (the Accepting of repentance), etc.

Second: Names of majesty:

They inspire within people's souls a sense of awe and fear from their Lord, as well as glorification and extolment of Him.

They carry the meanings of vanquishing, power, might, and greatness, such as: Al-'Azīz (the All-Mighty), Al-Jabbār (the Compeller), Al-Qahhār (the Superb Vanquisher), Al-Qawiyy (the All-Powerful), Al-Kabīr (the Great), and Al-Mutakabbir (the Supreme).

Third: Names of lordship:

These are the names which prompt the believer to feel humbled before his Lord and that he is weak and a created being by Allah Almighty.

They point to the lordship of Allah Almighty, such as: Ar-Rabb (the Lord), As-Sayyid (the Master), Al-Malik (the King), Al-Mālik (the Owner), Al-Khāliq (the Creator), Al-Bāri' (the Initiator), and Ar-Rāziq (the Provider).

Fourth: Names of divinity:

These are the names which prompt the believer to feel that he is a slave of Allah Almighty and that Allah is the One worthy of being worshiped alone.

They contain the meanings of divinity, such as: Al-Ilāh (the God) and As-Samad (the Eternal Refuge).

This classification is done on the basis of the meanings of these names. Yet all the names of Allah Almighty combine beauty, majesty, perfection, and greatness. They point to the Best and Most Sublime One to be described.

5. Each of these names establishes the attribute of perfection for Allah Almighty. Hence, His names are all beautiful, and His attributes point to His perfection, magnificence, and majesty, and His actions comprise wisdom, mercy, benefits, and justice.

6. None among the names of Allah Almighty signifies evil or deficiency.

Indeed, evil does not come from Him and is not part of His attributes or ascribed to His essence, and it does not exist in any of His actions. So, evil may not be attributed to His actions or attributes.

7. Allah Almighty commands His servants to supplicate Him by His names. He says:{Allah has the Most Beautiful Names, so call upon Him by them...}[Surat al-A'rāf: 180]This includes the supplications of worship and the supplications of requests.

{Allah has the Most Beautiful Names, so call upon Him by them...}

[Surat al-A'rāf: 180]

This includes the supplications of worship and the supplications of requests.

This is indeed one of the best and greatest acts of obedience and piety.

8. The beautiful names of Allah Almighty are not collectively listed in any Prophetic Hadīth.

We should stick to the rule that "the names of Allah Almighty should be derived from the Qur'an and Sunnah."

9. The second edition comprises commentary on ninety nine names among the beautiful names of Allah Almighty, as agreed between Shaykh Muhammad ibn Sālih ibn 'Uthaymīn, Dr. 'Umar Sulaymān al-Ashqar, and Shaykh 'Abdul-'Azīz ibn 'Abdullah ibn Bāz (may Alah have mercy upon them all) - or as agreed by two of the three.

In conclusion..

It has been accomplished with the help of Allah Almighty. I have collected what I could in this book, and I implore Allah to accept it from me and make it beneficial for everyone.

And may Allah's peace and blessings be upon Prophet Muhammad and his family and Companions.

And praise be to Allah, Lord of the worlds.

* It has been edited and proofread by Mr. Muhammad 'Abdul-'Azhīm and Mr. Muhammad 'Abdul-Latīf; typed by Mr. Mu'awwad Rizq; and formatted by Mr. Ahmad Kashouqah. May Allah reward them all and grant them success.

* Brief information about the author:

Born in 1378 AH (1967 AD), in Rahīmah, Saudi Arabia, 'Abdullah ibn Mushabbib ibn Musfir al-Qahtāni obtained a doctoral degree in Islamic Fiqh. He is a retired educational supervisor and the Imam and preacher of Abu Bakr al-Siddīq Mosque in Dammām, Saudi Arabia.

- Allah Almighty is the Close Companion of His Loving Servants 1
- Beautiful Names and Sublime Attributes of Allah Almighty from the Qur'an and Sunnah 1
- Dedicated 2
- Introduction of the Second Edition 2
- Introduction 2
- My Lord... 4
- Allāh Al-ilāh (Allah; the God) 4
  - Hearts deify Him and souls yearn for Him. 5
  - The greatest name: 5
  - So, be with Allah and He will be with you. 6
- Ar-Rabb (The Lord) 7
  - Knocking on the door. 7
  - His Lordship to His servants falls under two categories: 7
  - All praise is due to You. 8
  - Keys to the treasures. 8
  - O Lord! 8
  - Nonetheless, we do forget our Lord! 9
- Al-Ahad Al-Wāhid (The One and Only God) 9
  - Sound natural disposition.. 10
  - Clear evidence: 10
  - Allah is far exalted above what they say! 11
  - The universe attests to His Oneness: 11
  - Allah is the farthest from need to have partners.. 11
  - A Reminder. 12
- As-Samad (The Eternal Refuge) 13
  - The adequate answer. 13
  - Submission of the heart. 14
  - They responded to the call of their Lord. 14
  - Rest assured! 14
- Ar-Rahmān Ar-Rahīm (The Most Compassionate, the Most Merciful) 15
  - The mercy of Allah falls under two categories: 16
  - He is the Most Compassionate.. 16
  - Glad tidings! 17
  - Keys to mercy: 17
  - Do not let the devil daunt you! 18

- Al-Hayy (The Ever-Living) 18
  - Clear evidence: 19
  - Call of the universe 19
  - Hearts of lovers.. 19
  - Stand humble before Him! 20
- Al-Qayyūm (The All-Sustainer) 21
  - The only Deity worthy of worship.. 22
  - Rest assured! 22
- Al-Malik Al-Malīk (The King) 23
  - Let us pause here with the name "Al-Malik" (the King): 23
  - The devil enticed them.. 24
  - Sovereign of the Day of Recompense. 24
  - His dominion is absolute: 24
  - O the One Whose dominion never goes away! 25
  - Knock on the door of the King! 25
- As-Subūh (The All-Glorious) 26
  - You are more worthy.. 26
  - Obedient hearts. 27
  - Keys to happiness: 27
  - Glory be to You! 27
- Al-Quddūs (The Most Holy) 28
  - Glorified is He! 29
  - You are more worthy.. 29
  - Your share in this name 29
- As-Salām (The Source of Peace) 30
  - Let us pause here with the name "As-Salām": 30
  - Rewarding the lovers: 31
  - Your share in this name 31
  - Note.. 31
- Al-Mu'min (The Giver of Belief/Security) 32
  - Let us pause here with this great name: 32
  - Three aspects: 33
  - Your share in this name 34
- Al-Muhaymin (The All-Controller) 34
  - He is the All-Controller. 34

- Rest assured! 35
- The lifeline.. 35
- Al-'Azīz (The All-Mighty) 36
  - Sanctuary of the All-Mighty Lord: 36
  - For the seekers of honor.. 37
  - He will grant you honor.. 37
  - The keys to honor: 38
  - Contemplate! 38
- Al-Jabbār (The Compeller) 39
  - Do not dispute with Him! 39
  - Knock on the door of heaven! 40
  - Be kind and tender! 41
- Al-Mutakabbir (The Supreme) 41
  - Servitude of submissiveness.. 41
  - Consider the consequences! 42
  - The remedy: 42
- Al-Khāliq Al-Khallāq (The Creator, the Sublime Creator) 43
  - Magnificence of the Creator.. 44
  - The universe in harmony: 44
  - Rest assured! 45
- Al-Bāri' (The Initiator) 45
  - No coincidence.. 46
- Al-Musawwir (The Fashioner) 47
  - The strongest signs: 47
  - A last word.. 48
- Al-'Afuww (The Pardoner) 48
  - Allah's pardon is of two types: 49
  - He is the Pardoner.. 49
  - Turn back to Him! 49
  - The key to pardon: 50
- Al-Ghafūr Al-Ghaffār (The All-Forgiving, the Superb Forgiver) 51
  - The door is open.. 51
  - Do not despair! 52
  - Be humbly submissive to your Lord! 52
  - The lifeline.. 52

- Al-Kabīr (The Great) 53
  - At the doorstep. 53
  - The minds are falling short in this regard. 54
  - The most profound phrase.. 54
  - The key to approaching the King: 54
  - The honorable is the one who takes refuge in the Great Lord ... 55
- Al-A'la Al-'Aliyy Al-Muta'āl (The Most High - the High - the Exalted) ... 55
  - Where is Allah? 56
  - The path.. 57
  - You have achieved your wish. 57
- Al-Qāhir Al-Qahhār (The Vanquisher - the Superb Vanquisher) ... 58
  - He is the Superb Vanquisher: 58
  - Entrust your affairs to Him. 59
- Al-Wahhāb (The Bestower) 60
  - He is the Bestower: 60
  - At His doorstep.. 61
  - Return to the Bestower! 61
  - The secret lies in the beauty of supplication! 61
  - A gentle whisper.. 62
- Ar-Razzāq (The All-Provider) 62
  - Predestination had already been written. 63
  - His treasures are full. 63
  - Stop! 63
  - The keys to provisions. 64
  - Forgotten provisions! 64
  - A last word. 64
- Al-Fattāh (The Superb Judge) 65
  - Fact. 65
  - All keys are in His hand. 65
  - Turn to Him! 66
  - Special opening.. 66
- As-Samī' (The All-Hearing) 67
  - Indeed, He is All-Hearing and Near: 67
  - The keys to relief: 68
  - The All-Hearing protects you. 68

- A Reminder 69
- Al-Basīr (The All-Seeing) 69
  - The pleasure of compliance 70
  - A Reminder 71
- At-Tawwāb (The Accepting of Repentance) 71
  - What a Generous Lord! 72
  - A Reminder 72
  - Were it not that you commit sins 72
  - At the doorstep 73
  - Wake-up shakes 73
- Al-'Alīm (The All-Knowing) 74
  - He is the All-Knowing: 74
  - Allah's knowledge is perfect and comprehensive: 75
  - Fact 75
  - Your share in this name 76
- Al-'Azhīm (The Magnificent) 76
  - Glory be to You, the Magnificent Lord! 76
  - Raise your hands! 77
  - Whoever resorts to the Magnificent Lord is safe 77
  - The key to relief: 78
  - How should a Muslim extol his Lord? 78
- Al-Qawiyy (The All-Powerful) 79
  - Power comes from Him 79
  - The days of Allah 80
  - Shall I tell you?! 80
- Al-Matīn (The Strong) 81
  - Where are they? 81
  - Your wish comes true 82
- Al-Qādir, Al-Qadīr, Al-Muqtadir (The Able - The Omnipotent - The Supreme Determiner) 83
  - His ability is complete 83
  - Predestination had already been written 83
  - Do not wonder! 84
  - Everything has a measure: 84
- Al-Hafīzh (The All-Preserver) 85
  - Allah's preservation of His creation falls under two categories: 85

- He defends you.. 86
- A divine reward: 86
- Valuable advice: 86
- Glad tidings. 87
- Al-Ghaniyy (The Self-Sufficient) 87
  - The entire universe is in need of Allah Almighty. 88
  - The key to self-sufficiency: 88
- Al-Hakam Al-Hakīm (The Judge - The All-Wise) 90
  - A reward from the All-Wise. 90
  - Rest assured! 91
  - Beware! 91
- Al-Latīf (The All-Subtle/The Most Kind) 92
  - He is the Most Kind: 92
  - Do you not long for Him? 93
  - The key to happiness: 93
  - Be humbly submissive to the All-Subtle, the Most Kind! 93
- Al-Khabīr (The All-Aware) 94
  - The status of Ihsān (perfection): 95
  - The secret lies in the heart! 95
  - Being in the company of Allah: 95
- Al-Halīm (The Forbearing) 96
  - He is the Forbearing! 96
  - What a Forbearing Lord! 96
  - A whisper! 97
  - The pleasure of compliance! 97
  - In conclusion. 97
- Ar-Ra'ūf (The All-Kind) 98
  - The strongest signs: 98
  - A message to. 99
  - Hearts in humble submission.. 99
- Al-Wadūd (The Most Affectionate) 100
  - Pure benevolence: 101
  - Only for the lovers of Allah! 101
  - The proof of affection: 102
  - A sign.. 103

Al-Barr (The Beneficent) 103
    They are all appointed to serve you.. 104
    The kindness of the Beneficent Lord... 104
    Your share in this name... 105
Al-Qarīb (The Near) 105
    His nearness to His creation is of two types:... 105
    In Allah's protection... 106
    He is Near:... 106
    The reward of standing in need and in humble submission before our Lord.. 107
Al-Mujīb (The All-Responsive) 108
    At the doorstep.. 108
    A Reminder... 108
Al-Majīd (The Most Glorious) 109
    Our Lord likes to be praised.. 109
    All glory is due to You... 110
    Be with Him! 110
    The valley of success: 110
    The Throne: 111
Al-Hamīd (The Praiseworthy) 112
    Be humbly submissive to your Lord! 112
    Praise be to You... 113
Ash-Shākir Ash-Shakūr (The Appreciative - The Ever-Appreciative) 113
    He gives and then shows appreciation!... 114
    The greatest recompense.. 114
    There are two forms of thankfulness: 115
    The key to hearts:.. 115
Al-Karīm Al-Akram (The Generous - The Most Generous)... 116
    He gives and then shows appreciation: 116
    He is the Generous Lord: 117
    He does not need thanks.. 117
    He gives more than we wish.. 117
    The criterion:... 118
    A Reminder... 119
Al-Muqīt (The Keeper)... 119
    Rest assured! 121

Be thankful!	121
The pillars of self-sufficiency:	122
The way of the righteous.	122
Al-Wāsi' (The All-Encompassing)	123
The All-Encompassing Lord suffices you against your distress!	125
The deal is profitable.	126
The tears of the fearful.	127
Messages.	127
Ar-Raqīb (The Ever-Watchful)	128
He has succeeded.	129
The company of Allah:	130
A whisper.	131
Al-Hasīb (The Ever-Reckoner)	131
His sufficiency is:	132
He takes care of you during adversities!	133
Stick to it!	133
This statement means:	134
For the safety of the road!	134
A Reminder!	135
Al-Shahīd (The Witness) - Exalted be He	136
A fact:	137
The Day of Presentation!	137
Your duty!	138
Al-Haqq (The Truth) - Exalted be He	139
The conflict!	140
Where is the way?	140
Settle at the valley of salvation!	141
Al-Mubīn (The Evident) - Exalted be He	142
The people of intellects!	144
Al-Muhīt (The Encompassing) - Exalted be He	145
He is the Encompassing!	146
Rest assured!	147
Al-Awwal - Al-Ākhir - Al-Zhāhir - Al-Bātin (The First - The Last - The Outward - The Inward) - Exalted be He	148
He is close to you!	149

- Do not get bored of standing! 150
- A turning point! 151

Al-Wakīl (The Disposer of affairs) - Exalted be He 152
- To the truthful! 153
- To those who rely upon their Lord! 154
- Before going out! 155
- A Reminder! 156
- The path is from here! 157

Al-Nūr (The Light) - Glorified be He 158
- In His light! 159
- Take these words as a gift from me! 160
- The sweetness of His guidance! 160
- His Book is light! 161
- In a word! 162

Al-Kāfi (The All-Sufficient) 162
- He is the All-Sufficient: 163
- Stay at His door! 164
- A test 164
- The adequate answer 165

Al-Mawla Al-Waliyy (The Protector - The Guardian) 165
- He protects you as much as you obey Him: 166
- They are the people 167
- The path: 167
- The keys to acceptance: 168
- If He grants you His protection, He will surprise you! 168

Al-Hādi (The Guide) 170
- Allah's guidance to people 170
- The more you are guided, the higher you get elevated 171
- Knock on the door of the heaven! 173
- A last word 173

An-Nasīr (the Helper) 174
- Forms of help: 175
- The adequate answer 175

Al-Wārith (The Inheritor) 177
- The real ownership 179

- In supplications... 179
- Ash-Shāfi (The Healer) ... 180
  - Your refuge... 182
  - The way of the righteous... 183
  - Do not be sad! ... 184
- Al-Jamīl (The Beautiful)... 185
  - and too magnificent to be expressed in words! ... 186
  - The beauty of the worlds... 187
  - Longing... 187
  - Do not be ungrateful! ... 188
- Al-Qābid - Al-Bāsit (The Constrictor - The Expander) ... 188
  - A word before starting... 188
  - In the shades of His two names: Al-Qābid and Al-Bāsit: ... 189
  - The measure: ... 191
  - The greatest type of expanding: ... 192
  - A Reminder... 193
  - A whisper... 193
- Al-Muqaddim - Al-Mu'akhkhir (The Advancer - the Delayer) ... 193
  - Advance and delay ... 194
  - The true advance: ... 195
- Al-Hayiyy (The Modest)... 196
  - A fact: ... 197
  - How beautiful modesty is! ... 197
  - A last word... 198
- Ad-Dayyān (The Recompenser) ... 199
  - Consider the consequences! ... 200
- Al-Mannān (The Bestower of favors) ... 201
  - The blissful: ... 203
  - The course of the believers... 203
  - Do not consider what you do as favors! ... 203
- Al-Jawād (The Bountiful)... 204
  - Who could ever be more generous and bountiful than our Lord? ... 205
  - It is said: ... 206
- Ar-Rafīq (The Kind) ... 206
  - The kind ones: ... 207

- Your share in this name ... 208
- As-Sayyid (The Master) ... 209
  - In the shades of Allah's name "As-Sayyid": ... 209
  - Wrong thinking! ... 210
  - O masters! ... 210
  - The sanctuary of the Master: ... 210
- Badīʿ as-Samāwāt wa al-Ard (The Originator of the heavens and earth) ... 212
  - A call to the people of intellects! ... 212
  - Contemplate the universe! ... 213
  - A remedy.. ... 214
- Al-Muʿti (The Giver) ... 215
  - Allah's giving falls under two categories: ... 215
  - The keys of giving: ... 216
- Al-Muhsin (The Benevolent) ... 217
  - Complete benevolence: ... 218
  - Ihsān (perfection/benevolence) is of two kinds: ... 219
- Pauses of reflection upon the beautiful names of Allah ... 220
  - First: Names of beauty: ... 221
  - Second: Names of majesty: ... 221
  - Third: Names of lordship: ... 221
  - Fourth: Names of divinity: ... 221